Reporting Public Problems

An Analysis of Today's Issues

Reporting
Public Problems

An Analysis of Today's Issues

ROBERT D. MURPHY

Associate Professor and Chairman,
Newspaper Department,
School of Journalism,
Syracuse University

CHILTON COMPANY – BOOK DIVISION
Publishers
Philadelphia   New York

Published in Philadelphia by Chilton Company,
and simultaneously in Toronto, Canada, by Ambassador Books, Ltd.

LIBRARY OF CONGRESS CATALOG CARD NUMBER 60–5891

MANUFACTURED IN THE UNITED STATES OF AMERICA
BY QUINN & BODEN COMPANY, INC., RAHWAY, N. J.

Preface

Today's complicated public events often require that a reporter investigate a situation rather than cover a beat. Top reporters frequently find that their job is not only to report the outward manifestations of an event—what someone said or what papers were signed—but also to discover and report sufficient information so that a reader can understand the event in its true perspective.

With so many events and organizations seeking space in news columns, reporters must ask themselves, "What do readers need to know?" Then the reporter must seek out the answers.

This approach to reporting is fundamentally different from the more traditional one of covering certain places and certain officials and then reporting what transpires. Of necessity we shall always have a certain amount of this standby coverage, but it is quite evident that the trend among our leading newspapers is to cover situations of importance regardless of whether there are any events which signalize this importance.

Essentially, this means that our news media are covering public problems rather than public offices and officials.

In this book the author aims to help future reporters prepare themselves for this kind of reporting. The book does not concern itself primarily with structure; rather, it emphasizes the problems government is trying (or should be trying) to solve.

Much of the skeleton of public affairs is here: the organization of government, the who-has-what-information that every reporter needs to know. But the emphasis is not on the bare bones of government structure, but rather on the dynamics, the problems—because, after all, they are what reporters write about.

Such organization should help a teacher to force his students to pull together from all their college studies the knowledge and the techniques they need to report a changing world. An advanced reporting course should be a course in applied knowledge—the information and the insight gained in all other areas should be brought into a purposeful focus so that they can be applied to the substance of reporting public affairs.

Such a book cannot be compartmentalized entirely, any more than every story can be compartmentalized into a single news beat. Each area depends on every other area. Each student can be helped to see this and should be encouraged to introduce information and viewpoints from other areas to clarify reporting problems. Our government patterns are so varied that exceptions can be found to almost every generalization about them, so this text should be supplemented with local information.

Government structure is vital knowledge to a reporter, but even more vital is the understanding that problems of public affairs cross many lines and that reporters covering them must be prepared to do the same.

This book points out the formal machinery and informal arrangements by which various levels of government co-operate. Since joint action is increasing, it is obvious that more and more reporting will involve several levels of government in single articles.

This book also points out some of the informal agencies peripheral to government which frequently have much weight in decisions on public questions. These are worthy of coverage, and are beginning to receive it. Also unique in this book is a discussion of what is sure to be a continuing public concern—our education system.

The author is grateful to Syracuse University for a leave of absence which made it possible for him to finish this book sooner than he otherwise could have done it. He is grateful for contacts with students, newspapermen, and other teachers who have helped sharpen many ideas. To his colleagues at the Syracuse University School of Journalism the author is indebted for encouragement and help.

THE AUTHOR

Contents

PART TWO—LAW AND LAW ENFORCEMENT

PART THREE—INFORMAL AREAS OF PUBLIC AFFAIRS

PART FOUR—INDUSTRY IS PUBLIC AFFAIRS

PART ONE

Metropolitan Problems

I

Metropolitan Areas

Population Trends

Urban areas are spreading in all directions from our cities like lava from the center of a volcano. As the city-like developments grow they create new patterns of living which we do not understand, and they bring problems which we have only begun to solve.

For reporters working in metropolitan areas there will be many stories in the changes brought by the growth of population, the shopping centers, and the industry around the perimeters of our great cities. This "flight to the suburbs" is one of the significant stories of our times.

City people are moving to the suburbs. Country people are gravitating to the great population centers, but usually they stop short of the city and settle in the suburbs. The result is a decaying central city, with people living in the suburbs, shopping in outlying centers, and coming to the city, if at all, only to work. This movement is robbing the cities of commerce, wealth, and residents. It tends to weaken the city as a center of culture without providing any adequate new cultural centers. It puts a strain on rural governments, which must serve urban areas with political structures designed for villages or farm country.

Villages, towns, cities, counties—these are the local government units which we have used, and in general they have worked rather well. County governments have policed rural areas, kept the roads passable, and offered the few other governmental services which our rural areas wanted. Towns or townships in some of our states have served as subdivisions of the county.

As places became crowded they developed more needs—for additional policing, street lighting, water mains, sewers, and many more. To obtain

3

these services areas incorporated as villages or, if they were large enough, as cities.

This worked fine for a while, but eventually troubles developed. For reasons which we shall consider later most cities stopped annexing adjacent suburbs. Nearby cities grew until their borders met, and neither city wanted to be absorbed by the other. Residents in unincorporated areas resorted to special districts to obtain services, instead of forming cities or joining nearby ones.

As a result we have vast metropolitan areas without any unified government. People living in all parts of a metropolitan area have many of the same problems, but no common political organization to consider them. Problems of transportation, water supply, sewage, drainage, and land use usually can be solved most effectively if the planning is done for a whole metropolitan area, but most such areas have no way to act as a unit. Instead an area may be composed of two, three, or many cities, villages, and unincorporated areas which have city needs. The area may be in one or more counties and it may include parts of one, two, or three states.

In this chapter we will consider some of the metropolitan problems and how some areas are meeting them. In the next chapters we will consider the traditional forms of local government and how they operate. Reporters will find that, although they still get many good stories from the city and county governments, they will write more and more about metropolitan area problems.

This story from the *Boston Herald* is an example:

> A nationally-known research firm yesterday reported that Boston's downtown area holds the potential for great economic development and for a thriving "international headquarters."
>
> Arthur D. Little, Inc., found downtown Boston, because of its new highways and expressways and transit facilities, accessible and especially suitable for regional headquarters of firms that must draw on the Greater Boston Metropolitan area for a labor pool.
>
> Reporting on a preliminary survey of the economic status and future of the downtown retail area, the Little firm concluded:
>
> "That the retail core of the future will remain the largest in the area and can become the strongest economically if its activity is consolidated and if its physical layout is developed so that shoppers will be provided with convenient and pleasant surroundings."

The article closes with this quotation from the chairman of the local planning board:

> Much has been said about the shortcomings of retailing downtown, but the Boston retail core enjoys many advantages that cannot be matched by competing centers. Much has been said about the plight of Boston particu-

larly, but the decline in the ratio of retail sales in the central business district in Boston to sales in the total metropolitan area is virtually the same as the average decline experienced by the central cities of the other U.S. metropolitan areas.

The last paragraph quoted gives a key to much of the city-suburban friction—the defection of shoppers from the central city stores to new centers in the suburbs. The pain to the city is greater when it levies a sales tax which merchants outside the city do not have to collect.

What Is a Metropolitan Area?

All of us understand in a general way that a metropolitan area is a place in which a large population is concentrated in a fairly small space. The United States Bureau of the Census is very specific.

It considers as a metropolitan area any county or group of contiguous counties which has at least one central city of 50,000 or more population. Surrounding counties are included if they are sufficiently urbanized to form an integrated social and economic community. In New England the Census Bureau uses townships instead of counties in determining metropolitan areas. It is worthwhile noticing that this definition includes three specific areas: the central city or cities, their suburbs, and the city-like area beyond the suburbs (exurbia, as some of the population specialists call it).

The Census Bureau has designated more than 170 standard metropolitan areas in the United States. These include more than half of the country's population and only 7 per cent of the land area.

Growth of Metropolitan Areas

In 1850 only 15 per cent of the people of the United States lived in and around cities. In 1950, 64 per cent were urban dwellers. This long term trend is accelerating. From 1950 to 1956 the population of the country increased by 14.7 million. About 12.4 million of this increase, 85 per cent of it, was in the cities and their suburbs.

Another important trend further complicates urban problems. The suburbs and the fringe areas just beyond them are gaining population much faster than are the central cities. For example, consider the distribution of the 12.4 million population gain of the metropolitan areas from 1950 to 1956. Of this the central cities gained 2.3 million, suburbs 4.0 million, and urban-rural fringes 6.1 million. Some central cities are losing population while the adjacent areas are gaining it.

California gives us some idea of the tremendous impact of the metropolitan areas. Nine metropolitan areas in that state contain more than 84 per cent of its 14 million residents. In evaluating these figures it is well

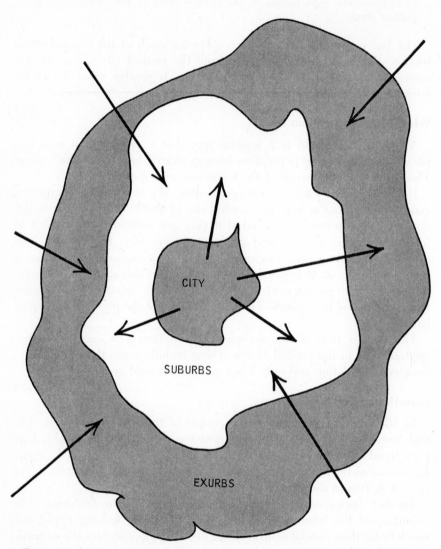

Fɪɢ. 1. People are moving from the city to the suburbs, and to the exurbs just beyond them. People are moving from the country, too, to metropolitan area jobs, but these people tend to stop short of the city itself, settling in the suburbs and the exurbs. The result—problems for the city, which is losing many of its residents with higher incomes, and problems for the suburbs, which often are not equipped to handle the sudden increase in population.

to remember that, although California has many large industries, it is also one of our important agricultural states.

Our population specialists expect this trend to continue. The best prophecies may fail because of unforeseen events, but certainly all signs point in that direction.

Farm mechanization is making it possible to produce more food with less labor, so farm jobs are declining. Industrial jobs in the cities are taking up the slack, so farm labor-saving devices have created more jobs in the long run because they have made possible mass production and consumption. Either factories have been enlarged or they have multiplied into more individual units. Both increase the concentration of jobs, and therefore population, in metropolitan centers.

Improved transportation facilities also contribute to the trend toward concentration of population. Better highways enable workers to commute more miles to their jobs. Better transportation in the future will further increase the commuting range.

The automobile also has helped create the metropolitan area problem by allowing workers to commute farther to their jobs. People can work in the central city and live in the suburbs, independent of public transportation facilities. This promotes a haphazard distribution of population growth and complicates still more the problems of a city trying to make adequate provision for traffic in and out of its limits.

It is impossible to predict what the transportation of the future will do to population distribution. The uncertainties of the situation are illustrated by the fact that Cape Cod businessmen gave thought to promoting their area as a residential center for high-income families whose wage earners work in Boston or New York. Helicopters might provide fast and convenient daily transportation.

Problems of Metropolitan Areas

Metropolitan areas offer many social, cultural, and economic advantages, but they are beset with problems. These are varied, but most of them stem from the fact that, while the problems are common to the whole area and can be solved only on an area-wide basis, there is no government with area-wide jurisdiction.

Highway construction and traffic control are good illustrations of problems that must be solved on an area-wide basis. Some villages have been faced with vast traffic jams as thousands of automobiles spilled off superhighways onto narrow streets originally intended for horse and buggy traffic.

Commuters furnish another version of the same problem. High-speed boulevards leading to the center of a city are almost useless as there is no place to park the cars of workers who drive in. A city government can control traffic only to its borders; the suburbs, too, have limited control. This need for area-wide planning helps to explain the added interest state governments have taken recently in planning arterial highways.

Water supply and sewage disposal are examples of projects of such magnitude that often the resources of an entire area are needed for adequate planning and financing. Certainly many suburbs are too small to operate these services efficiently.

Decisions about land use often cannot be made intelligently for pieces of a metropolitan area. What areas shall be used for residences? For industry? For commercial establishments?

Residential planning involves decisions about the type of homes or apartments which will be constructed in a given area. A city has a direct interest in the zoning regulations of its suburbs, for they control the approaches to the city. A residential area just inside the city limits may be carefully zoned for one-family residences with uncrowded lots, but it loses most of its appeal if a shantytown grows up adjacent to it, but just across the city line.

Intelligent residential planning cannot be done without considering transportation channels. Concentrated housing areas should not be built up without provision for highways or other transportation to take workers to their jobs and home again. The transportation and zoning riddles are part of the urban jigsaw. The fact that they are interrelated makes area-wide planning even more necessary.

Industrial land use, too, is difficult to control except on a metropolitan basis. Larger industries tend to build their plants just outside cities. It is not hard to understand why. Modern production line techniques call for a large floor space on one level. This requires a large piece of land which is hard to get in most cities. Large plants require space to park employees' cars, too. Large concerns tend to farm out less of their work to other plants; hence they have less need to be in the center of a city. There may be tax advantages, too, in the suburbs.

Whatever the reasons, this tendency of industry often causes problems. It deprives a city of a considerable amount of tax revenue, although the factories need city services and the chances are good that many of the workers live in the city. Such growth, too, makes it still more difficult for a city to control its approaches and keep its residential districts intact.

Baton Rouge, Louisiana, in a government reorganization plan which will be discussed later in this chapter, set aside two industrial areas. No homes can be built in these areas and the plants there are required to supply nearly all their own services, including fire and police protection.

Central parts of cities consist of major stores, office buildings, banks, professional men's offices, and other commercial establishments. Although we are used to the neighborhood grocery store, merchants in the center of the city are worried about the development of huge shopping centers which offer most of the goods and services of the downtown area and have become a strong counter-attraction for customers. Where these shopping centers develop outside of the city limits they are free, of course, from municipal sales taxes. The complexity of the problem is further illustrated by the fact that one of the major attractions offered by the outlying shopping centers is parking space, which is at a premium in the central areas of most of our cities.

Policing is not always regarded as a metropolitan area function. When all subdivisions of an area maintain adequate and competent police departments which cooperate with each other there may be no need for integration. On the other hand, part of the metropolitan area may be poorly policed and become a breeding spot for crime which infests the rest of the area.

Fire protection can often be provided by independent departments if they will cooperate in real emergencies. It is questionable, however, whether this gives taxpayers as much protection for each dollar spent as would an efficient larger organization.

One of the undesirable aspects of our present fragmented metropolitan area government is that it is so complex that few residents understand it. If one central government provided all governmental services it would be easy to find out who was responsible for poor public service. Ultimately the blame would rest on the shoulders of the chief executive of the government. Many residents have little idea of who is responsible for any given service under our present fragmented system.

A 1957 study of metropolitan Sacramento, California, for example, found that the average resident lives under ten different layers of local government. In addition to the county itself there are 5 municipalities, 45 school districts, and 157 special districts, or a total of 208 governmental units in the county.

Another West Coast metropolitan area, King County, Washington, has 189 independent governmental units. These include Seattle and 24 other cities and towns, 54 water districts, 35 fire protection districts, 26 school districts, 20 sewer districts, and 11 drainage districts.

It is expecting the impossible to ask newspapers to report adequately the activities of all these governmental organizations, and it is hopeless to expect the average voter to have any clear understanding of them.

Perhaps the most undesirable aspect of fragmented metropolitan area government is that it sometimes leads to feuding among different governments and to the growth of mutual dislike so that cooperation becomes difficult. City residents, for example, may feel that suburbanites are working in the city and enjoying its advantages without meeting any of its costs through taxes. Suburban residents, on the other hand, may feel that they have to spend much of their lives in areas over which they have no political control and whose governments are unfriendly toward them.

Bickering arises over many issues. A city sales tax often causes trouble because the city merchants see business disappearing to suburban centers where no tax is levied. City residents feel that the tax should be area-wide to equalize the burden, and suburbanites feel that the city is trying to dictate to them.

Sale of city services to the suburbs may cause trouble. City residents may refuse to sell water and sewer services to suburbs on the theory that to give outlying areas these services will make it advantageous for them to stay out of the city while still enjoying city services. Or the city may sell the services, but charge a much higher rate than is paid by city residents. Either situation is likely to cause resentment.

If such fragmented government is wasteful and undemocratic, why don't we throw it out and establish general purpose units of government with authority to plan on sufficiently large scale to deal with the problems? The answer is that tradition and sentiment work against such a sensible solution. So do some politicians and officeholders who fear they would suffer a decline in influence if established patterns and units of government were changed.

Instead, our public planners usually work through a series of compromise adjustments. The following are some of the proposed solutions.

The Special District

The special district is a unit which has governmental power in just one area, as opposed to the general units of government, such as cities, towns, and villages, which have general governmental power.

It is formed under provisions of state laws to provide one specific service, and it is given sufficient authority to accomplish its purpose. For example, residents of an area may desire street lights. They establish a district under procedure set up by state law. This district may be given power to have the lights installed and to maintain them.

Residents of an adjacent area may see the need for sewers, so they set up a special district with power to levy taxes, install sewers, and maintain them. There may be an area in which the districts overlap, so residents pay taxes for street lights to one district, for sewers to another. Most certainly they are in a school district, so they pay taxes separately for schools.

The districts may multiply so that the average citizen cannot begin to understand them. He may not even know that he is paying taxes to them.

The special districts have an obvious value—they furnish services which, without these districts, would be unavailable to residents under our present fragmented government. It stands to reason, however, that the same services could be provided more efficiently and with less confusion to the taxpayer by a general unit of government. A general government could do over-all planning, something obviously not possible on the piecemeal basis on which special districts are forced to operate.

The districts, although they are usually small, are neither close to the people nor democratic. Since the voters do not understand them and may not even know about them, they seldom vote in special district elections. In Sacramento County, California, where the average resident pays taxes to ten units of local government, it was found that few voters turn out for special district elections. While 50 to 75 per cent of the residents vote in a regular county election, 30 per cent is an unusually high figure for special districts, and 10 per cent is average.

In one year there were 94 special district and school district elections in Sacramento County. There would have been more except that elections are often eliminated when there is an uncontested slate of officers.

A Seattle study showed how undemocratic special districts can be. In one new real estate development the district boundaries were extended to include the homes of two families. Voters of these two families created a sewer district and elected three of themselves as commissioners. In another development three families moved in, and after they had met residence requirements the six eligible voters of the three families established a sewer district and elected the three men of the families as commissioners. These same six voters then held another election and authorized bonding the district for $1,800,000. These bonds will be paid eventually by about 4,000 families.

The special district is often useful in that frequently it is the only way residents of a given area can get a certain service. Too often, however, it has added so much confusion that it has become a problem in itself.

Metropolitan Districts

Metropolitan districts, often called metropolitan authorities, are big brothers to the special district. They have many of the same disadvantages, but planners resort to them sometimes for the same reason special districts are created—there is no other way to do a job.

Essentially, metropolitan districts are legal entities which have been established to do one or a few jobs for large metropolitan areas. Examples are the Port of New York Authority which cuts across state lines of New York and New Jersey, the Metropolitan Sanitary District of Greater Chicago which provides sewer service for a large area, and the Bay Area Pollution Control District of San Francisco.

Some of the metropolitan districts have made real contributions, which probably could not have been made without them. They can plan on a scale otherwise impossible when two or more states are involved. However, they are limited to a given segment of a metropolitan area's problems and therefore cannot be expected to do a truly comprehensive planning job. This is their essential disadvantage. Despite their large size and great resources they still represent only a fragmented approach to metropolitan area planning.

Among other disadvantages of the metropolitan districts are these:

They sometimes add confusion to the total governmental picture. Rather than simplifying an already complicated structure, they add another level of government. In most voters' eyes this is probably another level of confusion.

They are somewhat removed from popular control. Usually the commissioners are not elected and at times they have not been particularly sensitive to popular control.

Since they are separate from other planning agencies they may work at cross-purposes.

Despite these disadvantages the metropolitan district seems destined to be used more frequently in the future. It is sometimes the only way in which certain problems can be approached under our present governmental organization.

This story from the *San Francisco Chronicle* describes an attempt to consolidate several authorities:

> Mayor George Christopher yesterday swung his weight behind proposals to merge control of the Bay Area's bridges, harbors and airports into a single port authority.
>
> The Mayor took his stand in a letter to the Bay Area Council, which has hired an engineering firm to find out whether such an authority can be created.
>
> "It is my hope that this report will prove not only the economic feasibility of such a centralized jurisdiction but also the imperative need for such an effort," the Mayor wrote.
>
> Consolidation of transit facilities that tie together Bay Area communities would "cast out provincialism" and improve the efficiency of transit services, he said.
>
> "I don't see why we need both a Golden Gate Bridge Authority and a State Toll Bridge Authority to operate our bridges," he said.
>
> As for San Francisco's airport, the Mayor said, the city paid for it but in time it will belong to San Francisco "in name only."
>
> With population on the Peninsula climbing as it is, "Peninsula residents will derive greater benefit from it than we do," he said.
>
> "It is time," the Mayor concluded, "to look for a plan that would put all of these facilities under one jurisdiction. The Bay Area Council's report might be the sparkplug to do the job."
>
> The Mayor said he thought consolidation should stop short of San Francisco's water supply, however. He said long-term contracts to furnish water

to neighbor counties from Hetch Hetchy surpluses would be better than a water district.

Centralization of Functions

Sometimes it is possible to arrive at a piecemeal solution of some of the problems facing a metropolitan area by joining agencies of different governmental units, or by giving to one unit functions that were formerly assigned to two or more. Perhaps the most common example of this is the city-county health department. This one agency does the work formerly handled by two. This avoids duplication and makes it possible to achieve economies by better use of available staff and centralized buying and administration.

Central purchasing and personnel operations are also quite feasible. Research and planning are areas where central functions could give us better and cheaper local government. Indeed, any of the staff functions—those which service the operating departments—might be centralized without too much difficulty.

Little progress has been made in centralizing line, or operating, functions except in health and welfare, where the state governments have tended to be a more active and unifying force.

Centralization of function is not a final answer to the problems of disorganized government, but it allows a government reformer to approach a single problem at a time and have a somewhat better chance of getting something done about it. It does not add to the complexity of government, as does the addition of metropolitan authorities.

Annexation

Annexation is simply the extension of city boundaries to take in the urban areas immediately adjacent. The outside area becomes a part of the city, assumes its share of the tax burden, and receives in return the urban services which it needs and which the city is capable of offering. This is the ultimate, logical answer to fragmented metropolitan area government.

For a while this worked well. City boundaries at one time in our history marked the division between urban and rural communities. As city-like areas grew at the city limits they became, in fact, parts of the city through annexation.

This device has become increasingly unpopular in the twentieth century. Cities sometimes have expanded to the point where they have reached areas which have built up as village centers. These centers have identities of their own which they are reluctant to lose. The residents outside of the city may fear that annexation would force them to pay more in taxes. Some experts feel that part of the trouble is that city authorities have been inept at "selling" annexation to adjacent areas. State laws, too, tend to make annexation difficult.

Alabama has given its cities some control of the area just outside their limits. Cities of 6,000 and over can enforce police and sanitary ordinances within three miles of the city limits. Smaller cities can do the same within a mile and a half of the city limits. Cities are also empowered to levy business license taxes in the same area at a rate no higher than that within the city. Cities may also control subdivision plats within five miles of the corporate limits.

Federation of Local Units

Under the federation plan a central government is established to deal with problems affecting the whole area, while smaller units are left to handle strictly local matters. Usually the central government consists of representatives of the smaller units. When the smaller units are known as boroughs this is sometimes called the borough plan.

This is still pretty much in the experimental stage, but it is working well in Toronto and a few other places. It seems to be the plan that is gaining favor most rapidly. Much depends on two fundamental questions: the system of representation, and the division of powers.

The federation plan shows promise of providing a solution in many areas. For example, several cities in a metropolitan area are not likely to desire to surrender their individuality and their powers to another level of government. The federation plan allows the cities to keep their individual governments to handle local issues, and to have a voice in area-wide decisions through representatives to the central government.

Most often the county unit is the one modified and used as the central unit under the federation plan. This makes for easier adoption. The county unit is already firmly entrenched, so it is easier to modify than abolish it. Also there is less of a sense of radical change and fewer voters are frightened.

Consolidation of City and County

For practical purposes the city and county governments are one in New York City, New Orleans, Philadelphia, and Boston. In most of these places some county offices still exist as such, but most of the functions are performed by a single administrative unit with over-all power.

This is a practical solution, but some difficulties are met in putting it into effect. It involves the abolition of a well-established form of government, and some officeholders will be out of jobs. They naturally object, and residents often do, too, just because they don't like to see familiar landmarks disappear.

Consolidation is often made difficult by state laws. The city of Baton

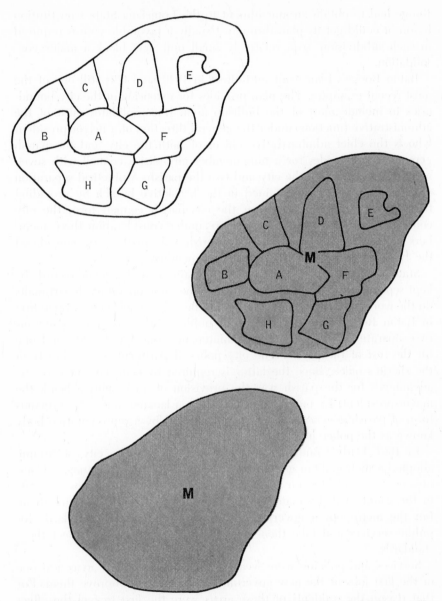

Fig. 2. Political development in our metropolitan areas often lags behind economic developments and communication. (*Top*) Eight incorporated areas (A, B, C, D, E, F, G, H) in a metropolitan area may have no common government except that of a county, which offers only minimum services. (*Center*) Under a federated system, one government (usually the county) is granted additional powers to direct metropolitan-wide functions, while the incorporated areas maintain strictly local functions. (*Bottom*) The logical (but seldom achieved) development: one metropolitan-area government controls the entire area.

Rouge had to obtain an amendment to the Louisiana State Constitution before it could get its plan through. Usually a favorable vote is required in each subdivision, so a relatively small unit may block a major consolidation.

Baton Rouge's plan went into effect in 1949, and it is still one of the most recent examples. The plan provides for extension of the city boundaries to include most of the built-up area. It consolidates most of the administrative functions under the general direction of a mayor-president who is the chief administrative officer of both the city and the parish (county). It provides for a nine-member city-parish council with seven members representing the city and two the parish. A practical separation of city and parish is maintained in the legislative branch by providing that the city representatives on the city-parish council form the city council. When purely city matters are under consideration these members meet as a city council. When parish-wide matters are considered the two parish representatives join the meeting.

State law in Louisiana requires that certain tax and revenue records be kept separately by city and parish. Since the same operating departments do the work, the separate records tend to be only a bookkeeping operation in Baton Rouge. The department of public works, however, maintains two separate divisions for street maintenance, one for the city and one for the rest of the parish. The city police department is separate from the sheriff's office, since the latter is required by state law. One of the advantages for the parish was the provision of an executive head, the mayor-president. Executive control had been lacking under the previous form of parish government, which was headed by a representative body known as the police jury.

In 1957 Dade County, Florida, which includes the city of Miami, adopted a metropolitan government headed by a county manager. Commissioners are elected on a nonpartisan basis. The 26 city governments in the county will be maintained as long as the residents desire them, but the metropolitan government can enforce minimum standards for public services and take them over if municipalities fail to meet these standards.

Services and policing were weak in the unincorporated areas and one of the first jobs of the new government has been to improve them. For that reason the residents of these areas were the first to feel the effect of the new plan. Miamians were happy because the metropolitan government planned to set up special service tax districts and tax only the residents who would benefit from police and fire protection, street repairs, and similar services. Miami residents felt that they had been paying county taxes for services to the unincorporated areas of the county.

No new government can take over without disputes as to its powers, particularly when it conflicts with other governments whose officials have been accustomed to more autonomy. These two articles from the *Miami Herald* illustrate the problem:

Dade County's new Metropolitan government Friday won broad powers to enforce its traffic laws and all other laws inside the county's 26 cities.

Circuit Judge Pat Cannon's ruling was immediately appealed, however, to the Supreme Court by the Village of Miami Shores.

Shores officials had asked the court to say just what powers were left to the cities and what were supreme with the county under the Metro Charter.

Cannon left no doubt in his lengthy ruling.

The Metro charter, he said, supersedes all city laws except in fields where the charter specifically gives the power to the cities. These fields include the setting of zoning standards higher than Metro standards, and the right of cities to amend their own charters.

But, Cannon emphasized, cities are not free to ignore such countywide laws as the new Metro traffic code.

Dean Claussen, member of the Shores Council and president of the Dade League of Municipalities, did not express concern over the ruling.

"The suit was filed," he said, "strictly for clarification on provisions of the charter. We thought there might be a possible discrepancy between the Metro charter and the constitutional amendment on which it was based."

If the Supreme Court upholds Cannon, he said, "I'm not sure it will have any great effect on the cities."

County Manager O. W. Campbell viewed the ruling as only one of a series he expects to secure Metro's position.

"Maybe," he said, "ultimately, people will believe that the charter means what it says."

He said the county will wait for final Supreme Court ruling in the case before making any changes. There is money in the new budget, he said, to expand Metro court to take over all traffic violations.

"We can go either way, depending on what the court rules," he said.

Cannon permanently enjoined Miami Shores from further enforcing its own traffic laws and ordered it to follow the Metro law. Village police, however, will enforce it.

And the Shores court and judges were ordered to stop trying traffic violations, except those now pending.

That would send all traffic offenders to Metropolitan Court. It now operates only in the unincorporated area and in Opa-locka and South Miami, which voluntarily agreed to recognize the Metro code.

Once in a while the citizen may be caught in conflicting rulings:

Drivers will be caught in the middle Friday when Metro begins its crackdown on cities still issuing their own auto inspection stickers.

Miami and Miami Beach are the main targets.

But it's the man behind the wheel who can be arrested, if Metro officials carry out their threat to start arresting motorists who buy city inspection stickers after Aug. 1.

County Manager O. W. Campbell and Public Safety Director Thomas Kelly made the threat Monday, in announcing that no new stickers except those issued by Metro will be recognized as valid beginning Friday.

The crackdown is expected to lead to a court fight.

Miami Beach already has informed Metro it will continue issuing its own stickers unless the court orders it to do otherwise.

Miami has not openly balked at the order. But Assistant City Manager Ray Williams said Monday the city can't comply without a resolution by City Commissioners. And they are not scheduled to meet again until September.

Involved in the dispute will be motorists whose present stickers already have expired or which will expire in August.

If they go to any except the nine presently approved stations, they'll get stickers that Metro police will consider invalid.

Consolidation has existed in some places for more than a hundred years, and generally has worked well. Getting it adopted elsewhere has been difficult.

Separation of City and County

In other areas an attempt has been made to get better government by separating the city entirely from the county. Virginia law provides that cities of more than 5,000 population shall be separate from the county in which they are situated, except for a court system. Cities larger than 10,000 have separate courts. Baltimore, San Francisco, St. Louis, and Denver are also separate from their counties.

One major disadvantage of separation is that cities are frozen within their boundaries, with very little chance to expand. Rural areas, too, are often placed at a disadvantage because much of their most valuable property is taken off the tax rolls by separation.

Separation seems to develop most often when urban residents feel that they are paying more than their share of the costs of county government.

Separation in states other than Virginia is usually a complicated process and frequently it results in difficulties in apportioning representatives to a state assembly.

At best it seems to quiet the bickering between city and county as to the proper division of tax burdens. It leads to no basic solutions and causes problems of its own. Contiguous rural and urban areas together make up an economic unit. Rural residents need the urban area as a shopping center and for many other services. Many urban areas, too, are such only because they serve the economic needs of the surrounding area. Separation certainly contradicts the economic realities, and economic considerations are fundamental to political ones.

The Future of Metropolitan Areas

The migration to cities and our increasing population portend a change in many of our institutions and in our national outlook. We have been an urban nation for years, but we have not wanted to admit it. We have rural beginnings, and, like the country boy who makes good in the city, we like to think that we're really country folks.

This viewpoint will change as urban-oriented generations grow up, and part of the change will be increased attention to improving our metropolitan areas. We will see in a later chapter how our state legislatures and our national Congress have overrepresented the country areas. This has resulted sometimes in unsympathetic treatment of urban problems. Eventually this will change because political control will shift, although slowly, with changes in population.

Some political scientists predict a closer relationship between metropolitan areas and the federal government, with a corresponding decline in the influence of state governments. Others see state governments as the agencies which will eventually bring unity to our urban tangle.

Certainly reporters will find that more and more of their stories involve several levels of government. It seems almost certain that the devices mentioned in this chapter will be used, with infinite variations, as our urban areas try to bring order to their governments. The plain fact is that we are trying to govern huge areas and large populations with controls that were designed for rural populations which needed far fewer government services. The result is not only expensive and inefficient government, but also undemocratic and unnecessarily complicated government.

What Is the Reporter's Job?

Times of swift change bring more responsibility and more opportunities to newspapers and their reporters, as well as to political leaders. Most of the individuals participating in the revolutionary population shift we have been considering do not understand it or its consequences.

As Americans, we have a curious tendency to be extreme about our attitudes. We tend to hang on to things because they are old, without examining their value, or we tend to welcome change as "progress," again without examining its value. In our move to suburbia and exurbia we have added chaos to confusion by mixing up our two contradictory viewpoints. We seem to think that in 50-foot suburban lots we will recapture the country graces of earlier days and maintain the advantages of a city job and city social contacts.

Sometimes it seems to work that way; at other times we get the disadvantages of both country and city. The contempt of some planners for much of our new development is expressed by their common term for it—"urban sprawl."

Nevertheless the suburbs and the metropolitan area problems will undoubtedly continue to grow and require more attention from newspapers. It is likely that expert reporting will be needed here more than in many other areas in the years just ahead because of the rapid changes which appear to be in the offing.

Reporters need to see that each metropolitan area is in reality a unit, and to help their readers understand this. Some newspapers have a tendency to think they are doing their job when they report the government and politics of their city. When the city is just the hub of a great urbanized area this is entirely inadequate. Newspapers should not feel that they are responsible only to those who elect the mayor and city council. They should feel accountable to all the people in the area in which they circulate. Since most city newspapers circulate throughout their entire metropolitan area they have an opportunity to serve as a unifying force. In some areas they seem to be about the only agencies which profess area-wide allegiance.

Area-wide reporting in depth is needed. Reporters will have to do more than summarize reports and speeches. They will have to find out what is going on, what forces are shaping the metropolis, and how these forces affect newspaper readers. The sources of this information are census reports, public officials, public records, and private and public research agencies. Reporters may sometimes find that all of these sources do not give them the information their readers need, and that they must do primary local research, using social scientists' methods. Reporters will have to talk with many people to add human interest to figures and trends.

One year after the Miami area's metropolitan government went into effect, Juanita Greene told of its effect on one family in this article in the *Miami Herald:*

> The Rowland Finks are one of those happy families.
>
> They're happy with each other, happy with Miami, and happy with their city government.
>
> And they're happy, too, with Metro—they think.
>
> "There isn't much we want from the county," said the young mechanic, who lives in one of the older sections of Miami, at 225 NW 35th Ave. "Our biggest hope is that it will lower taxes."
>
> "Yes," put in Mrs. Fink, a lively young mother of two. "We voted for it because we were told it would eliminate duplication—whatever that means."
>
> So far their lives have been untouched by the new Metropolitan government, which started operating a year ago. And even in the future, when Metro really gets rolling, they'll notice less change than the people in the unincorporated area and most of the other cities.
>
> The benefits will be there, but most will be indirect.

The Finks already get good service, from the City of Miami.

"We have a library, a playground, and a swimming pool nearby," Mrs. Fink pointed out. "Our street is in good shape and we have sidewalks."

"Even the police protection is good," added Fink. . . .

Why, then, did the Finks, so content with their lot, vote for Metro?

"It sounded like a good idea," said Fink.

"The day may come," predicted Fink, "when Metro can give us better service than the city does. If that happens, I wouldn't mind if it took over. We don't care who does the job, as long as it doesn't cost too much."

The *Christian Science Monitor* describes and evaluates suburban life in this extract from an article:

The suburbs are church-going communities. In most suburbs family attendance at church is regarded as right for the children, and parents feel the responsibility for encouraging their attendance. Result: the whole family goes. The suburban church, often interdenominational, provides many social, counseling, and recreational services. Whether the growth of the suburban churches indicates a true religious movement is debated by some churchmen, but no one denies that people who never went to church when they lived in the city become regular church attendants at church or synagogue in the suburbs.

Families do more things together in the suburbs. Evenings often see the whole family take off, clad in country club clothes, for a jaunt through the shopping center. Here, the car conveniently parked, they look over all the new temptations—the backyard play apparatus; the terrace furniture; the kitchen labor-savers; the new model tricycle—and plan their next involvement in installment purchasing. (No wonder Fortune magazine calls this market "Big and lush and uniform.")

Suburbia believes in education. It does not always support it as it should, lacking the tax base which industry gives a city, but it definitely wants its children to get a good high-school education and go to college. The percentage of high-school seniors who express their intention of going on with their education is much higher in the suburbs than in the city, judging by the Chicago area. Is Suburbia's trend toward informal, sociable, extrovert living to be welcomed? To the extent that it brings a sense of open-air freedom, of friendliness, of more congenial family living into the American culture, the answer is "Yes." On the other hand, the city has much to give—in cultural opportunities, in intellectual stimulus, in time for thought—which the suburban home, with its many calls to work and play, does not encourage. The final answer is that each can benefit by the influence of the other. We need both.

REPORTING ASSIGNMENTS

Write an article designed for publication in your local newspaper based on these reporting assignments:

1. Define the population area. If you live in one of the "standard metropolitan areas" explain to your readers what this means. Tell how many people live in the area, how the population is distributed, how it ranks with other population centers in the state or nation.

2. Describe population trends in your area for the past 50 years. Have residents been moving into the city? Out of it? Has the suburban area been growing? How does this compare with state and national trends?

3. Describe the governmental units in your area. How well are they designed to meet present governmental problems?

4. Assess your city as a social and cultural center. Do people come into the city for concerts? To visit museums or libraries? Are there drama programs? Lectures?

5. Describe the distribution of population in your state. How many residents are city dwellers? How many suburbanites? How many rural? How many metropolitan areas are there in the state?

6. Tell how much industry is situated in your city, as against the amount outside the city but nearby.

7. Interview a company executive to find out why his plant is inside or outside the city. If possible, select a company which has recently moved into the area.

8. Compare views of three officials as to what areas get the best break on taxes in your district. Interview a county official, a city official, and an official of a village or town outside the city, but in the county.

9. Describe the level of governmental services in the unincorporated areas of the county. Compare services there with services in the villages and other incorporated areas.

10. Describe the amount of cooperation between city and county governments in your area. Are there any joint departments? Is there joint operation of any facilities?

2

Units of Local Government

Every editor wants his paper to do a good job in covering the affairs of the local government. Since nothing can compete with a newspaper in describing city and county affairs, reporters face a special opportunity and a special responsibility.

The newspaper's dominant position in local news coverage means an opportunity because it makes the newspaper indispensable to each of its readers. After all, no one can get along without a knowledge of what is happening in his own community. The newspaper's responsibility comes from the realization that a constant flow of information about local government is essential to a democracy.

For these reasons the reporters who cover local government are usually the most skilled ones on a newspaper. They are often just as capable as their colleagues in the state capitals and in Washington. The local reporters seldom write stories of national significance, but to home-town readers the copy they produce often is more important.

Reporters covering local units of government need an understanding of government in general, a detailed knowledge of how their local units operate, and that special skill of every good reporter—the ability to find out how the organization chart is translated into human patterns.

The city charter describes the formal procedure which must be followed in transacting public business. Underlying this is a web of personalities and politics which determines the course of action. This is true of any organization—the men who run it and their interrelationships shape its policies. A reporter must try to understand the men who run his local units of government. Perhaps members of the majority party iron out their disputes before council meetings so that they can present a united front at the session. Perhaps the mayor takes advice from one councilman, and rejects it from another.

In other words, the men who hold public office determine how the jobs are performed. What a reporter has to describe is the activity of a highly-complicated, always-changing, and very human machine for making and implementing decisions on public policy. How this machine works and what it accomplishes are the business of the local newspaper reader as a citizen.

In this chapter we will describe the units of local government and how they are usually organized. Local government is infinitely varied and each reporter has to become a student of his own particular government system.

Local government units are cities, counties, towns, boroughs, villages, and a bewildering array of special districts. Before we consider them separately it is well to consider the source of their power, for this is a key to their general duties and their relationships to other government units.

The Power Framework

The federal Constitution grants certain powers to the central government. The Tenth Amendment provides that "The powers not delegated to the United States by the Constitution, nor prohibited by it to the States, are reserved to the States respectively, or to the people."

Since the power to establish and control local government is neither assigned to the federal government nor forbidden to the states, it is clearly a function of the states. This means that the powers wielded by the local governments come from the states. Although a state constitution may provide for a considerable amount of local autonomy, the state is still supreme. An amendment to the state constitution can take the power away from local government. Just the same we have a strong tradition of local self-rule which would make it difficult to centralize power completely.

Local units come into being in two ways: either at the volition of the state, or by the action of the local electorate with state approval.

Counties exist in all our states except Connecticut, Louisiana, and Alaska. Connecticut had them from 1666 until 1959 when they were abolished. Louisiana has districts, corresponding to counties, which are called parishes. Farmers of Alaska's constitution took a horrified look at counties and overlapping units of local government in the other states and tried to keep the same thing from happening there. Later in this chapter we shall consider what they did about it. Most of the territory in the United States, however, is inside one of the more than 3,000 counties.

Counties are geographical subdivisions of the state; they were created by it, and they exist to carry out duties it assigns.

Cities exist because residents of an area felt the need for an urban government and asked the state to issue a charter. The charter usually specifies the type of government and grants certain powers.

Thus the city is more a creature of the local residents than is the county. Usually its officers have more discretion and wider functions, although in a few places which have adopted metropolitan government this distinction is being obliterated.

The other units of local government resemble either the county or the city in these aspects.

City Government

More than half of America's citizens are affected more directly by the city than by any other form of government.

For these millions the city government furnishes vital services—police and fire protection, health and sanitation, garbage collection, street maintenance—all of which are essential to life in a metropolis. When city services break down, city hall and newspaper offices hear the clamor at once. And why not? Who wouldn't complain if firemen were tardy, traffic unregulated, garbage uncollected?

Newspapers and news-conscious radio stations realize that they have a ready-made mine of interest in their city government. They know, too, that it is one of their prime responsibilities to keep their readers informed about it.

Although they have a considerable amount of power, city governments are still creatures of the state. A heavily populated area may become a city with the issuance of a charter by the state legislature. This charter is a conditional grant of the state's authority. It gives the city certain powers while the state retains others, and the whole grant is revocable. For example, the governor will send the state militia to an area in which local authorities are unable to maintain law and order.

The charter becomes the working blueprint of the new city. It defines the type of government the city is to use and describes the functions and powers of its officials. It is required reading for a reporter or editorial writer who hopes to explain the functioning of his city.

In the early days of our national life our cities were influenced by the example of the federal government. If the system of checks and balances was good on the federal level, it was assumed that it also was good on the local level. Thus we developed a pattern of municipal government featuring a legislative body to make policy decisions, an executive to carry them out, and a separate judiciary. The executive was called a mayor, and often the legislative body was divided into two houses, called a board of aldermen and a common council. The bicameral legislative body proved very cumbersome for city governments and has almost disappeared from American cities.

The division of powers between an executive and a legislative branch seems to be impossible on the local level, although newer forms of city government often seem to achieve workable distinctions. What is the exact difference between a policy decision and an administrative decision? We have come to believe that budget-making, major expenditures, over-all planning, and extent of municipal services are matters for legislative decision. The decisions necessary to implement the policy are administrative.

Three kinds of city government are in general use in the United States today. They are mayor-council, commission, and council-manager. Mayor-council is of two types: strong mayor and weak mayor.

MAYOR-COUNCIL. Under the mayor-council plan the voters elect a council and a mayor. In general the mayor is the executive and the council makes policy decisions. In most governments of this type the distinction is not very clear-cut. In fact, the mayor is often expected to be a leader in policy formulation.

The mayor may or may not be a member of the council. In smaller cities and villages he is likely to be the presiding officer.

The difference between a strong mayor and a weak mayor government is best discovered by asking a series of questions:

How do the other administrative officers of the government get their jobs?

In a strong mayor government they are appointed by the mayor and are responsible to him. He can fire them, too. In a weak mayor government these officers are appointed by the council, or they are elected.

Who has the deciding power in budget-making?

In a strong mayor government the mayor prepares the budget and submits it to the council. The council may have power only to accept it or reject it. This puts the mayor in a very strong position because councilmen cannot delete separate items, and they cannot refuse to pass the budget except in extreme cases because that would shut down the city government. If the council prepares the budget the mayor may still be in a strong position if he has an item veto. This means that he can eliminate any item. In a weak mayor government the council may have almost complete control of the budget. Most cities are somewhere between these extremes.

Can the mayor veto council actions?

Obviously he is stronger if he can.

Does the council, through its committees, try to run the operating departments of the city?

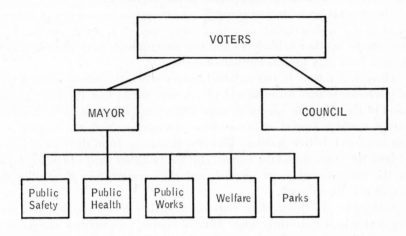

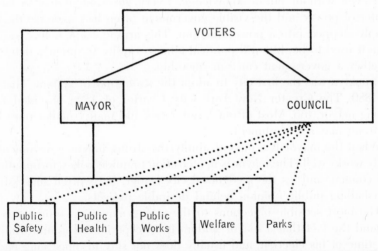

Fig. 3. Under the *strong mayor system* of city government, the council, with the mayor, determines policy, but the mayor supervises the operating departments. Under the *weak mayor system,* the council assumes more control of the operating departments. The mayor's power may be decreased still further by direct election of some of the operating heads, and by removal of his control over the budget.

In some weak mayor cities the committees of the council really run the city. In strong mayor cities the committees usually have to content themselves with making suggestions to the mayor.

The general term "mayor-council" covers so many varieties of government that it is descriptive only in a vague way. A reporter moving from one city to another is likely to find the governments very different, even though both may be labeled mayor-council.

There was a time in our national history when the mayor-council type of government was so inefficient that it was not in fact the true government of the city. The mayor in some cities was powerless to do anything except wield a trowel at cornerstone ceremonies, and the council was not in a much better position. This situation arose from the lack of power of both the council and the mayor, and the fact that most operating heads of the government were elected and thus responsible to neither the mayor nor the council.

Such cities got things done only because they had an undercover government which gave directions. This, of course, consisted of the political boss and his coterie. If, as often happened, the boss was able to dictate who was elected to office, it was obvious who controlled the government.

This was a bad arrangement because it resulted in a secret or semi-secret government. Decisions often were made without public discussion and even without public knowledge. Every government has to have a center of power and the visible government often had none, so the boss simply stepped into a power vacuum. This arrangement is less common than it used to be, but still political alliances quite frequently determine whether a government can run smoothly.

Brooklyn was the first city to adopt the strong mayor system. That was in 1880. The Greater New York City Charter of 1898 provided for a strong mayor, too. Most of our larger cities and many smaller ones have a strong mayor government.

When the mayor is a man of ability the strong mayor government usually works well. The mayor is in a position to guide policy formulation in the council, and, as the recognized city leader, he is often successful in marshalling public opinion behind desirable projects.

The most sensible objections to the strong mayor government center around the fact that a mayor seldom is an experienced administrator at the time of his election, and usually does not stay in office long enough to develop a high degree of administrative skill. In addition to his administrative responsibilities, the mayor is chief policy-maker. In this capacity he works with the general public and the city council. In addition, the mayor is the ceremonial head of the government, which means that he has to present a welcoming speech every time the state's radish growers come to town for a convention. With all these duties any administrator would have too little time to run the huge establishment required by even a medium-sized city.

This criticism applies to a state governor and even to the President of the United States. Its truth varies with the individuals involved and their particular situation, but it is a valid criticism of many units of government. In some cities the mayor has been given an administrative officer or executive to shoulder most of the purely administrative work. In a few places this officer is responsible to the council. Among the cities which have used such an official are San Francisco, Los Angeles, New York, Boston, and New Orleans.

The weak mayor government seldom works well in cities of any size. Authority is so diffused among officials, committees, and commissions that it is difficult to get anything done or to place responsibility.

THE COMMISSION FORM. Galveston, Texas, is usually credited with originating the commission form of city government. Its mayor and council were inadequate to deal with the aftermath of the disastrous flood of 1900, and the citizens turned to a committee of businessmen. They proved capable, and the "Galveston Plan" was widely hailed.

Actually several cities had experimented with similar plans during the last quarter of the 19th century. They included New Orleans, Washington, D. C., Memphis, and Mobile.

The essential elements of this plan are that the citizens elect a commission, usually of five men. They are elected at large instead of by ward or election district, and each one heads a major operating department of the city. The commission meets to make policy decisions. The old theory of separation of administrative and legislative powers is abandoned. The commissioners individually are operating heads of the government; together they form the policy-making body.

Gradually flaws became apparent, and the commission form of government is on the way out. Too often the commissioners who were good enough politicians to get elected were not good enough administrators to handle a large city department. Popular election of administrators made it impossible to be sure that trained talent would be running the government.

In Newark, New Jersey, and some other cities, the commissioners got into the habit of accepting each other's recommendations for their departments. This meant that there were five governments instead of one. Staff functions, such as purchasing and personnel, were often not centralized and sometimes salary scales differed from one department to another. A majority of the commission—three members—got together in some cities and favored their own departments for political reasons rather than for the general good.

In short, the commission form of government proved particularly sensi-

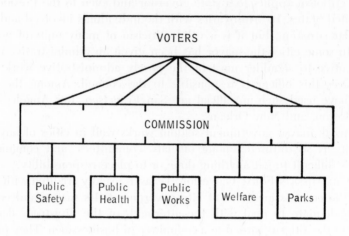

COMMISSION GOVERNMENT

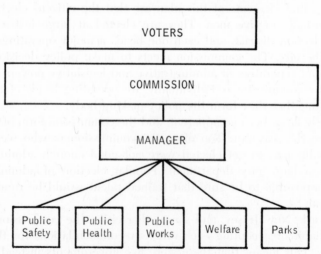

COMMISSION-MANAGER GOVERNMENT

Fig. 4. In the *commission* form of city government, voters elect members of a commission, which is the policy-determining body. Separately, each commissioner heads an operating department of the government.

In the *commission-manager* form of government, the commission determines major policy and hires a manager who runs the operating departments. (Operating departments vary from city to city.)

tive to the quality of the men running it. When the commissioners were men of great skill and devoted to the public good it worked well. It is fairly easily shaped to the desires of political opportunists, however, and fails miserably when poor administrators are at the helm.

Perhaps its greatest contribution was that it started experimentation which led to the council-manager form of government. Accompanying the commission form, too, were experiments with short ballots, initiative, referendum, and nonpartisan election of city officials.

COUNCIL-MANAGER GOVERNMENT. The council-manager government consists of a small council, usually five members, that hires a professional city manager. The council is the policy-making body; the manager is the administrator—the man who puts the council's decisions into action.

Staunton, Virginia, was the first city to have a manager. Charles E. Ashburner was appointed to the post there in 1908. The city did not have a council-manager government in the way we understand it today because it retained a bicameral council and a mayor.

In 1911 the New York legislature turned down a plan drafted for a city manager for Lockport, New York, but the "Lockport Plan" served as the basis for plans later adopted by Sumter, South Carolina, in 1913, and by Hickory and Morgantown, North Carolina, soon after.

In the typical manager plan the council determines the budget, sets the salary scale, levies taxes, and makes appropriations. The council is supposed to keep its hands off the administrative affairs of the city. It is the manager's duty to hire and discharge personnel, within the civil service stipulations, and to coordinate all the departments of the administration.

Usually the council is elected at large on a nonpartisan ballot.

The council-manager plan has proved successful in many places, and is gaining favor. Cincinnati is the largest city with a manager government.

Where the manager form has failed, it has been because the council was unwilling to forego politics, interfered with the administration of the city, or failed to hire a qualified manager. Poorly-drawn charters have sometimes been a contributing factor.

City Functions and Departments

We have examined the various types of city government. The variety of forms is great, but there is much more uniformity in function. Basically the city is a service organization, providing certain needs of its residents. The major functions are handled by departments.

PUBLIC SAFETY. The traditional concept of the public safety department includes a commissioner of public safety or a board charged with overseeing the police and fire departments. The idea was that a layman might well head the police department as the President, a civilian, heads the

United States armed forces. The commissioner or the board might be elected or, more often, appointed by the mayor or council.

More commonly now the chief of police and the fire chief are responsible directly to the mayor or city manager. The police department is discussed in Chapter 9.

Fire departments figure in some of the most dramatic stories that newspapers print. Many newspaper offices used to have extensions of the fire alarm system in their offices. Now this early information on fires is more often obtained from a man at police headquarters or over the police radio. Big fires are dramatic stories and in small communities even little ones are treated briefly for the record.

Other rich sources of stories, sources too frequently neglected, are found in this department. Recruitment, promotions, training programs, new equipment—these and many more make good local copy. Also important are the "trend" stories which can be developed from reports and fire department records. These stories may include the number of fires reported, with total and average damage, the cost of fire protection as compared with that in other cities of the same size, and comparative insurance rates. Fire prevention work, too, is highly deserving of attention.

PUBLIC HEALTH. Usually directed by a commissioner of health, this city department concerns itself primarily with preventive medicine. Sanitation, nutrition, disease control, eradication of rodents, and inspection of public eating places and food handlers are among its primary concerns. Visiting nurses and free clinics are among the services usually maintained. Bureaus found in health departments are those for communicable disease control, school inspection, tuberculosis control, child hygiene, nursing, laboratories, vital statistics, food, and sanitation.

Thanks to the efforts of health department staffs across the country, stories originating here seldom have the dramatic impact of an epidemic. For this reason the health department is sometimes neglected by the news media, which emphasizes stories from the fire and police departments because such stories are easy to dramatize. It takes dogged hunting for stories, careful interpretation of facts, and a flair for turning out readable copy, but the stories from the health department are potentially among the most interesting and important to be gathered from the city government.

EDUCATION. An important concern of all levels of government, education is still primarily locally controlled, although state and federal governments offer grants by which funds are made available to school systems on condition that certain requirements be met.

In all but a few American cities members of the school board are elected by the voters. This, together with a considerable amount of independence in financial matters, gives the school system much autonomy.

The school system is a big operation in a fair-sized city. It has a big physical plant, many employees, and spends a great deal of money. School board meetings can be complicated affairs, but the news they generate is vital to any community. So is the news from the superintendent's office. Chapter 4 is devoted to education.

PUBLIC WORKS. In a public works department are grouped a multitude of the service functions inherent in the city government. It is usually the public works department which hauls away trash and garbage from householders' doors. It is the public works department which maintains the streets, the sewage system, and the public buildings. An efficient public works department may be half-forgotten by the public, but if services are not maintained readers will look to the newspaper for an explanation.

WELFARE. Since the depression of the 1930's, welfare has not been regarded as a purely local function. The county poor farm has given way to elaborate welfare programs aimed at making as many persons as possible self-sufficient and at taking care of those unable to fend for themselves. State and federal governments supply part of the funds and supervise some aspects of the program. Joint city-county welfare departments are fairly common.

PLANNING. Civic planning is a function of all branches of government, including all the departments of a city government. Estimating future needs and making intelligent provision to meet them is as much a community function as it is a function of a well-ordered family life.

Many cities have a group specifically charged with planning, but some parcel it out to a housing commission, a traffic board, a parking authority, and to any number of other agencies. When there is a planning board or commission it usually carries over-all responsibility for making surveys, interpreting results, and co-ordinating the planning of other agencies. Most news media realize the story possibilities in planning. Zoning is one phase of planning.

HOUSING. Many cities now maintain some kind of a housing authority or agency which is charged with the continuing responsibility of providing low-cost public housing for underprivileged families. This involves many other aspects of city life, including planning and urban renewal. Since the state and federal governments are active in financing this kind of development the housing director is likely to spend much of his time negotiating with them. This will lead to many stories involving all three levels of government, as considered in Chapter 3. One of the interesting recent trends is toward building housing especially designed for older people, who make up a larger proportion of our population each year.

County Government

The counties, as we noticed earlier, differ from the cities in that they were created to carry out state functions and are agents of the states. It is strange, therefore, from an administrative point of view, that their officers are usually elected by the people of the county. This contrasts with a centralized system in which the county officials would be appointed by the state government and removable by it. Although county officials get their jobs, usually, by local election, their state responsibilities are pretty well spelled-out in state law and presumably state officials could remove them on sufficient cause. Our traditions of local government are so strong, though, that most state officials would attempt this only as a last resort.

Counties have been regarded as one of our weakest forms of government. Typically, the county is governed by a board of elected commissioners who form both the legislative and the executive heads of the government. In addition there is likely to be a large number of elected officials and boards which direct certain phases of county activity and are under the control of the board only when it comes time to get their budget approved. It is small wonder that political scientists like to call the county "our headless government."

Alaskans intend to do without counties in view of all the difficulties with them in the other states. Much of the vast area of the 49th state is still so sparsely inhabited that county government is not needed anyway. Where some such level of government seems necessary the proposed constitution provides for a "borough" system. Alaskan planners hope to gain cooperation between boroughs and any cities within them by requiring that borough councils shall include some members of the city councils, and by establishing intergovernment bureaus.

To avoid duplication of functions through special districts the general purpose units—cities and boroughs—will supply all services. Where only a portion of a borough needs a given service an agency may be established to supply it in the borough government or under the supervision of the state legislature. Thus only two levels of local government are permitted.

In another attempt to keep local government simple and flexible, Alaska's proposed constitution provides for a boundary commission in the executive department of the state government. This commission is empowered to change boundaries of local units subject to a veto by the legislature.

Many of our counties are still rural, needing few government services. For these the traditional county government is more or less sufficient. Many counties now, however, contain much urban area, often outside the city limits, and there is much pressure on the county government to provide services similar to those offered by municipal governments. In these metropolitan counties the old form of government is not adequate.

The county is usually the state court district, and county judges and lower court judges may be elected or appointed on a county basis. County governments also require other court and law enforcement officers which are described in the chapters on police and courts. These officers include the sheriff, the district attorney, perhaps a public defender, and a coroner.

Besides law enforcement, the county is charged with collecting taxes, assessing property, maintaining roads, supplying a health service, providing public welfare, and serving as the official record center for property transfers, vital statistics, citizenship papers, and many types of business records.

In addition to these standard duties many counties are having to assume additional functions by the force of the metropolitan movement. People are moving into county areas near large cities, failing to incorporate with the city, but demanding that the county or some government provide them with city-like services. The most common demands of this nature are for water and sewage services.

Once counties have been established it is difficult for the state legislature to change the boundaries. Although it has the power to do this, political considerations may make it almost impossible. The result is that throughout the country there are many counties with too small an area and too small a population to function effectively. Many states laid out their counties years ago on the principle that it should be possible for every resident to travel to the county seat and home again the same day. Modern transportation has enlarged this distance, but counties have not changed. One political scientist suggested that Oklahoma residents could be served better and at less cost if the state's present 77 counties were redistricted into 12 larger ones.

ORGANIZATION AND OFFICIALS. The organization pattern for the county is usually simple. It consists of an elective board plus a series of elective officers who handle specific jobs, such as welfare and law enforcement.

In almost half of the counties in the country the governing board is made up of three persons; in more than 100 counties one person does this job; and in about 300 counties there are 10 or more commissioners or supervisors. Where the county boards are larger they usually are composed of the supervisors of the townships within the county. This township representation system is followed in Michigan, New York, and Wisconsin.

In Tennessee the justices of the peace meet to form the county governing board. In Maine, New Hampshire, Massachusetts, and South Carolina the members of the state legislature from the county adopt the county budget, set the tax rate, and in general oversee county financial operations. Many states have some kind of supervision over county finances.

In most states the county board sets the budget, levies the taxes, approves major purchases, plans major public works such as new buildings, and supervises the affairs of the county which are not delegated by law to another elective official.

In counties which have no real administrative head the chairman of the board of supervisors often partially fills this gap by taking over some of the administrative work, usually assisted with the details by the clerk of the board.

Other county officials include:

The *county treasurer.* He keeps the county's money, disburses on order from the board, and is general financial officer.

The *auditor* or *comptroller.* This official conducts post audits to make sure the money was spent as authorized.

The *tax collector.*

The *assessor,* who evaluates real property for tax purposes. In some states this function is handled by city and town assessors. In that case there is usually an equalization board which allows for different appraisal systems so that each town will pay an equitable amount of the county tax.

The *county engineer,* who usually advises or supervises construction of roads and bridges and their maintenance.

The *county clerk* or *recorder of deeds.* His staff keeps records of property ownership, liens against property, records of time purchases, court judgments, citizenship papers, and sometimes vital statistics.

Sometimes there is a register of wills, a *surrogate,* or a *probate officer* who records wills and may hear cases involving contested wills.

The *jury commissioner,* who compiles and maintains lists of prospective jurors.

Road commissioners.

The *sealer of weights and measures* tests scales and other measuring devices used in stores and other commercial establishments.

Election commissioner or a *board of elections* keeps records of voter registration, sets up polling places, and in general supervises elections.

The *county health commissioner* heads a department that in some places is combined with the city health department and primarily is concerned with preventive medicine.

The county *welfare board* or *welfare director* manages one of the county's important historic functions. Much of the money distributed by county agencies comes from state and federal sources. As we noticed earlier, city and county welfare offices are combined in many places, or the county office has assumed responsibility for the city, too.

Often the welfare director will have general supervision of a home for the aged or a hospital. In a large county he supervises the expenditure of large sums of money. Newspaper stories usually center around payments of money to the welfare department from the state government, amounts disbursed, institutions run by the departments, changes in welfare payments, and number of persons receiving various kinds of welfare aid.

Newspapers seldom print the names of persons receiving welfare payments. In places where newspapers have vigorously asserted their right to examine welfare rolls it has usually been for the purpose of discovering illegitimate use of funds rather than for revealing the names of persons receiving aid.

A few counties have managers and are organized much like the council-manager form of city government. A few others have administrative officers, without all the power of a county manager, but with some administrative power. Cook County, Illinois, and some other counties, have elective chief executives with powers similar to that of the mayor. Chapter 1 described the plan used in Baton Rouge, Louisiana, where the mayor-president is chief executive of the city and parish.

Other Units of Local Government

The towns are strongest in New England where they perform many of the duties elsewhere assigned to counties. New York and Wisconsin, as well as New England, call these units towns; in most of the 14 other states where they exist they are called townships.

The annual town meeting is still held in many of the New England towns and in a few other states. Here, in one of the few survivals of direct democracy, the voters pass laws, levy taxes, and elect officials. In New England the management of the town between annual meetings is entrusted to selectmen. Other officials include the town clerk, whose office handles most of the records kept in county offices elsewhere, the road commissioner, the overseer of the poor, the town treasurer, the constables, and, in the larger towns, other officials.

In some of the states there is a chief officer in the township. In New York he is called the supervisor and represents the town on the county board of supervisors. He is called town chairman in Wisconsin, and trustee in Indiana, Missouri, and Kansas.

In New England some of the towns include highly populated areas which demand, and get, urban services from the town government. In other states town functions have gradually been shifted to the counties or to urban governments. Sometimes towns serve only as election districts.

One peculiarity of the township is that occasionally it appears in only part of a state. South Carolina has two townships and the state of Washington has only a few.

The town or township is quite different in various parts of the country, but it often resembles a miniature county. It performs functions delegated by the state and it most often owes its origin to state action.

Villages and boroughs are incorporated places whose governments perform some of the functions of cities. The special district, another unit often found in local areas, was discussed in Chapter 1.

Covering Local Government

Local governments furnish many points of coverage that need to be reported regularly and thoroughly.

One of these is the meeting of the council, the commission, or other legislative body. Good coverage requires a reporter to understand the board's organization, its powers, and the political alignment and personal predilections of its members. Since the members know what is coming up, sometimes the issues are not fully explained in the session; the reporter needs to do some homework, too. This will make him familiar with the issues which are likely to arise in the meeting, make his understanding quicker at the session, and save him time when he writes his story. The time will be precious if he is up against a deadline.

Most legislative bodies at any level of government do the bulk of their work through committees. A reporter needs to know the committee system and what members are on each committee; he should cultivate sources of information on both. This will allow him to predict with greater accuracy the actions of the entire body, and prepare for such action. It will also allow him to give his reader an inside view of what is going on.

Sessions of public bodies are ordinarily open to the public. Usually the law requires that they shall be. Occasionally members will try to transact business in secret. Newspapers have two means of combatting this. One is to seek a court order requiring that the meetings be kept open. This works if there is a statute requiring the meetings to be open to the public. The other method is to publicize the fact that meetings are closed and that public business is being conducted in secret. This usually brings enough pressure to bear so that meetings are opened up. Of course, any board can go into executive session or act as a "committee of the whole" in which, technically, no public business transpires. The only real weapon against this is for the newspaper to make it undesirable from the legislator's own point of view. This can be done by bringing public pressure or by finding one or two members who are willing to tell what happened and so report the meeting anyway.

Other regular checkpoints in covering city government are the more important city offices. The mayor may hold regular press conferences. If he does not, he should be available regularly to reporters, as should council members and heads of the city departments. Commissions, such as the planning group, are frequently sources of good stories. The city clerk is a good source of news, for he usually keeps the minutes of the council and has an ear to city business in general.

The sources are somewhat parallel in county government. The officers of the board of commissioners, or the supervisors, are especially important where there is no designated county executive. The clerk of the board of supervisors, or whatever parallel officer exists, is helpful in preparing for and covering sessions of the board, and in many other matters, for he often wields authority for the board and transmits its orders. In some places this function is taken over by the county clerk. The county clerk's office is a natural source of many routine stories and trend stories which are obtained from the numerous records of which he and his staff are custodians.

One of the problems of covering any legislative body is that of being sure that participants are quoted correctly. When a member says he has been quoted incorrectly it is difficult to prove the charge or disprove it if there is no verbatim transcript of the proceedings. Even if there is an official record this may not always save a reporter because many bodies (including the United States Senate and the House of Representatives) allow their members to change their remarks for the record. Usually it is the very remark which a legislator decides to change which will make a good story.

Editor & Publisher tells how one reporter tried to solve this problem. After Mayor George R. Clough of Galveston, Texas, accused reporters of misquoting him, Joel Kirkpatrick carried a tape recorder to a meeting of the board of city commissioners. He finally took the machine out after the mayor called police and got the board to forbid the use of the recorder.

Such incidents raise interesting questions as to whether there is any valid difference between reporting by the use of a reporter's memory, aided by pencil notes, and reporting by the use of a tape recorder. Until a few months before the incident Mayor Clough had owned a radio station and had been in the habit of recording commission meetings and playing them back over his station.

It seems likely that a mechanical means of recording information will eventually become commonplace, for it has the advantage of giving a complete record. There are disadvantages, too, and one of them is the time required to use tapes in writing a story.

Coverage of public meetings, regular checking with important local officials—these are the beginnings of good coverage. Too often, however, this results only in good routine coverage. If this is all a newspaper does it is likely to print only what the public officials want to see in print. The newspaper's real job is to find out what its readers need to know and print that. This may be different sometimes from what the officials want readers to know.

To tell its readers what they need to know, a newspaper should view its local government from at least five aspects and supply information regularly in all five areas:

1. *A basic description of the city and its functions.* How is it organized? What does it do? What is the job of the mayor? What does he do in an average day? What is the job of the common council? Major department heads? What terminology may be new to readers?

To a reporter covering city hall regularly this seems so elementary that it hardly needs repeating. Just the same many of his readers, and intelligent ones, will not have this information. Some who knew it once will have forgotten. It is a test of a reporter's skill to make this information interesting. It is obviously useful. Feature stories including personality sketches will be useful. Many newspapers which have printed this kind of series have been amazed at the reader reaction it brought.

2. *City facilities available to residents.* A good city does many things for its readers beyond the routine services of garbage collection, sewage disposal, water supply, and the rest. Many cities have magnificent libraries, good concerts, beautiful parks, free clinics, adult education programs. As a simple service to its readers a newspaper should keep them informed about these opportunities—and not just when some city official asks for help.

3. *Financial structure.* This is discussed in detail in Chapter 5. Here it is enough to say that a newspaper needs to be vigilant to tell the taxpayers how their money is being spent, and what kind of financial shape their local government units are in.

4. *Comparative studies.* A newspaper should be alert constantly to find examples which can be helpful at home from units of local government in other places. This can range from studying the effect of a new charter in a neighboring community, to sending reporters all over the country to study other forms of local government and how they might be applied at home. The *Denver Post* did just that to form part of a series of articles discussing possibilities of a new city charter.

5. *Citizen participation.* A newspaper should actively try to keep its readers interested and participating in the affairs of their local units of government. This is a big order, but newspapers can help. After all, local communities are more than governments and charts and statistics; they are places where people live. To most of their residents they represent

"home" and many of the good things of life. To newspapers as well as to other civic leaders belongs the job of holding up a vision of a finer hometown and helping its readers to achieve it.

The *Kansas City Star* under William Rockhill Nelson is credited with helping to pull Kansas City out of the mud and turn it into a city of parks and boulevards. Other newspapers are doing the same sort of thing every day for their cities.

REPORTING ASSIGNMENTS

1. Cover a meeting of the legislative body of your city. Write the story for local publication.

2. Do the same for the legislative body of your county.

3. Write a story or series of stories for local publication describing the structure of your city government.

4. Do the same for your county government.

5. Tour the office of the county clerk (or town clerk) and write a story about it.

6. Interview the head of one of the operating departments of the city or county and write a story about the department.

7. Interview the head of the civil service commission of your city or county for a story on recruitment of personnel. If there is no such official find out who does the hiring and what policies are followed.

8. Visit a fire station, and talk with firemen for a feature story on how firemen live and work.

9. If your city has a centralized planning agency visit it and find out what is being done to insure future orderly growth of the city.

10. Write a feature story or a series of stories describing your city as a cultural center.

11. Write a story describing the zoning regulations used in your community and tell how they are administered.

3

State and Federal Activities

State and federal governments have been gradually increasing their control over local units through the years. This long-term trend has been accelerating since the early 1930's and so it is natural that more and more local news stories come, in part at least, from state and federal sources.

Is the city seeking to revamp its charter? State law controls the possibilities and procedures.

Is the sewage system inadequate? State officials may insist on a new one and will certainly have to approve its design.

Is a new hospital needed? Perhaps state and federal funds can be tapped. If they are, minimum state and federal standards will be applied.

Has an industrial slump thrown local men out of work? The state employment office, supervised to some extent by the federal government, will become an important news source.

Is the city trying to eradicate the slums? The federal government may help, if it approves the plans.

In this chapter we will examine some of the ways in which state and federal governments are intervening in local affairs, and some of the methods they are using. Here we will only illustrate the trend and the coverage problems; it would take many volumes to cover the subject thoroughly. It is a subject of importance to reporters, for it seems inevitable that they will have to cover an increasing number of local-state-federal stories.

State and federal governments are also increasing their direct activities in relation to the citizens. These are the functions which officials administer without the participation of another level of government. State health department officials work with local officials on many projects, but they also have jobs to do directly and without help from local units.

Such activities may include restaurant and hotel inspection and licensing of many professions. Likewise the national government often co-operates with state and local units, but also has its own independent jobs to do. The Post Office, for example, has daily contact with millions of citizens.

In this chapter we will consider relationships between levels of government, and local activities of the state and federal governments, for both produce many important news stories.

Types of Control

It is convenient to discuss interrelationships as two phases: legislative and administrative control. Legislative control is one phase of the state-local relationship, and is the direct expression of the state legislature's power to control the destiny of the local units. The administrative control is more subtle, but often more important. Administrative control is exerted in several ways, as we shall see, and it is woven into the relationships among all three levels of government. The national government may exert control over a state; through the state it may exert control over local units; the federal unit may control local units directly; or the state may use administrative controls over the local unit.

This is an area of government little understood by the general public, and no wonder—it is subtle and complicated. This makes it all the more important that newspapers do a good job in reporting it, for in many respects it is more important than the more direct methods of control.

It is tempting to describe some of the forms of administrative control as "administrative co-operation" among the levels of government, because often the relationship seems, on the surface, to be purely co-operative. But control is still the right word because the highest level of government, if its officials are reasonably energetic, nearly always imposes its standards.

Originally the state government worked almost entirely through legislative control, but gradually this has shifted over so that the emphasis is on the administrative and "co-operative" aspects. In the hands of capable, conscientious administrators this shift is good because control is more flexible and can be more intelligently applied in each situation. Its dangers are that it can lead to a hierarchy of government "experts" who exert a great deal of control over decisions. They may be intent on imposing a given system without much regard for local wishes, and without being under public control to the extent that an elective body would be.

The federal government has from the start worked more through the administrative process to influence state and local governments. It had to because the Constitution strictly limits its direct power in these matters.

The administrative control may often sound soft and seem to be ad-

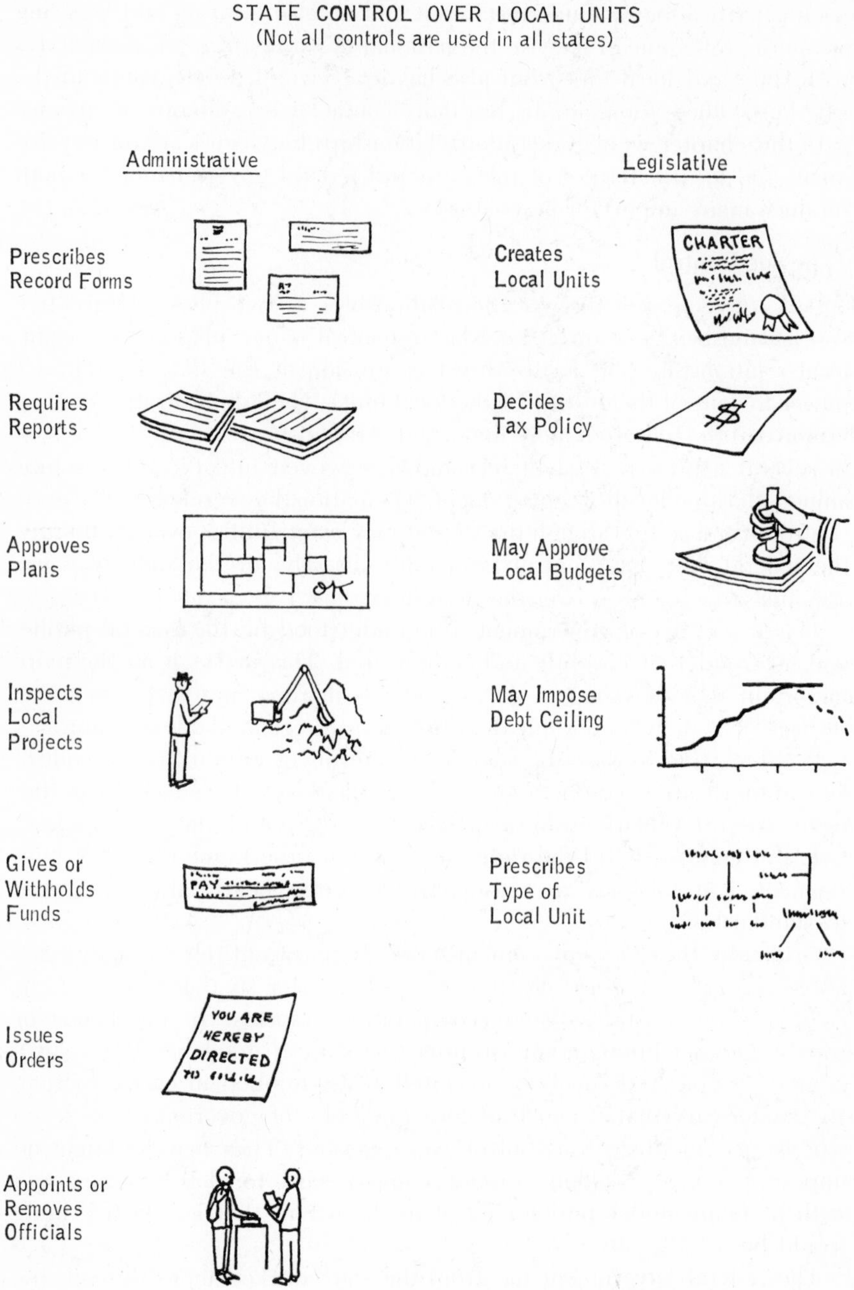
STATE CONTROL OVER LOCAL UNITS
(Not all controls are used in all states)
Administrative
Legislative
Prescribes Record Forms
Creates Local Units
CHARTER
Requires Reports
Decides Tax Policy
$
Approves Plans
OK
May Approve Local Budgets
Inspects Local Projects
May Impose Debt Ceiling
Gives or Withholds Funds
PAY
Prescribes Type of Local Unit
Issues Orders
YOU ARE HEREBY DIRECTED
Appoints or Removes Officials

Fig. 5

visory, but it is control, just the same, and has much power to shape our local and state governments. In essence the administrative control has been used to impose minimum standards on local units. It also tends to level government services throughout a state or the country by taxing the more prosperous areas to supply minimum services to the poorer places.

LEGISLATIVE CONTROLS. Since local units are creatures of the state, the legislatures have much power over local affairs. Their authority may be limited in two ways: by court decisions and by state constitutions.

Courts have sometimes upheld local self-rule as an inherent right, but more often they have held that local units have no power except what is granted by the state. This is the general rule today.

During the 19th century there were few constitutional restrictions on legislative power over local governments. Cities usually gained their powers by special act of the legislature. This often led to political log-rolling and inefficient city government.

Delaware and Florida still set up their municipal governments by special acts, but most state constitutions now require that legislatures deal with municipalities by general law. For this purpose cities are classified, most often by population, and legislation must apply to all cities within a given classification. Some legislatures defeated the purpose of classification by making classes so small that each might contain only one city, but courts have generally declared this unconstitutional.

Another phase of legislative control came into vogue with the "home rule" movement. Under this system the constitution provides that cities may adopt or amend their own charters. Sometimes this is permitted without any intervention by state officials, but more often approval of the legislature or the governor is required. Sometimes home rule provisions have been so difficult that many years have passed between the passage of home rule legislation and the establishment of even one home rule city in a state.

New York and some other states provide, in addition to home rule, several optional plans of organization.

New Jersey law permits cities to select from three basic plans of government: mayor-council, council-manager, and small municipalities plan. The choice is widened by including in these alternatives six kinds of mayor-council government, five council-manager types, and four of the small municipalities type.

The Wisconsin state constitution provides for home rule. Connecticut, Florida, Georgia, Iowa, Mississippi, North Carolina, and South Carolina grant fairly large home rule powers to local governments by legislation. Minnesota, Oklahoma, and Washington have short home rule statutes which confer broad powers on local governments.

Whatever the constitutional provisions, the state legislature is sure to be influential in guiding the affairs of local governments.

ADMINISTRATIVE CONTROLS. Both state and national governments control local units through administrative devices. These are more flexible than legislation.

Methods of administrative control range from such a subtle device as offering advice, to the definitely unsubtle one of putting the function into the hands of state officers. In between are methods which vary in strength. Some of them are supplying information, requiring reports, lending personnel, licensing, requiring that state officials approve plans, giving or withholding funds, and appointing and removing officers.

These powers are sometimes used conscientiously by state and federal officials to promote good local government. Sometimes they are used for political purposes. Quite often they are used carelessly. If the statutes require the state health department to receive reports from local units this may be a useful power or it may be a farce. If the reports are carefully filled out, if they are read when they get to the state office, and if use is made of the information on them, they are useful. On the other hand, the state department may take no notice if local officials fail to send in the reports. Or the reports may simply be filed away by a clerk, then forgotten. The possession of a power as stipulated in a statute does not necessarily mean that it is being used intelligently if at all.

Reports may be required simply to insure that certain records are kept and that they are maintained in a certain way. This, in itself, is a measure of control.

State governments often require reports from local health departments. State fiscal agencies also require reports from local agencies. Some states require that cities accept state supervision of their accounting practices; in other states such a system is optional. Often local governments will accept an accounting system provided by the states to avoid the trouble of setting up one of their own. When this is combined with state inspection, a considerable amount of control is present.

Federal-State-Local Co-operation

Grants-in-aid are used by both state and federal governments to help local units improve their services, and also to control the quality of those services. The principle is simple: The state or federal unit offers money for a given purpose with the provision that the funds will be withdrawn unless certain standards are met. This raises standards of local services throughout an area and also increases the control by the central unit.

One interesting aspect of the grant-in-aid is that it often involves three levels of government. The federal level makes funds available to states for specific purposes. The state is usually given general supervision of how the funds shall be spent, subject to the approval of federal officials. State or federal agents assist local agencies in drawing up plans, and make frequent inspections to insure that work is kept up to standards.

The Hill-Burton Act, for example, provides federal funds to help communities build hospitals. State and federal governments share costs with the community. Responsibility for planning as well as supervision is diffused through the three levels of government.

Urban Renewal: A Study in Federal Aid

Edward J. Logue, who has directed New Haven's battle against its slums, views urban renewal as an entirely new approach to city problems. He wrote in a *New York Times Magazine* article that it "focuses on the city as a whole and treats all urban problems as interrelated, both in their origin and their solution."

While many state governments are active in housing and slum removal programs, the major effort now being made in the country is sponsored by the federal government. It involves direct grants from United States funds to cities which meet specified conditions.

Boston, Hartford, and some other cities have been making great efforts with a combination of public financing and co-operation from business, but some cities feel that the costs of slum clearance are beyond their means, even with federal help. The cost of clearing slum land is nearly always more than the land is worth. Another difficulty is that owners of slum property often can make tremendous profits by renting small units to large families at high rents. Often the taxpayers foot the bill because many of the slum dwellers are public charges.

This problem of slum owners being unwilling to either tear down or fix up their lucrative property is illustrated in a long story by Wayne Phillips in the *New York Times*. Here are the first few paragraphs:

> New York City is spending more than $45,000,000 a year that is in effect a subsidy of slums.
>
> This money—a third of all that is spent on public assistance—goes into the pockets of landlords, much of it to pay for some of the worst housing in the city.
>
> Catering to welfare clients, for whom the city picks up the rent bill, has become a lucrative business for many slum landlords.
>
> Buildings that are among the most miserable in the city are tenanted almost exclusively by welfare clients. The rents they pay are as high or higher than those in much better housing.
>
> The Welfare Department is helpless to control the steadily rising rent bill it is forced to pay, or to compel landlords to provide decent housing for the taxpayers' dollars.

Its only alternative is to permit its clients—the poorest of the city's poor—to be dumped into the streets.

"We have no choice," Henry L. McCarthy, the city's Welfare Commissioner, said recently. "This is a profiteering situation and we are the victims of it."

One of the reasons owners of slum property can sometimes make exorbitant profits on it is that the property is in such poor condition that realistic appraisal of its worth leads to low property taxes. Added to this is the fact that it usually costs more to acquire and clear the land than it is worth. For example, the city of Baltimore paid three million dollars to buy and clear 30 acres near Johns Hopkins Hospital. It then leased the property on the basis of a $600,000 evaluation. Thirteen acres of New York City's slums cost nearly six million dollars and were resold for one million.

But slum clearance has dollars and cents justification. New construction on former slum land always results in higher assessments and thus more revenue for the city. Cities stand to save, too, in costs of municipal services. Slum areas, which produce the least in taxes, cost the city far more than any other areas because they require more policing, more fire protection, more clinics, and more services of almost every kind.

One 41-block area in Norfolk, Virginia, for instance, paid less than $40,000 in taxes, officials estimated, while the city spent $250,000 to provide municipal services. The area has now been cleared of slums.

Despite the social and humanitarian values, as well as long-term financial reasons for removing slums, many cities have felt that the job was too big for them. The mayor of St. Louis told a Senate committee that taxpayers of his city had voted more than a hundred million dollars for capital improvements over a period, and yet rebuilding the city was too big a job for local resources.

The federal government has stepped into this breach by making money available as loans and outright grants to buy land, raze buildings which are substandard, and prepare the site for other uses. The idea is that then it can be turned over to private investors who will develop it according to residential, commercial, or industrial uses designated by the city.

The federal government will absorb two thirds of the cost of making the land available; the city is allowed to provide its share in land, cash, or services. Thus New Haven estimated it would take $22.5 million to buy and clear 140 acres of its downtown slums, and that the federal government would pay $15 million of this. Mr. Logue figured that New Haven's $7.5 million share amounted to about $45 per resident "to get itself an entirely new downtown." The federal government will also pay the costs of preliminary surveys.

Control comes in the form of approval of plans and inspection of work to make sure it meets federal standards. In addition the Federal Housing and Home Finance Administrator must approve a program for the city's redevelopment—a major factor in city planning.

Considering the magnitude of the projects, it is not strange that progress under the federal program was slow at first. There were inevitable complaints by local officials that the federal government required too much red tape—approval by too many agencies, each with its own set of standards. Some legislators retaliated by complaining that a few city officials simply seemed to want a blank check on the federal treasury. Progress is speeding up and the impact of the federal program is likely to be felt in every city in the country.

The following story in the Newburgh, New York, *News* was obviously written after consultation with city and federal officials:

> Newburgh's $1,167,000 federal aid reservation for its Urban Renewal program is in danger of cancellation in another six months, if a new policy of the Urban Renewal Administration is followed through here.
>
> Walter S. Fried, regional administrator of the Housing and Home Finance Agency, disclosed Saturday that capital grant reservations for any UR project will automatically expire two years after approval of the preliminary application if the municipal or other local agency has not filed and obtained federal approval of more complete plans and a grant contract.
>
> Newburgh's preliminary application was approved 18 months ago.
>
> Lawrence Herbst, Newburgh's Urban Renewal director, said today that the city has moved as fast as possible on its project. The preliminary planning phase of the slum clearance and rebuilding project has been completed but approval of the preliminary report on project eligibility and relocation is still awaited from the FHHA. It's expected by the end of the month, Mr. Herbst said. The final planning stage should take from six months to a year, it is estimated by city officials. Then a final decision must be made by the City Council on whether to make final application for a UR grant.
>
> Both Mr. Herbst and City Manager Albert J. Abrams said today that Mr. Fried's comments would need more study and investigation before their significance can be determined.

Federal Highways

Another federal program which is local news for every newspaper in the country is the interstate highway system. Plans call for a limited access highway system to connect all the major population centers of the country. The federal program is paying 90 per cent of the cost, and sets uniform standards. The federal government has always been interested in highways. Article I, Section 8 of the Constitution gives Congress power "To establish Post Office and post Roads."

Despite this direct grant of power Congress has usually preferred to work through the states and to achieve control through conditions attached to grants.

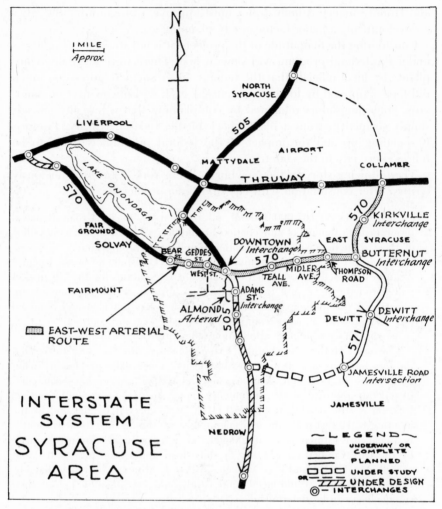

Fɪɢ. 6. The *Syracuse Post-Standard* used this map to illustrate the new highway system in its city, a project which involved the co-operation of local, state, and federal units of government. Highways are an increasingly important source of news. (Courtesy, *Syracuse Post-Standard.*)

Other Federal Stories

At times the federal government intervenes in local affairs in a very positive fashion and the result is a good story—locally and nationally.

When the United States Supreme Court held that separate schools for different races violated the Constitutional privileges of citizens, the government took positive action to force the Southern states to integrate their schools. The result varied from place to place. In Little Rock, Arkansas, federal troops and later United States marshals were used to force the government's program. This story could not help but have world-wide significance.

This direct intervention in local affairs even at the cost of violence is within our constitutional pattern because the Constitution requires that the federal government protect citizen's rights from being violated—even by their state governments. After the Supreme Court's decision that the rights of U.S. citizens were being violated the duty of the government was clear.

International relations, controlled by the federal government, often have local repercussions in border states. The St. Lawrence Seaway is exerting tremendous influence on the economy of New York, Illinois, and all of our states in its area. Division in Congress delayed the beginning of the project for 30 years after Canada became actively interested. The Seaway is a local story for many cities, but our participation is controlled from Washington.

Federal government activities of many types make local stories. The Tennessee Valley Authority has been a continuing local story in the states in which it operates, as well as a national story for the rest of the country.

Facts collected by federal agencies and released by localities are often good local stories, as these paragraphs from the *Baltimore Sun* illustrate:

> The cost of living in Baltimore reached an all-time high during June, the Bureau of Labor Statistics of the Department of Labor reported yesterday.
>
> Higher prices for food, housing and medical and personal care more than offset declines in transportation and recreational costs, the agency said. Apparel costs remained unchanged.
>
> The bureau's price index reached 124.8 per cent of the 1947–1949 average. This means it cost almost a quarter more to buy what could be purchased for a dollar ten years ago.
>
> June living costs for the city were .6 per cent over those recorded in March and 3 per cent more than this time last year.

Notice the lucid explanation of the price index in the second sentence of the third paragraph.

Local Federal Offices

The federal government is making news in almost every city every day. It is doing it through the broad programs such as those already mentioned and through the local offices of its various branches. The listing "United States Government" in the telephone book of any fairly large city will explain why most city editors keep a reporter on the "federal beat," covering the local offices of the federal government.

From time to time, nearly all these offices are newsworthy. The Post Office affects our lives directly and so its activities are interesting to readers. The law enforcement agencies of the federal government are discussed in Chapter 9. Along with local police agencies they deserve careful coverage.

The armed services have recruiters in all major population centers and they are good for occasional stories. The Immigration Service is represented at ports of entry.

Other important federal offices found in most cities include: service branches of the Department of Agriculture; Department of Commerce offices, usually including the Weather Bureau and the Civil Aeronautics Administration; the Federal Housing Administration; the Department of Health, Education and Welfare, including Social Security and Old Age Survivors Insurance offices; Labor Department offices of Apprenticeship Training and Wage and Hour Division; and Treasury Department offices, including the Internal Revenue Bureau and the Intelligence Division.

The list varies with each city, and the importance of each office varies with the type of community. Agriculture Department offices are much more important in farming centers, for example. In general the list of federal offices increases with the size of the city and with its importance as a communications center for an area.

State Administrative Devices

State governments, especially in times of emergency or when local officials are negligent, can exercise a considerable amount of direct authority in local matters.

Under certain conditions state officers can appoint or remove local officials. During the Nineteenth Century it was not uncommon for governors regularly to appoint and remove local police chiefs. This practice exists in a few cities today. The governor's power to remove officials found negligent varies from state to state. It is strongest in Florida, Maine, Michigan, and Pennsylvania.

In a few places state officials can issue orders that are binding on local officials. This is most common in education, public finance, and health. The New York Public Health Council, part of the state Department of Health, issues health regulations which are binding on all local health officials throughout the state except in New York City. The regional health directors supervise work of local officials.

Sometimes a state will take over a local function permanently or during an emergency. Massachusetts requires that local governments use the state personnel system in their recruitment. New Jersey has made such a service available to local governments, but has not required them to use it.

LOCAL STORIES COME FROM STATE AND FEDERAL
SOURCES

	State Government	Federal Government
Roads..................	Plans and builds state routes.	Finances highways as part of federal system.
Hospitals...............	Helps plan and finance some community hospitals.	Helps plan and finance some community hospitals.
Employment.............	State employment office will have local figures.	Provides over-all figures for comparison.
Urban renewal...........	State acts directly or helps local units with planning and financing.	Helps local units directly with planning and financing.
Sewage disposal..........	Sets requirements for local units. Insists on minimum standards.	Has some power through control of interstate waterways.
Public health............	Maintains inspection and sanitation services.	Provides advice and assistance. Operates veterans' hospitals and research facilities.

Other Local News from State Officers

State administrators have control over many kinds of activities. This means that there are likely to be many state offices in every large city and that the activities of state agencies often make local news. These offices are a regular port-of-call for local reporters. Sometimes the local story develops as a result of an inspection trip by officials from the capital, or in hearings before state officials.

Public utility regulation often becomes a matter of local interest. If the bus company wants to increase its fare or eliminate bus routes, it will have to obtain the consent of a state agency. Since this is important to many local people, hearings are likely to result. Often city officials will appear at these sessions. The news possibilities are obvious.

Public utility commissions must be consulted, too, when railroads want to change their service—whether it is to eliminate some trains or reduce the number of stops.

State activity in road construction is of local importance. There has been a tendency over the years for the state to take responsibility for a steadily increasing number of what were formerly town or country roads. The federal government is also important as a road-builder, as we have seen.

This story from the *Pittsburgh Post-Gazette* shows that this trend is continuing and tells why some local units like it:

County commissioners yesterday were advised to turn over 50 per cent of the county highway and bridge system to the state.

The transfer, if effected, would produce annual savings of at least $2,000,-

000, according to a study prepared by the Allegheny Conference and the Pennsylvania Economy League. . . .

Transfer of the highways, the report said, would enable the county to divert the savings to the growing demand for more services in other areas, such as health, libraries, garbage disposal and sewage treatment.

The recommended shift would give the State Highways Department administrative control and financial responsibility for 252.84 miles of highways and 257 bridges. The county would retain the rest, or exactly the same number of road miles and the same number of bridges.

Notice how information from state and city officials is woven together in opening paragraphs from a story in the *Louisville Courier-Journal*:

A new approach to the proposed New Albany bridge, using a strip of the Louisville flood levee as part of the roadbed, is being worked out by State engineers.

The new route, as compared with the Bank Street approach considered earlier, would disturb no houses or other buildings in Louisville, would do less damage to Shawnee Golf Course, and would probably cost less, City Works Director W. W. Sanders said.

The following paragraphs, taken from the same story, show that the federal government is also interested in the project. The story also illustrates the number of approvals necessary for projects in several jurisdictions.

The works director said the plan has the approval of Louisville officials and those of both states involved. Still needed is approval of the Federal Bureau of Public Roads and the Army Corps of Engineers, which is responsible for flood protection here.

The construction plans would in effect widen the levee toward the river to make room for four or six lanes of traffic.

Col. E. D. Comm, district engineer for the Corps of Engineers, said his office would have to inspect completed plans for the project to decide whether they would jeopardize the effectiveness of the floodwall. The levee's resistance to seepage of water must not be weakened, he said.

J. C. Cobb, Kentucky district engineer for the Bureau of Public Roads, was away from his Frankfort office yesterday. He was quoted earlier by the *Louisville Times* as saying of the new approach:

"We like the plan. It looks like it might be a better one than the Bank Street route."

The *Pittsburgh Post-Gazette* cites state and county officials as the source for figures on unemployment:

Claims for unemployment compensation and public assistance in the state and county are still rising—but at a decelerated pace.

This was indicated yesterday in reports from John F. Adams, executive director of the State Bureau of Employment Security, and George P. Mills, executive director of the county public assistance board.

State health departments are often very active in carrying out their own functions as well as supervising local units. Most state health departments are information centers for their states on the number of cases of communicable diseases; usually the health departments report this information by cities, towns, or counties, so it is important local news.

The health department is an educational department, too, with displays, literature, and often a speaker's bureau to promote healthy habits.

Health department officials are empowered to investigate water supply systems, dairy farms, and milk processing plants, and to supervise sanitary conditions in hotels, restaurants, rooming houses, and slaughter houses. The health department tries to avoid pollution of rivers and lakes. It is usually the state agency charged with licensing physicians, dentists, barbers, nurses, pharmacists, and embalmers. New York State licenses x-ray operators as a means of controlling the use of this device.

In all these activities, and many more, the average state health department is vital to the people of the state it serves. It is a good news source, and one that is often neglected.

The state insurance department or insurance commissioner usually has wide powers to regulate insurance companies. For example, when the Pennsylvania insurance commissioner approved rate increases for three Blue Cross plans in his state he ordered a broad program to lower costs and curtail unnecessary hospitalization. It involved study of plans in Pennsylvania and other states to cut costs and reduce hospitalization abuses. State insurance departments can use their regulatory powers, too, to insist that companies live up to the terms of their contracts.

State governments often exert a considerable amount of influence over labor relations through control of working conditions, safety devices, hours, wages, and especially child and female labor. This is considered in Chapter 20.

Agriculture departments collect farm statistics, including regional market prices which are very important news to the farm readers of a newspaper. The departments maintain agricultural experiment stations which test new techniques and equipment. Usually a service is provided for testing soil and fertilizers, the inspection of plants for disease, and general control of plant and animal disease within the state.

Agriculture departments and state agricultural colleges have men in the field helping farmers with their problems. These departments also conduct institutes and extension courses. Home demonstration agents have been an important factor in helping to raise the standard of living in rural homes by demonstrating better methods of canning and freezing food and other homemaking skills.

Another large area of state responsibility is conservation. State agencies charged with this job have general responsibility for developing state forest areas, preservation of fish and game, forest fire control, irrigation of arid lands, drainage of swamps, and many other activities often conducted in co-operation with the United States Department of Agriculture.

Highway construction and maintenance, already mentioned, is probably the most newsworthy activity of states in the area of public works, but often it is conducted by a highway department, distinct from the department of public works. Where this is done the public works departments still have a wide range of activities, including supervising state parks and playgrounds, monuments, dams, reservoirs, and public buildings. In New York and a few other states canals are still an important freight route.

Teamwork Gets the News

One of the satisfactions of newspaper reporting is that often stories can be covered and written by one person. The reporter has the satisfaction of seeing in print a fairly individual product, rather than being forced to merge his identity with that of the team in so-called "group journalism."

On the other hand there are many stories which do require joint activity by two or many reporters. Often stories like those suggested in this chapter come from enough different sources so that several reporters may do the spadework, to find information which later is woven into a story by one of them or by a rewrite man.

Co-ordination in reporting is particularly required when a story involves all three levels of government. Part of it may come from Washington, part from the state capital, and part from local sources. Inquiries in Washington and at the state capital can be made most efficiently by the newspaper's regular correspondents in those places, or by a reporter for a press service which represents the paper. When all the information is in, a local reporter can usually do the best job of putting it together into one story or series.

The complex nature of government relationships means that a reporter, even on the local scene, has to be sophisticated about affairs in the capital and in Washington. Here, as elsewhere, the wider a reporter's knowledge, the better the job he can do.

REPORTING ASSIGNMENTS

1. Interview the official in charge of the local office of a state agency in your city. Write a story describing the work of his office.
2. Do the same for a federal agency.

3. Write an article or a series of articles on urban renewal problems in your city.

4. Write an article about employment trends in your area, using local, state, and, if necessary, federal sources.

5. Interview either a city health official or a state health official stationed in your city and write a story telling how these units co-operate to provide local services.

6. Do the same for welfare units.

7. Write an article or series telling how much home rule your state government allows its cities. Use your city and other local units as specific illustrations.

8. Interview an official of a local utility and write an article telling how state or federal regulation affects his business.

9. Write an article telling how much of the highway system in your county is maintained by the state and how much by local units.

10. Write a story on local activities of either the state or the federal government, showing how many persons are employed by that unit in your area and what percentage this figure is of the total number of employed workers.

4

News from the Classrooms

Schools have long been a concern of America. We know that the rudiments of an education are necessities for intelligent participation in the political process.

For many years our ancestors felt that an elementary education was the rightful privilege of every child. Lately we have expanded our horizons—now nearly everyone can go to high school. Eventually our public and private colleges and universities will be able to give a college education to everyone intelligent enough to profit from it.

Education is tied up with our notions of democracy. We need educated citizens to build a better country. A basic education for every child is also a part of our concept of equality of opportunity.

Schools—good schools—are tied in with the American dream.

We have neglected our schools, played hookey from them when we were young, and underpaid our teachers, but today we spend more money and more argument on them than on almost any other institution of our society. We know very well that the progress of our country is tied to the success of our schools.

Few governmental functions touch our lives so intimately and are so important to each of us as our schools.

A news story? One of the best!

Organization for Education

Local school districts are the basic units in our public education system. State organizations are important supervisory units, and in most areas there is a "middle layer" of administration which is gradually losing its influence.

Although they have delegated much power to local districts, our state governments have final control over education. Officers of a school district (legally, at least) serve as the agents of the state government in administering schools in their district. Most of the states prescribe minimum standards, then allow local boards to develop their schools pretty much as they wish within these limitations.

The thousands of school districts in the United States vary in size from tiny rural districts supporting one-room country schools with one teacher to large urban areas—a few with hundreds of schools.

A majority of the states has organized school districts independent, both geographically and politically, of other local units of government. The districts frequently cut across town lines, although cities usually will constitute a single district. When a school district covers the same area as a city, it usually is independent of city officials.

In a few states regular government units have school responsibility. These are chiefly in New England, where the towns are the units for school administration, and in some of the southern states, which use the county.

More often than not, the districts are truly independent of the other units of local government. Not only are their officials elected independently, but also they often have independent taxing powers and complete control over the school budget. Of course there are exceptions to this. Sometimes, when school districts coincide with city or county boundaries, officials of the other government will have power to review school budgets and otherwise exercise control.

This story from the *Hartford Courant* tells of regular city officials reviewing a school budget:

> The $9,884,490 budget request of the Board of Education for the coming fiscal year bounced Monday.
>
> City Manager Sharpe turned it back to members of the Board and school officials meeting at City Hall, with a stern request for review and revision downward.
>
> The request is $1,175,830 higher than current spending, an increase of about two mills.
>
> Sharpe told members the administration anticipated an increase of some $500,000 above current spending. He noted that this is the second million-dollar increase requested in as many years.
>
> It is apparent at City Hall that if the board refuses to slash the amount requested Sharpe will do so. And if the manager does not slash, the City Council will—by some $300,000.

Local Organization

Control of a school district is vested in a group commonly called the School Board, although it may have the official title of Board of Education, School District Directors, or Board of Trustees. The school board is the true operating head of the schools in its district, and as such is primarily responsible for their quality. Naturally it is an important source of news.

Members of school boards usually are elected by voters in their district and serve without pay. In a very few places boards are appointed by city or county officials.

Board members are often elected in nonpartisan elections separate from those for other local officials. Ordinarily they are nominated by petition of qualified voters. Where they represent political parties and are elected at regular elections, the usual partisanship prevails; otherwise, the school boards usually keep out of partisan politics.

Five- and seven-member boards are most common, although small districts often have three-member boards. Terms of office commonly range from three to six years, with election times rotated so that there are always some experienced members. Indiana is unique among the states in that the township trustees serve *ex officio* as school board members.

It is routine procedure for reporters to cover meetings of a school board. Sometimes school district elections are fairly tame, with no real clash of issues; at other times they develop into real contests. In either situation a reporter needs to emphasize the importance of the election and to define sharply whatever issues are presented.

School board members often come in for a considerable amount of criticism, and sometimes they deserve it. Nevertheless, in general, we have been fortunate in the caliber of individuals serving on school boards. Persons of ability and with a desire to serve the public seem to be attracted to them. This is fortunate, for the school boards determine to a large extent the quality of our school programs. State education departments can demand minimum standards and can encourage better programs, but superior programs come from local interest as expressed through the board of education.

In districts of any size the board of education hires a superintendent who serves as the executive officer of the board, carrying out its decisions and running the school system in its day-to-day activities. As does any executive officer, he frequently makes recommendations to the board and influences its actions in other ways. The amount of control exerted by the superintendent varies with the personalities involved. He is one of the best news sources in the local school system.

Many states provide for annual meetings, open to all qualified voters in a district. These meetings hold final local control. Usually they approve the annual school budget, set the tax rate, authorize the purchase of real estate, and determine district policies in general within powers granted by the state. Such meetings are more common in suburban and rural districts.

The Middle Layer of School Administration

Many states provide for a "middle layer" of school administration between the local and the state levels. In most states this is at the county level, although in some there are special supervisory districts.

About 30 states have county boards of education. In the states which use the county as the school district, the county board and the county superintendent are very influential officials, with much of the same authority that a city board and the superintendent have in most of our city districts.

More frequently, the county board advises the local school district and serves as an administrative unit for the state department of education. It usually hires a county school superintendent who also functions as an adviser to the local schools and as a fact-reporting agent for the state department. Often this county office distributes state money to the local districts according to the state formula. The county superintendent may visit local schools as a state inspector, and to give whatever help he can.

County superintendents, at their best, stimulate local boards and teachers to build better schools by helping them to consider long-range plans and by interpreting state policy. Often they help their schools to hire teachers.

State Education Departments

Although the states have final authority and final responsibility for the educational system, they usually delegate much of the power to the local boards, as we have seen. Delaware is the only state which has a truly centralized state-wide system for education. Other states set minimum standards, then delegate to the local boards authority to operate the schools.

A few states provide detailed syllabuses for the basic courses. New York goes a step farther. In its state-wide Regents examinations it provides a uniform testing service.

Late in 1957 the Connecticut State Board of Education issued a statement announcing its plans for developing "suggested basic requirements" for courses in mathematics, science, English, social sciences, health and physical education, foreign languages, art, and music. It also planned increased aid to local schools in testing and guidance programs.

Minimum standards commonly maintained by the states cover such areas as the number of school days required each year and the subjects taught. States usually set the standards required of teachers and serve as the agent for certifying them. Usually the state board must approve plans for new buildings, and it may require that inadequate facilities be replaced.

We have seen that boards prevail on the local and intermediate level of school administration in this country. They are used just as frequently at the state level, for supplementary education programs as well as schools and colleges.

Typically, central educational authority is assigned to a board composed of from 5 to 15 members, who select a professional educator as the state's principal education officer and the executive arm of the board. Sometimes this board is purely regulatory in that it does not concern itself with the operation of any educational unit, but determines over-all policy. Sometimes it combines this policy function with the job of operating some or all of the state units of higher education.

Usually the governing boards operate only one institution, perhaps the state university, although many boards have responsibility for several institutions. The Oregon State Board of Higher Education operates all the state's institutions of higher learning. Governing boards usually have corporate powers—that is, they can sue and be sued, borrow money, and perform the other business operations necessary to running an institution.

The Council of Chief State School Officers recommends 7 to 12 members as the ideal size for boards of education, and more than half of the state boards fall within this range. A few boards are much larger; one has 102 members. Larger boards are generally regarded as impractical.

Members of the state boards of education are usually nonprofessionals serving without pay, although they may receive their expenses when they attend meetings. They may be elected, or appointed by the governor or the legislature. A 1946 statute of the state of Washington provides a unique method: Members of the state education board are elected by a convention of school board directors of the state. This method has resulted in the election of leaders among local school board members.

States which allow the governor to appoint members of state boards of education usually require confirmation by one or both houses of the legislature. Usually, too, terms are staggered so that it is difficult or impossible for a governor to appoint a majority of the board during one term of office.

In about one third of the states the boards appoint the chief education officer, sometimes known as the state director of education. More states are likely to adopt this practice in the opinion of specialists in the United States Office of Education. In a very few states the chief education officer is elected by the voters. Others provide for election by the legislature or appointment by the governor.

Financing the Schools

As we have seen, local school boards have much autonomy in financial matters. Often they can determine their own budgets and set their own tax rate. This is added to the general property tax, and, while the tax collector may act as the school board's agent in receiving the money, he has no function other than to turn it over to the board. The school tax is still the chief source of revenue for local school districts, although every state now supplies some financial help, and the trend is toward increased state aid.

Education is important as measured by the amount of money we spend on it. More local taxes go to schools than to any other single item. For example, the Tax Foundation reports that in one recent year local government spent almost twice as much for education as it did for the next three most expensive services combined.

But the vast sums of money we spend on education do not automatically guarantee an adequate educational opportunity for every child. Frequently one section of a state may have excellent public schools while those in another part may be inadequate. State grants are often used to help equalize facilities in different parts of the states. There is some danger, however, if state grants are used recklessly. It has been found that aid without provision for local participation may paralyze local effort.

For example, Senator Leslie Westin of the School Aid and Reorganization Commission of St. Paul, Minnesota, said that the income tax, as used for school purposes in Minnesota, has caused some problems. The tax is dedicated to school purposes, and the state has collected more money than it has paid out. This has led to tremendous pressures to increase aid, "to the point that we now have many, many districts that have virtually no local effort at all. . . . We have some 1,400 closed school districts able to send their children to adjoining districts and financed on the state and equalization aid they receive. We have created a bad situation in Minnesota because we have been pushing the aid beyond local efforts."

One solution, or partial solution, to this problem is the requirement that local school districts match or supply a certain percentage of the amount given by the state. Sometimes the requirements are based directly on the district's ability to pay. For example, the district may be required to raise a certain number of mills for each dollar of assessed valuation within its boundaries. Ohio has set a certain millage requirement which each district must meet before it is eligible for state aid.

One of the figures used in determining the proper size of a school district is the amount of assessed valuation per student. It is obvious that this figure must reach a certain minimum before the district can provide an effective school system.

Differing assessment rates, which are discussed in Chapter 5, pose problems in connection with the distribution of state aid. If the assessors in one district value the property for tax purposes at one half of its actual value, while the assessors in another district value property at three-quarters or full value, it is obvious that a millage requirement will work a hardship on the district appraised at full or nearly full value. The only solution to this seems to be a state-wide equalization program.

One of the dangers of state aid, or of any aid from outside the school district, is that it is too easy to think that money from the state is gravy. All of us know that state and federal revenues come from the same source that produces local revenue—the taxpayer. But it is easier for school boards, hard-pressed for funds, to turn to the state rather than take the issue to the voters.

Sometimes a negative vote on a school bond issue will discourage citizens who clearly see the educational needs of their communities. This is where state aid can be helpful. If it is withheld until the district raises a certain percentage of the funds, it can bribe local voters to bond themselves for part of the money to get the rest the "easy way" from the state government. But the "gravy train" psychology can be carried too far. Eventually it leads to lack of interest and to government far removed from the citizens. Newspaper campaigns for school bond issues can be a very effective device for educating citizens in their basic school needs. Voters are likely to consider the issues carefully if they are being asked to increase their own taxes to pay for better schools.

This story which appeared in the *Philadelphia Evening Bulletin* in late 1957 discusses the state's share of the school expenses in neighboring New Jersey. It offers a brief explanation of New Jersey's "foundation program," which is widely discussed in school circles.

Trenton, Nov. 19—(AP)—The New Jersey Department of Education today estimated local school districts will receive $87,643,040 in aid from the state during 1958–59—an increase of less than $3.5 million over the current fiscal year.

Earlier estimates had predicted a rise of about $6 million.

Education Commissioner Frederick M. Raubinger said leveling off in state school aid was caused by inflation.

He said inflation has caused the market value of real estate to increase, bringing about a rise in the municipal share of school costs.

Direct aid to local school districts is figured on a formula which is pegged to a "foundation program" of $200 for every pupil in average daily attendance.

The municipality's share of this is based on the equalized value of its tax ratables. The state pays the remainder, but not less than $50 a pupil in each school district.

Raubinger said half of the school districts in the state would be receiving only the minimum state aid.

"School costs are falling back on the local property owner," he said.

Raubinger said his estimates were based on an estimated average daily enrollment of 930,606 pupils.

The department also pays 75 per cent of the cost of approved school transportation through an aid program.

Federal Aid—the Issues

The federal government has supplied little aid to schools. It maintains the Office of Education in the Department of Health, Education and Welfare, which compiles statistics and conducts many valuable studies. It has supplied direct financial aid to a very few schools which have been faced with an influx of children from new federal installations in their districts. Although it has been our tradition to keep the federal government out of education, the question keeps coming up regularly in Congress, and federal aid has many influential adherents.

Those who want the federal government to help finance our public schools are of the opinion that it is "discriminating against" the schools because it supplies money for highways, poor relief, and many other things, but none for the schools. Those who oppose federal aid say that it is impossible for the federal government to supply money without taking control away from the states and the local districts.

A study committee report of the Commission on Intergovernmental Relations summarized the arguments. Here is their essence:

For federal aid:

1. A minimum level of educational opportunity should be available to every child in the country.

2. A number of states need federal help to provide more educational facilities.

3. Added mobility of the population justifies federal aid to keep standards high.

4. Adequate educational facilities are necessary for national defense and the general welfare.

5. The federal government aids other services, so in not aiding education it is discriminating against it.

6. Only federal assistance can assure adequate schools in all states regardless of variations in wealth and taxpaying ability.

Against federal aid:

1. Although critical problems exist, our present system has nonetheless done a remarkable job, and we should consider carefully before abandoning it.

2. Less wealthy states are rapidly improving their ability to meet the costs of an adequate educational program.

3. Variations in taxpaying ability to support schools are greater within

individual states than among the states. Some states have equalized educational opportunities, others have not. Federal aid would inevitably bring federal control since it would be impossible to supply funds without requiring equalization within the states.

4. Federal taxes, after all, come from the states, and nearly all the taxable assets of the federal government are also available to the states.

5. The states and their school districts have the fiscal ability to meet their own school needs if they choose to do so. This is true even of the least wealthy states. It is a matter of desire, not ability.

6. Federal aid would mean a sacrifice of local responsibility and participation. This would be in conflict with our basic principles. Much of the strength of our education system has been possible because of our decentralized system, which leaves the ultimate responsibility in the hands of the people.

The study committee concluded that federal aid to education is neither necessary nor desirable. The argument is still far from settled, however, and we can expect to hear much about it in future sessions of Congress.

How Big Should a School District Be?

In frontier days one-room schoolhouses were a necessity. Pupils walked to school, and districts were sparsely settled. The school buses and highways of today have changed that and made large districts practical. There is no question that larger schools are cheaper to operate and generally better, and many educators have applied themselves to the task of consolidating districts.

State school officers have put their weight behind consolidation programs, usually employing what they call voluntary methods. This description is not quite accurate because, in most cases, the "voluntary" aspect of the proceeding is made questionable by the fact that districts refusing to comply are usually given less state aid than they would otherwise receive.

A Kansas statute of 1945 established a system which was frankly compulsory. The law created a state division for school reorganization and a school reorganization committee was appointed by the board of supervisors of each county. These committees were ordered to draw up school reorganization plans with the aid of the state division, and, after prescribed hearing procedure, to put them into effect. Dissatisfied persons could appeal to the court. This law was eventually declared unconstitutional on the grounds that it provided for an illegal delegation of legislative powers. While it was on the books, however, many districts were consolidated, and this was upheld by the courts. Later consolidation proceeded under a similar system, but on a "voluntary" basis—voters were given the opportunity to accept or reject the new system, but were faced with the knowledge that, if they rejected it, state aid would be cut.

With such programs several states have dramatically reduced the number of school districts. Illinois, for example, has less than a fifth of the districts it had in 1948.

Much resistance to enlarging districts is encountered locally because many people believe that larger districts lead to less local participation. The opposite viewpoint is expressed by James E. Allen, Jr., New York State Commissioner of Education, in a letter responding to an editorial in the *Syracuse Herald-Journal*:

> I quite agree that bigness in school districts does not make for quality.
>
> On the other hand, all our evidence over the years does show that, other things being equal, size does make a real difference in the kind and quality of education which a school can provide.
>
> You state that centralization decreases local control. I don't believe this is the case.
>
> In fact, in small districts, especially those where the education of children is provided through contract with an adjoining district, there is much less opportunity for exercise of local control.
>
> Our experience has shown that where the district is large enough to have a full education program the citizens take a deeper and more active interest in the affairs of their schools. . . .

With good roads and school buses it has become practical to enlarge the districts for more efficient administration. The question is: How large should the districts be?

Local factors tend to preserve the established districts. School officials have a tendency to try to keep them because they fear loss of prestige or authority if districts are changed. Parents may like the established districts because they want to send their children to nearby schools with children they know.

Are there natural factors which indicate the best size for a school district?

The district should be large enough to support an adequate program efficiently. A commonly quoted estimate is that there should be a minimum of 1,600 pupils in a system which operates schools from kindergarten through the twelfth grade. This makes it practical to maintain adequate laboratories, shops, a gymnasium, an auditorium, and other facilities.

If the district is too small, one of two things happens: Either the program is too thin or it becomes unnecessarily expensive. There is no economy, either, in letting the district become too large, for then facilities have to be duplicated.

Small districts are expensive. This is shown in study after study. In

Texas, for example, it was found that $25,550 will educate 120 children a year in large districts, but only 100 a year in small districts.

It is also cheaper to provide classrooms in larger districts. In Pennsylvania it was found that a high school for 900 pupils can be built for $1,700 per pupil, while a comparable high school for 300 pupils will cost $2,000 per pupil.

It is easy, though, to create districts which require children to ride too far and make the school seem far removed from the home. What should be the maximum period that children ride on a school bus? Some of our enlarged districts have pupils riding an hour in the morning and another at night. This can work real hardships. The bus-riding time adds little or nothing to a child's education.

These considerations raise critical questions in many places. For instance, does it doom children in sparsely settled areas to an inadequate education or to one that is ridiculously expensive?

By the standards described here, thousands of our school districts are too small to do an adequate job. Are the standards correct? Are there ways in which small schools, where they are unavoidable, can be operated efficiently and with as good a program as larger ones? Have our experts, in their enthusiasm for schools of a certain size, shut their minds to ideas for enriching the programs of smaller schools? Are large schools essential just because our teachers' colleges are turning out a certain kind of product? Do we need to make a special effort to identify potential teachers with more than average versatility, and train them for smaller school systems?

If a district has enough pupils, the next question is: Does it have enough wealth to support an adequate program? Wealth is measured in taxable assets, a favorite expression of school planners.

Many of the newer suburban communities are almost entirely residential, so that the school tax falls heavily on home-owners. Some school districts which contain industrial property are relatively small, and the tax paid by the industries covers a large part of the school costs. It is a question as to how fair this is to surrounding districts which often house the families of workers in the industries. This unequal distribution of taxable resources is one of the strong arguments for state aid to education.

Still another factor considered by school planners is that a school district should reflect the natural political and social boundaries.

Curriculum Planning

What subjects shall be taught? In the early days of our country, the schools, of necessity, kept pretty much to the essentials—reading, writing, and arithmetic, the famed "Three R's." Our offerings have grown richer, and now many schools even teach vocational subjects. This is a change which is still developing in our secondary school and college system.

Many trades which in former days were taught by a system of apprenticeships are now taught in school. Beauty culture and shopwork are examples.

The trend is easy to understand. We have become committed to the idea that all our children are entitled to a high school diploma. But as more pupils stayed in school, it became apparent that many did not want to study the traditional courses. Furthermore, many students were not adapted to these courses. The schools changed to fit their pupils' needs. This trend is also apparent at the college and university level, as college degrees become more common.

Some people feel that these changes have diluted the quality of our education, but this is not necessarily true. If we can give more adequate vocational training in the schools, this is all to the good. There is no reason why this cannot be done while providing a liberal education for all who have the will and the talent to profit from it.

Another subject often debated in the local school meeting is the size and nature of auxiliary services. How many dances shall the school sponsor? How many clubs? Will there be an activities period? Should secret societies be tolerated?

School facilities are used during the summer for recreation programs, often sponsored jointly by local agencies and by the state.

Keeping Teachers in the Classroom

Problems make news, and today's schools are rich in problems. Finance is one we have already discussed. The other controversial subjects we have talked about are problems, too.

Perhaps the schools' most publicized problem is that of maintaining an adequate staff of qualified teachers. With enrollments climbing rapidly, more teachers are needed every year just to keep up with them. Grade school enrollment, 27.5 million in 1955, is expected to hit 35 million in 1965. High school enrollment, 7 million in 1955, is expected to rise to 12 million in 1965.

We not only need more teachers, we also need more good teachers. Many persons teaching in our public schools do not meet certification requirements of their states. School administrators hire them because they cannot hire better teachers.

As our society improves, we need constantly improving teachers. Howard E. Wilson, secretary of the Educational Policies Commission of the National Education Association, put it this way: "A democratic and technological society . . . demands a steady upgrading of the educational level . . . if the economy is to continue expanding and if citizen participation in the democratic process is to be a reality." President Eisenhower was talking about the same thing when he told Congress that, "Solutions to all the other problems in education will be empty achievements indeed if good teaching is not available."

What are we doing to get better teachers?

We're beginning to pay them a little better, and we're giving them a little bit more of the respect which is due them. There is still a long way to go. Teachers' salaries still have not recovered from the days when teaching was regarded as an occupation for women, and when there were few other career opportunities open to educated women. Since our standards for teachers have risen faster than our salary scales, many of our best potential teachers have found that they can earn more money in other fields.

A few schools have tried merit rating systems to pay better salaries to better teachers. Despite the argument that this system works well in industry, some teachers are opposed to it. They say that an essentially subjective system is dangerous to teachers' morale. The Massachusetts Teachers' Union went on record as opposed to it, and asked access to the personnel files of teachers who were awarded merit increases. Those who favor the system claim that it would make it possible to retain the better teachers by paying them better.

School administrators are trying to induce more gifted high school students to consider teaching as a profession, through special scholarships and demonstrations of the advantages of teaching. Many older women already holding college degrees are being urged to take short, intensive teacher-training programs and become teachers. Administrators are enthusiastic about their ability in the classroom.

Another way in which the schools are trying to combat the teacher shortage is by using television, motion pictures, and tape recorders to increase the number of students who can be taught by one teacher. Some people are enthusiastic about the results and predict that soon the country's most gifted teachers can, through television, reach millions in classrooms and homes throughout the country. Others say that education will be sure to suffer from these devices because they reduce or eliminate the essential classroom give-and-take between student and teacher.

Some educators say that larger classes are possible in many subjects, and that the traditional notion of classes of 25 to 30 students should be altered. Classes with as many as 100 students are practical in some subjects, they say, arguing that children learn more in large classes taught by good teachers than in small ones taught by poor teachers.

The problem is most acute in science and mathematics, because persons qualified to teach in these areas have especially enticing job offers from industry.

The Gifted and the Unwilling

How can we select persons with native ability in the humanities and sciences and train enough of them to keep our complicated civilization going? We have been warned for years that Russia is turning out more scientists, engineers, and doctors than we are. Former President Hoover cited figures showing that relatively few of our high school students are being trained in higher mathematics or even in elementary physics. He suggested that we allow our high school students too much leeway in selecting their own subjects. Instead, he said, we should require them to sample some of the more difficult fields since the average 13- or 14-year-old does not seem inclined to do so on his own volition.

An Associated Press story tells how one group of educators in New York State sought to find a solution:

ALBANY (AP)—A group of professional educators recommends a program of extra summer training of talented students to be tested in a few communities of the state.

Training emphasis would be on science and mathematics.

The group of 22 educators proposes special state aid to support the programs.

They met here yesterday for a conference to explore ways of accelerating science-mathematics education and of making greater use of school personnel and facilities to meet the challenge posed by Soviet Russia's advances in missiles development.

The conference was called by Education Commissioner James E. Allen, Jr.

Allen said that, while the conference advocated greater use of school facilities in summer, it came to "no definite conclusions" on establishing a regular 12-month school year.

After the conference, the educators issued a joint statement that:

1. Urged establishment of pilot programs "leading to greatest year-around use of schools" to enrich the education of talented students.

2. Called on colleges and industry to make their facilities and personnel available to keep school teachers abreast of scientific developments, through seminars and other in-service training courses.

3. Urged the State Education Department to expand its services designed to help public schools identify especially talented youngsters.

Making proper use of our highest talent is an important problem of the schools. To do this, schools must be geared to decrease the number of "dropouts" and to encourage the best children to continue on to college. In 1957 less than one half of those graduating in the top fifth of their classes went on to college. More inspiring teachers in high school is part of the answer. More scholarships for talented youngsters is another part.

Our increasing standards of education have brought with them some problems of their own. For example, generally we now require children to continue in school until they are 16 or 17 years old. For most pupils this presents no problems. A few, however, find school dull and have no desire to continue. This leads to misunderstandings and sometimes to open revolt. Schools in slum areas are particularly vulnerable. Some "problem schools" in New York City find it difficult to keep an adequate faculty, because most of the teachers want to teach in better districts where they have more tractable students and less challenge to classroom discipline.

Good teaching is needed here as much as anywhere else. Perhaps children in these schools are even more in need of talented teachers. There is no question that an understanding teacher can do much in underprivileged sections to lead children to happy and successful lives. Nearly all the children in the "tough" schools profit from the teaching of gifted persons who understand them and are concerned about them. Our teachers' colleges might be persuaded to make a special effort to train teachers for these assignments. They are less desirable, certainly, in general, but they can be as rewarding as teaching anywhere else.

Charles G. Spiegler, a teacher in one of New York's "tough" schools, has put the problem well in an article in the *New York Times Magazine:*

> I teach in a "tough" vocational high school. And, although we have our full quota of switchblade kids, card sharks and probationers, the fact is that for every ineducable in my school there are fifty who will vie for the honor society; for every window smasher there are 100 who resent his anti-social behavior; for every child who is so emotionally crippled that he does not belong within school walls there are many hundreds of potentially good, solid young Americans going to school to learn how to make a better living and how to live better.
>
> There is, admittedly, a hard core of boys—perhaps 2 per cent—who respond to neither reason nor warmth nor decency, however abundantly offered. They wander through the school shooting craps wherever they please, selling dirty postcards, drawing scenes on lavatory walls that would make Krafft-Ebing blush. I have heard drunkards and drug addicts vilifying teachers. It takes only one boy to wreck a lesson by rising in class and inviting his colleagues: "Come on to my house, see my gun collection, take one—get the teacher." A dozen such boys can carry on a guerrilla war that will demoralize an entire student body and faculty.
>
> But the typical student in a "tough" school is not evil. He is difficult and he is different—different from anything textbooks warned the teacher to expect. You can't, for instance, get him to read Shakespeare, though he'll gladly stay up all night to read "The Spirit of St. Louis." You bore him in economics when you quote him Gresham's law. But turn to installment buying and up he perks. In science he cares little for the precise definition of "matter." What matters more to him is how one gets rid of acne, how you "soup up" a hot rod, what makes sputniks spin.
>
> His I.Q. is more in his hands than his head. He is a master builder with a

hot rod and can name you (and spell you) its most intricate part. Yet ask him what a bachelor of arts is and you hear, "He's a guy who got away by staying single." A doctor of philosophy? "That's a crazy doctor—like the one my Uncle Joe went to once." This is not a fresh or a stupid boy. This is a non-academic boy.

In 1900 a New York high school teacher would hardly ever have met such a boy. Of 500,000 children in elementary schools only 14,000 ever got to high school, generally the bright, the scholarly, the well-to-do. Today everybody goes—until the age of 16 or 17. The compulsory education laws in almost every state of the Union say they must.

As if this were not problem enough for the average, academically trained, middle-class oriented teacher add this: Of the 700 boys in my school fully 40 per cent come from broken homes.

What Makes a Good School?

Every school system should evaluate itself—the effectiveness of its program and its teaching. Every newspaper should be interested in this, too. How can it find out and tell its readers whether they have good schools or poor ones?

This is not easy to answer, and a newspaper which cannot go to the trouble of doing a thorough and fair job should not try at all, because it would do more harm than good.

One kind of evaluation is the cost per student. This will vary with the size of the school system, the adequacy of the facilities, and the salary scale. Every taxpayer is interested in this figure, but it is a poor yardstick because it tends to emphasize the negative. Education should be economical, but, more important, it should be effective.

Some administrators will object to the cost-per-student yardstick as a measure even of cost. Another yardstick which is sometimes used is "cost per teaching unit"—the cost of maintaining one teacher and one class. Some administrators say this is a fairer method of evaluation because it may cost almost as much to maintain a class of 14 as it does to maintain one of 30 children. The high cost for the smaller class may not be any fault of the school administration.

One measure of the success of a school system is the number of its graduates who are admitted to college and the number who are successful there. This is partly determined by the community in which a school is situated. Higher-class neighborhoods can be expected to produce more potential college graduates than lower-class neighborhoods. On the other hand, there is no question that talented teachers and vocational counselors can and do lead more children to college and successful careers.

Another measure of the success of a school is its acceptance by a recognized evaluating group.

There are intangible things which are still open to evaluation by a skilled reporter. Some schools emanate enthusiasm. The administrators show it, as do the teachers, and children come home radiant after a day's work. We have no way of measuring these things and perhaps never will. But a good reporter, given enough time and encouragement, can find such enthusiasm and report it. Parents often spot such a school simply by talking with their friends. Talk with a few parents who have moved to a community recently and see how often "good schools" was the reason for the change.

Colleges and Universities

Elementary and secondary schools have always been the cornerstone of our education system. In today's world that cornerstone is inadequate by itself. We must add the colleges and the universities.

We simply cannot afford to maintain a system in which going to college is a privilege open only to those who can afford to pay the bills. Earlier in this chapter it was pointed out that only one half of the highest fifth of our high school graduating classes is going to college. This is a waste of some of our best talent.

We need trained scientific minds to devise and man the machines which may save our civilization in a new war. We need trained minds, too, in the humanities, to help keep our civilization worth saving.

We need scientists for peacetime uses, too. We need them to help raise our standard of living. Perhaps we will need them to keep us from starving. Better health habits and living conditions are giving us longer lives and a higher birth rate, so our population is increasing. It is predicted that the United States will have 38 per cent more inhabitants in 1976 than it did in 1956. This increase is likely to be even more dramatic in other countries. To support this population we will have to rely more on synthetic foods, and we will have to find new sources of water and other essentials. These jobs will require more scientists.

In our race to train scientists we may forget that social sciences and the humanities are just as necessary to give us the breadth of understanding which science, by itself, cannot supply. We need people who understand and practice the skills of communicating ideas from one culture to another, from scientists to nonscientists. We need scientists who can write and talk about their work, and we need writers who can understand and interpret science.

This need was pointed out by one of our leaders in basic research, Dr. André Cournand of Columbia University. Dr. Cournand, a Nobel Prize winner, is chairman of the National Heart Institute Committee which distributes many millions of dollars each year in funds for further research. He said:

My greatest worry for the future is that there are not enough young investigators who can write good English. More and more of them can put together new devices, but many are totally unable to express themselves or to use the devices imaginatively. We must educate people to develop a taste for ideas.

If you derive satisfaction from seeing how a great literary mind works, that gives you a facility for dealing with great ideas in science and other areas. If you do this early in life, then the taste for ideas becomes like eating and breathing. To provide basic research you must emphasize all human culture.

We must expand facilities in our great universities. We must find a way to increase general respect for intellectual things, and for the people who deal with ideas. The basic scientific researcher is as important to us as the man who takes the result of basic research and makes a refrigerator or a radar system. We have thousands of uses for electricity, yet they all sprang from the basic research which first helped men to understand it. The scientists who produced the basic knowledge were not even sure that it would have a practical application.

Universities face many of the problems of the secondary schools. Resources are often inadequate. Their faculties are often drained off by private industry which can afford to pay higher salaries. Facilities sometimes are so limited that they cramp teaching and research.

Private universities have felt the pinch particularly. Most administrators, however, have been unwilling to turn to the government for aid. The tradition of the private institution is strong, and many people feel that private institutions can offer unique contributions—essential variety and the opportunity to test new ideas in education. They are necessary, alongside the public institutions of higher learning.

Many businesses are responding to the need by contributing to the support of private colleges and universities. This support takes several forms. It may be direct grants to be used at the discretion of the university's president and board of trustees. This is the most useful, for it helps administrators to use the money where it is most needed and to develop the institution along the lines they wish. Other grants from private business take the form of grants for special purposes—to erect buildings, to buy certain types of equipment, to endow a chair for a specific purpose. A business may grant scholarships to its own employees or to sons and daughters of employees. One increasingly common way in which business supports private universities is by paying the costs of basic research which is of interest to the industry.

Educators have suggested that government, state and federal, can help by giving scholarships to talented students for use in any accredited institution. This would not subject private institutions to government control. Such scholarships should be matched by grants to the university since tuition fees do not cover costs of educating a student. Otherwise the university would lose money on each additional student enrolled.

Unlimited funds would solve some of the problems of higher education, but not all of them. Finding and training enough good teachers will always be a problem. Our population is increasing and so is the percentage which attends college. Dr. Frank H. Bowles, president of the College Entrance Examination Board, predicted that there will be 10 million students in college in 1968—three times the number there in 1959. Finding the faculties and facilities to teach this increasing number of students is as great a problem for our colleges and universities as it is for our elementary and secondary schools.

Reporting the Schools

Joseph Mayer Rice, a reporter for the *Forum*, and the magazine's editor, Walter Hines Page, are given credit for helping to launch the progressive movement in education. Rice spent the first six months of the year 1892 touring 36 cities to investigate school conditions. The articles which resulted painted a black picture of American education. For the most part Rice reported schools which were strangled by corrupt politicians who appointed untrained teachers, and which were stifled by public apathy.

He found a few bright spots, including "progressive corps of teachers" at La Porte, Indiana, Minneapolis, and the Cook County Normal School in Chicago.

Newspapers generally commented favorably on the *Forum's* series, but many educational journals were outraged. Dr. Nicholas Murray Butler, later president of Columbia University, defended the articles.

Coverage today is usually less sensational than that of Joseph Rice, and for a good reason—schools are generally free from political control and run by competent, conscientious teachers and administrators. Perhaps the worst charge that can be made against education coverage today is that sometimes it does not go deeper than the routine. Education coverage is becoming a well-recognized specialty. The Educational Press Association of America, founded in 1895, has helped raise coverage standards.

Often a reporter is not to blame if he covers only the more obvious stories. He may have too large a beat to allow him time to report the more complicated ones. Some school administrators are inclined to discourage thorough reporting of the schools. They may have had their work misrepresented at some time. Often they can be won over by a reporter who shows that he is capable of doing a good job and is really interested in the problems of the administrator.

Whatever the cause of surface reporting of schools, conscientious editors are realizing not only that thorough coverage of the educational

SCHOOL NEWS
Where It Comes From

School Board Meetings

School Administrators

Annual School Meetings

Budget and Other Documents

State School Officials

Teachers and the Classroom

School Events

Citizens' Groups

FIG. 7

system in their communities is an obligation they owe their readers, but also that it pays off in stories with high readership.

The routine stories have usually been well covered. They are reports of the annual school meeting, meetings of the school board, the school budget and resultant tax adjustment, new teachers and resignations of old ones, enrollment figures, sports, honor rolls, P-TA meetings, course changes, and many other similar items.

These stories are important; they are the routine items which develop from systematic, although unimaginative, coverage. They are the backbone of the local paper's school coverage, but to do the job right a reporter should venture farther into the schools and their problems. This requires considerably more understanding and investigation. Deeper coverage cannot be obtained by simply stating what happens at a meeting, rewriting a story from the principal's office, or putting a lead on a list of names on an honor roll.

A reporter on the school beat should be aware of the objectives of his community's schools and their problems. The areas discussed in this chapter are a beginning. How well have the local school officials analyzed their objectives? How well do the people of the community understand them? What are the population trends in the community? Are school officials making long range plans in accord with expected school enrollment? Most schools are beset by problems discussed in this chapter, and by other problems as well. It is the school reporter's business to know and relay to his readers the problems and plans of local school officials.

School administrators are always faced with questions as to how good a school program they can sell to the community, and what specific aspects of a school program are most acceptable to parents. The emphasis desired for vocational subjects will vary from community to community. Every school needs to keep in touch with the people, finding out what aspects of the school program are most popular. To some extent the school should be guided by this, but it cannot forsake reasonable standards for the sake of popularity. It has a communication problem in its community. The superintendent and the principal need to know community thinking, and they need to explain the reasons for the program they maintain. A reporter can and should help them. He can explain the program to his readers, and he probably can interpret community thinking to the administrators since he should be a student of opinion on the subjects he is reporting.

The reporter should seek to give his readers an impression of the schools—the same impression they would get if they had the time and the skill of the reporter.

A good reporter learns to get the "feel" of a place. He should be able to visit a school and spend enough time there so that he knows what kind of a place it is. Is it filled with pupils and teachers who are bored with their work and are just waiting to get out? Or does it reflect devotion and enthusiasm? Usually it will be somewhere in-between in its tone. A good reporter can do his schools and his readers a service by sensitive reporting. It takes much time and much understanding. A reporter who lacks either should not try it.

A reporter should tell his readers what sorts of people are running the schools. Sketches of principals, the superintendent, and the teachers, which help to humanize them for parents and explain their philosophy, will do a service for everyone. What kind of people are our teachers? Perhaps a reporter can visit classes to find out "what it's like" to go to a particular school.

Newspapers can be helpful in school controversies. An editor and his reporters are sufficiently informed about their readers (or should be) to understand their views. They should be able to understand the professional staff, too. Thus, newspaper people are ideally placed to find areas of agreement. School controversies, like others, must be reported objectively, but it is reasonable to emphasize the areas of agreement so that settlements can be reached more easily. Schools are so vital to our way of life that anything which insures their smooth and effective functioning is a valuable public service.

In town after town newspapers have helped school leaders to explain the need for new schools. When a newspaper editor is sure that requests for new facilities represent real needs he has an obligation to the community to help it achieve these facilities. In the process he is likely to educate a great many voters.

In general, the newspapers need to report the world of education for what it is—a world of ideas. The ideas represented in our school system are as broad as our culture, and our schools have much to offer the adults in their communities. One of the avenues for this cultural enrichment should be the newspaper. Teachers, with the thorough training many of them receive and frequent refresher courses, have valuable information and opinions about local situations. In capitalizing on this, the newspaper will gain many good stories and it will help to integrate the schools and their teachers into the life of the community.

Where a college or a university is within the area covered by a newspaper, the same type of reporting is useful. Too often the people of a city feel far removed from the academic life of the institution. This has bad effects on the life of the college and of the town. They have much to offer each other, and lack of understanding and of real contact sometimes causes unnecessary friction.

Any college is a fertile source of stories. It takes digging to get them, but the reporter who does it performs a useful service—especially in this period when some individuals profess a distrust for all "eggheads."

REPORTING ASSIGNMENTS

1. Write a story or series on trends in school population in your community. How do today's enrollment figures compare with those of previous years? What are estimates for the future? If growth is predicted, what plans are being made to handle the larger number of students?

2. If possible attend an annual school meeting and write a story about it.

3. Write a story comparing school costs in several area districts.

4. Write a personality sketch of a local teacher or school administrator.

5. Write a story telling how many graduates of your local school system go to college. Compare this with other districts.

6. Analyze the sources of revenue of your schools. Tell how much comes from local sources and how much from the state.

5

Government Finance

Financial Decisions Are Policy Decisions

Public finance affects everybody's pocketbook and everybody's way of life. How the government collects the money it needs determines who will pay the greatest share. How it spends its money helps to determine what kind of communities we have.

Government costs us all a great deal of money. We pay some directly, some indirectly. A person cannot pay his income or real estate taxes without knowing it; but other taxes are hidden. Manufacturers pass on the cost of their taxes to consumers and we tend to forget that part of the price we pay for a car or a washing machine goes for taxes.

By sheer amount alone government finance is important. It is estimated that a family with an income of less than $2,000 pays more than a quarter of it in taxes. Families with income of more than $10,000 pay more than a third of it in taxes. Families with larger incomes pay even larger percentages.

These figures include the direct and indirect taxes and those levied by federal, state, and local units of government. Families in the lowest income groups pay few income taxes, but the government collects from them in excise taxes which are hidden in the costs of consumer goods, and in real estate taxes which are included in rents paid by families who do not own property.

The large slice of the national income skimmed off by government cannot help but affect every aspect of our economy. The Tax Foundation estimates that a family with an income of $4,500 pays $1,393 in taxes. This is money which would otherwise be put into the economy to increase the market for goods and services, or else saved and used for venture capital to help finance established businesses or start new ones.

For our taxes we get many things: national defense, including experiments with the atom and artificial earth satellites, public roads, police and fire protection—the list is endless.

Major finance decisions determine our government policy. The more the government takes in taxes, the less there is left over for private uses. The more the government takes in taxes, the more activities it can participate in, and the fewer the fields that are left for private endeavor. We have moved a long way from the *laissez-faire* theory in which government was only an arbiter. Now we expect government to perform many services for us. The question is: Just what is a legitimate public enterprise and what should be left for private operation?

In a socialistic economy the government would own all wealth, run all enterprises, and apportion rewards to workers. We do not accept this theory, but we have come to believe that there are certain functions which can best be performed by the government. Among these are maintenance of streets and parks, supplying water and sewage services, and police protection.

Some enterprises are in a twilight zone, with considerable disagreement as to whether they are public or private functions. Among these are the industries generally known as the public utilities, which supply electricity and gas, and telephone and transportation service.

These are the areas in which we have decided that competition is either too wasteful, or impractical for some other reason. Two telephone systems in the same town would complicate our existence. Public transportation which duplicates service would be wasteful and confusing. If a private company is granted a monopoly it is required to submit to more detailed regulations than apply to most businesses. Rates and quality of service are usually controlled by a government agency to protect the public, on the theory that the company should submit because of the special privilege granted it.

Tax and spending decisions put into effect the public policy. If Congress votes to establish a Tennessee Valley Authority to produce public power this means that some of the power industry is taken out of private hands. That decision must be supported by public funds until the project reaches the point where it can be self-sustaining and perhaps return revenues to the government treasury.

Since the powers to tax and to spend are so fundamental to our economy, and since they are interwoven with social decisions of all kinds, an understanding of public finance is vital to an understanding of how our public policy is implemented. However, financial operations are difficult to explain and often difficult to understand. Many persons are bored by details of tax and budget procedure, despite the fact that they affect their own pocketbooks so closely.

That is why newspapers need to work especially hard in this area of public affairs. Writing the details of a city budget so that the public can understand it takes skill. Just understanding the financial operations of a city takes a good background plus the willingness to work hard at the job. This chapter will describe some of the problems and some of the procedures. A reporter who works in this area will learn much every day from his job, but he should take pains to acquire a thorough background and to keep up to date in current public finance procedures.

Where Do Taxes Come From?

This question is easy to answer in general—from the people, of course. A few details are also worth considering.

We pay taxes to three levels of government: local, state, and federal. This leads to many complications, all centering around one question: Which level of government should tap which source of revenue?

The only way in which the answer to this question can be understood is historically. Certainly there was no logical development.

SOME OF OUR TAX SOURCES

Tax	Used by		
	Local	State	Federal
General property........	Yes	Indirectly	No
Income................	Sometimes	Sometimes	Yes
Sales.................	Sometimes	Often	No
Import duties..........	No	No	Yes
Excise................	Sometimes	Yes	Yes

One of the difficulties with the Articles of Confederation, under which the United States was governed from 1781 until the Constitution took effect in 1789, was that the Continental Congress had no power to force states to pay the tax levies placed against them.

Article I, Section 8 of the Constitution provides:

"The Congress shall have Power to lay and collect Taxes, Duties, Imposts and Excises, to pay the Debts and provide for the common Defence and general Welfare of the United States; but all Duties, Imposts and Excises shall be uniform throughout the United States."

Alexander Hamilton was the first secretary of the treasury, and his handling of the national debt and the first tax program under the Constitution put the national government on a firm financial basis. Direct taxation was not always popular. One of Hamilton's taxes was on distilled liquors. It took 15,000 soldiers to put down some conscientious objectors to this tax in western Pennsylvania in 1794. This may have been a straw in the wind, for federal agents still have a considerable amount of difficulty taxing the product of small stills.

The most productive source of revenue for the federal government up to the time of the Civil War was the duty on imports. This was relatively easy to collect, and the power belonged solely to the federal government. When this revenue became inadequate, the government turned to excise taxes on admissions and tobacco, and eventually on automobiles, gasoline, and many other items. Eventually the income tax, opened to the national government by the Sixteenth Amendment in 1913, became the most important source of revenue.

While it is true that the purpose of most taxes is to raise money, it is important to realize that taxes can have other purposes, too. Customs duties, for example, are frequently used by this and other nations to protect home industry. Products made by cheaper labor abroad may flood our domestic markets and threaten our own producers. A customs duty can remedy the situation if it is high enough to make the cost of imported products as high as or higher than that of domestic products.

Congress has always been subjected to much pressure to provide "protective tariffs" for many manufacturers. The fostering of a sound domestic economy is a worthwhile end, particularly if the protected industry has a strategic wartime importance. On the other hand, it must be done with care, lest we make enemies abroad.

The imposition of a direct tax may have other than revenue purposes, too. For example, proprietors of gambling establishments are required to buy a tax stamp from the Internal Revenue Bureau. Since gambling establishments are illegal in most of the states, it seems that this requirement may have had something other than pure revenue purposes. There is a tendency, too, for the federal government to feel more free to tax luxury items than necessities. Thus cosmetics, jewelry, and furs are frequently subjected to special federal taxation.

The federal government so far has left to state and local governments two important sources of revenue: sales and general property taxes.

There seems little question that the general property tax will remain the province of the local government, with supervision by the states, and sometimes with the requirement that the revenues must be shared with the state. This is because the general property tax is most easily administered locally. As we shall see later, it gives plenty of trouble, even to county and state governments. It would be even more difficult to administer on the national level.

Congress is under pressure from time to time to adopt a sales tax as a convenient source of revenue. So far the state and local governments have been able to stave off such a tax. A direct tax on sales is collected more easily than many other kinds of taxes, and many states use it as an important source of income. Other states, such as New York, permit local governments to levy it. Localities which use it soon find it to be an important source of revenue.

The federal unit is not the only one which places heavy reliance on the income tax. New York State uses it, and other states assign it to local units. Most of the cities in Kentucky, Ohio, and Pennsylvania, as well as St. Louis, use local income taxes. Philadelphia derives about a third of its income from a payroll tax.

At every level of government there is some revenue from nontax sources. These include fees from licenses and permits, profits from utilities run by the government, and income from the sale of property and from gifts.

Intergovernmental Payments

The centralization and mobility of industry have made it more difficult for local units of government to collect taxes. Sometimes an industry will build a plant in the suburbs. This means that the city cannot tax it, even though the industry may draw on the city's labor pool for its workers, and may require many other city services. Often industry builds outside of cities, not to escape taxes, but because no adequate building sites are available in the city. But industry's good motives do not solve the city's tax problem.

Good transportation may sometimes make taxing difficult. Taxes on bank accounts are not too effective because it is easy to move balances to a bank in another jurisdiction.

Sometimes it is the suburbs which suffer from small tax districts. If most of the industry in an area is situated inside the city and most of the workers reside in the suburbs, the outlying areas will find that they are housing the workers, but are getting no tax help from industry. This is the problem facing many new suburbs, which are hard pressed to find enough revenue to support schools and other essential activities.

Even a metropolitan government may not be large enough to levy some kinds of taxes efficiently.

The result of all this is that the state governments have collected an increasing proportion of tax revenues. But it does not necessarily follow that because the state is the best agent to collect a given tax it is the best one to spend it.

State governments turn back to the local governments large amounts of money. Sometimes there is strict control by the state of how the money shall be spent; sometimes it simply goes into the general fund of the local government.

This same process is going on between the federal and the state governments, with some federal funds being turned over to the states to use and some destined for ultimate local use. In addition there is an increasing tendency for the national government to supply funds directly to the local units.

In one recent year the total revenues of the state and local governments were about equal, but the total expenditures of the local governments were double that of the state governments. Local units combined have about the same number of civilian employees as the federal government plus all the state governments.

Notice the financing relationships of the three levels of government, as described in this story, datelined Washington, in the *Pittsburgh Post-Gazette:*

> Pittsburgh officials are reconciled to 50–50 rather than 90–10 Federal-State matching for construction of the less than one-half mile piece of Crosstown Boulevard, they intimated here today.
>
> Mayor David Lawrence, Richard K. Mellon, Park Martin and Pennsylvania's United States Senators Edward Martin and Joseph S. Clark today asked Federal Highway Administrator Bertram D. Tallamy to include the short but important bit of boulevard in the "interstate system" of Federal highways.
>
> This is the 41,000-mile grid of most important highways, established by Congress, to connect the most important cities of the country and to be of strategic use in case of war. All but 350 miles of the 41,000 has been assigned.
>
> Mr. Tallamy told the Pennsylvanians he must hold that 350 miles in reserve for perhaps a year, and then dole it out carefully to the most worthy cases. He did not foreclose the inclusion of the Crosstown Boulevard in it, but he did not promise anything, either.
>
> Mayor Lawrence said after the meeting he believes the group "made progress." But with the next breath he said, "If the state administration will agree, there is no doubt we can get 50–50 matching, the sort reserved for the primary system of Federal aid highways."
>
> He said the cost of this short bit of boulevard would be between six and seven million dollars. High land acquisition costs make this section of road perhaps the most expensive in the state.
>
> But the city had already pledged $1.5 million to it. So even if the 50–50 matching formula were used, the state would have to put up no more than $2 million.
>
> The officials insist that the function of the short bit of highway, linking Bigelow Boulevard with the Boulevard of the Allies, is so important it really should have interstate system treatment.

In the whole tax picture the federal government dominates. It has a superior legal position which makes it possible for it to pre-empt a tax source if it so desires. Many of the same sources taxed by the federal government are taxed also by states and local units. It is doubtful whether the smaller units can threaten the federal revenues by imposing the same kind of tax, but certainly the federal government can make it difficult for the other levels.

Income taxes are a good example. As we have seen, the central government and some states and some cities derive a large portion of their revenues from this source. The federal taxes are higher than local or state charges, and the federal government is in a better position to increase its rate. Local units and even states are in danger of losing tax resources if they raise rates too high. Industries may hesitate to build new plants in states which have a high income or sales tax, or a high corporation tax. Individuals may move out of cities or metropolitan areas which have an income tax. Merchants complain that customers go to other cities to buy when local governments use a sales tax. Thus there are some very definite limits to the ability of a local unit to levy taxes. On the other hand it is much more difficult to move away from a tax imposed by the national government, and for many businesses and individuals it is impossible.

The advantages are stacked in favor of the federal government in still another way. For example, a businessman might not find a 2 per cent sales tax oppressive, but a 2 per cent local tax on top of a 3 per cent federal tax might drive him to a place where he would have to pay only the federal tax. This would be particularly true during slow business periods when profit margins are smaller.

In the opinion of most tax specialists federal taxation has not so far "dried up" many sources of state and local revenue, but it has made it difficult to expand local taxation. There is some agitation for the federal government to return some of its tax sources to state and local units, but with the federal government constantly battling a deficit, this seems unlikely to happen. There is certain to be a clamor against allowing the federal government to tap new sources of revenue, since hard-pressed local units are exploring every possible source.

With the federal government, and, to a lesser extent, the state governments, tending to monopolize the best sources of revenue, two trends are occurring:

1. Increasingly the state and federal governments are pouring money back to the local governments. This is being done in several ways which we will explore.

2. State governments in particular, but the federal government to some extent also, are taking over what used to be local functions. Some of these

are administered directly by the higher level of government with its own officials. Others are managed by local officials acting as agents of the state or federal government.

Each of these trends quite effectively lessens the influence, prestige, and importance of local units. There are serious questions as to whether this is desirable.

Some local and state officials pretend that they see an evil plot in Washington to supplant them. The central government, no matter which party is in power, has seldom been hesitant about taking over added revenues and functions, but it has often been pushed into it by economic trends plus lack of long-range planning by state and local officials.

Concentration of power in federal hands was given tremendous impetus during the early 1930's, when first local and then state government broke down in the face of unemployment and consequent sudden large demands on welfare funds. When state funds were exhausted the federal government was forced to step in. Gradually much of the control over welfare by the federal government has been handed back to the states, but few states have made any adequate preparations to face a similar emergency in the future without massive federal aid.

One of the vital questions of government is to sort out the functions which can best be performed at each level of government and to insure that each level has sufficient revenue to do the job.

Many functions need federal planning and direction at least in part. Some of the more obvious ones are highway construction, flood control, improvement of waterways, control of water pollution, construction of air terminals, civil defense, and disaster relief.

The amount of federal control and financing should depend on the size of the project and the area concerned. Flood control districts may cover several states. There is obvious need for uniform standards for airports. Water pollution and water control are likely to affect residents of several states. The amount of water which the city of Chicago is permitted to divert from Lake Michigan has even international ramifications, for it affects the level of the Great Lakes bordered by Canada.

It is easy to assume that federal control of a function leads to the most efficient operation, but often the reverse is true. If local residents are taxed by the federal government which then performs a local service, it is quite obvious that several layers of officialdom and therefore expense are involved which would have been avoided by local operation.

This pyramiding of overhead is not the only disadvantage of federal operation of local functions. Federal grants are often used with the idea of equalizing facilities throughout the nation. Few will dispute the desirability of guaranteeing minimum standards in health, education, and relief for every resident, no matter where in the country he lives.

But equalizing on a national level sometimes leads to unnecessary expense. Salaries are likely to be higher for federal officials than prevailing local rates. This makes it difficult for state and local governments to keep their workers and leads to added expense. Prevailing federal rates are geared to large metropolitan areas where living expenses are higher.

Equalization programs at times have led, not so much to equalization, but to spending more money on a given activity by all units concerned. The methods of estimating need are not adequate.

Another criticism of the state and federal grants which require local matching is that sometimes local funds are simply diverted from other equally or more worthy functions to match the grant.

Federal leadership sometimes is not as good as it should be, either. Civil Aeronautics Administration officials insisted on a rock subbase as a replacement for part of a concrete apron at Kansas City, Missouri, despite objections of local engineers. When, as local engineers had predicted, it proved impossible to lay such a subbase CAA officials agreed to the substitution of a sand base. The apron rested on river sand, but the CAA officials insisted that four inches of sand be dug out and replaced with four inches of sand which had to be hauled to the site.

Sometimes local officials responsible for a program will welcome federal or state standards as a means of insisting on doing a job a given way. When professionalism is built up in a given area of public work the officials may feel more loyalty to their counterparts in the state and federal governments than to the people they are serving. Professionalism in government is essential, but obviously it should not be used to thwart local political initiative or control.

Despite the objections raised to federal control, it is clear that payments from the federal or state government to the local units have resulted in improvements and better service than many communities would have gotten on their own. On the other hand, some local leaders will argue that the jobs could have been done better in their communities by local efforts if enough tax sources had been left free for the local unit to raise the money by itself.

The tremendous dominance of the federal unit in taxing and spending is a development of the twentieth century. In 1900 the revenues of the local governments in the United States were about equal to the combined revenues of the states and the federal government.

"Grant-in-aid" is the commonly used expression for federal and state payments to local units. Some local officials insist that this is a misleading term, since often the money which changes hands is a return by the state government of money which it collected for the local units. At other times the state pays the local units to perform what is essentially a state service. When this happens the aid is really from the local unit to the state. Often the grant may result in added burdens on the local unit. Some students of local government prefer the expression "intergovernmental payments" rather than "grant-in-aid."

The form in which the payments are made helps to decide what area will get a larger portion of the revenues returned by the state to local governments. New York, for example, used to have a state-collected, locally-shared tax system, which provided that certain percentages of some of the taxes collected by the state would be returned to localities in which they originated. This meant that areas with large tax resources would get a larger return from the state than those with smaller ones. Now the state has abolished the shared tax and substituted grants to cities, towns, and villages on the basis of population. It is easy to see that the new system tends to equalize tax resources, and favor areas with large populations but less wealth.

States Control Local Taxing

State governments are the agencies which authorize local governments to tax. We have a strong tradition that the general property tax is an important source of local revenue, but it is collected in many states by county authorities acting as agents of the states.

Not only do the states decide what taxes the local governments can use, but they can and often do supervise local revenue procedures in detail.

Some of the state legislation seems aimed primarily at guarding state tax sources from exploitation by local taxing authorities. Pennsylvania, in effect, permits its cities and boroughs to tax anything which is not taxed by the state.

New York State has a list of "permissive taxes" which may be used by localities at their discretion. These include a 2 per cent retail tax, a 3 per cent levy on receipts of food and drink sales in restaurants and bars, a tax of up to 3 per cent on utility bills, a levy of up to 25 per cent of the state license fee on alcoholic beverages, a tax of $5 to $10 on passenger vehicles, a levy of up to $\frac{3}{5}$ of 1 per cent of gross business receipts, and a levy of up to $25 a year on "coin operated amusement devices."

From the point of view of sheer efficiency it might be more effective for the states to collect most of the taxes, and then return a portion of the revenues to the local units in the forms of shared taxes or grants. There is a trend in this direction. Sometimes local officials encourage it because it is always easier to let the state collect taxes than to ask the local voters to tax themselves, either through increased rates on property, or though a new tax such as a sales or income tax. Voters seem to like this, too, because they can always hide behind the pleasant fiction that "the state" is spending the money. Although they know well that the money originally came out of their own pockets, they may prefer to think that it is a windfall from state or federal units.

This kind of thinking is dangerous in that it may lead to extravagant and inefficient government. Eventually it will mean the withering away of local functions, with more powers being transferred to the state and federal units, and with local citizens feeling that government is far away and out of their control.

Portions of three newspaper articles illustrate three aspects of federal-state-local financial relations. The first, from the *Louisville Courier-Journal*, shows the problems of a state government in accepting additional funds from the federal treasury. It is worthwhile noticing that the difficulties result from an awareness on the part of businessmen that they ultimately will pay the costs. The taxing and spending relationship is not always so obvious. Notice that the reporter backgrounded the issue well and explained federal-state relations:

A new scheme to pay extra unemployment benefits out of State funds instead of federal strengthened the possibility Wednesday that Governor Chandler may call a special legislative session.

The proposal came from Economic Security Commissioner Vego E. Barnes, who has opposed borrowing federal funds to increase jobless pay.

Barnes asserted at a meeting of business groups here that the State could finance extra benefits from its own unemployment trust fund, if the Legislature would give him authority.

The unemployment-trust-fund balance is now about $104,000,000—down from its peak of around $146,000,000 in 1954. Last fiscal year, about $15,-000,000 more was paid out of the fund than was paid into it by employers who are taxed to finance the entire jobless-insurance program.

In the January-June period alone, about $10,000,000 more has been paid from the fund than has been paid into it.

Whether or not the Governor summons the General Assembly into extraordinary session depends, first of all, upon final outcome of a lawsuit.

The suit aims at finding out whether Kentucky can legally accept federal funds provided by Congress and pay up to 13 extra weeks of jobless benefits to persons who have exhausted their regular benefits and are still out of work.

Circuit Judge W. B. Ardery ruled Saturday that only the Legislature could empower the State to accept the offer of federal funds to pay the additional benefits. His decision has been appealed.

Chandler told two groups representing business and industry—the Kentucky Chamber of Commerce and Associated Industries of Kentucky—that he will take no action until the Court of Appeals has handed down a final ruling on the question.

The businessmen had come to plead with the Governor not to accept the federal money and not to pay the extra jobless benefits, even if the courts should rule that he can do so legally, because this would mean an increase in employers' federal unemployment taxes, starting in 1963.

Later in the same story Commissioner Barnes voices an argument often used by state officials with regard to federal aid (and sometimes by local officials with regard to state aid):

> "I am opposed to borrowing from the Federal Government when we have $104,000,000 of our own, and turning over the right to them to say how much we shall pay and who shall get the benefits—and they'll set up review boards to check on how every dollar is spent, maybe even in Kentucky."

The following story, also from the *Louisville Courier-Journal*, describes one type of federal control over federal-state joint programs. This is simply the requirement of a report to see whether federal conditions have been met. The controversy arose after a candidate for governor was allowed to address a meeting held for people receiving welfare. The story is from the *Courier-Journal's* Washington bureau:

> On demand of regional officials of the Federal Department of Health, Education, and Welfare, Vego Barnes, Kentucky commissioner of economic security, has filed with them a four-page detailed report of the series of meetings he has held for recipients of public assistance.
>
> George N. Narensky, regional director of public assistance in the office at Charlottesville, Va., said he and his associates are studying the Barnes report, which reached them Wednesday.
>
> After they evaluate it to determine if there were infractions of the public-assistance law or if the meetings, although valid, were "inappropriate," they will send the Barnes report to Washington for final decision on what action, if any, to take.
>
> "All we have known until today about the meetings," Narensky said, "is what we got from newspaper clippings sent to us. From this distance, it doesn't make a very pretty picture. Certainly nothing like those meetings has been held anywhere else.
>
> "There have been cases in other states where recipients of public assistance came together to hear the program discussed, but nowhere else did they listen to speeches by political candidates. Nowhere else was there such an atmosphere of political campaigning thrown about them.
>
> "With our office, it isn't just a question whether there was or was not an infraction of the law. It's just as important that we keep the public-assistance program clear of political implications as it is that we follow the letter of the law.
>
> "That's why we became more and more concerned about the meetings Mr. Barnes was holding all over Kentucky. Finally, we decided we ought to have an official version from him.
>
> "So on July 15 we sent Mr. Barnes a telegram asking him about the meetings, who was invited to attend, who was invited to speak to the welfare recipients, what the purpose of the meetings was.
>
> "When a week had passed without response from him, we sent a second

telegram last Monday. Today we got his response. It covers four pages and has 10 exhibits. While we haven't had a chance to study it thoroughly, it appears that Mr. Barnes has made a full response."

The *Christian Science Monitor,* in covering a San Francisco meeting, gives some background on local-federal relations in financing slum removal. It tells, too, how some cities have managed to tackle the job by using local resources:

If you want to see your city progress in ways such as getting rid of slums, get your business leaders on the job.

This is the "success" formula American Mayors spotlighted at the California Chamber of Commerce's statewide conference on urban redevelopment here in San Francisco.

Speakers deplored the useless years San Francisco has spent in planning slum-clearance projects without turning a spadeful of earth. Some authorities laid it to California's "needlessly" complicated state laws.

Just why "there has to be a law" for cities to progress by tearing down slums and building fine new buildings isn't clear to the average citizen. The reason, as explained by a recent article in the magazine, Business Week, is this: "Unfortunately, the redevelopment of slums offers no profit incentive to private capital on its own."

The profits from slum properties are said to be proportionately higher than on high class real estate because slum properties are taxed so lightly. Slums yield high rental profits. Low taxes on slums keep slumland prices so high that builders can't make sufficient profits developing the land.

Under the Federal Housing Act, cities are permitted to acquire blighted areas, tear down the squalid buildings, and resell the cleared land for less than it costs private developers. The federal formula calls for the government to put up two-thirds of the land-price difference and the city one-third.

Mayor Haydon Burns of Jacksonville, Fla., told the conference his community's version of the slum clearance "success" story. When his city launched its slum war under the housing act, Jacksonville "was stopped cold by a Florida Supreme Court ruling." The court held it was unconstitutional to "take property from one citizen with the intent of selling it to another citizen."

The "taking" comes from the fact that slum property owners in Jacksonville priced their land so high that the only way to acquire it was by the condemnation process known as the right of eminent domain.

This did not stop Jacksonville's city authorities. They devised a system of independent land acquisition financed by a combination of special sales and use taxes including what Mayor Burns described as a "city utilities tax of 10 per cent added to the customers' bills, with a sliding scale to large users of lights, water, gas and telephones."

"The result has been that everything we have undertaken has had to be done solely by local governmental entities or private enterprise without one penny of federal aid," said Mayor Burns proudly.

This "solution" adds $1,900,000 to the living costs of Jacksonville citizens. Other tax sources for implementing Jacksonville's new look include expressway tolls "and a portion of the community's share of gasoline taxes, pledged through 1990." The new look includes plans for a "beautiful, spacious and convenient County Court House and new jail."

Mayor Burns also cited a 12,000 seat sports Coliseum that will displace "old slum buildings." He credited the local Chamber of Commerce and a committee of 100 civic leaders for their "teamwork" and close cooperation with the city government.

In the same article the reporter describes Pittsburgh's plan to persuade businessmen that not all civic expenditures are costs, but capital expenditures instead. Pittsburgh officials have held that the extension of municipal services, transportation, and the rest, has increased the value of property. Since the increase in value was due to municipal services, they said, the city was entitled to the profit. Under this theory the value of the sites was taxed heavily, while the tax rate on the buildings was dropped by 50 per cent. This revenue enabled the city to finance new projects and to abolish other taxes.

One of the angles which helped to persuade businessmen that this was a good business proposition was the increased value of property in redeveloped areas. Before the Golden Triangle was rescued from obsolescence, properties there sold for an average of 15 per cent below their assessed value. Afterward sales prices averaged 20 per cent higher than assessed values.

Local Budget Procedure

To properly interpret local finance to his readers the reporter needs to understand the complexities of intergovernment payments. He also needs to understand local budget procedure, for here policy decisions are put into practice.

The city or county budget is often the most important single story in a year about a given level of government. It is more than a story of dollars and cents. It represents the plan of a city or town for the coming year. A low budget and correspondingly low tax rate may not necessarily represent good government—it may represent a low level of municipal services, and a government which is letting its resources decay. By studying a budget the reporter and other citizens can tell what the city management thinks is important—because whatever it is, money will have to be provided for it.

The budget is a blueprint of city plans for the coming year, and it is also the most important single control for executive management of the city. Too often reporters allow their readers to forget all about the budget once it has been passed. It is just as important to make regular checks to see whether the officials are living up to their budget. The *Yonkers Herald-Statesman* publishes regular reports on the financial condition of the city just as most newspapers publish the financial position of the United States Treasury. The local figures are just as important as the national ones to local readers.

A budget can be a simple document, although most municipal ones are prepared in such detail that they look rather formidable. In essence a budget is simply an itemized list of income and expenditures expected over a given period in the future.

Local Finance Officers

Specialists in local government recommend a unified finance department with the officers appointed by the chief executive officer and responsible to him. Many cities do not follow these suggestions, and there is wide variety in organization for financial operations. Sometimes, as we have seen, the council or commission has considerable influence in preparation of the budget. Often financial officials are elected by voters and consequently are not accountable to either the council or the chief executive officer—the mayor or the manager. Most cities, however, have the officers described here, even though they may not be organized into a single department with a head who is directly responsible to the mayor or the manager.

DIRECTOR OF FINANCE. When such an official exists he usually heads a unified finance department containing the officials listed below. The director of finance is responsible to the executive officer or to the legislative body. This is true in theory, even though he is sometimes elected.

BUDGET OFFICER. This position sometimes goes by other names, but the job always has to be done. This official is directly responsible for preparing the budget by working with department heads.

CONTROLLER. This official is the general accounting officer. In addition he preaudits all expenditures to make sure that they are legal and that there is money in the treasury to cover them.

TREASURER. Custodian of public funds, the treasurer collects the revenues, keeps them on deposit at banks, and spends them when he has proper authorization from the controller. In earlier days treasurers were often paid by being allowed to keep any money they could earn in interest.

ASSESSOR. When a tax is based on the value of real or personal property one of the critical jobs is to place a value on each piece of property taxed. We shall pay more attention to the assessor's duties later in this chapter.

PURCHASING AGENT. Private business and many units of government have provided evidence that central purchasing is economical and efficient. A central purchasing agent can save money by buying in large quantities those supplies which are used by many departments. He can also require tests to determine the quality of the products he is buying. Not the least of his values is that he serves as a clearing-house for purchases, thus making it difficult for other department heads to show favoritism to certain vendors.

In addition to the officials listed above, who are often found in a central finance department controlled by the city executive, there is often an *auditor* (sometimes called a *controller* or *comptroller*) who is responsible to the legislative branch. It is his job to audit the expenditures after they have been made to insure that funds were spent legally. Sometimes this official is elected by the voters. Private accountants are called in to do this job in some places, and in small communities the legislative body itself may perform the postaudit.

This story from the *Cheektowaga Times* of western New York shows a change in procedure:

> Cheektowaga's Town Board voted itself out of the auditing business Monday night. By a unanimous vote, the board members present authorized the hiring of Holloway & Co., a firm of certified public accountants, to conduct the annual audit of town fiscal affairs.
>
> Previously, the board has conducted the audit itself.
>
> The resolution which authorized the hiring of the Holloway firm also set forth ground rules by which the audit will be made. Presumably they are stricter than the rules the board was accustomed to setting for itself.
>
> The new procedure was carefully reviewed by Town Atty. Thomas Delahunt. The Holloway firm will check the accounting for all money received and disbursed by all town officers and employes by examining books, records, receipts, orders, warrants, vouchers and cancelled checks having to do with receipts and disbursement of town funds.
>
> They also will examine the civil and criminal dockets of the justices of the peace to determine if fines and fees have been turned over to the proper officials.
>
> But the Town Board set down firm boundaries which the auditors must not cross. They are not to investigate:
>
> 1—The correctness, legality or propriety of the action of any official or employe where not directly related to receiving or disbursing town funds.
>
> 2—The correctness, legality, regularity or propriety of the police blotter or other police records, informations, warrants, orders, tickets, etc., not related to the receiving and disbursing of town funds.

Assessment Procedure

Arriving at a fair appraisal of property is difficult under ideal conditions. A fair appraisal is even less likely in many places where the appraiser or assessor is elected; he thus cannot be expected to have any professional competence, and is subjected to political pressures.

In cities which tax all personal property the chances to hide some of it are obvious. Where bank accounts are taxed officials have noticed that balances migrate during appraisal periods to other areas where there is no tax. Valuation is supposed to bear some relationship to the actual cash value of the property. For some kinds of property this can be determined fairly readily. Assessors can examine sales records to find out selling prices of houses in a given area and thus set up a reasonably equitable standard of valuation. But factories, stores, and other commercial property cannot be evaluated so easily. It is difficult to place a fair value on household goods or the contents of an office building.

Appraisers used to park in front of a piece of property and, from their knowledge of general conditions, place a value on it. Some places still let their appraisers follow this practice. In others, a careful system has been developed in which the community is mapped and a value is placed on each running foot of frontage, with the amount determined by the area of the city. The value is determined after an examination of sale and rental prices. Standard procedures are developed, too, for adjusting the price of corner lots and those which are more or less than the standard depth.

New England towns and cities compile a "grand list" of taxable property. In other places the list may be called the tax roll. Whatever the name of the list, the total valuation of property makes a good story. Here is one such story from the *Pittsburgh Post-Gazette:*

> Tax value of Allegheny County's real estate increased $120,132,516 in the last 12 months with Baldwin's $7,561,282 gain in assessments taking the lead for all suburban communities, it was reported yesterday.
>
> The County Board of Assessment listed the total value of county real estate at $2,962,790,199, representing an all-time high.
>
> Top gains in assessments following Baldwin were these suburban communities:
>
> Castle Shannon, $5,261,000; White Oak, $5,436,808; Penn Hills, $5,229,-540; Whitehall, $5,139,467; Monroeville, $4,522,290; Moon Township, $4,420,560.
>
> New home building in the suburbs, in addition to a sweeping review of assessments on older dwellings, was held responsible for the increase. In the city of Pittsburgh the gain was $15,227,637.
>
> The review of out-of-date assessments was carried out in several communities in the southern part of the county, resulting in upgrading of property valuation by several million dollars.
>
> Property assessments went up by $4,285,215 in Elizabeth Township, where angry taxpayers hanged County Board Chairman John J. Kane and Mayor Lawrence in effigy in protest against the re-appraisals.

The last paragraph quoted shows why it is difficult to keep assessments in line with the true value of property—it is just plain unpopular, and officials take their political lives in their hands when they do it. The result is that the assessment for tax purposes is seldom the full value of the property. When a given amount of money is to be raised through the property tax the rate has to be set proportionately higher, with the tax-payer paying the same amount of money anyway. Somehow the low tax valuation seems to make the property owner happy, perhaps because he likes to think that his property is the most undervalued one on the rolls. In times of increasing property values this problem is likely to be more acute. It is reflected in the first two words of the article quoted above. Notice that the writer says "tax value" of Allegheny property, without making any guess as to what the "real value" is.

Serious undervaluation of property means that a community can raise less in tax money because there is usually some state limit on the rate—so much per thousand dollars of assessed valuation. Chronic undervaluation is sometimes used, too, to attract new residents to a given town, where property is assessed by town rather than county appraisers.

It is easy to see how differing assessment practices can lead to unfair taxation. If property in Town A is valued at 40 per cent of full value and property in Town B at 65 per cent of full value, it is easy to see that tax-payers in Town A will pay less than their full share of the county-wide tax unless some means is found to equalize the burden. The same situation has led to unequal division of state-wide tax burdens among counties and to "equalization plans."

Equalization boards or officials are often found at county and state levels to determine the level of tax assessments in different areas and establish a ratio which will even up the assessments for state-wide or county-wide equity.

In our previous illustration, for example, if equalizers determined that property in Town A was assessed at 40 per cent of full value and that in Town B at 65 per cent, they would apply a ratio which would raise Town A assessments to the proper level for county tax purposes.

On the state or local level this is a highly complicated process. It is hard to explain it to taxpayers and therefore officials are frequently charged with political manipulation. The following story from the *Chicago Daily News* illustrates the problem at the state level:

> The thorny—and politically potent—tax multiplier was up for discussion Tuesday between Gov. Stratton and his revenue director, Richard J. Lyons.
>
> The mysterious multipliers have multiplied themselves into a major concern among some downstate political leaders.
>
> They are protesting plans to boost the multipliers an average of about 10 per cent across the state.
>
> It is Lyons' State Department of Revenue that slaps on a new multiplier each year for each of the state's 102 counties.

In theory the multiplier—or equalization factor—is supposed to equalize property tax assessments among the counties.

Some downstaters have charged that the multiplier was hiked so that more money would have to be collected at the county level for schools and less would have to be shelled out from state coffers.

This, they maintain, would pretty-up the Illinois budget picture since the state is obliged to make up deficits in areas where local funds are insufficient.

Not so, said Lyons.

"Gov. Stratton never spoke to me about the budget or anything else," he added. "He always said, 'Do what is proper, Dick.'

"He's never interfered with the operation of the department. He never mentioned anything about the budget."

So far Lyons' department has certified multipliers for 90 counties. Cook county's is not expected until early next year. Sixty-five of the 90 have been made final and 25 are tentative.

"In my meeting with the governor," said Lyons, "we'll take up those counties that have brought us sufficient proof that the multiplier is too high."

He said that includes about 10 or 15 counties.

Reducing multipliers is not out of the ordinary, Lyons said.

Later in the story the writer explains how the state equalization officials arrive at their figures:

Through the year field men from the department pore over records in county courthouses.

From deeds—or revenue stamps on deeds—they determine the selling price of various kinds of property.

On the basis of many such transactions, the department determines a median figure of the difference between the assessed valuation and what the properties actually sold for.

They use data from several years and check it against construction cost indexes, land costs and the like.

It is up to the director, then, to decide what multiplier will be applied to any particular county.

"A director aims at a very conservative figure as to full valuation," said Lyons.

Later on the story tells that, although Cook county property is assessed on a county-wide basis, most Illinois property is assessed by township officials. The state equalization process does not clear up the inequities resulting from this, but county boards of tax appeals have been asked to apply an equalization factor in their counties.

Dependence on general property or real estate taxes has led some towns to try to zone out new housing which could not be assessed high enough to support at least the additional costs it would bring to the community. Faced with an influx of families with school-age children the communities have been hard put to provide classroom space and teachers, especially when many of the new families are in relatively cheap houses. Perhaps this is an argument that the general property tax is antiquated.

Antiquated or not, the general property tax is usually the one that takes up the slack in local government revenues. Even when other taxes are used, the property tax rate is the one which is usually adjusted to provide the revenue found necessary when the budget has been compiled.

Making the Budget

Arthur Bromage, a specialist in local government, lists eight steps in the preparation of the budget in his book, *Introduction to Municipal Government and Administration*. Each step is good for at least one newspaper story. Here they are:

1. The chief fiscal officer distributes instructions and forms to the department heads for them to use in preparing and presenting their budget requests.

2. The department heads submit their budget requests with supporting data.

3. The chief fiscal officer prepares a statement showing the amount that will be necessary to pay interest and retire principal of the local debt, plus any other fixed costs of the city which will not show up in individual budget requests. He also estimates revenues.

4. The chief fiscal officer assembles the budget and summarizes it.

5. The city manager, mayor, or county executive and the chief fiscal officer confer with department heads to determine the validity of and need for budget requests.

6. The chief executive makes his decision on what to allow and what to throw out and balances the income against proposed expenses.

7. The legislative body receives the budget and holds public hearings.

8. The legislative body revises and adopts the budget.

In small communities all of these steps may not be so clear, but they are the processes which must be followed formally or informally in preparing a public budget. The procedure is similar to that of a private business organization.

Once the budget has been adopted neither the mayor, the manager, nor the newspapers can afford to forget about it. Since it embodies the carefully thought out plans of the government for the following year, it is important that it be administered carefully. Newspaper readers need to be reminded, too, that the budget is an administrative tool, and they should be told frequently how the city is living up to its plans. Often the individual departments will not be allowed to spend more than a given portion of their appropriations during a certain period. The year may be divided into quarters and the departments allowed to spend only a quarter of their budget during each period. Sometimes monthly periods are used.

Seasonal variations will change this somewhat. For example, the public works department will often have extra-heavy seasonal expenses, such as snow removal in winter.

Reporters need to understand the kind of accounting methods used by their local governments. Two key words here are cash and accrual.

Under a cash system of accounting, money due is not added to the books until it is actually received, and expenditures are not subtracted from the books until the money is actually spent. Under the accrual system, money is added to the books when it becomes due and expenditures are subtracted as soon as the commitment has been made. Thus, under the cash system, tax revenues are not added to the books until the city has collected the money. Under the accrual system, the money is added as soon as the taxes become due. Under the cash system, if the city agrees to buy a fire truck the money is not subtracted until it is actually spent. Under the accrual system, it is subtracted as soon as the city agrees to the purchase.

Many cities use the safest method of accounting—the cash system for income and the accrual system for outgo. Under this system receipts are not credited until they are actually in hand, but expenditures are subtracted as soon as the city is committed to them.

Local Debt

Like the federal government, many of our cities are chronically in debt. A few have made a success of "pay as you go" plans, but sometimes this has been at the expense of municipal improvement. Judicious use of borrowing is not regarded as poor financial policy, although short term debts usually do mean that the city is not managing its money very well.

Tax anticipation warrants are the commonest kind of short term municipal debt. They are notes for short periods by which the city pledges uncollected taxes for funds to meet operating expenses.

In an entirely different category are bonds issued to cover the expenses of capital improvement—new schools or other public buildings, parks, or other long-lasting city resources. These will be a major improvement in the city and citizens will gain benefits from them for many years. Bonds should be paid off some time before the effective life of the improvement is spent, but usually that period is at least 20 or 25 years. Occasionally one finds a city which, through refunding, is still paying for public improvements which were worn out years ago.

Ideally a city would avoid all interest charges by paying for public improvements either out of current revenue or by saving in advance. Very large cities may be in a position to pay for capital improvements out of current income, if they undertake only one major project at a time.

Few cities collect enough taxes to do this, and they must rely on either borrowing or saving. Building up a reserve for capital improvements is usually difficult. There is always constant pressure for tax relief, and it is that much harder to resist if a city has "money in the bank." There are many groups, too, with pet projects, and if a city has a capital reserve fund they are likely to regard this as an invitation to agitate harder than ever to get it spent for their project.

When cities or other units of local government borrow money they usually do it through one of four types of bonds:

GENERAL OBLIGATION BONDS. These are the responsibility of the municipal corporation and its general revenues are pledged to repay the bonds.

REVENUE BONDS. Such bonds are payable from income of specific property, such as a municipal water system, an electric plant, or some other facility. The money borrowed is used to construct or renovate the plant.

SPECIAL ASSESSMENT BONDS. These bonds are paid wholly or in part by the revenue of a special assessment levied against property-holders who benefit from an improvement. Thus, a city may borrow to install sidewalks in a given section, assess the land owners in the section, and pay the bonds from the revenue. Sometimes water lines are paid for in this way. Lighting and sewage systems are other examples.

SPECIAL-GENERAL BONDS. These are bonds which are payable from the revenue of a special assessment, but with the added backing of the credit of the municipal corporation, pledged on a contingent liability basis. This means that if the revenues from the special assessment are inadequate to pay the bonds, the regular city revenues will have to be used to pay them off. Bonds of this type have come into use as the result of a series of defaults on special revenue bonds which made it difficult to sell them. In boom times special assessment bonds might be issued to extend water to undeveloped areas with the anticipation that houses would be built. If a depression followed, the subdivision might not be built up; there then would be no taxpayers to foot the bill for the water.

Bonds can also be classified as to whether they are registered or coupon. The city keeps a record of the owner of every registered bond and sends the interest when it is due. If a bondholder sells a bond, he signs it over to the new owner, who sends it to the city which then makes out a new bond in the name of the new owner and sends it to him. The city keeps no record of the owners of coupon bonds. When the interest is due the bondholder clips a coupon and mails it in, whereupon the city pays the interest. Owners of registered bonds find it easier to collect if the bonds are lost or stolen.

Some bonds, called sinking fund or term bonds, are sold so that the principal all becomes due at once—perhaps 20 years from the date of issue. Other bonds, called serial bonds, may be issued so that part of the principal is due every year. Sinking fund bonds require that the city set aside a certain amount each year in a sinking fund to retire the principal when it comes due. The serial bonds do not require a sinking fund since part of them is retired each year. The serial bonds generally are preferred because cities sometimes have mismanaged their sinking funds, and bondholders have found when the bonds were due that there was no money to pay them. A default on a serial bond becomes apparent at once if one year's payment is missed.

The *San Francisco Chronicle* tells about efforts to float municipal bonds in this story:

> Four municipal bond issues on the November 4 ballot were endorsed yesterday by the Citizens Bond Screening Committee—but the $3.6 million for the Palace of Fine Arts barely made it.
>
> The Palace restoration project received a luke-warm 9-to-8 endorsement by the committee headed by Banker Jerd F. Sullivan, Jr.
>
> Three other propositions, including $7,225,000 for the rehabilitation of the Civic Auditorium, received overwhelming support from the committee.
>
> A proposed $1.5 million bond issue to build a new maintenance yard for the Department of Electricity and $1.3 million issue for expansion of the department of Public Works' maintenance yard each passed by a 15-2 vote, the same as the Civic Auditorium.
>
> A new courthouse and City Hall rehabilitation bond issue of $22,150,000 and a Ferry Building Park project of $2,785,000 had previously been endorsed by the committee, which is composed of leading businessmen and representatives of labor and civic organizations.
>
> Meanwhile the City indicated yesterday it will adopt a "go slow" policy in issuing voter-authorized bonds.
>
> Reason for all the concern is a sudden shrinkage of San Francisco's credit.
>
> Controller Harry Ross said yesterday it will be necessary to work up a priority list for proposed projects.
>
> The bond-selling slowdown was forced by an "agonizing reappraisal" this week of the city's financial picture.
>
> On Tuesday, the City had permission from its voters to sell $95.3 million worth of bonds to finance projects ranging from firehouses to Hetch Hetchy power turbines.
>
> The Charter-imposed ceiling on the amount the City can owe to bondholders at any one time is 12 per cent of the assessment roll. On Tuesday, that was $272 million, with $167.7 million outstanding and a margin for new sales of $104.3 million.
>
> But on Wednesday, the new assessment roll showed a $285 million drop in taxable bank accounts. This automatically dropped the debt limit by $34 million.
>
> The result: a new ceiling of $70.3 million, with $95.3 million in approved bonds still on hand.
>
> There is no immediate crisis, Ross said yesterday.

For one thing, the City is redeeming bonds at the rate of about $15 million a year. For another, Ross carefully balances the market and the City's projects, selling only when the money is needed.

Most cities have some debt ceiling, and problems like San Francisco's are not uncommon. Three quarters of the states have debt limits which they impose on municipal governments. Other limits are imposed in city charters. The limits came as the result of heavy municipal indebtedness and bankruptcies which did much in the nineteenth century to injure municipal credit standing.

Total local debt in the United States was $27.5 million in 1843. By 1860 it had risen to $200 million. In New York the total indebtedness of the cities was 10 per cent of the total assessed valuation. In New Jersey it was 11 per cent. Some cities had debts equal to more than 25 per cent of their total assessed valuation, and a few big-spending municipalities had outstanding bonds equal to more than their total assessed valuation. Some of the bonds had been issued to buy railroad stock, to induce the railroads to build through their town.

The depressions of 1873 and 1874 put a number of cities into bankruptcy and caused many states to impose debt ceilings. The average limit now is 5 per cent of assessed valuation, with some between 5 and 10 per cent, and a few higher than that.

Sometimes the limits have been unrealistic, particularly in light of the tendency to appraise property at something less than the market value. This led to various dodges by which cities sought to escape debt limits. Often courts have been liberal in interpreting these provisions.

One of the ways in which cities have expanded their debt limits is by establishing separate authorities for special purposes. An authority with power to issue revenue bonds may build a city building and the city will pay off through a lease arrangement. Usually the city will have the privilege of buying the building for $1 when it is debt-free. The same sort of arrangement may be made with a private concern. Courts have held in some cases that a city's debt amounts each year only to the sum called for by the lease.

Sometimes a city will set up one authority after another so that there may eventually be several separate authorities, each indebted up to the limit. While these are, in a sense, separate organizations, the property which is used to secure the bonds is the same, so the actual debt limit may be doubled or tripled in this manner.

Newspapers and Public Finance

Newspapers have an obvious watchdog function where public funds are concerned. There is sometimes a tendency to keep careful track of funds at the state capital or in Washington, but to forget local financing—at least in watching day-to-day details. Once-a-year coverage of the budget does not give voters enough information about the financial condition of their local governments. Weekly financial statements, perhaps even daily ones, would help to make readers conscious of the need for care in local financing, and would help local officials to remember the need for constant appraisal of the financial condition of their government.

In addition to being a watchdog, the good newspaper works hard to explain public finance in terms the reader understands. The reader will catch on fast if the reporter succeeds in telling him what a financial venture at any level of government will mean to his pocketbook. Will taxes go up or down? What will that mean to the man who earns $110 a week?

"Hidden taxes" is a common expression, but it needs constant explanation. How much of our income goes in taxes? How much that we do not know about?

Different types of taxes need to be explained. What are the relative advantages of a sales tax as against an income tax? Who pays more of each—the high income or the low income person?

What is the effect of intergovernmental payments? To what extent should the process of equalization be carried out by taxing rich areas and transferring the funds to poorer ones? Should it be carried out in some fields such as education, health, and welfare, but eliminated in others?

Because public taxing and public spending are tied so closely to public policy the newspapers need to bring their readers all the information available as to the incidence of taxing and spending programs. What is the result of levying a sales tax? Should the state or local government collect it? Why? Where should welfare functions be situated—in local, state, or federal units? All these are tax and revenue questions which involve deep-seated problems of public policy.

Presenting the routine of finance on any level of government so that readers will understand how it applies to them and how it is intertwined with public policy, is a job worth the efforts of the best reporter.

REPORTING ASSIGNMENTS

1. Write a feature story describing the process of preparing the budget in your city.

2. If possible attend a budget hearing and write an article on it suitable for publication in the local newspaper.

3. Interview city officials to find out how the budget is enforced throughout the year; then write an article about it.

4. Write a story analyzing the strength of various officials in preparing the budget. Who has the most control—council, mayor, some board, or another official? How is this control achieved?

5. Write a story about the debt position of your city. How much is the debt? What kinds of bonds are used? What is the per capita debt? What is the percentage of debt to assessed valuation? How does this compare with other cities?

6. Write a story describing the process your city must go through before incurring a debt.

7. Find out whether your city has a central purchasing agent. If so, write a story about his work. If not, describe its methods of buying supplies.

8. Write a series of articles analyzing the tax sources of your city and town or county governments. What percentage of the total revenue comes from each source?

9. Write a story telling how much money your city, county, or town receives from the state. Tell in what form the money is paid (as state-collected, locally-shared taxes, grants, or other method) and what restrictions there are on the way it is spent.

10. Write a story or a series showing how federal money is spent in your locality.

6

Public Health

Early Public Health Problems

After the Royal Court moved from London to Windsor to escape the plague of 1625, a gallows was promptly erected at Windsor to hang anyone else who arrived from London.

This prudent measure was not unusual in those days. When an epidemic broke out the privileged persons usually fled, and then tried to prevent further spread of the disease by forbidding anyone else to leave the infected area.

The *Gazette de Hollande* described conditions in Marseille during an outbreak there of the plague nearly a century later, in 1720. The paper quotes doctors as describing the city as:

> . . . a hospital in which there are more than 500 dying patients, abandoned without the slightest aid and not even with water to drink, a mass of unremoved bodies between the wards of the hospital; a town stricken and despairing; whole families destroyed; nearly all the doctors and surgeons dead, the Brethern and Sisters of Mercy reduced from eighty to four, of whom three have fled; the neighborhood of the town swarming with looters and thieves who rob the farms of the better class and with these latter not knowing how to escape either the plague or the robbers.

French authorities used desperate measures to try to keep residents from escaping from Marseille. A ring of sentries was ordered for the area "sufficiently close together to communicate with each other and patrolling all night." Anyone who escaped was "to be chased, taken back to the spot from which he escaped and have his head broken in the presence of his neighbors as an example to them."

This early form of quarantine was reported in *Nouvelles d'Amsterdam* for October 17, 1721.

The terror of the plague was intense and well justified, and it is small wonder that extreme measures were used to control the plague.

Ships often carried diseases from country to country, and so they came to be suspect in all major ports. Often sailors and passengers were forced to spend many days in quarantine before they were admitted to the port city.

"Bills of health," now obsolete, were used as early as 1300. Shipmasters could usually avoid quarantine only by producing an official document certifying that their last port of call was free from certain diseases (plague, yellow fever, and cholera). Often this document had to be countersigned by the consul of the country in which the ship was arriving to guarantee its veracity. This came to be known as "a clean bill of health."

Such were some of the crude beginnings of the public health programs which are so important today in helping us to live longer and stay healthier. The connection between public health and the health of each individual is so obvious that public health stories have long been important news.

Today's public health officer has been described as a doctor with just one patient—the community. Preventive medicine is his chief job, but often it is hard to draw the line between preventive and curative medicine. Hospitalizing persons with infectious diseases and seeing to it that they have the best of care is preventive medicine from the community standpoint, because it may keep the disease from spreading; but for the disease-ridden individual it could hardly be called preventive.

What Is Public Health Work?

Many jobs are assigned to public health officials. The more important jobs are these:

1. *Control of epidemics.* This involves isolating persons with contagious diseases and treating them. It requires tracing the source of the epidemic, and may mean immunization clinics to protect the rest of the population.

2. *Environmental sanitation.* Sanitarians and sanitary engineers are trained to recognize health hazards, and are empowered to see that they are corrected. Dumps may be breeding grounds for rats; swamps may breed mosquitoes.

3. *Preventive medicine.* This includes the operation of clinics. Among the most common are those for babies, children, and expectant mothers.

4. *Health education.* Some health department officials spend most of their time teaching good health habits. Most state health departments are prepared to send out speakers, exhibits, or films on good health habits. Some officials devote their time to preparing materials and displays to sell the public on good health.

PUBLIC HEALTH PROBLEMS

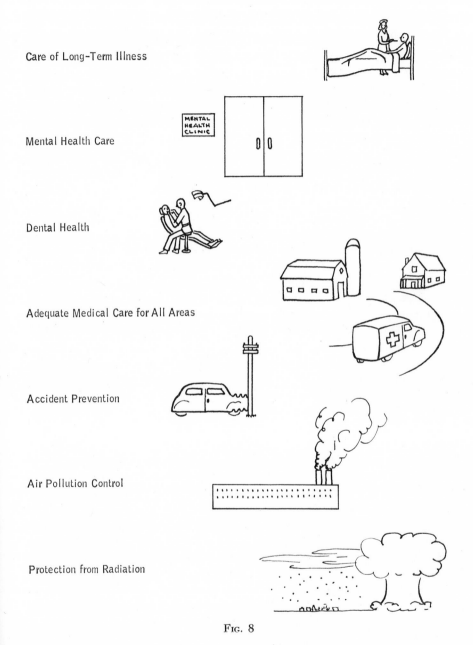

Care of Long-Term Illness

Mental Health Care

Dental Health

Adequate Medical Care for All Areas

Accident Prevention

Air Pollution Control

Protection from Radiation

Fig. 8

5. *Inspection services.* Public health officials examine food sources and other things of importance to the public's physical well-being. Milk inspectors may visit the dairy farms which supply a city's milk, and without their approval a farmer cannot sell his milk in their city. Meat supplies are inspected. Restaurants must be approved by public health officers. Pollution of streams and lakes, and garbage and sewage disposal, are in the province of the health department, as are the sources of a community's water supply.

Some idea of the wide range of public health activities can be gained from the fact that the field includes 150 separate vocations, with new ones being added constantly. The military services recognize 42 different health and medical categories of military duty.

Public Health Agencies

In most of our communities the local health department is the central public health agency. All the states have health divisions and the United States government is active in the field, but the day-to-day public health activities are usually carried on at the local level.

Cities and counties may have separate health departments, although, as was pointed out in an earlier chapter, combined city-county health departments are not uncommon.

Often the local unit is headed by a board of health which consists of appointed or elected members (often five) who serve as the general control body. They often serve without salary, and they may have general power to enact health regulations with the force of local law. They may appoint the local health officer, and they have general control of his activities.

The health officer heads the health department, which performs the essential local health functions. The size of the department varies with the size and nature of the community. Some health authorities feel that a population of 50,000 is necessary to support an adequate health department, able to employ enough people to provide full service.

About one third of the counties in the United States have no local public health service, but they are the sparsely settled counties and include only about 10 per cent of the population.

Several counties in California have contracted with the state to supply essential public health services. Local officials select the services they desire and the state supplies them at a given cost. Usually the health officer is a local official, but the state hires public health nurses, sanitarians, and whatever other workers are needed. These people are on the state payroll, but live in the communities they serve and work under the general direction of the local health officer.

In Vermont the responsibility for the control of infectious diseases has been delegated to the state health department. Six supervising nurses are in charge of twelve district offices. Where there are local public health nurses, the state nurses work with them to provide more adequate service.

State Health Departments

State health agencies cooperate with local units and to some extent supervise them. Normally state health agencies run a state health laboratory which is available to local units. The state health department collects health information, records it, and interprets it to the public.

The state health department supervises health problems which affect more than one community. For example, the pollution of a lake or stream is likely to be of concern to a number of communities.

The state unit is charged, too, with general supervision of many sanitation functions. Sewage disposal systems usually require state approval; so does the sanitary condition of water at public bathing beaches. Some state health departments supervise industrial hygiene.

The state health department is almost always active in the educational aspects of health work. Persuading the people of its state to adopt good health habits is one of its primary jobs. Benjamin Disraeli expressed the state's interest in the health of its citizens in these words: "The health of the population is really the foundation upon which all their happiness and all their powers as a state depend."

The state department stands ready to help local units in the control of epidemics and will, if the local unit fails, take over its job until the emergency is over or local service can be restored.

New York State Health Commissioner Dr. Herman Hilleboe has suggested that regional health departments may be the next step needed to provide adequate services to our mobile population.

Federal Health Activities

The federal government is not involved directly in operating a health service for the general population. This is considered to be the job of the local units, with the aid of the state. The federal government sponsors a considerable amount of research, and is ready to advise state and local units and aid them if called upon. It does run a large health program in the Veterans' Administration and in the medical service of the Bureau of Indian Affairs. It cares for service-associated disabilities of veterans and provides medical programs for Indians living on reservations. Crippled children are also aided by the federal government.

The U.S. Public Health Service, headed by the Surgeon General, runs a fairly extensive research program in the National Institute of Health at Bethesda, Maryland. The Health Service, a division of the Department of Health, Education and Welfare, also collects and analyzes vital statistics, participates in some cases in decisions on stream pollution, milk, and general sanitation problems. The Service is also charged with the responsibility of clearing ships from foreign ports to make sure that they are bringing in no contagious diseases. Yellow fever, cholera, smallpox, plague, and some other diseases are still subject to quarantine.

World Health Organization

The World Health Organization, an international organization of about 75 nations, expresses the goals of public health work in its constitution:

> The enjoyment of the highest attainable standard of health is one of the fundamental rights of every human being without distinction of race, religion, political belief, economic or social condition. . . . Governments have a responsibility for the health of their peoples which can be fulfilled only by the provision of adequate health and social measures.

The World Health Organization is a clearing house for health information and stands by to aid governments in solving their health problems, but cannot participate in internal affairs of a nation without invitation.

It directs most of its attention to international problems concerned with the control of epidemics, the establishment of international standards for keeping vital statistics and preparing medicines, the aid of backward countries, the advising of governments, and the control of traffic in opium, cocaine, heroin, and other drugs.

It has helped to control diseases which used to spread all over the world, as a result of the pilgrimages to Mecca. The pilgrims from all over the world converged on the Holy City, bringing cholera, plague, and smallpox which spread rapidly because of the overcrowding and unsanitary conditions at the Holy Places. World Health Organization representatives helped check the spread of contagion by establishing observation posts at places passed by the pilgrims on the way to Mecca, and using epidemic control devices such as international control of sanitation, quarantine, and vaccination.

Intergovernmental Cooperation

This review of public health organizations has been general, and is intended to be suggestive. Every reporter can discover the public health organizations in his area without much difficulty. The local patterns achieve more significance when they are fitted into state, national, and international schemes. Like most community problems, health questions often require the attention of more than one level of government. Contagion does not stop at the borders of a city or state any more than crime does, and frequently cooperative measures or control from a higher level of government is the only effective way to deal with it.

In addition to the public agencies, many private organizations are concerned with health problems. Many large foundations give grants for research in health. On the local level one of the common activities for private organizations is to provide visiting nurses for persons unable to pay for this service themselves. In Richmond, Virginia, the private nursing organization was combined with the public nursing service to provide more adequate care with available resources.

New Directions in Health Service

The Pilgrims enacted a law in 1636 providing, "if any man shalbee sent forth as a souldier and shall return maimed hee shalbee maintained competently by the Collonie during his life." Maimed and disabled veterans were given pensions by Massachusetts Bay Colony, Maryland, New York, Rhode Island, Virginia, and Pennsylvania. Shortly after the Revolution the Continental Congress provided pensions to disabled Revolutionary soldiers.

Our first thoughts in this country were for veterans, but gradually we have enlarged our ideas of medical care to include the concept that no one should be denied adequate care because of lack of money to pay for it.

We have not reached this goal in practice, and probably will not for some time. It will take more resources than we have—more buildings, more equipment, more personnel.

World attention to public health problems has paid off amazingly already. Raymond B. Allen, educator and doctor, described progress in these words:

This century has witnessed the greatest advance in knowledge of health and diseases of any period in history. It can be strongly argued that greater progress has been made in medical science in the past fifty years than in the previous five thousand. Even though this may be an exaggeration, it is most certainly true that before another fifty years have elapsed, the necessary knowledge and skills will have been acquired to deal with most if not all of the principal problems of disease and health not presently understood. These include cancer, poliomyelitis and the virus infections in general, the degenerative disorders of the aging, and the emotional and mental disorders of the psychoneuroses and psychoses. . . . Medicine has long since moved beyond the problems which have to do with infectious diseases. Although continued vigilance is necessary to control these diseases, the major problems of preventive medicine of the future lie in the fields of occupational disease, malnutrition, maladjustment, psychoneurosis, social deficiencies in general, and health education.

With control of the infectious diseases not demanding all the efforts of our health departments, what will be some of their problems of the future?

One important problem has directly to do with the news media, because it involves explaining scientific information to the public. The question is simply how we can persuade the public of the need for taking advantage of medical progress.

If often seems ridiculously difficult for health officials to persuade large numbers of people to do the obviously important things. For example, polio vaccine programs were carried out through the schools, in public health clinics, and in doctors' offices. Despite the wide availability of the vaccine, many persons failed to give their children this protection or take it themselves. In 1959, six years after the discovery of the Salk serum, less than one half of the population under 40 years of age had taken the basic three injections, and more than a third had received none of the vaccine. The public health ramifications of this become more obvious when we remember that each person who protects himself through immunization also protects the general health, because he makes it unlikely that he will give the disease to others.

This story from the *Denver Post* gives the governor and the State Health Department a chance to stress their interest in getting everyone to take polio inoculations:

> It is "one of the duties of citizenship" to take a full series of inoculations against polio, Gov. Steve McNichols declared late Thursday.
>
> Commenting on the disclosure that only about 38 pct. of Colorado's population has been fully immunized, the governor said:
>
> "You hardly have a right to carry around a communicable disease. This problem can become critical again if people are going to be lax about it."
>
> He said he, Mrs. McNichols and their five children all are scheduled for an annual "booster" shot within the next week, remarking, "Some people think you can't catch polio if you're over 40, but it isn't true." McNichols is 44.
>
> "I am urging all citizens to take a full series of shots," he said. "This illness can be a tragic, crippling thing. Just think of your kids catching it."
>
> The State Health Department disclosed Thursday that more than 1 million Coloradans have not had the full series of three shots which gives 95 pct. protection against paralysis resulting from polio. Only about one-third of the 1 million have had any shots at all, said Dr. C. S. Mollohan, director of communicable disease control for the department.

Another problem which will confront our public health specialists increasingly in the future is how to prevent long-term illness and how to care for it when it is inevitable. Surveys have shown that one of the biggest worries of our older people is that they will be beset by illness which will make them helpless and drain away all the resources they have saved over a lifetime.

Health specialists are becoming increasingly interested, not only in helping people to live longer, but also in making the years productive. This also brings up the question of how care of elderly persons shall be financed. We are committed to paying the hospital bills of those who are destitute, but this frequently works a hardship on persons of small resources, who have to lose everything before they are eligible for public help. Gradually we are reexamining our ideas on this subject.

One answer is voluntary health prepayment plans. Some private companies offer such policies, but complete protection is too expensive for many individuals. Congress has given some consideration to including hospital benefits in a social security program. It has been estimated that this would cost a billion dollars a year at the start. Other suggestions have been privately run plans closely supervised by the government.

There are objections to all these suggestions, but one thing is certain. With the elderly people becoming an increasingly larger proportion of our population we are sure to feel more pressure to take this hazard out of retirement years. Proper financing is part of the answer. Special attention to medical needs of the elderly is another part.

One of the problems with health insurance programs is that some people who have policies enter hospitals when they do not need to. Sometimes people with insurance policies covering surgery will even have operations they don't need. This increases the cost of the insurance, sometimes making the premiums beyond the means of the average wage-earner—the class most needing the protection. It also crowds hospitals to the point where some do not even have room for emergency patients, and community leaders are trying to find resources to build new hospitals.

Writer Jim Bishop discusses the problem in connection with the Blue Cross insurance plan, in this portion of a column:

> It (the Blue Cross) is caught between some irresponsible doctors, some greedy patients, and some hospitals which would close their doors if it were not for Blue Cross money. Doctors are recommending institutional care in cases where, if the low-income patient didn't have Blue Cross, two or three house calls would suffice.
>
> Surgery has gone a little wild. Hysterectomies, gall bladder operations, Smithwick sections and resections are on a medical conveyor belt. The patients are worse. A family head will have one policy in his place of business, one at home, and collect from both and pocket the difference.
>
> Hospitals add wings to their big structures and put in 75 or 100 additional beds. Still, bed space is at a premium. Are we getting sicker as a nation? Hardly. Our doctors are slamming more people into hospitals with less reason.

One of the brave men who speaks out is J. Albert Durgom, executive vice president of the Hospital Service Plan of New Jersey. This state has but one Blue Cross Plan, and, in 1957, had 2,083,415 members. Mr. Durgom is one of the early fathers of Blue Cross. He knows the field.

He says that the United States, in 25 years, has gone from "empty hospital beds to an all time over-use of hospitals now."

. . . "The answer," says Mr. Durgom, "lies basically in the hands of the medical profession. . . . Such authority must remain within the professional judgment of the physician who bears the responsibility for the care of his patient, but such decision must extend beyond the sheer convenience of the patient and the physician, with a disciplinary set of standards by the medical staff of the hospital. . . ."

He does not indict medicine as a profession for these abuses. Some doctors are careless, just as some lawyers are—or engineers. Mr. Durgom claims that organized medicine will police and discipline its careless members or face the threat of government regulation.

Mental illness has reached such proportions that it is clearly one of the public health problems of the immediate future. Half of the patients in our hospitals at any given time are suffering from mental illness. Much public money is spent maintaining hospitals for the mentally ill. General public understanding of the problems of mental health is needed before treatment can be as effective as it should. One of the problems is that it is difficult for a person who has been in a mental hospital to adjust to society. This sort of difficulty may produce a relapse, which would not have occurred if the public had been ready to accept him. "Half-way houses" have been used in a few places as an intermediate stop before full release to society. This allows a more gradual adjustment period.

Public health specialists are becoming increasingly interested in accident prevention. Persons under 35 years of age are more likely to die from accidents than from any other single cause. Among the total population, accidents rank fourth among the causes of death.

Since the public health specialist is concerned with prolonging life and keeping people healthy, it is easy to see why he should be concerned with accidents. Younger persons, who are most likely to die in accidents, are a particular loss to the community because they should have ahead of them many productive years. The magnitude of the area opening up to public health authorities in accident prevention suggests many new developments in the years immediately ahead.

Public health authorities are sure to devote even more attention in the future to control of pollution of the air and water. Increasingly concentrated populations and nuclear energy will make these problems more complicated. Closely akin to them is the task of protecting the population from radiation, and the disposal of radioactive wastes. This will become a local problem in many places, and reporters covering the story are likely to find that they will have to collect their information from several different government agencies.

Another problem of the future concerns the proper utilization of our facilities. How many new hospitals do we need? We know now that many persons are confined to hospitals, not because they need the facilities available there, but because they cannot obtain adequate nursing anywhere else. Many of these patients, doctors say, would be better off at home if there were some way to give them proper care. Others could be cared for just as well in nursing homes, if adequate homes were available.

Obviously it is cheaper to take care of people in their homes or in nursing homes than in hospitals which are designed to care for the seriously ill. A proper balance in facilities and more adequate provisions for home nursing would take some of the strain off our hospitals.

Area-wide planning is taking place, too, with regard to facilities. Patients need to have specialists available. Doctors in small communities need the stimulation of working with their colleagues. In a few places we have developed medical centers with a system for sending interns into smaller hospitals in the area, and with an accepted system for transferring some patients to the central hospital or medical center where special facilities and medical specialties are available. The center's specialists also travel occasionally to the smaller hospitals in the area to consult and operate.

The concept may include refresher courses to help doctors keep abreast of the latest findings in their ever-changing field.

Covering Public Health Problems

Public health problems are sure to take many new turns in the years directly ahead, and require adjustments, new techniques, and decisions on fundamental public policy. This will require an imaginative approach from those who control our public policy and the health personnel who implement it. It will require the same imaginative approach from those who report and interpret it to the public.

The routine stories will still be important, such as the number of cases of communicable diseases, personnel shifts, and stories on pollution control.

This story, from the Gloversville-Johnstown, New York, *Leader-Herald,* shows how the reporter covering Common Council is likely to find himself dealing with public health problems:

> Owners of property which constitutes a health, fire or safety hazard are going to have to reckon with the combined powers of all city departments in the near future.
>
> Buildings committee chairman Henry J. Scribner recommended at a meeting of the Common Council last night that the fire chief, sanitary in-

spector and building inspector file reports on abandoned or unsanitary buildings or property.

Property owners will be notified that the condition is considered illegal and will be ordered to correct law violations within a specified time. City Atty. George W. Gloning, Jr., will be directed to take legal action which could lead to condemnation of property if corrective steps are not taken.

The move represents the first concrete action by the city since Planning Consultant Russell D. Bailey called attention to the "derelict buildings" situation in January.

In this story, the Los Angeles *Mirror News* covers one aspect of another public health problem, air pollution:

If a diesel locomotive begins to heave and belch smoke, you just don't run it into the nearest garage for repairs like an automobile.

You head it for the yards and hope that an Air Pollution Control District Inspector doesn't hand out a ticket under that section of the Health and Safety Code that puts a limit on smoke.

A Pacific Electric diesel developed a defective fuel injector while wheeling along Santa Monica Blvd. last summer and PE was hauled into court for the smoke violation—a $25 rap.

And back in December, 1955, Southern Pacific was fined $500 because of a smoking diesel ticketed between Broadway and Spring Sts. along the Los Angeles River.

The fine was suspended to $150 and a year's probation, but it's on the records.

This preamble is by way of answer to an Alhambra reader who feels The Mirror News is guilty of ducking its responsibility by failing to point out "the willful neglect of the railroad industry to help fight smog."

The fact of the matter is, when the railroads junked steam locomotives in favor of diesel equipment, they eliminated a lot of air pollution.

The smoke from their boilers was not the kind of stuff that contributed to eye irritation; it was the sulfur dioxide that smells like rotten eggs.

"We cite 'em when we catch 'em," said an APCD enforcement officer. "Actually, the railroads are not a large contributing factor. They'll have an occasional breakdown.

"Within a year's time, if we get three or four citations, it will be a lot. . . ."

Many of the stories will center around important policy decisions. Some of the policy questions are: Should the government assume more of the costs of health care? What jobs properly belong to the local units? Should state and federal governments supply more direct services to the public? What can be done to keep the costs of medical treatment within the reach of low-income families? Socialized medicine will surely come in for more rounds of discussion.

As our society tries to answer these questions, reporters for all the news media will distribute the information the public needs to make valid decisions. It will take reporters with thorough understanding of the social problems as well as a scientific approach to comprehend the specialists.

Medical and public health research has done spectacular things for everyone by lengthening our lives and keeping us healthier. Its contributions will certainly be as great in the years ahead. The writer who can interpret this research to shop clerks, factory workers, farmers, teachers, and to all the other nonspecialists, will be doing his community a great service.

Cathy Covert, a writer for the *Syracuse Herald-Journal,* described research at the Upstate Medical Center of the State University of New York in a series. Here is part of one article which shows how she explains medical concepts in understandable terms:

> It probably will never replace baseball.
> But diagnosing virus disease has turned into another great American pastime.
> "Probably some virus," your friends will chorus hopefully, as you take to your bed with anything from influenza to mumps.
> In the case of those two diseases they'd be right. Viruses also cause polio, rickets, measles, yellow fever, rabies and cold sores.
> For your doctor, diagnosing your case of influenza isn't so easy.
> He'll probably have to go largely on your symptoms. Unfortunately your sore throat, fever and aching back could mean a lot of other things besides influenza.
> And the only reliable laboratory tests for a disease like influenza have taken weeks to complete.
> By that time the patient is usually well, and past much effective help.
> So the rapid test for influenza being developed by Dr. Seymour S. Kalter at the Medical College of the State University of New York may be of considerable value.

REPORTING ASSIGNMENTS

1. Interview the administrator of a local hospital for a story on costs of running a hospital, and how these are reflected in fees charged patients.

2. Write a story on your local public health department, telling the reader how it is organized and what it does.

3. Write a feature story on public health nurses. If possible spend a half-day or a day with one for a first hand understanding of her work.

4. In a feature story tell what facilities are available in your area to help unwed mothers.

5. What public clinics are available to citizens of your community?

6. How is your city's supply of milk and other foods guarded by public health inspectors? This may be worth more than one article.

7. What provisions do your state and city have for insisting on minimum housing standards for all citizens? How are they enforced?

8. Inspect the death certificates for your county for a period long enough to include 200 deaths, and write a story about the most common causes of death in your community.

9. Write an article or series of articles assessing your community as a medical center. What facilities are available? How adequate are they for the needs of the people? Interview doctors, and public health and hospital officials.

10. What medical research is being conducted in your area?

PART TWO

Law and Law Enforcement

7

The Nature of Law

Laws are the formal, enforceable rules under which we live. The power to make and enforce laws is one of the attributes of a sovereign nation. Law-making and law enforcement take up much newspaper space, and many reporters spend their lives covering these aspects of our society.

Basic laws, from which all others flow, come about by common agreement or by dispensation from a higher source.

Authority in early America was often established by a grant of power from the reigning monarch of England. Here is an extract from Queen Elizabeth's charter to Sir Walter Raleigh, dated March 25, 1584:

> Elizabeth, by the Grace of God of England, Fraunce and Ireland Queene, defender of the faith, &c. To all people to whome these presents shall come, greeting.
>
> Knowe yee that of our especial grace, certaine science, and meere motion, . . . we give and graunt to our trustie and welbeloved servant *Walter Ralegh*, Esquire, and to his heires assignes for ever, free liberties and licence from time to time, and at all times for ever hereafter, to discover, search, finde out, and view such remote, heathen and barbarous lands, countries, and territories, not actually possessed of any Christian Prince, nor inhabited by Christian People, as to him, . . . shall seeme good, and the same to have, holde occupie and enjoy to him, . . . for ever, with all prerogatives, . . . thereto or thereabouts both by sea and land, whatsoever we by our letters patent may graunt, . . .
>
> And . . . we . . . do give the graunt to the said Walter Ralegh . . . that hee . . . shall, within the said mentioned remote lands . . . have full and meere power and authoritie to correct, punish, pardon, governe, and rule by their and every or any of their good discretions and pollicies,

as well in causes capital, or criminall, as civil . . . all such our subjects that shall at any time hereafter inhabite any such landes, countries, or territories. . . .

Early American history provides us with another illustration of basic law—the general agreement. The Pilgrims, having no charter, signed the Mayflower Compact on November 11, 1620, as their ship stood off Cape Cod. In the brief document the Pilgrims agreed to

> . . . solemnly and mutually in the Presence of God and one another, cov-
> enant and combine ourselves together into a civil Body Politick, for our
> better Ordering and Preservation, and Furtherance of the Ends aforesaid;
> And by Virtue hereof do enact, constitute, and frame, such just and equal
> laws, Ordinances, Acts, Constitutions, and Offices, from time to time, as
> shall be thought most meet and covenient for the general Good of the
> Colony; unto which we promise all due Submission and Obedience.

The Mayflower Compact was never intended as a constitution, but the Pilgrims never obtained a charter, so it remained the only semblance of such basic law that the colony ever had.

Our federal Constitution gained its force, as we know, by mutual agreement. It became effective with the "Ratification of the Conventions of nine States," as provided in Article VII.

Charters, constitutions, compacts, articles of confederation—these are some of the basic grants of power. Legislation is based on them.

Written laws usually are statutes enacted by Congress, a state legislature, or the legislative body of a city. We get our laws in other ways, too. Judicial decisions have the force of law, and *precedent* (decisions in earlier similar cases) guides a judge when he ponders a case. Executives sometimes issue laws by decree. This is more true in dictator-run countries, but our own executives can issue proclamations which have the force of law. Congress often gives to executive agencies the power to formulate rules which are binding law.

WHERE LAW COMES FROM

1. General Agreements
   Compacts
   Constitutions
2. Dispensation from higher sources
   Charters
   Executive decrees
3. Acts of legislative bodies
4. Precedent
   Legal decisions in previous cases

Legal Distinctions

Here are a few of the broad legal distinctions the reporter must understand:

CIVIL LAW AND CRIMINAL LAW. Civil law governs relationships between individuals. This will be discussed in Chapter 13. The important thing to remember now is that it involves no criminal charges, and is used to straighten out differences between parties in accordance with prevailing law. Criminal law deals with the punishment of persons who commit acts defined as crimes.

Two characteristics identify criminal actions:

1. A representative of the state (usually the district attorney or county prosecutor) brings charges in the name of the state or the people of the state.

2. Punishment is sought. (Civil actions usually seek damages or restitution.) Punishment may take the form of a fine, a prison sentence, the death penalty, or something else. The basic notion is that a person found guilty is made to suffer for a misdeed.

PRIVATE AND PUBLIC LAW. Private law governs the relationship between individuals. It is more often called civil law. Public law deals with the state and its relationship to individuals. It is divided into constitutional law, administrative law, criminal law and procedure, and international law.

ADJECTIVE AND SUBSTANTIVE LAW. Adjective law governs procedure—how the courts operate, what evidence shall be admitted, and all the rest. Substantive law defines the crimes, the rights, and the punishments. Another way of differentiating is to say that substantive law is the body of rules administered by the courts, while adjective law defines the procedure by which the laws are administered.

Adjective law, as well as substantive, is important to a reporter. Often a case may be determined by the interpretation of a given rule of procedure, as, for example, by a ruling to admit or to bar a given piece of evidence. Moreover, a reporter must have at least a rudimentary knowledge of procedure to understand what is going on in a courtroom.

COMMON AND STATUTE LAW. Common law usually refers to the body of precedent which we derived from early English law. Common law derives its authority from precedent, as opposed to statute law which is written by the legislature. In some states many of the common law concepts have been reaffirmed by legislative act. A judge may apply a common law concept without any specific legislative act for support. Certain crimes, for example, called common law crimes, are not defined in the criminal codes of all the states, but are regularly punished by the courts of those states. Common law has additional meaning in some jurisdictions, but this is its most important one.

Officers of the Courts

The people who run the courts are important to a court reporter. Usually they supply the information for his stories. The more important court officers are:

The *judge* is the presiding officer and is responsible for the smooth running of the whole trial. He makes decisions on legal questions, and his decisions are final as far as the conduct of the trial is concerned. If a judge makes a serious error a trial verdict may be upset by a higher court, or a new trial ordered, but during the trial itself the judge's word is the final one. A lawyer who disagrees with a ruling of the judge can argue the point, and if he loses can ask that his exception be noted in the record in case he wants to make it the basis for an appeal to a higher court. The judge has control over the participants in a trial and the spectators in his courtroom. This power is summarily enforceable through his contempt power, which will be discussed shortly. He may order a given spectator to leave the room, or he may clear the courtroom. He rules on the admissibility of evidence and all the other legal questions which arise during a trial. In some cases he may judge the facts of the case in addition to the law. He may sometimes set aside the verdict of a jury or modify it, if he regards it as unreasonable or clearly out of line with the weight of the evidence. In the higher courts panels of judges will hear cases without a jury, since their decisions almost always involve interpretations of the law, rather than a judgment on facts.

An *amicus curiae* or *friend of the court* sometimes plays a role in courtroom dramas, although usually only in the more important cases. Such a person may be an expert in a field in which the judge feels the need of help, or he may simply be a person whose opinion is valued by the judge.

More often *amicus curiae* refers to a person who represents an organization interested in some aspect of a case being tried, but which is not a party to the suit. The lawyer requests the court to allow him to file a brief as *amicus curiae*. If the permission is granted the brief is filed, or perhaps the lawyer is given permission to argue orally before the court. Thus, when the Associated Press was being tried on a charge of violating the antitrust laws, lawyers for the *Chicago Tribune* filed a brief as *amicus curiae*.

The *prosecuting attorney* is a public official charged with bringing actions against persons indicted for felonies or charged with misdemeanors. It is his duty to prepare the case against the defendant and present it in court.

The *defense attorney* represents the defendant. It is his duty to present the best possible defense for his client within the rules of the court. Like the prosecuting attorney, he is regarded as an officer of the court.

The *public defender,* found in some states, is an official whose duty it is to defend a person, accused of crimes, who cannot afford to hire a lawyer. In states which do not have such an official the judge appoints a lawyer to defend indigent persons accused of crimes.

The *bailiff* maintains order in the courtroom, takes charge of prisoners on trial, and carries out the orders of the judge. Often he is a deputy sheriff permanently assigned to the courts.

The *clerk of the court* keeps the *calendar,* a listing of the cases in the order in which they will appear before the court, and has charge of the records. Lawyers file papers with the clerk, who is an information clearing center and thus of great importance to a reporter. A friendly clerk who recognizes a good news story can be a great help.

The *stenographer* makes a transcript of proceedings. Court stenographers are highly skilled, and they are well paid by comparison with the average stenographer.

The Contempt Power

Courts have certain special powers which often produce good news stories. Some of the powers are defined in statutes, but most judges assume that the courts have these powers, whether or not they are spelled out in statutes. The common law theory is that these special powers come to the courts naturally and that even the legislature cannot abrogate them.

The contempt power affects newsmen in the course of their work, and supplies them with stories, too. It is the power to regulate the conduct of persons before the court. Just how far this power extends is a matter of controversy.

There is no question that it extends to control over persons actually in the courtroom or adjacent to it. This is called *direct contempt,* and it is necessary to the operation of a court system. A judge could not hold a session of court if he did not possess this power. If it were not for the contempt power, friends of an accused person might "pack" the courtroom when he was on trial and create such a disturbance that the trial could not proceed; or they might intimidate the witnesses. As it is, the judge can order the bailiffs to clear the court. Anyone who disobeys the judge in the courtroom can be thrown into jail without further judicial proceedings.

The contempt power is also used to force the attendance of witnesses and others necessary to a case. If a person disregards an order to appear in court he, too, may be punished summarily, that is, without a trial.

There is some argument about the *constructive contempt* power of a court. This is the power to punish an action which is not committed in the presence of the court, but is "construed" by the judge to be contemptuous. This is sometimes called *indirect contempt.*

The contempt power of the courts affects newsmen in three ways:

1. It gives the judge power to regulate the activities of reporters and photographers in the courtroom, and thus controls to some extent how they cover a story. This is most important for still photographers, and newsmen using tape recorders and television cameras. If a judge feels that these activities are making it difficult to conduct the trial he can order them suspended. Some judges bar photographers entirely, while others generally tolerate them. Photographers using modern cameras and film can take pictures without disturbing the proceedings, often without participants realizing they are being photographed. Some judges still regard photographers as impeding the course of justice. Sometimes the rules of a court will open or close the proceedings to photographers; sometimes the judge will decide.

2. Contempt power may be used to punish a reporter and editor for things published in the newspapers which the judge regards as likely to prejudice the outcome of a trial. In accident cases, reporters are careful not to mention the fact that one or both of the participants are insured. Witnesses at the trial are not allowed to mention this, either, on the theory that it will unduly influence the jury. Editorials "advising" the judge or jury how a case should be decided have been held contemptuous. This, of course, is constructive contempt.

3. A judge may use the contempt power in an effort to make a reporter reveal the sources of information he used to obtain a story. In Newburgh, New York, for example, Douglas V. Clarke, then city editor of the *Newburgh News,* and a reporter for that paper, spent some time in jail when they refused to tell where they found information about gambling conditions in the city. They felt, as most reporters do, that their obligation to respect the confidence of the persons who gave them the information could not be violated. They were released on a technicality.

In 1957 Marie Torre, radio-television columnist for the *New York Herald Tribune,* was ordered punished when she refused to reveal the source of her information for an item about Judy Garland. The issue became important to the courts when Miss Garland sued the National Broadcasting Company, and needed Miss Torre's testimony to support her case. A circuit court of appeals upheld the decision of the lower court which had held Miss Torre in contempt and the United States Supreme Court refused to hear the case. Miss Torre spent a few days in jail.

Twelve states have laws recognizing a "confidential relationship" between a reporter and his source of news. This is comparable to the legally accepted confidential relationships by which a husband cannot be forced to reveal things told him in confidence by his wife, and vice versa. Other recognized confidential relationships are between a clergyman and his parishioner, a doctor and his patient, and a lawyer and his client. These are justified on the theory that they are in the public interest because they help to maintain a more stable society.

Since the power to make a reluctant witness testify is vital to a court, it is understandable that legislators are not eager to extend the confidential relationship. Just the same, many newspapermen feel that such a confidential relationship between reporters and their sources is also in the public interest, because it would help newspapers to get more information for the public good than they otherwise could.

At the time the U.S. Supreme Court refused to hear an appeal on the Marie Torre case, Oxie Reichler, editor of the *Yonkers Herald Statesman*, stated the newspaperman's view in an editorial:

> Every once in a while a newspaper reporter turns up information as to dereliction on the part of a public official, particularly failure to enforce the law. Obviously, the first thought of such an official is to hop on the reporter, make his life miserable and perhaps even send him to jail unless the reporter exposes his sources. In such a situation, law enforcement is overlooked, while those who want justice to prevail (in this case the reporter) are persecuted. . . .
>
> There are good reasons why some legislators have qualms about a confidence law—principally because of the cloak of protection it might give to gossip columnists. On the other hand, there stands the rock-ribbed First Amendment, guaranteeing freedom of the press, safeguarding freedom of information. If anyone can dry up the sources of information by handicapping the press in its printing the news that citizens need, that citizens must have if they are to protect their freedoms, then we may be in trouble.

Extraordinary Remedies

The extraordinary remedies of the courts are powers which came to the early English courts from the King. The most common ones are:

1. *Habeas corpus,* a power by which a court can order an official to produce a person in court or explain why he should not do so. This may result in a *habeas corpus* hearing. A lawyer may seek such an order when a person is arrested and held incommunicado. It originated in the Magna Charta.

2. *Mandamus* (we command) is an order by a court to a public official commanding the performance of an act which the official is required by law to perform. The request for a mandamus is usually brought by a citizen whose rights have been violated because an official refuses to act.

3. *Quo warranto* (by what authority) is a writ by which the King inquired into the rights of persons to hold a given public office. A modified form of this writ is still used occasionally in the United States to test the right of a person to hold office, or the powers of a government corporation.

4. *Certiorari* is an order from a higher to a lower court ordering the lower court to send up a record for examination in the higher court. This is one way a lawyer may appeal a case—he asks the higher court for a *writ of certiorari* ordering up the record for review. The United States

Supreme Court, for example, holds sessions at which it announces its decisions on many requests for *writs of certiorari*. The notations usually are simply "writ granted" or "writ denied." They mean the court has agreed to hear an appeal or has refused to do so. A refusal, of course, leaves undisturbed the decision of the lower court.

5. A *prohibition* is an order from a higher to a lower court requiring the lower one to cease action on a case because some portion of it exceeds the court's jurisdiction. It is not used very frequently.

The Court System

In each of the states there are two court systems—the state and the federal. The federal system handles cases involving federal laws and treaties and the Constitution, suits between states or citizens of different states or involving diplomatic personnel, crimes committed on federal property, and appeals from decisions of certain federal agencies. The rest of the cases is left to the state courts.

Most cases go without question to either a federal or a state court. Law enforcement generally is the responsibility of the states, and so the state courts get most of the routine cases.

Overlapping occurs in areas into which the federal government has extended its authority. Bank robbery, for example, has been traditionally a crime punishable by the state governments, and therefore prosecuted in the state courts. When the Federal Deposit Insurance Corporation was created to insure bank deposits, it became a federal offense to rob a bank insured under it. Since most banks are so insured, it is both a state and a federal offense to rob them. Usually local, state, and federal police go to work on a bank robbery, and if the federal men capture the robbers they bring them to federal court. Otherwise the suspects are prosecuted in a state court.

Usually cases are clear-cut. There are state and federal game laws. Violations of either are prosecuted in the appropriate court. The federal courts are filled with cases involving immigration rules, postal fraud, narcotics regulations, naturalization proceedings, antitrust laws, regulations of a multitude of federal agencies such as the Interstate Commerce Commission, and other federal laws.

Sometimes the federal courts will try a criminal case because the crime was committed on federal property. Often there is no federal law which applies, so the judges will apply the laws of the state in which the court is sitting.

Cases are sometimes appealed from the state courts to the federal. This can be done if the federal courts agree that a federal question is involved. The cases which get the most publicity are those involving civil rights. They often come to the federal courts for a decision on whether there was a violation of the First or Fourteenth Amendments to the United States Constitution. The Fourteenth Amendment makes citizens of the states citizens also of the United States, and obligates the United States government to protect their rights from violations—even by the states.

Jurisdiction

One of the first things a reporter needs to know about a court is its jurisdiction. Jurisdiction means area of control. A teacher's jurisdiction extends over his classroom. A judge has jurisdiction, or control, over the actions of persons in his courtroom. The jurisdiction of his court is defined by the kind of cases it can try. From the foregoing discussion it is obvious that an important question in determining a court's jurisdiction is whether it is a federal or a state court. Other questions are:

1. Is the court civil or criminal? A court may have the power to try both civil and criminal cases, or it may be empowered to try only one or the other.

2. Is the court original or appellate? Courts of original jurisdiction can try only new cases as they arise. Courts of appellate jurisdiction can hear appeals from lower courts. Some courts have original jurisdiction only, some have appellate only, some have both.

3. How important a case can the court try? In civil cases the jurisdiction of a court may be limited by the amount of money being sought in damages. In criminal cases it is common to break the jurisdiction between felonies and misdemeanors, with the lower court having jurisdiction only over misdemeanors. Thus, the lower courts in New York State can try misdemeanors only, while the county courts may try even the most serious criminal cases.

4. What are the geographical limits to the jurisdiction of a court? Some courts can try offenses committed within a given city, while others have county-wide, district-wide, or even state-wide jurisdiction. The geographical jurisdiction of the United States Supreme Court is limited only by the boundaries of the country.

In addition to these general questions, there may be all kinds of special limitations on the jurisdiction of a court. A civil court, for example, may be limited to actions in law or in equity. These distinctions will become clear as we discuss criminal and civil law.

Structure of the State Courts

The variety of court structure among the states makes it impossible to pick out any typical structure or terminology. Often counties are primary court districts, with county courts having general original jurisdiction, but often the courts will have different names.

Sometimes the same court will have criminal and civil jurisdiction; sometimes there will be separate civil and criminal courts; sometimes one court will have separate civil and criminal terms.

Always, however, some orderly appeals system is provided and the jurisdiction of each court is spelled out. If he knows these two things a reporter can soon understand the system of his particular state.

There is sure to be a state court of final appeal, which is roughly equivalent in its state to the United States Supreme Court in the federal system. Often the states call their highest court the supreme court, but in New York it is called the Court of Appeals. To make it more confusing for the outsider, New York has a Supreme Court which has general original jurisdiction, but is not a court of last resort. The state is divided into ten Supreme Court districts.

Although a state court system is likely to appear confusing at first glance, it is not difficult for a reporter to gain a thorough understanding of it fairly rapidly. Fortunately, procedure, which is described later in this book, tends to be more uniform among the states than is the structure of the court system.

Structure of the Federal Courts

Compared with many state court systems, the federal judiciary is a model of simplicity, consisting of three levels, with well-defined jurisdictions.

Most of the cases arise and are settled in one of the more than 90 Federal District Courts. These have original jurisdiction over most of the federal cases. Each district has one or more judges, a United States attorney, a United States marshal and a United States commissioner. The commissioner is the preliminary hearing officer in criminal cases, and decides whether prisoners shall be held over for the grand jury. Other officers are a clerk and his deputies, referees in bankruptcy, and probation and parole officers.

The next level consists of the circuit courts of appeal. There are ten judicial circuits and the District of Columbia. Each circuit court has at least three judges, and two judges constitute a quorum. The circuit courts were established to relieve the Supreme Court of its heavy load of appeals; they filter out most of the cases which do not involve interpretation of the basic law. They have original jurisdiction in cases arising under rulings of certain federal agencies.

At the top is the Supreme Court, the only one specifically provided for in the Constitution, which says: "The judicial Power of the United States, shall be vested in one supreme Court, and in such inferior Courts as the Congress may from time to time ordain and establish" (Article III, Section 1).

The Supreme Court consists of a chief justice of the United States and eight associate justices. Six justices constitute a quorum. Its term begins on the first Monday in October of each year and continues until May or June.

As the highest federal tribunal the Supreme Court has the power to declare void acts of Congress or the state legislatures if, in the opinion of the justices, these acts run counter to the Constitution. The doctrine of the separation of powers, holding the judicial department to be equal to the other two great departments of the government, the executive and the legislative, gives the United States Supreme Court tremendous power and prestige.

It will not render advisory opinions—that is, tell the legislature in advance whether it will hold some act constitutional—but decides the matter only when it is tested with a real issue in litigation. If one party sues another in the lower courts, depending on a new piece of legislation, the person sued may argue that the act is unconstitutional. If the Supreme Court agrees to hear the case it will decide on the question of constitutionality. If the act is declared unconstitutional it will remain on the statute books unless Congress or the state legislature repeals it, but it is a dead law because everyone knows that the courts will refuse to enforce it.

REPORTING ASSIGNMENTS

1. Write a story naming the local courts in your area; briefly describe the jurisdiction of each.

2. In a feature story tell how the judges in your state get their jobs (by appointment or election), how much they are paid, what retirement provisions they have, how they can be removed, and so forth.

3. Interview a lawyer specializing in criminal work for a feature story about him, and his work, and why he chose that specialty.

4. Do the same for a lawyer specializing in civil work.

5. Find out if there have been any recent proposals for changes in the court system in your state. If there have been, write a story telling what they are and why they were suggested.

8

Criminal Law

The Nature of Crime

Crime is antisocial activity regarded as grave enough to be punished by government. Technically, an act is a crime because it is defined as such in statutes or common law. Crimes are punished by fine, imprisonment, or death. Sometimes a judge will devise a novel penalty, such as sentencing a traffic violator to attend lectures on safety or to visit the county morgue to see bodies of persons killed in accidents.

The exact definition of a given crime will vary from state to state. Sometimes a crime will not even be defined in the statutes. In this event the courts will be guided by precedent handed down from the common law. The court reporter needs to know how each crime is defined in his state.

What is a crime in one place may not be in another. It is a crime, for example, in each of the United States to have more than one wife at the same time. In certain other countries, having several wives is a mark of wealth and distinction. This sometimes gives a protocol expert some trouble, especially when a foreign dignitary arrives with several wives for a state visit.

Society's view of what is criminal changes. For example, some places have laws making it an offense to drive *under* a certain speed on given highways, on the theory that the slow driver causes accidents. Old-fashioned "blue laws" define as criminal acts which are no longer considered as such. As our social concepts change so do our notions of what constitutes crime, although our laws always lag behind our changing habits of thought.

Certain things, however, are usually true of criminal acts:

134

1. Usually crimes injure someone other than the perpetrator.
2. Often they injure the public.
3. Sometimes they injure the government.
4. Often they are regarded as immoral.

When a certain act has been defined as a crime, it means that the government will assume the responsibility for punishing persons who commit the act. This was not always true. At one time in England the only restraint on murder was private vengeance. This led to private wars—clan fighting and feuding.

Today our machinery for enforcing the criminal law is huge and complicated. It consists of (1) a police system, (2) a judicial system (the courts), and (3) a punishment system.

Crimes are divided into two categories: felonies and misdemeanors. The exact classification into which a given crime will fall is determined in the United States by each of the state constitutions or criminal codes.

More serious crimes are felonies. In many states a felony is defined as "any public offense upon conviction for which the offender is liable to be sentenced to death or to imprisonment in a penitentiary or state prison."

Misdemeanors are crimes not regarded as serious enough to be felonies. In general, punishment for a misdemeanor is either a fine or a sentence in a county jail. Most misdemeanors do not require indictment by a grand jury, although more serious misdemeanors may.

The easiest way to study the major crimes is to classify them according to the particular harm done. This is also the traditional way of classifying them. Every classification of this nature contains some overlapping, and there are slight differences. However, the system which follows will serve the purposes of the reporter:

1. Crimes against the person.
2. Crimes against habitations.
3. Crimes against property.
4. Crimes against morality and decency.
5. Crimes against the public peace.
6. Crimes against public health and safety.
7. Crimes against the government.

Crimes Against the Person

1. *Criminal homicide* consists of four degrees:

First degree murder is the unlawful killing of a human being with intent and deliberate planning in advance. First degree murder includes, too, killings done in connection with another serious offense (frequently called *felony murder*).

Second degree murder is usually defined to mean killing in which there was no elaborate preliminary planning, but nevertheless there was an intent to kill formed instantaneously in the mind.

Voluntary manslaughter is the unlawful killing of another without malice, either expressed or implied, in sudden heat or passion, as when two persons fight in a sudden quarrel and one kills the other.

Involuntary manslaughter is a killing without intent or malice during the commission of an unlawful act, or in the commission of a lawful act without proper safeguards and caution.

In some states the two degrees of manslaughter are classified as *first* and *second degree manslaughter.*

2. *Simple assault* is the threat of violence or an unsuccessful attempt at violence, such as a blow which falls short.

3. *Battery* (or, as it is called in some states, *aggravated assault*) is the unlawful application of force to the person of another. Usually battery implies absence of the other person's consent. Certain football plays, for example, are regarded as good playing, but the same act on the street might be regarded as battery or aggravated assault. The difference is simply that the football players give tacit consent to being tackled. However, too violent an act could be considered battery even if consent were given. For example, maiming a person so that he could not do his work would be battery.

4. *False imprisonment* is the unlawful restraint of another's liberty.

5. *Abortion* is unlawfully causing fetal miscarriage.

6. *Kidnaping* is the forcible stealing away of another person. This crime overlaps with false imprisonment and abduction.

7. *Mayhem* or *maim* is the unlawful disfiguring or dismembering of another.

8. *Abduction* is the unlawful taking of a female for purposes of marriage, concubinage, or prostitution.

9. *Rape* is the unlawful carnal knowledge of a woman without her consent. *Statutory rape* is the crime of sexual intercourse with a girl below a certain age (called the age of consent), even though she permits the act.

Crimes Against Habitations

1. *Burglary* is the breaking and entering of the house or property of another with intent to commit a felony therein, whether or not the felony was actually committed.

2. *Arson* under common law was the willful and malicious burning of the dwelling of another. Many states now include under arson the crime of burning one's own house to collect insurance or if it endangers the house of another. Arson is regarded as more serious if committed at night

or if the structure burned was a habitation. If a person dies in a fire set deliberately the person responsible may be charged with murder instead of arson.

Crimes Against Property

Crimes against property form a crazy-quilt pattern, but all involve the basic idea of theft. Historically this pattern developed from the idea of *larceny,* divided into *grand larceny,* where the value of the goods was more than 12 pence, and *petit larceny.* At one time 12 pence was about the value of a good sheep, but of course money depreciated through the ages, so that 12 pence is now less than 25 cents. The penalty for grand larceny in early England was death. Judges were naturally reluctant to impose the death penalty for petty thefts. Thus there developed new crimes which allowed some punishment less than execution. The result has been a series of more or less overlapping crimes, so that a district attorney has to make a careful evaluation of evidence to determine what charge to lodge; even then he may find that a trial develops evidence to indicate a crime other than the one charged. The resulting miscarriage of justice has led a few states to revamp the criminal code to include nearly all crimes against property under a new crime such as "theft," with various degress.

Most states, however, cling to the traditional classification:

1. *Larceny* is the unlawful taking and carrying away by stealth of another's property with intent to convert it to the taker's use. The difference between *grand* and *petit* larceny is set in the statutes at an arbitrary valuation.

2. *Trespass,* in its most limited sense, is unlawful entry on another's property. In a very wide sense it can mean almost any unlawful act, committed with actual or implied violence.

3. *Robbery* is the taking of property from another's person or immediate presence by force or threat of force.

4. *Embezzlement* is the taking, for one's own use or benefit, of property or money which has been entrusted to him.

5. *False pretenses* is making false statements with the intent to wrongfully obtain money or goods.

6. *Receiving stolen property* is a crime which makes theft profitable. "Fence" is the common name for a person who knowingly buys stolen property.

7. *Malicious mischief* is the deliberate destruction or injury of another's property.

8. *Forgery* is falsely making or altering with intent to defraud of any writing, which, if genuine, might be the basis of a legal obligation. The most common illustration of the kind of "legal obligation" involved is a

check which creates a duty to pay money. Also a crime is *uttering a forgery,* that is, offering as genuine a document known to be false with intent to defraud.

Crimes Against Morality and Decency

1. *Adultery* is voluntary sexual intercourse of a married person and someone other than the offender's husband or wife.

2. *Fornication* is sexual intercourse between two unmarried persons.

3. *Bigamy* is the crime of knowingly contracting a second marriage (or going through the form of contracting a second marriage) while a former marriage is still existing.

4. *Incest* is sexual intercourse between persons so closely related that marriage is forbidden by law.

5. *Seduction* is the crime committed by a man who induces a woman to commit unlawful sexual intercourse by persuasion, promises, bribes, or other means short of force.

6. *Statutory offense* is the way newspapers often report the unnatural sex crimes. These include unnatural sex relations between persons, and *bestiality,* carnal copulation with a beast.

7. *Prostitution* is the crime of a woman who permits any man who will pay her price to have sexual intercourse with her.

8. *Obscenity* refers to words or actions which are offensive to chastity. *Indecency* may mean the same thing with the addition of anything which is outrageously disgusting.

9. *Blasphemy* is the malicious reviling of God, His name, His attributes, or of religion.

Crimes Against the Public Peace

1. *Affray* is the crime committed when two or more persons fight in a public place "to the terror of the people."

2. A *rout* occurs whenever two or more persons try to perform an act which, if completed, would be a riot.

3. A *riot* is a tumultuous disturbance of the peace by three or more persons assembled by their own authority.

4. *Vagrancy* is the charge sometimes lodged against persons who, although able to work, go from place to place in idleness, with no visible means of support, depending on handouts.

5. *Disturbing the peace* is a charge sometimes used to cover any of these offenses.

Crimes Against Public Health and Safety

Many acts which cause a restriction of the rights of others are classed as *nuisances,* and generally are regarded as misdemeanors. They are classified as *public, private,* and *mixed,* depending upon the number of persons affected. The list of acts which have been classed as nuisances is almost endless. Common nuisances are obstructing roadways or waterways, polluting the air or water with dangerous or vile-smelling substances, maintaining a junkyard in a residential section, and running noisy machinery at night in a residential section. There are many others.

Crimes Against the Government

1. *Treason* is an attempt at violent overthrow of the government, or the betrayal of one's government to a foreign power. The Constitution says, "Treason against the United States shall consist only in levying war against them, or in adhering to their enemies, giving them aid and comfort." Treason can be committed by citizens and resident foreigners.

2. *Sedition* is the act of urging, in speech or in writing, the alteration by illegal means, or the violent overthrow, of the government.

3. *Perjury* is knowingly giving false testimony under oath, as in a judicial proceeding.

4. *Subornation of perjury* is inducing another person to commit perjury.

5. *Bribery* is giving a public official something of value to influence him improperly in the performance of his public duties.

6. *Counterfeiting* is copying something without authorization and with intent to defraud. This offense usually involves the making of fake money.

7. *Embracery* is the attempt to influence a jury illegally.

The foregoing list of crimes includes only the more common ones. The police reporter needs to understand these as a start. If he stays on the police beat very long he will become familiar with more. It is important to remember that the crimes may be defined differently in different states. If a reporter moves to a new state he will need to familiarize himself with its criminal statutes.

Juvenile Offenders

In many states persons under a certain age are given special treatment when they are arrested for criminal activity. Unless their offense is extremely serious, they may be allowed to plead as juveniles, which means that their case is assigned to juvenile court and they are given the benefit of especially designed counseling and parole services. They are more likely than older offenders, of course, to be given suspended sentences.

The record of some of the juvenile courts is excellent, and the best ones are rehabilitating many young offenders. One aspect of their activity which has annoyed newspaper editors is that the records of juveniles are often kept secret, thus shutting off the flow of news about them.

Editors have argued that this provision sometimes causes a dangerous situation in a community, especially when it shields persons who are actually hardened criminals, although they may be under a given age.

In a speech before the New York Society of Newspaper Editors, Malcolm Wilson, then a New York State assemblyman and later lieutenant governor, argued against such closing up of records. He said that if any records were to be closed it was much more logical to shield first offenders, no matter what their age, on the theory that there was more hope of rehabilitating them than many of the habitual offenders who were under age.

REPORTING ASSIGNMENTS

1. Look at the records of your local police court or whatever court has jurisdiction over misdemeanors. Write a story telling what crimes are charged most frequently.

2. Examine the record of your local court which has jurisdiction over felonies and write the same kind of story.

3. Examine a report on national crime statistics and compare these with statistics in your own area.

4. What special treatment is given juvenile offenders in your area? Write a story about it.

9

Covering the Police

Pick up any newspaper or listen to any newscast and you will find that law enforcement is part of the news. One of the prime responsibilities of any local government is to curb crime. For any local newspaper or radio station the police department is an important source of news.

One of the things that makes a town a good place to live is effective law enforcement. It means less crime and a safer, more pleasant community. Local government is close to the citizens, and one of the ways in which it affects them most directly is through law enforcement.

How is the police department doing? This is a logical question for any resident to ask, for on the answer depends his security and perhaps his life. In seeking the answer he turns frequently to his newspaper and to radio and television newscasts.

Police work, like most other vocations, has become specialized. The men who run a big city police department are experts in administration, and they control an organization composed of experts in crime detection, traffic control, first aid, communications, and subdivisions of these fields. The reporter who covers local police needs an understanding of these specialities and how they fit together into the policing pattern. And he needs the basic equipment of any reporter: an inquiring, orderly mind, and the knack of getting along with people.

The job of enforcing the law in the United States is the responsibility of every level of government: local, state, and federal.

This is not true in every country. France and Belgium, for example, have highly centralized police systems, with one office controlling police activities throughout the country. These are in sharp contrast to the United States where each city, within its charter powers, has responsibility for law enforcement. The state government can assume control in emer-

gencies, but that power is seldom used. Aside from possible state intervention, the local police department runs its own affairs, subject to control
by voters. Voters exercise their power through a mayor, or sometimes
through a police commission or a commissioner of public safety.

Despite the emphasis on local enforcement the police function is diffused through the three levels of government. This, together with the
fact that we have an amazing array of local governments and several
police agencies, means that a local newspaper may cover five or more
police agencies as a daily routine.

City Police Departments

In most fair-sized cities, the bulk of the crime news comes from the
municipal police department; day in and day out, this agency gets the
most thorough coverage from most daily newspapers and radio stations.
Many papers assign at least one man to full-time coverage of the city
police department. In some places he may make his headquarters the press
room of police headquarters, phone in his stories, and show up at the office
only on payday.

City police departments range in size from a two- or three-man operation in a tiny city, to New York's department which employs nearly 25,000
policemen and civilians.

Police departments are made responsible to the people in several ways.
Some cities still maintain a board of public safety which is directly in
charge of police and fire departments. In a few instances this board is
appointed by the governor of the state. More frequently it is locally appointed or elected. More often the police department is under the general
direction of a civilian police commissioner, who makes major decisions
and is responsible to the mayor. In many cities the chief of police is
the top departmental official and works under the general supervision of
the mayor or the manager. Usually the chief has a deputy chief or two,
and in most cities captains are directly responsible for the operating
units of the department: the traffic control bureau, the records and identification bureau, the detective bureau, the juvenile bureau, and some
catch-all division which handles personnel, purchasing, training, public
relations, and other staff functions.

Of prime importance to reporters is the records system, for it is the
source of many story tips. The captain's desk or sergeant's desk, where
prisoners are booked, is another important checkpoint. Here the central
record of any police system is kept. It is variously called the jail register,
the arrest record, and the blotter. When a prisoner is brought to headquarters or a precinct station after his arrest, the essential information
about him is recorded in this book. This includes his name, address, age,

circumstances of arrest, and the name of the arresting officer. Eventually the disposition of the case will be recorded, but by that time the reporter will probably have the information from police court records.

Where the police department is very small, successful coverage depends on maintaining good relationships with each member of the department. The volume of news generated by the police department in such a small city will be sufficient to justify only simple coverage—perhaps one visit and two or three telephone calls during the day. The reporter needs to develop a system for checking the records, so that no story will be missed because a patrolman forgot it or didn't think it was worthwhile.

As police departments become larger they naturally become more complex. Still they are organized around the three major aspects of police activity: patrol, investigation, and traffic control. Connected with these functions and supplementing them are many other duties, frequently represented in separate divisions of the force.

In the larger cities the police department may be organized on a geographical basis. This is true of New York City.

Normally the "private" of the uniformed patrol is called a patrolman. Fairly typical structure makes the next higher officer a sergeant. Then comes the lieutenant, and then the captain. They are sometimes followed by inspectors, deputy chief inspectors, and a chief inspector, as in the New York City system.

A reporter should understand the organization of the particular department he is covering. A formal chart may not be available, but it will be relatively easy for him to formulate one in his mind as he discovers the organizational pattern.

Here are some of the important units in most police departments:

RADIO ROOM. Most police departments of any size now use radio to relay orders and information to cars out on patrol. As complaints are telephoned to the department a dispatcher will assign cars to investigate. The radio room is the first place where the police department becomes aware of information which may result in news stories. Thus the persons in the radio room are important sources of information for the police reporter. Usually there will be a radio in the newspaper office tuned to the police band.

DETECTIVE BUREAU. This bureau takes charge of criminal cases which require investigation. Record systems used by detectives are not standardized, and in some departments they may be only personal memoranda kept by the investigators themselves. Much of the work of the detective bureau will not result in stories—at least until a case has been solved. Just the same the reporter who is friendly with the detectives will get stories that might not otherwise be published. He will also get advance information about other stories, information that will help when they finally break.

IDENTIFICATION BUREAU. Fingerprint files and photographs are the major contribution of most identification bureaus. Modern fingerprint identification systems, co-ordinated on a nation-wide scale by the Federal Bureau of Investigation, make it practically impossible for a previous offender to hide his identity. It is standard practice to fingerprint all persons arrested. Prints are sent to the FBI central file in Washington, which checks to see whether the person being held is wanted by any police department in the country. Many habitual offenders are caught in this way and returned for trial in another jurisdiction.

Fingerprints have noncriminal uses, too. Ordinary citizens are often fingerprinted, and police experts are called on to identify bodies of persons who died accidentally and who might not be identifiable otherwise.

CRIME DETECTION LABORATORY. Scientific crime detection involves more hard work and less glamor than movies would indicate, but science has solved many murders.

Fingerprint identification is one of the most effective of the scientific crime detection methods.

Ballistics, the scientific study of firearms, has convicted many killers. By its use, experts can identify the weapon which fired a bullet, can estimate the distance from which a shot was fired, and the type of gun used.

Moulage is used to make permanent records of clues that would otherwise disappear. A footprint which would wash away in the next rain or be trampled over can be preserved in the form of a cast.

Chemical analysis of hair may lead to the person who shed it. Chemical analysis of stains in clothing has helped solve many crimes.

Photography is a routine tool of the criminal investigator.

Alert crime laboratories even maintain files of such prosaic things as laundry marks. The identification possibilities here are obvious. A central file may save hours, and mean the apprehension of a criminal.

Many departments maintain files which list the working methods of known criminals. These files may help a force to narrow an investigation down to a few suspects, who have the "working" habits displayed in a crime police are trying to crack.

A good friend in the crime detection laboratory is a boon to a police reporter. Sometimes a paper can reveal what is going on and so provide interesting stories on a case. It is frequently a good source of feature material.

POLICE COURT. Though not really a part of the police department, the police court is frequently on the police reporter's beat. It is often situated in the same building which houses the police department, and its work is tied in very closely with that of the department.

The police court is covered in the chapter on criminal courts. All we need to notice here is that it is the lowest court of criminal jurisdiction in most state court systems. It is empowered to try misdemeanor cases, but has authority to act only as a court of preliminary hearing in felony cases. This means that it can dispose of cases involving minor crimes—petty larceny, drunkenness, and the rest. In more serious crimes it can determine only whether there is enough evidence against a suspect to warrant holding him for action by the grand jury or a higher court.

A police court reporter's function is usually to cover the disposition of cases from the records after each court session. He will be familiar with many of the cases already, having reported the arrest. At times an important trial may be held in police court, and a reporter will cover it in person and produce something more dramatic than the usual routine account. In some states, for example, it is considered a misdemeanor to operate a gambling device, and dramatic copy may result from trials of alleged proprietors of gambling establishments. Good copy results, too, from misdemeanor trials involving prominent persons.

This partial cataloging should not obscure the primary fact that most of the news comes from the biggest day-to-day operation of any police department—the patrolmen in cars, motorcycles, and on the beat.

A metropolitan police force is subject to more temptation than almost any other group. Profits of illegitimate activities are tremendous, and racketeers are always ready to use large sums of money to buy protection from the police. From patrolman to captain this temptation is always in sight. When salaries are low the temptation is redoubled.

A reporter covering police headquarters has to know the department better than most policemen do. He has to be a friend of the people who can give him news, but he cannot be so friendly that he overlooks his primary duty—to tell his readers how honest and effective their police force is.

County Police—Sheriff's Office

Each state government has primary responsibility for maintaining law and order within its own state's boundaries. Traditionally this function has been exercised through a sheriff in each county. As we noticed earlier, the sheriff is finding his duties being taken over by the city police departments as urban populations grow, and by the establishment of state police systems. However, the county sheriff is still an important law enforcement officer.

The sheriff is in a rather strange position since he is charged with enforcing state laws, but is elected by the people of a county. Thus his official responsibility is to the state government, whose laws he is bound to enforce. At the same time he is dependent for continuance in office on the good will of the electorate of his own county. This does not lead to as centralized a law enforcement system as some state officials might desire. It does have the advantage that the sheriff keeps law enforcement geared to the wishes of the voters who live in his area.

Duties of the sheriff are civil as well as criminal. Civil duties include calling juries and supervising them when a judge orders them "locked up," serving processes, guarding prisoners being held for court action, and executing judgments of the civil courts. This last duty sometimes leads to a sheriff's sale of property to satisfy a judgment.

These duties, vital as they are to the functioning of the courts, are not as dramatic and generally not as newsworthy as the criminal functions of the sheriff. The sheriff is the principal law enforcement officer in the less urbanized counties. For practical purposes his jurisdiction is usually limited to the rural areas of his county. City police departments assume the law enforcement job within the corporation limits. Like a city police department, the sheriff's operation is big or small, depending on his community. It may consist of the sheriff and one part time deputy, or it may be a large force equipped with radio cars, a crime laboratory, and all the trappings of a modern police force.

Other Local Police Agencies

Some counties, including Westchester, New York, and Hudson, New Jersey, maintain separate parkway police units. These are assigned to highway patrol on parkways which may bisect a unit administered entirely by another police agency. The possibilities for confusion are easy to imagine. For example, some of the parkways in Chicago are patrolled by special park police, although in some areas these parkways resemble any other street and are lined with normal business establishments and dwellings. This leads to confusion and makes it necessary for a reporter to have an intimate knowledge of the policing system.

Although they are vanishing from the American scene, village and rural constables may sometimes become sources of news. These constables are usually part time officials, and frequently they devote little time to law enforcement.

As areas gain population and become urbanized, they often replace constables with a village police system. As communities grow these agencies assume the characteristics of city police forces.

State Police

Sheriffs are elected by people of the counties, and city police are responsible to the mayor or another elected city official. Thus neither is accountable directly to the governor of the state, who is in theory the head of a sovereign unit of government. This is one of the reasons states have founded their own police forces.

The governor of Indiana is said to have been forced to call out the state militia to enforce a statute against gambling when sheriffs refused to do so.

Former Governor Pennypacker of Pennsylvania gave this explanation of the formation of the Pennsylvania state police:

> In the year 1903, when I assumed office of chief executive of the state, I found myself thereby invested with supreme executive authority. I found that no power existed to interfere with me in my duty to enforce the laws of the state, and that by the same token, no conditions could release me from my duty so to do. I then looked about me to see what instruments I possessed wherewith to accomplish this bounden obligation—what instruments on whose loyalty and obedience I could truly rely. I perceived three such instruments—my private secretary, a very small man; my woman stenographer; and the janitor, a Negro. So I made the state police.

The earliest state police was established in 1835 in what was then the Republic of Texas. Massachusetts was next with the creation of a few "state constables" in 1865. They were superseded in 1879 by a state detective unit, which was absorbed by the Department of Public Safety, created in 1920.

Established shortly after the turn of the century, the Pennsylvania "State Constabulary" became a model for many of the later state police forces. Its most distinguishing characteristic was the wide power granted to the superintendent, who was responsible to the governor. It operated from troop headquarters and substations as do many of the state police units today, and specialized in protecting the people of the rural areas. The New York State Police, established in 1917, closely followed the Pennsylvania pattern.

Some of the states have highway police forces whose powers are limited to patrolling highways and enforcing traffic laws. In some states such a body exists alongside other state police forces, almost inevitably with overlapping functions. The long-range tendency seems to be for the highway patrol to either (1) extend its jurisdiction to general police work, or (2) unite with a body with general police powers if such an organization exists with state-wide authority.

State police forces range from relatively weak, undermanned units devoted primarily to traffic control, to well-developed police arms of the states. In New York State there is, connected with the state police, a Bureau of Criminal Investigation, which functions as a state-wide detective agency. It also operates a crime laboratory, which aids local police agencies on request.

In common with most police forces, a state unit is likely to become the repository for miscellaneous duties, many of which have little direct relation to the police function. In some states it supervises the tests for drivers' licenses. In others, state policemen serve as game wardens or as bailiffs for justice of the peace courts.

Usually organized on a military basis, the typical unit is under the control of a single official, appointed by the governor, with line and staff assistants. The state is broken down into geographic areas with a division head in charge of each area. The New York State Police calls each division head a captain and puts him at the head of a "troop." Inside each area there are smaller zones headed by lieutenants. Stations and substations are under the supervision of a sergeant or a trooper.

State police forces, typically, are modern effective police organizations, equipped with radio cars, crime laboratories and all the rest of the paraphernalia of up-to-date police work. Their record systems—and for this a reporter can be grateful—are usually well organized and intelligently kept. They frequently backstop local law enforcement agencies by close co-operation and, by the loan to local officials of the facilities of crime laboratories, and skilled personnel.

To a newspaper, the state police is a prime news source. In addition to the obvious news of local crime and highway control, the state officers can supply incidental information which develops from their patrol of the highways and their broad communications system. Weather conditions, traffic problems, and tips on crimes and accidents handled by other police agencies are examples.

One of the first things a police reporter in a new state should do is to find out the organization picture of the state police and its habits in giving information to the press. In most state police systems, officers in charge of a region are permitted or encouraged to co-operate with reporters. This attitude almost inevitably results in a friendly press and mutual benefit to the police and the newspaper, with the general public the ultimate beneficiary.

State police systems were ahead of most municipal systems in adopting strenuous training programs, which have resulted in capable policemen.

Most newspapers do not cover the state police as thoroughly as they do city police. The state police do not generate as much local news and their bureaus often are outside cities. Routine coverage is often by a call twice a day to the nearest state police headquarters, and by a monitor on the state police radio. Reporters should visit the state police offices as often as possible to build a friendly relationship.

Overlapping jurisdictions are a headache for police reporters as well as for officers. For example, if the state police and the sheriff both have patrols on a given highway, which office should a reporter call to get the story of an accident? The answer is either or both, although there may be an informal gentlemen's agreement which determines jurisdiction.

Federal Police

Reporters in large cities find that many police agents of the federal government are at work in their communities. Even in smaller cities federal police work is becoming common.

Here are two illustrations to show how federal police work has expanded through the years:

1. The Federal Bureau of Investigation is empowered to investigate robberies of banks which are insured under the Federal Deposit Insurance Corporation.

2. The same agency has been given power to enter kidnaping cases after 24 hours under an amendment to the Federal Anti-Kidnaping Law of 1932, the "Lindbergh Act."

Under our Constitution the states have retained the power to investigate and punish crimes. The federal government investigates and punishes violations of federal statutes and the federal Constitution. This police power has been expanded by judicial interpretation of the power to regulate interstate commerce and the "elastic clause" of the Constitution. The Lindbergh law gains its legal justification from the assumption that a kidnaper is likely to cross a state line if he has not been apprehended after a certain period.

The best-known of the federal police agencies is the Federal Bureau of Investigation, which has complete jurisdiction over all federal crimes which are not the special province of another federal police agency. The FBI is the only general police agency of the federal government. It is the best developed and, through its central crime reporting service and central file of fingerprints, it offers wide service to other federal, state, and local police units. It also has established a training program to which a limited number of local policemen may be sent, and it maintains an extensive crime laboratory which is available to other agencies. It is a part of the Department of Justice and has regional offices all over the U.S.A.

Five other federal police agencies are frequently of importance to a local reporter:

1. The immigration Border Patrol maintained by the Department of Justice.

2. The Secret Service Division of the Treasury Department. Famous as the agency which guards the President and his family, the division is also concerned with forgery and counterfeiting, and with certain other federal crimes. The movies have glorified its agents as "T-Men."

3. Postal inspectors investigate mail fraud and other violations of the postal laws.

4. Narcotics investigators in the Treasury Department are designated to help control the traffic in illegal drugs.

5. Customs investigators, also an arm of the Treasury Department, are concerned with smuggling and illegal imports.

In addition numerous other federal agencies have a police power, although a reporter comes in contact with them less frequently. These include agencies in the Veterans Administration, Department of Commerce, Federal Trade Commission, Securities and Exchange Commission, Federal Communications Commission, Interstate Commerce Commission, National Parks Service, Public Health Administration, and others.

In general a local reporter has a more difficult time covering the federal police agencies than in working with state and local police.

Federal police have no local ties, and frequently local agents are shifted around so that it is difficult for a reporter to build up contacts over a period of time. Often agents are instructed to avoid stories in the local papers. Sometimes this makes it almost impossible for a reporter to cover a locally committed federal offense until someone is arrested or indicted, when it will become a matter of record.

Often agents of the FBI will seek the co-operation of local policemen. They may need them to augment their own manpower or because the local police know the area better. Or they may ask local help as an expression of courtesy to the local department. When this happens a reporter can often get a report through his contacts with local policemen.

Newspaperman Jack Lait, for example, got an exclusive story of the FBI roundup and killing of a notorious gangster because he had once befriended the father of a rookie Chicago policeman. The rookie was one of the policemen selected to aid the FBI as they closed in on the mobster. Chicago newsmen had been unable to find out when the police would close in, but the young policeman telegraphed Mr. Lait, then working in New York, to come to Chicago if he wanted a good story. Mr. Lait followed the suggestion and so witnessed and reported a spectacular event of the war on Chicago's gangland.

In giving the FBI jurisdiction over kidnapings and bank robberies, Congress has added somewhat to the confusion of overlapping jurisdictions. Since a bank robbery is now a federal as well as a state offense, state, federal, and local police may all go into action on the same crime. The case may be tried in either federal or state courts. The FBI's jurisdiction extends only to robberies of banks insured by the Federal Deposit Insurance Corporation. Today, however, that includes most banks.

There is usually at least the show of co-operation among the police agencies in such circumstances. There is plenty of competition, too. Whether this is good or bad is something for the police expert to figure out. For the newspaperman trying to report the story it means more sources to be checked and compared, a harder coverage job.

The justification for extending the federal jurisdiction is that local and even state police cannot operate on a large enough scale to deal effectively with some crimes. Modern transportation works to the advantage of the criminal because he can move easily across state lines, something that a state or local officer cannot do without running into complications. The FBI, organized on a national basis, can better combat the fast-moving criminal.

News Coverage Problems

Offhand it would seem that the local police agencies would be the easiest to cover because they are locally responsible. It is impossible to generalize, however, because of the tremendous differences in quality of local police departments. Some are efficient, public relations minded, and accurate record keepers. Others are the opposite. Some regard newsmen as an intrusion.

Newspapers have to adjust their coverage to the conditions they find, although they do have the responsibility of persuading the police chief that fair reporting of police news will benefit the department and the public.

Usually the man stationed at police headquarters makes a routine check of the reports which have come in since he went off duty the previous day. Then he checks sources the chief has suggested and those he himself has developed for news in the different departments. He should have friends in the detective bureau so that he can keep posted on stories as they develop, and is prepared when an investigation produces a raid or an arrest. He needs to check the chief's office and personnel officers for routine news of the organization: promotions, recruits, organizational changes, and all the rest.

With this routine behind him, the police reporter settles down to the job of keeping close to the sources of information so that he will have a story on a fast-breaking development. This he does by listening to the broadcasts to police cars and by frequent checks of the booking desk.

When a newsworthy story, such as a holdup, develops, the police reporter probably calls his office to report what is happening, then follows his city editor's instructions. Usually he is told to stay at headquarters to cover new developments there, while the editor sends a reporter from the office for on-the-spot coverage. Or the police reporter may go to the scene himself.

Police headquarters is a first class source of tips about all kinds of activities in the city, and it is the job of the headquarters reporter to be alert to them and sort out the ones which might make a good story. These he reports to the city editor. Sometimes he will get a report of a fire before anyone else on the paper. It is routine to phone in the information.

Sometimes the police reporter finds his job dull. Much of it is "protective"—to be on the spot in case something does happen. Just the same there is excitement and a chance to write plenty of usable copy every day. Some reporters spend a lifetime on the police beat. Many others who have graduated from it regard it as one of the best training spots. It gives a young reporter a wide range of stories to write, and practice in dealing with varied and frequently difficult news sources.

Newsmen frequently co-operate with law enforcement officers in withholding news when publication would hamper police work. Alexander F. Jones, executive editor of the *Syracuse Herald-Journal*, cites two such cases in the following editorial:

> The capture of the two kidnapers who held a San Francisco realtor for 64 hours under the threat of death if a $500,000 ransom was not paid is another illustration of newspaper cooperation with the police.
>
> The fact that not a line was printed by the San Francisco newspapers until the vicious thugs were handcuffed and in jail is being called "the best kept secret in newspaper history."
>
> It was an excellent performance by the police and the newspapers, but the same pattern has been followed in numerous kidnaping cases, one of which I was in on nearly 20 years ago—the William Hamm case in St. Paul, Minn.
>
> Dealing with kidnapers is a harrowing business. Waiting for ransom messages, hanging on mysterious telephone calls, watching the frantic family, torn between a desire to cooperate with the police and a fear of never seeing their loved one again, those midnight trips by silent representatives of the family, with or without packages of money, and the denouement with the kidnapers captured or a dead body found is a chilling experience, with every minute seeming like hours.
>
> But the record in many cases proves that a story is not the only concern of a newspaper. With a life at stake, a fortune involved, and the slightest slip either way the possible determining factors, the press has always cooperated with either the police or the F.B.I.
>
> In the San Francisco case the Moskovitz family was notified in a note in the 36-year-old son's handwriting (under threat of emasculation) that he would be killed unless $500,000 in old money was paid and that notification of the police or a story in a newspaper would also be fatal.
>
> The family notified the police—a brave decision with so much at stake.
>
> The police called in the newspapers and explained the situation. For two days there was not a line to indicate that anyone outside the family knew of the kidnaping.
>
> Then came a traced telephone call, a vigil to wait for the next one, the arrest and confession, and the man was back with his family before a line was printed.
>
> The same pattern was developed in the Hamm case. We were called in, two of us stayed at the home for nearly three days. In that case the $100,000 ransom was paid and the notorious Touhy gang arrested and tried and found not guilty. Later a local gang was convicted of the crime.

It is a strange feeling to have a story like that under your hat and not a word appearing in print. But one look at the agonized family and a newspaper story does not seem important.

The police of every city can tell of countless crime stories where newspapers have gone all the way to help catch a culprit—even to the point of printing misinformation to give the criminal a sense of safety while the noose was actually tightening.

I cannot help but think of them sometimes when charges of sensationalism are being hurled about.

The San Francisco case, and all the others, just come under the head of public service.

Should Newspapers Print Crime News?

Some people argue that newspapers should not print the routine crime news. Their arguments go like this:

1. Crime news tends to glamorize criminals and to make others fall into a life of crime.

2. Crime news hinders the work of police by tipping off suspects about police theories and clues.

3. Crime news makes it impossible for a person charged with a crime to get a fair trial. The newspapers, say these critics, have convicted the person before his case ever comes to court.

4. Crime news serves no socially useful purpose. It is printed merely to increase circulation and therefore it should be eliminated.

Each of these arguments has just enough validity to be appealing to a person who does not take time to study them.

The first three arguments apply to certain undesirable kinds of crime coverage, and they are avoided by conscientious reporters. They are worth some attention, however, as guides to a newsman. They indicate that he should:

1. Make a special effort to picture crime for what it is—tawdry, dirty, unpleasant—and criminals for what they usually are—unintelligent, cowardly, unhappy. These adjectives do not apply to all crime and all criminals, but they apply much more often than do romantic concepts. When they do apply it is up to the reporter to make that clear, or at least to refrain from painting in flashy characters and false glamor.

2. Refrain from tipping off criminals. The modern reporter does not fancy himself a gangbuster. He lets the police nab the criminal, and he sees to it that his copy does not make it harder for the policemen to do their job.

3. Make his copy fair to all parties. Sociologists have presented cases of what they call "trial by newspaper," and in some of them newspapers were clearly at fault in printing too much incriminating detail. Sometimes the fault has been partly that of police chiefs or district attorneys,

who are so hungry for publicity that they release more details than is desirable. In a competitive situation it may become very difficult for a news medium to withhold such information, with the knowledge that a competitor has it and will publish it since it comes from a qualified source. This does not justify such publication.

Those who argue that crime news serves no useful purpose seem to want to ignore the unpleasant aspects of their community. The job of a newspaper is to help its readers understand what is going on so that they can reach intelligent decisions about public affairs. Unfortunately crime is one of the facts of community life, and if we do not know about it we shall never get rid of it. Arguing that newspapers should ignore crime news and let their readers do the same is like arguing that we should ignore germs because we cannot see them.

News media can offer some sound arguments for the necessity of printing crime news. One of the best rationales for printing it was offered by Arthur Hayes Sulzberger, publisher of the *New York Times,* in an address to the graduating class of the FBI National Academy in Washington, as reported in *Editor & Publisher:*

> Crime news, in my opinion, is an important deterrent to crime because, either directly or inferentially, it carries the warning that crime does not pay. If there is any foundation in psychology for our assumption that repetition is effective, surely the press stories of arrest, conviction, sentence, and execution appearing day after day must make some impression on the minds of the criminally inclined.
>
> Moreover, crime news aids in the apprehension of those who have committed offenses. It permits the widest dissemination of personal descriptions. It exposes the criminal to an army of volunteer intelligence sources, and forces the criminal to slow his movements if he is escaping.
>
> Crime news puts the public on guard against the perpetrator of crime, or against the perpetration of like offenses by other criminals.
>
> Crime news provides a penalty for many offenders more feared than the penalties of the law. Those who would laugh off fines or even short imprisonment if they could pay the one or serve the other in obscurity, fear the penalties of public reproach. A short experience in dealing with those who try to keep their names out of crime news would persuade any press critic of the powerful influence of this deterrent upon many people. The confirmed criminal, the hardened lawbreaker, may be indifferent to this penalty, but thousands of persons, who might otherwise proceed from minor to major crime, are influenced by it and avoid the repetition of offenses that have led to painful publicity.
>
> Crime news has one other function upon which I have not yet touched. It is the responsibility of the press to keep the processes of justice under constant public scrutiny. Full news coverage of agencies of justice provides assurance against discriminatory practice, or corruption in office, both on the part of enforcement officials and of the courts. It is a protection for

the good official. It is an assurance against abuses of authority by bad officials.

Let me acknowledge that the police are not without their legitimate complaints against newspapers, some of which play up crime news and the salacious aspects of it with no thought except increased circulation. I need not remind you, however, of the human interest in such stories. A good, juicy murder is exciting reading—why deny it? A rough check indicates that 25 per cent of all fiction published in book form last year was made up of detective stories. And so-called "surveys of readership" conducted during the war indicated that men, only slightly less than women, favored a local crime story over reports of air and land battles. That is undoubtedly the reason why overzealous reporters and editors may sometimes complicate the problems of enforcing the law.

Routine Crime News Is Only the Start

News of criminal activity and police action in combatting it is very important to any community, but a newspaper which stops there is doing only half its job.

Once a system is established it is fairly easy to pick up and write the routine police news, but it is not easy to paint the rest of the picture the readers need.

Police activity touches on so many aspects of community life that the possibilities of background features are limitless. One activity which has been getting more coverage in recent years is the fight against juvenile delinquency. The police department is only one agency which deals with young delinquents, but it is an important one. And the police are likely to have records which are significant.

The number of juvenile offenders as compared with previous years is in itself an interesting subject. When the reporter starts digging and producing reasons, trends, expert opinion, then his story begins to achieve stature—it may become a creative contribution to community betterment. Skilled, sympathetic interest in the problems of juvenile offenders seems sometimes to work miracles. A delinquent boys' center in New York State, for example, is reported to have treated 200 delinquent boys in six years with every graduate going straight. The cost is high—$3,200 a year for each boy. No one can doubt that such rehabilitation is cheap at any price, but a truly informed public might be able to correct the conditions which allow boys to run afoul of the law.

Any reporter who doubts his own social obligations has only to reflect that it is mostly through himself and others in his profession that the public gains enough insight to correct conditions which breed crime.

Trend stories of all kinds are available to the reporter who will take the time and has the understanding to make sense out of statistics and report them in attractive form. The crime level for comparative periods is often reported by police departments. With this as a springboard a reporter can find many story possibilities.

Comparisons between our city and others of the same size offer a sound basis of thought for any citizen. Do we have more crime than city X? What crimes are most common here? How does this compare with other cities? In what ways are conditions different here and what is the likely effect? What is expert opinion on the subject? These are a few of the questions that may produce topnotch stories.

Costs of policing a city are logical story material. The question may not be so much, "Are we paying too much for our police service?" as, "Are we getting all the police service we are paying for?"

If city X has a lower crime rate does it pay more for its police service? If so, what does it do with the additional money? Absolute costs of running a police department mean very little. Figures are usually reported as so many dollars per thousand population. Even this figure is likely to be unfair. One city may be easier to police. Perhaps it is more compact. Perhaps it has a penitentiary which periodically empties habitual offenders into its streets. Perhaps it has more help from the state police. Perhaps its population is more (or less) law-abiding than that of another city. All these factors and more need to be considered. Nonetheless they do not invalidate stories on comparative costs. They indicate only that they should be used with caution and scrupulous fairness.

Reports of studies by criminologists are an often overlooked source of worthwhile material. Such studies are often found in papers read at conventions, in professional journals, or in new books.

Under the headline, "Does the Victim Invite the Crime?" the *New York Times* printed a story based on this kind of research:

> The enterprising businessman who finds himself duped by a smooth-talking oil-stock salesman has unwittingly set the stage for the crime, suggests Dr. Hans von Hentig of Yale, whose specialty is criminology.
>
> "Often victims seem to be born," he says. "Often they are society-made. Sometimes the most valuable qualities render us easy victims; in a sense, the victim shapes and molds the criminal."
>
> After studying in detail the trend of the year, week and hour of the day in which most crimes are committed; the age, sex, occupation and physical characteristics of the criminal, and certain traits and tendencies of the victim that foster aggression, von Hentig reaches these conclusions:
>
> Forty-five per cent of all homicides occur between 6 P.M. and midnight.
>
> Most burglars are arrested between 2 and 4 o'clock in the morning; the next greatest number of arrests occurs in the following two-hour period.
>
> Crimes of violence and the serious sex crimes culminate on Saturday, Sunday and "blue" Monday.
>
> Most women commit suicide on Sunday, most men on Monday.

Burglary tends to increase from Friday night on, and Saturday night criminality "is obviously caused largely by alcoholic and other excesses."

The articles goes on, but that is enough to give an idea of its flavor. The police department of any city has the records with which such a story could be localized. Or perhaps the local university has a criminologist who has made similar studies or other types just as interesting.

Newspapers, Police, and Gambling

A reporter cannot always refrain from writing stories critical of the police department. If he values his "contacts" at the police department so much that he refuses to write a story critical of it he has abdicated one of his most important functions.

Frequently stories a reporter writes on gambling imply criticisms of the police department. Gambling is one of the most delicate problems that a police chief has to face. For one thing, it is big business, with assets sufficient to make a policeman's salary look microscopic. Enough policemen have weakened, and enough police departments have been corrupted, top to bottom, for the average citizen to be likely to view his own police department with skepticism as far as gambling enforcement is concerned. For another thing, while most forms of gambling are forbidden in most states, the public isn't quite sure that it opposes gambling.

This second factor is the more important one. A conscientious chief, backed by a city administration eager for a clean slate, can keep the police department uncorrupted; but when the public resists enforcement of gambling laws the police department may find its efforts ineffectual. The American public sometimes displays the attitude that there should be laws forbidding gambling, but it is all right to gamble now and then. Policemen are caught in the middle of this Jekyll-Hyde personality of the public.

Some newspapers go along with popular sentiment and ignore gambling so long as it is "kept in its place," which seems to mean so long as nobody makes too much fuss about it. Others feel that it is their duty to keep insisting on the enforcement of the laws on the books. It is difficult to see how any newspaper editor can do otherwise.

When a reporter finds evidence of gambling he can follow one of several courses:

1. He can ignore it. This is the easiest way, but it means that the reporter is doing less than the job his readers have a right to expect.

2. He can, if his editor agrees, rush into print. This may be the wisest course, but only if immediate public disclosure seems most likely to bring about a cleanup, and only if the reporter is sure he can prove his information in court.

3. If his editor consents he may report the information to the police chief or the district attorney and offer to withhold it pending a police investigation. This is the wisest course if the police department has shown that it is sincerely interested in controlling gambling. It also saves the reporter from the frequent police charge that, by printing such information before giving it to the police, the newspaper has made it impossible for them to make an arrest. If the police raid a place the story on that is just as good as the original one would have been.

On the other hand, if the police department is lethargic about gambling, the reporter's only alternative may be to print the information. He should bear in mind that there is a real difference between knowing that something is true and being able to prove it in court. Falsely accusing someone of running a gambling establishment is libelous, and it may be very difficult to prove a charge, especially if the police do not co-operate.

Gambling is just one of the areas in which the newsmen may find that his ideas of his public duty conflict with the wishes of the police chief. When this happens the reporter needs to act cautiously and to be sure that his editor is fully informed and supports him. Final responsibility for the contents of a newspaper rests, of course, with the editor and publisher.

Access to Records

Legal problems of the police reporter center about two main areas: the right to see and quote police records, and the dangers of libel actions resulting from published stories.

The right of access to records is confused in the United States, because many states do not have any laws on the subject and those that do often disagree. There are not enough judicial decisions, either, to produce anything better than a twilight zone.

In general the proceedings of legislative bodies, courts of record, and certain administrative agencies are regarded as public records, open to public inspection and inspection by reporters.

A few states have provided that certain police records shall be open to public inspection, including the police blotter. Many states have not.

Where statutes open none of the police records to public inspection, the reporter must rely on co-operation from the persons in charge of the records.

When police officials close the records, newspapers often try to open them up, by printing articles and editorials describing the situation and arguing that the officials are abrogating the public's right to know. This appeal is quite often successful, especially if all the news media in an area take it up. Sometimes a request to the mayor will be effective.

Since the legal status of police records is in so much doubt, there are

Form D-141   POLICE DEPARTMENT   DR No...........................

To Chief of Police, ... }   BURGLARY REPORT   Class...........................
                     .... }

Bus. Name..........................Bus. Address...Phone.........................
Victim................................Res. Address.................Phone.............Race............Occup. ....
Date and Time Occurred.. Day of Week........................
Location of Occurrence.. .... Between ....
Date and Time Reported....................194...., ...A. M. ....P. M. Reported To..................
Reported By ....
              NAME   ADDRESS

Type of Premises Entered (One Story Dwelling, Two Story, Drug Store, etc.) ....
Entered Thru ....
Method and Instrument Used to Gain Entrance (Cut Screen, Broke Glass, etc.) ....
Where Were Occupants (Absent, In Bed, In Yard, Entertaining Guests, etc.) ....
Other Acts of Suspects (Burned Matches, Ransacked, Assaulted Occupants, Prepared Exits, etc.)...............

Juveniles Suspected? .... Why? ....

SAFE BURGLARY: Explosives.............. Torch.......... Punch............ Rip............ Broken Open............... Carried Away...........
Fingerprints?.............. F. P. Bureau Notified?.............. Other Physical Evidence......................... Crime Lab. Notified?...............

Suspects ....Gun or Other Weapon Used..
           NUMBER   SEX AND COLOR
Vehicle Used (Describe) ....

Suspect No. 1   Name or Alias... Address.............................. Race..............
Age.............. Height.............. Weight................. Build.............. Hair................ Eyes.............. Complexion..............
Identifying Marks and Characteristics (Scar, Left Handed, Dope Fiend, Disguises, Glasses, Teeth, Speech, etc.).............

Clothing ....
Occupation .... Descent....................... Arrested?..................... Arrest No.................

Suspect No. 2   Name or Alias... Address.............................. Race..............
Age.............. Height................ Weight................. Build.............. Hair.............. Eyes.............. Complexion..............
Identifying Marks and Characteristics (Scar, Left Handed, Dope Fiend, Disguises, Glasses, Teeth, Speech, etc.)...........

Clothing ....
Occupation .... Descent....................... Arrested?..................... Arrest No.................

Witness..................................... Address................................. Phone.............
Statement (Can Identify Suspects, etc.)...
Witness..................................... Address................................. Phone.............
Statement (Can Identify Suspects, etc.)...
Is the Property Covered by Insurance?...
Complainant Can Be Seen.......... .... When?......................... .... Where?......................... Will Prosecute: Yes☐ No ☐

Further Details of Complaint (Also Itemize and Give Value of Each Article Taken, List Articles with Serial Numbers First, Names and
Initials Next)

                                                                              Total Value $...............

Evidence or Property Left Behind by Criminal — Disposition of Same

Approved By.. Officer.. Date .... Hour...........
              (If additional space needed tumble sheet and use other side)

FIG. 9. Police records are an important source of news. Here is one form of burglary
report.

many conflicts between newspapers and police departments on this point. A case from Schenectady, New York, furnishes a good example.

The police chief of Niskayuna, a town near Schenectady, closed the records. H. R. Ekins, managing editor of the *Union-Star*, hammered away at the story in the news columns and within a few days the records were opened up. Mr. Ekins asked for an opinion from the State Attorney General, Louis Lefkowitz. In an informal opinion the attorney general said that he could find no statutes on the point and that judicial rulings were not very decisive. Nevertheless, he said that it was his opinion that police officials should keep the records open to reporters whenever they could do so without endangering the public interest.

Some newspapers regarded this as a victory for the right to know. Others thought it made it clear that the right was in danger. The *Knicker-bocker-News* of Albany called for a statute opening up the records.

The Police Reporter and Libel

Every reporter and deskman has to keep part of his mind aware at all times of libel dangers. For the police reporter particularly, libel is a constant bogeyman.

It is libelous *per se* to falsely accuse a person of a serious crime. It is libelous even though the accusation resulted from an honest error. These two statements explain the danger from libel that is inherent in police news.

Police reporters are constantly writing about persons accused of crimes. This is not libelous if it is true, but in the routine a reporter may make a mistake and name the wrong person. At once the story becomes a libel hazard. The paper is still liable even if the reporter merely copied a policeman's mistake. The paper might, if sued, offer the policeman's error to prove that it had no malicious intent and thus try to lessen damages, but this would not protect it from the suit since the policeman's report is not a privileged document.

Mistaken identity is another danger. Sometimes persons arrested give the name of another person, or their true name may be the same as that of a law-abiding citizen. If the law-abiding individual can prove that people thought he was the person accused of crime he has a libel action. This is just another argument for a careful check of all facts that go into a police story, and for adequate identification of all persons involved.

It is this danger which leads many newspapers, when reporting arrests, to use such expressions as, "a man booked as John Doe" or, "he gave his name as John Doe." This is not a sure-fire defense against a libel action, although it might possibly lessen damages if the jury thought it were an indication of good faith.

When a particularly atrocious crime has been committed, a city police

Form D-143

POLICE DEPARTMENT DR No.............................

To Chief of Police,..
....} CRIME AGAINST THE PERSON REPORT

Type of Offense (Assault, Sex, Kidnapping, Att. Suicide, Misc. Injury, etc.) ....

Victim ....Res. Address........................ Phone............ M. F..........
Bus. Address .... Phone .... Occupation...................... Age......... Race...........
Date and Time Occurred... Day of Week...............
Location of Occurrence .... Between ....
Date and Time Reported.........................,...
Reported By .... Address........................... Phone...............
Reported To ....
Type of Premises or Location of Victim (Describe)..
(AUTO, PEDESTRIAN, DWELLING, UNDERPASS, BUSINESS ESTABLISHMENT, ETC.)

Murder, Assault or Kidnapping, Force or Means Used (Knife, Gun, Poison, etc.) ....
Reason (Revenge, Quarrel, Ransom, Attempted Rape, etc.)...
Other Acts and Circumstances (Disputes, Drunken Quarrel, Organized Gang; etc.) ....

Sex Offenses: How Did Suspect Approach Victim? (Accosting From Auto, Promises to Child, Renting Room, etc.)...........

What Did Suspect Say? (Exact Words)..

What Did Suspect Do? (Exposed Person, Committed Degeneracy, Attacked Child, etc., Explain).........................

Method Used (Bodily Force, Consent of Victim, Intoxication, Gun, etc.) ....

No. Suspects ....Vehicle Used (Describe) ....
               AGE   COLOR
....Gun or Other Weapon Used................................

Suspect No. 1 Name or Alias....................................... Address... Race...............
Age.............. Height.................... Weight.................... Build............ Hair.......... Eyes............ Complexion..................
Identifying Marks and Characteristics (Scar, Left Handed, Dope Fiend, Disguises, Glasses, Teeth, Speech, etc.).................

Clothing ....
Occupation .... Descent............................... Arrested?.......................... Arrest No...............

Suspect No. 2 Name or Alias....................................... Address... Race...............
Age.............. Height.................... Weight.................... Build............ Hair.......... Eyes............ Complexion..................
Identifying Marks and Characteristics (Scar, Left Handed, Dope Fiend, Disguises, Glasses, Teeth, Speech, etc.).................

Clothing ....
Occupation .... Descent............................... Arrested?.......................... Arrest No...............

Witness .... Address.. Phone...............
Statement (Can Identify Suspects, etc.)..
Witness .... Address.. Phone...............
Statement (Can Identify Suspects, etc.)..
Further Details of Complaint..

Evidence or Property Left Behind by Criminal — Disposition of Same...

Approved By.. Officer... Date.................. Hour...................
If additional space is required, use plain paper and carry DR No. in Upper Right Corner.

FIG. 10. A police department's crime against the person report.

department may be under great pressure to find the guilty person. This sometimes pushes police officers into premature announcements that they have found the guilty person. In one instance a police lieutenant in charge of an investigation kept turning up a new suspect every day or so, and each time he announced that this man was guilty. He was taken off the case before it was solved, but the newspapers which published his statements were threatened with libel suits. In such situations the police officer might possibly be sued for slander, but it is much more likely that the newspaper would be sued for libel. After all, it is widespread publicity which causes damage to reputation, and more money can be collected from the relatively great resources of a newspaper than from the average policeman.

This serves to point up the fact that police officers, even chiefs, commissioners, and district attorneys, are not privileged sources. The fact that a policeman or a high official says something does not make it safe from a libel suit.

Privilege is an important defense in a libel action. There are two kinds. *Absolute privilege* is granted to participants in certain events, such as a trial in a court of record; sessions of Congress, state legislatures, and other legislative bodies; and sometimes to public hearings of the committees of some of these bodies. It frees the participants from libel damages resulting from things they say during official sessions of privileged bodies. *Conditional privilege* is granted to newspaper accounts of the proceedings of such bodies. The conditions are that such reports be *full, fair,* and *accurate.* In other words, a newspaper cannot be sued for libel for a full, fair, and accurate account of a court of record. Without such privilege many courtroom stories would not be printable. There is much variety from state to state in designating what public bodies and public records shall be privileged, so a reporter has to be familiar with the laws and judicial decisions of his own state. It is sometimes easy for a reporter to think that a statement to the press by a high offical is privileged. However, this is not true.

Reporters should do two things to avoid libel: (1) be sure they can prove the truth of the stories they print, and (2) know the libel laws of their state and discard dangerous material.

A reporter needs more than mechanical accuracy. He must be able to copy correctly the spelling of a name, yes; but he needs, too, the critical mind which catches "facts" which don't quite add up, the sensitive nose which detects the faint odor of garbled information. He needs enough energy so that he does not shirk making 20 calls, if necessary, just to make sure that his suspicions are *not* justified.

Potentially libelous material appears in print, especially in the more sensational newspapers. Some newspapers print this type of material, and take a calculated risk. Often they get away with it. Some persons arrested have no reputations to lose; therefore it would be hard for them to collect in a libel suit. Many others do not have the means to start a libel suit, or they might not want to sue because they don't want the publicity it would bring. When newspapers take advantage of this merely for a sensational story, they reflect no credit on the profession.

Other newspapers may take calculated risks in the public service. It is dangerous to impute that a public official is not doing his duty. Nevertheless, many newspapers have done it when they felt that the public interest demanded it.

REPORTING ASSIGNMENTS

1. Tour your city police station and write a feature story about it.

2. Do the same for the county sheriff's office.

3. Interview a state police officer for a story on his work.

4. Interview a postal inspector and write a story about his work.

5. Check the records of the police station or sheriff's office showing the arrests for an 8-hour period, and write whatever stories you think are worth printing.

6. Interview an oldtimer on the detective force for a story on how crime detecting methods have changed during his years of service.

7. Write a feature story on some department of the sheriff's office or division of the police department, such as the records division, the training school, the crime laboratory, or the traffic bureau.

8. Interview a police official who has worked with juvenile offenders for his views on how to cut down teen-age crime.

10

Arrest and Indictment Procedure

Arrest

Newspaper stories about law enforcement often begin with an arrest, and later stories may follow a case through the pretrial events and the trial itself.

MAJOR STEPS IN A CRIMINAL PROCEEDING

Arrest
Booking
Preliminary hearing
Grand Jury action
Arraignment
Trial
Appeal
Sentencing

Procedure is fairly uniform among the states, although there are many local variations. This chapter tells what happens to a person arrested for a crime from the time of his arrest until his trial opens. It has two purposes—to illustrate a somewhat typical procedure, and to use in its normal setting some of the police and legal terminology every reporter has to know.

Although private citizens can make arrests under certain conditions, police officers make nearly all of them. An arrest is the act of taking a person into custody.

A policeman may make an arrest when he sees evidence that a crime has been committed, and has good reason to think that the person he

164

is arresting committed it. A private citizen is empowered to make an arrest in New York State and most of the others if a crime is committed or attempted in his presence, or if the person arrested has committed a felony, even outside his presence. Citizen arrest has gone out of vogue because it is dangerous, and because of the danger of being sued for false arrest.

A police officer who has a warrant to arrest a person does not have to worry about seeing evidence of a crime, since he is merely carrying out the order of a judge who signed the warrant. A judge can sign a warrant ordering an arrest when he has good reason to think that the person named has committed a crime.

Booking

The next step is, or should be, to bring the person arrested before the proper judicial official, who will determine whether the person should be held. Arrests are often made at night, however, when no judge is available, and so the person arrested is booked at police headquarters and detained in jail until the judge is available in the morning.

"Booking" is taking the arrested person before the desk sergeant or other booking officer, who records his name, address, age, circumstances of arrest, and perhaps other information. The person arrested has to surrender all personal possessions except his clothes, and is taken to jail. The record blank is still sometimes called "the blotter," although it is now more often called the jail register or something similarly unromantic. At any rate, in most police headquarters reporters inspect it frequently and it often gives them their first tip on a story. In small towns the newspaper may print the names of everyone taken to jail; in big cities only persons already widely known will receive publicity. In most places reporters have access to the records, but in big cities the material may be summarized and sent down every few hours to reporters in the press room.

One other aspect of arrest and booking procedure which sometimes makes news stories is the amount of time, after a person is arrested, that he can be held without being brought before a magistrate. The longer a person is held, the more opportunity the police have to question him, and the more opportunity is presented to gain a confession. Policemen and some theorists seriously defend the practice of holding persons for a period without bringing them before a magistrate, on the grounds that police work cannot be effective without some such opportunity for questioning.

A long period of this sort may be tempting to an unscrupulous police force, for it gives police a chance to apply a bit of pressure to induce a suspect to confess to a crime. Prolonged questioning itself may become a form of pressure, for it puts the suspect at a definite disadvantage. Such practices as shining a bright light in a suspect's face as he is questioned certainly begin to sound like third degree methods. Sometimes these relatively mild forms of pressure lead to threats of violence and actual torture. It is impossible to guess how prevalent this practice is, but there is evidence that it crops up. When this is found by a news reporter it may be a good story, if he can prove it. Proof is usually impossible, however, and that is one of the reasons why the practice persists.

At any rate, the time that a person is held between his arrest and his hearing before a magistrate may be significant. Most states provide that the hearing must be within "a reasonable time." Some have established a definite number of hours. Unscrupulous police departments may get around such requirements by neglecting to book a suspect until sometime after his actual arrest.

Some police departments will occasionally round up a group of drifters for questioning, without any intention of bringing them before a magistrate. This seems to work only because the type of persons thus arrested are without resources, and perhaps are small time crooks who cannot afford to offend the police or cannot afford to hire a lawyer.

This practice of holding persons for questioning without a charge, or on an "open charge," is fairly common. It cannot be defended on theoretical grounds, but many police officials will defend it as one of the ways necessary to make police work effective. The same is true of "stool pigeons," individuals who may engage in petty crime, but are tolerated by the police because they supply information about underworld activities, thus allowing police departments to function more efficiently.

Preliminary Hearing

The preliminary hearing or preliminary arraignment is the appearance before a magistrate of the person arrested for a crime. The magistrate has the duty to see that the prisoner understands the charge, knows that anything he says may be held against him, and realizes that he has a right to counsel. If he cannot afford a lawyer the magistrate has the obligation to appoint one to defend him.

This hearing may be before a justice of the peace or a police court judge, or the official may have some other title. Usually his powers are to try misdemeanor cases, but only to hold the preliminary hearing in felony cases.

If the charge is a misdemeanor, the judge can accept a plea of guilty or not guilty. If the plea is guilty he can sentence on the spot. This type of crime usually involves a small fine or a short jail term. The judge may sentence, or he may give a *suspended sentence*, which means that the person will be free on good behavior, but may be jailed without further trial if he is arrested again during the time of his sentence. Sometimes the judge orders the prisoner put on *probation*. (This is discussed in Chapter 12.)

If the person pleads not guilty the judge may listen to arguments, hear the evidence, and reach a decision. Or he may set a time for trial later when the person accused has had time to engage an attorney and prepare his case. In such circumstances, the accused is usually freed on *bail*, which means that he puts up a given amount of money or property to guarantee his appearance for trial. (This is often done through a professional bondsman who charges a fee for the service.) When the time set for the trial arrives, it is held before the same judge.

If the crime charged is a felony, the powers of the lower court are limited to deciding whether there is enough evidence to warrant holding the accused for grand jury action or trial in a higher court. The duty of the lower court judge is not to determine whether the accused is guilty, but simply whether the evidence warrants holding him for further action. If the judge decides the evidence is insufficient, he orders the prisoner freed. If he decides the evidence is sufficient, he orders the prisoner *bound over* for grand jury action, or held for trial in a higher court.

Indictment Procedure

Article V of the United States Constitution provides that, "No person shall be held to answer for a capital or otherwise infamous crime, unless on a presentment or indictment of a Grand Jury, except in cases arising in the land or naval forces, or in the Militia, when in actual service in time of War or public danger." A capital crime is one punishable by death, and an infamous crime is generally interpreted to mean one punishable by a term in a penitentiary. In other words, capital and infamous crimes comprise those we regard as felonies. The constitutional provision, therefore, requires a grand jury indictment before a person can be prosecuted for a felony in the federal courts.

About half the states now provide that persons accused of all but the most serious crimes can be brought to trial on an *information* prepared by the district attorney, instead of by a grand jury indictment. Most of the criminal cases coming to the Superior Court in Connecticut, for example, are brought there on informations filed by one of the state's attorneys. The Connecticut Constitution provides, however, that a person must be indicted by a grand jury before he can be tried for a crime punishable by death or life imprisonment. Connecticut statutes provide, too, that a lower court, finding itself without jurisdiction to try a criminal case, can in most cases order an accused person held over for the Superior Court without resorting to grand jury action.

When a person is ordered held for action in a higher court or for the grand jury he can be freed again on bail unless the charge is a very serious one.

At this point in the proceedings the city police department, if it has held the prisoner, will turn him over to the county sheriff. We have police forces attached to many levels of government, but the machinery for holding prisoners, gathering and presenting evidence, and conducting trials is, to a large extent, controlled by the county. The county acts in the name of the state. The federal system is, of course, separate.

This machinery for meting out justice consists of the county sheriff and his deputies, the district attorney and his staff, a grand jury system in many places, and the courts.

The district attorney is known in some places as the county prosecutor or the state's attorney. In most of the states this official is elected by the voters of a county. In Connecticut, however, the judges of the Superior Court appoint state's attorneys for the various judicial districts. In most places the district attorney is not the same as the county attorney. The county attorney is the county's lawyer in civil matters, while the district attorney or prosecutor is charged with law enforcement.

The prosecutor works closely with the sheriff and city police because they can bring in evidence to help him convict an accused person. In addition, the prosecutor is likely to have his own staff of investigators, and sometimes even his own detectives. In a heavily populated county his staff may resemble a small police force. He has assistant district attorneys who help in the preparation of cases and in court work. He is likely to have representatives in the lower courts throughout his county to press cases against persons accused of crimes. In the smaller counties the district attorney may work with few assistants; sometimes he has only a secretary.

Whatever the size of his establishment, the district attorney or prosecutor is an important news source. He may be the best source of information about what is going on in the grand jury room, and he may be willing to tell what cases he will present to the grand jury. The district attorney's job is often used as a political springboard, too. Thomas E. Dewey's first fame came as a racket-busting district attorney in New York City. This helped carry him to the governor's mansion at Albany and to two nominations for the presidency. Many persons prominent in state and national politics used the county prosecutor's job as a starting rung. As a dramatic figure in local trials, the prosecutor has a good chance to win popular approval.

He conducts investigations, sometimes presents evidence at preliminary hearings, presents cases to the grand jury or draws up informations to be used as the basis for prosecution, and then prosecutes the case in court.

The Grand Jury

The grand jury is one of the traditions we inherited from England, although it no longer functions there. As it existed in early England, it consisted of knights of the neighborhood who met and, out of their own knowledge of local affairs, brought indictments against persons they thought should be tried in the courts. In the United States today the grand jury hears evidence presented by the district attorney and decides whether the persons accused should be forced to submit to a trial. Usually it conducts a routine inspection of the county jail and sometimes of other public facilities. It may also investigate the conduct of officials at its own volition or if asked by the district attorney to do so. Sometimes special grand juries are impaneled to investigate gambling or vice. A special federal grand jury investigating communism indicted top communist leaders in this country and resulted in the famous trial of the communists in the late 1940's.

The number of grand jurors will vary from one jurisdiction to another, although some states cling to the common law numbers—12 to 23. The federal government and New York State require from 16 to 23, although juries usually have 23 members. In Oregon and Utah, 7 jurors are used; in South Dakota, 6 to 8; in Texas, 12; in Idaho, 16. Under common law 12 must vote to bring an indictment, and that is the number required in the federal system and in New York.

Grand jury members are selected, either from regular jury lists or from among persons thought especially well qualified. In some places where the latter system is used the grand jury is called a *blue ribbon* jury.

The jury elects a foreman and a secretary from its own members. The district attorney will have cases ready to submit to the grand jury when it meets, and he will present evidence to support his case and ask for an *indictment* or *true bill*. If the grand jury fails to bring an indictment sought by the district attorney it is said to have brought in a *no bill* or an *ignoramus*.

Evidence presented to the grand jury usually is *ex parte* (one-sided); it tends only to prove the guilt of the accused. This is justified on the grounds that the grand jury is not considering whether a person is guilty of a crime, but simply whether there is enough evidence against him to justify bringing him to trial. A person who is accused, however, may appear before the grand jury to tell his side of the story by signing a waiver of immunity. This is a document by which he agrees that any material he discloses before the grand jury may be used against him later if a trial is held. Evidence is presented before the grand jury as it is in regular court—through witnesses, documents, displays, and other ways to be discussed later.

If one grand jury refuses to indict a person, his case may be referred to a later grand jury by order of a judge if new evidence has been found. An accused person cannot be tried twice for the same offense under the doctrine of *double jeopardy,* but he is not considered to be in jeopardy when his case is considered by the grand jury.

Some jurists commend the grand jury system on the grounds that it keeps the laws closer to the thinking of the people. Juries have sometimes refused to indict persons just because members of the grand jury disagreed with the law or felt that the person accused should not be punished. One person told the grand jury that he had been taking money from the bank for which he worked. He said he had confessed to his superiors at the bank and was making restitution systematically out of his income. The bank officials had agreed not to bring charges if the grand jury did not indict him. He described the peculiar circumstances which had tempted him, and said that he thought he had suffered sufficiently already. Apparently members of the grand jury agreed, for they refused to indict him, and the man was never brought to trial.

This is entirely in keeping with our notions of the wide discretion of the grand jury. Its original purpose in England was to prevent the king's courts from enforcing unpopular laws as well as to protect citizens from irresponsible prosecution.

Sometimes a grand jury will start investigations of its own, independent of the prosecutor, and some grand juries have defied the prosecutor as the members sought to find corruption in law enforcement agencies or other sensitive places in government. This is the kind of grand jury which the newspapers usually label a "runaway grand jury."

The grand jury usually expresses its power through the courts. A person refusing to testify before the grand jury will normally be cited for contempt in a court. However, under common law theory, the grand jury has a contempt power of its own, quite independent of the courts.

Covering the Grand Jury

The grand jury is an important and reasonably prolific source of information, but it can be a difficult one for a reporter to cover.

One of the difficulties arises from the fact that the grand jury proceedings are, by law, held in secret. The district attorney and witnesses may be in the room when the grand jury members hear evidence, but no person, not even the district attorney, can be present when the members are deliberating. Thus first hand coverage is impossible.

The second difficulty for reporters arises because the grand jury sessions are not privileged. This means that there is no special protection against a libel action for a newspaper which prints the proceedings of a grand jury. Since the material considered by a grand jury would often be a libel against someone if it were not true, it is almost always dangerous for a newspaper to report proceedings of the grand jury.

The third difficulty for reporters is the fact that they may be held in contempt for reporting grand jury proceedings, even if they succeed in finding out what went on and are willing to risk libel dangers. Contempt is considered in more detail in Chapter 7. The fact that the grand jury possesses this power means that a newspaper and its employees can be summarily punished for actions which the members regard as contemptuous. Such actions might include publication of the proceedings of the jury.

Despite these difficulties there are some stories which can be written about grand jury proceedings. A reporter who keeps good records will know that certain cases, bound over for grand jury action, will come up, and that should be part of the story announcing the convening of a new grand jury. The district attorney may be willing to announce what other cases he will present to the grand jury. Often he will not tell about all the cases he is presenting, and he may have very good reasons. For example, if he is asking the grand jury to indict someone who has not been arrested or charged and does not know the district attorney is seeking an indictment, a newspaper story would simply tip him off so that he could leave the jurisdiction of the local courts.

Sometimes a district attorney will tell reporters what is going on in a grand jury room, and this material, if it is not libelous, can usually be reported. Then, too, there is nothing to prevent a reporter from sitting outside a grand jury room and observing who enters it. This may be a giveaway as to what cases the grand jury is considering. The reporter may even ask the witnesses as they leave the grand jury room what they told the jurors. Often a district attorney or grand jury foreman will caution witnesses not to talk to reporters. Results of interviews with witnesses can be printed only after careful consideration about the possibilities of libel and contempt.

Despite all these difficulties in covering the grand jury, some surprisingly detailed accounts get into the newspapers. The following story from the *Times-Herald* of Middletown, New York, tells who testified and fills in the background:

> The Orange County grand jury yesterday heard testimony of four witnesses in connection with the May 19th shooting of a berserk Air Force enlisted man in a Florida tavern.
>
> Witnesses at the jury session were Miss Mary McInnes, a waitress at the Gaiety Inn; Joseph Zingale, owner of the bar, Chester Kowaleski, a patron at the time of the incident, and BCI Sgt. William Adams.
>
> Miss McInnes and Mr. Kowaleski sustained serious wounds when S/Sgt. Paul E. Taylor, 32, attacked the waitress with a pocket knife in the tavern.

Taylor was fatally shot a few minutes later by Florida Police Chief Leo Bilvin.

On May 21, the Florida village board conducted a hearing on the shooting and subsequently commended Chief Bilvin for his action in connection with the case.

Miss McInnes and Mr. Kowaleski have initiated negligence actions against Mr. Zingale. They each are seeking $100,000 damages for injuries . . . they charge, were received from his negligence in protecting them from the attacker.

This story from the *Louisville Courier-Journal* tells of two persons held for the grand jury on lottery charges:

Thomas M. "Pat" Crawley, Jr., was held to the grand jury in Police Court yesterday on charges of creating a nuisance and possession of lottery tickets.

He was released under $1,000 bond for hearing before the jury August 26.

Crawley, 39, of 604 Floral Terrace, is accused of circulating handbills attacking a police officer here.

An employee of a printing shop identified Crawley as the man who gave the shop an order for 1,000 of the bills a month ago, and Maxwell Allen, a private investigator, testified a signature, "James Monroe," on an order sheet appeared to be in Crawley's handwriting.

Police said they found lottery slips in Crawley's home when they served the nuisance warrant.

Crawley did not testify. He previously denied the charges.

Also held to the grand jury on a lottery charge was Webster F. Kirkpatrick, 63, of 726 W. Walnut. His bond was set at $500 for hearing August 26.

Police said Kirkpatrick sold a lottery ticket to Eugene Townsend, 72, of 2408 W. Chestnut at Eighth and Walnut on July 11. They said Townsend told them he was supposed to have won $100 on a previous lottery ticket, but hadn't been paid.

Townsend was fined $25 for disorderly conduct amended from purchasing a chance on a lottery drawing.

The *Chicago Daily News* tells of a federal and a county grand jury investigating the same set of circumstances:

The Cook county grand jury investigation of Municipal Judge Edward M. Koza has been sidetracked temporarily to await results of a federal inquiry.

This decision was announced by Frank Ferlic, first assistant state's attorney, after State's Attorney Adamowski spent 28 minutes before a federal grand jury Monday.

The federal jury is expected to resume its investigation Thursday into a charge that Koza solicited a $25,000 bribe from Lawyer Irving N. Stenn Sr. to "fix" an assistant U.S. attorney in a 1956 federal investigation of ambulance chasing.

Koza himself was closeted with the federal jurors for the third time Monday morning for 96 minutes.

He returned in the afternoon for an appearance of 4 minutes and one of a mere 30 seconds sandwiched around Adamowski's session with the jury. Stenn, who specializes in personal injury cases, appeared before the federal jury 45 minutes.

He reportedly was excused from testifying before the county jury to await the outcome of the federal case.

None of Monday's witnesses would comment on the jury proceedings.

The rest of the story fills in more background.

A West Coast grand jury recommended better care of a public building in this article in the *San Francisco News:*

Something has to be done about the Civic Auditorium—and now.

That was the imperative recommendation today from the San Francisco Grand Jury.

The jury cited a "critical need of major repairs," and made these further points:

*Upper floors should be remodeled to provide more meeting room—so the massive building "will conform more nearly to the requirements of a convention center."

*Movement of the city real estate office and other departments into the auditorium should be stopped. "The movement," a jury committee stressed, "is contrary to the building's primary function."

*A substitute should be found "immediately" for the canopy over the main arena.

"Removal of the canopy," the jury noted, "is listed as critical and funds have been provided for its removal; however, no substitute remedy is planned at the moment and unsightly roof beams will be exposed to view, aggravating an already undesirable condition."

The jury suggested a bond issue may be necessary to finance the refurbishing.

The *Atlanta Constitution* describes a Fulton county grand jury's criticism of the Atlanta police department in a front page story:

Atlanta officials have failed to clean up the police department and to take disciplinary action against policemen who allowed the lottery to operate unhindered, the Fulton Grand Jury charged Friday.

The May–June term jury, in stinging term-end presentments, declared that the operation of lottery over an extended period "should be taken as evidence of the laxity, if not actual corruption within the police department."

Lottery operations are still going on in the city "on a reduced scale," the jury added, and some large operators are only waiting until the "heat is off" to resume big-time business.

Asserting that its probe of police protection and lottery "has met with frustration in every direction," the jury said the investigation is "still far from complete." It recommended to the incoming jury "that the investigation of the lottery and protection rackets be continued."

In its lead story the same day, the *Constitution* reports other parts of the grand jury's charges:

> The Fulton County grand jury Friday accused Alderman Ralph Huie of trying to intimidate the grand jury "by discrediting the foreman in the eyes of some of its members."
>
> Mayor William Hartsfield's office supplied documents and pictures used in the attempt, according to Huie's own statement to two jurors, the grand jury said in its presentments.
>
> Under the heading, "Grand Jury Intimidation," the jury found that Huie failed in his attempt to discredit the foreman.
>
> "The grand jury has complete confidence in Mr. S. L. Brooks as foreman and believes that he has pushed the investigation of police activities as diligently as possible," the grand jury said.

Either during or immediately after a grand jury session the indictments are given to the judge of the court which has jurisdiction to try the offenses. The persons charged are arrested, if they are not already in custody, and brought before the court. This story from the *Syracuse Post-Standard* tells of one such appearance:

> Michael M. Wynn of Yorkville, promoter of bingo games in Syracuse, Utica and New Britain, Conn., entered unconcernedly in county court chambers at 3:15 P.M. yesterday a plea of not guilty to a three-count misdemeanor indictment. The bill the grand jury reported about five hours earlier in the day to Justice Clifford H. Searl in supreme court was the only one resulting from a John Doe investigation covering four days, with a total of 60 witnesses sworn.

Newspapers often publish a story at the end of a grand jury session listing the number of *open* and *closed* indictments. Open indictments may be reported at once, but closed ones remain secret until their contents are revealed, usually after the arrest of the persons indicted.

REPORTING ASSIGNMENTS

1. Write a story describing how persons are booked at your local police station.

2. Interview someone who has served on a grand jury locally, preferably as foreman, for a story on his views on the importance of the grand jury.

3. Interview an official of the police department or the local district attorney's office for a story of the number of people arrested compared with the number eventually brought before a judge, and the length of time individuals are held in jail before they appear in court.

II

Criminal Trial Procedure

Criminal courts supply more high drama than any other regular source of news. A spectacular murder trial has everything to make a good story—high stakes, emotionally charged material, dramatic courtroom situations, mystery, suspense, and often a sex angle.

Add to these attractions the privilege which allows a reporter to reveal information that may not otherwise be printable, and it is easy to see why a murder trial is a good circulation builder.

But the criminal courts are much more than the mere scene of absorbing human dramas; they are at the same time one of the great cogs in our law enforcement machine and a bulwark protecting our civil rights. A criminal court proceeding, with competent counsel on both sides, a good judge, and a fair jury is the best device we have been able to invent for determining the guilt or innocence of persons accused of crime.

Three Great Protections

Three great legal protections are thrown around a person being tried on a criminal charge:

1. He is presumed innocent until he is proved guilty. This means that a jury should not convict a person unless the prosecutor proves the person's guilt. The *burden of proof* is on the prosecutor, and if he fails to prove guilt the accused must be set free. Another way of saying it is that the accused does not have to prove his innocence, but simply has to discredit any evidence the prosecutor brings which tends to prove him guilty. This may sound like a legal technicality, but it is a matter of great importance, and cases are often won or lost on the basis of it.

2. The accused is given a chance to confront his accusers. In our Anglo-American legal system a person cannot be convicted on the basis of

175

secret informers. The right to confront the prosecution witness in open court is a mighty weapon in the hands of an attorney skilled in the art of cross-examination. Witnesses may sometimes lie about an accused person's guilt because they have been told to do so by an unjust prosecutor, because they are confused, because of malice, and sometimes even to get reward money. The chance to question them in court is an important safeguard against deceitful witnesses.

3. The accused is not required to testify against himself. This great protection of our civil liberties brings up important questions as to the use of a confession. A judge will throw out of court a confession which was obtained under duress.

Another great protection for the accused and for the system of justice itself is provided by the Sixth Amendment which says, "In all criminal prosecutions, the accused shall enjoy the right to a speedy and public trial. . . ." This Constitutional recognition of the public interest in our judicial system makes it possible for reporters to attend trials as a part of the general public. Thus reporters extend the walls of the courtroom, so that more of the public may know what is going on.

Occasionally a court will order the public, including reporters, barred from a trial. Usually a higher court will reverse such a ruling. Such an instance occurred during a trial of a charge of pandering in Ohio. At the request of the E. W. Scripps Company, the Ohio Court of Appeals ordered a lower court to be opened to the public. The defense attorneys had asked that the public be excluded on the grounds that it would be easier for the attorneys to get a witness to tell the truth if she were examined in private.

In ordering the court opened, the Court of Appeals said:

> Courts are public institutions and they are maintained by the public as a necessary part of the process of government in maintaining and adjudging the legal obligations and rights of the people. Judicial power in a criminal case is exercised by an action in the name of the state in which action all have a deep and abiding concern. Any suggestion that law enforcement has any private aspects as to the manner in which justice is administered is completely without foundation.
>
> To permit trials of persons charged with a felony to be held in secret, the order for secrecy being based entirely on defendants' requests, would take from the court its most potent force in support of the impartial administration of justice according to law.

The Ohio court strengthened its position with this quotation from a federal court discussion of an attempt to bar the public from a trial:

> We are satisfied that the framers of the Sixth Amendment believed it to be essential to the preservation of the liberty of the individual that to the

extent and within the limits which we have indicated, members of the general public should be admitted to every criminal trial even though it might appear that in a case such as the one before us, most of them came only out of morbid curiosity.

The Ohio court concluded that ". . . a defendant has no right . . . to a private trial. . . ."

The "public trial" principle is well established in America; secret trials have been out of fashion in the Anglo-American system since the days of the hated Star Chamber which was abolished by Parliament in 1640.

Now and then criminal trials make history. The Scopes trial in Dayton, Tennessee, in 1925, pitted Clarence Darrow, defense attorney, against prosecutor William Jennings Bryan. J. T. Scopes, a public school teacher, was being tried on a charge of teaching Darwin's theory of evolution in violation of a state law which forbade such instruction. The trial attracted the attention of civil liberties groups, and of almost everyone who read newspapers. Now it is a part of our history.

The natural drama of the courtroom is often transported to the stage or screen by playwrights and film writers. Motion picture and television viewers can testify to this. Serious playwrights sometimes make use of the natural drama of the criminal trial. Two examples of powerful courtroom scenes are those in George Bernard Shaw's "Saint Joan" and John Galsworthy's "Justice."

With all the natural drama of the courts recognized by writers, it is not strange that a real trial competently reported is good newspaper copy. It may have all the drama of a situation in a play, plus the tremendous added impact of being real and present. The newspaper reader knows that he is sitting on the sidelines of the drama. Given this set of circumstances a good reporter cannot fail to turn in stories which will interest many readers.

A reporter's eyes are just as important as his ears in covering a trial. Much of the drama may come in gestures and expressions (perhaps a lawyer makes a point by shaking his head). It is easy to take down an account of the verbal proceedings and from that write a story of sorts, but the good reporter serves as the eyes as well as the ears of his readers. What does the witness look like? How does he act? What kind of performances are the lawyers turning in? What does the courtroom look like? The trial is an event played on a stage. Often the action is as absorbing as that of any play, and often the lawyers and other participants are as good in their roles as any professional Thespian. A reporter cannot put his reader into a spectator's seat unless he remembers to report what his eyes tell him as well as what he hears.

But the drama in the court is really only a means of achieving an objective—a just decision. A good lawyer is likely to be a dramatic actor in the courtroom, but this is only to drive home his points. If he wanted to play dramatic roles for their own sake he would be in a Broadway theater and not arguing issues in a courtroom.

What we have been saying applies to the more important trials. The beginning reporter will be lucky to cover court at all, and then he will probably get only the small cases which tend to be routine. Misdemeanor hearings are usually dull events, with little news value, although there are occasional exceptions. Many trials involve excursions into unwholesome layers of criminal life. Many of them get only brief coverage or no coverage in the daily newspapers. Some newspapers cover as many trials as possible simply as a matter of record.

The main steps in a felony proceeding after the indictment are: reading of the indictment, impaneling the veniremen, selecting the jury, opening statements by the prosecutor and the defense, presentation of evidence, summing up by attorneys for both sides, the judge's charge to the jury, the jury's deliberations, announcement of the verdict, and sentencing. Each of these parts of a trial may produce many good newspaper stories.

MAJOR STEPS IN A FELONY TRIAL

1. Selection of a jury.
2. Opening statements.
   Prosecutor first.
   Then defense.
3. Prosecution case.
   Presentation of evidence.
   Cross-examination by defense.
4. Defense case.
   Presentation of evidence.
   Cross-examination by prosecution.
5. Closing statements.
   Defense first.
   Then prosecutor.
6. Judge's charge to jury.
7. Jury deliberation.
8. Announcement of verdict.
   Loser may ask that jury be polled.
   If verdict is *not guilty* prisoner is dismissed.
9. Sentencing by the judge.
   Usually at a later date after the judge has studied the case.

Reading the Indictment

As we saw in Chapter 10, a grand jury hands its indictment to the judge of the court which has jurisdiction over the crime charged. The judge orders the person indicted to appear before him in open court, and has the indictment read to him. The judge tells the person that he has a right to an attorney if he does not have one already, and tells him how he can plead. Usually this is *guilty* or *not guilty*. In some cases a judge can accept a plea of *nolo contendere*. This means that the accused does not, technically, admit guilt, but he does not deny it, either. He just throws himself on the mercy of the court.

In most cases a person can plead guilty and thus avoid a trial. Accused persons may do this if they think the evidence against them would make it difficult to win an acquittal. They hope that the judge will let them off with a lighter sentence because they have saved the government the expense of a trial. Sometimes deals are arranged whereby a person agrees to plead guilty on the promise of the district attorney to get him a lighter sentence. Judges may make such arrangements to save the public the expense of conducting a trial or sometimes to reward a prisoner who has furnished valuable information to the police.

If the person indicted pleads guilty, the judge usually sets a time for sentencing far enough in the future to allow him to study the case. Then on a "sentencing day" he will pass sentence on several persons at one session.

If the person indicted pleads not guilty the case is put on the calendar and the prisoner is either freed on bail or returned to jail to await trial. A person cannot plead guilty to an offense punishable by the death penalty.

The Jury Panel

Before a jury term of a criminal court begins a panel of jurors must be selected. This is done by different methods in different localities. Sometimes the voting list is used, with every *nth* person on the list called to jury duty. The interval (n) will depend on the number of names on the list and the size of the panel required. Perhaps every thirtieth name will be drawn, perhaps every hundredth. Whatever the interval, this method assures a fairly representative sample of the list.

In other places lists of property owners and renters are used. In still others the official in charge of selecting juries (sometimes called a commissioner of jurors) gets a list together as best he can by seeking volunteers. Once a person is called to jury duty he is required by law to serve unless he has an excuse which is sufficient in the eyes of the judge.

Members of the panel selected in this way are called *veniremen*. From their number are selected the jurors who actually serve in the trial.

Selecting the Jury

The first step in an important criminal trial is the selection of the jury. Each prospective juror is brought in and may be questioned by the prosecutor and the defense attorney. Either lawyer, if he does not want that particular person on the jury, may *challenge* the juror, which means that the person challenged is excused from serving.

There are two kinds of challenges, *challenge for cause* and *peremptory challenge*. Each lawyer may use an unlimited number of challenges for cause. This means that he has found a legally recognized reason for excusing the juror, and the judge agrees with his interpretation. The accepted reasons are ones which show that the prospective juror is likely to be prejudiced. If the prosecutor can show that a man is a relative or even an acquaintance of the accused, this is usually sufficient for a challenge for cause. In first degree murder trials prospective jurors are often asked whether they believe in capital punishment. If they say they do not, they may be excused on the theory that they would be inclined to vote for acquittal simply because they do not believe in the death penalty.

A lawyer may use his peremptory challenges at his own discretion, without assigning any reason, but the number of such challenges is limited, varying with the seriousness of the crime. For example, New York State allows 30 peremptory challenges on each side in crimes punishable by death. If the crime is punishable by 20 or more years of imprisonment, 20 are allowed; and five are allowed in every other criminal case. A lawyer may use a peremptory challenge, not because he particularly wants to get rid of the person he is challenging, but because he thinks he may find someone else in panel who will be more favorable to his side.

In his book *Courtroom* Quentin Reynolds tells that Samuel Leibowitz, in his days as a criminal lawyer, would investigate the background of the people on the jury panel to try to find things which would enable him to pick a jury which would be influenced by the arguments he intended to use. One case, for example, involved some technical arguments, so Leibowitz made sure that among the jurors were two men who had enough technical background so that they would understand the testimony and explain it to the other jurors. Such tactics made other lawyers complain sometimes that Leibowitz "had the jury in his pocket" before the trial began, but it came from Leibowitz's hard work and diligent preparation of all aspects of his cases.

The selection of the jury in an important criminal case is often a dramatic period, with each attorney working hard to get the most favorable jury possible. With much at stake, each lawyer may challenge so many jurors that the panel is used up before the jury is filled. Then more prospective jurors must be selected. The new panel members are called *talesmen,* from the Latin words meaning like or similar men—men like the ones on the original panel. In some cases judges have filled the vacancies on a panel by impaneling spectators in the courtroom or sending out deputy sheriffs armed with subpoenas to serve on people they meet in the neighborhood of the courthouse, compelling them to appear forthwith for jury duty. This is seldom done any more, and is not regarded as good practice.

The business of selecting a jury may take several days, and good reporters write dramatic accounts of the proceedings.

Opening Statements

Once the jury has been selected, the prosecutor must *open the case,* by making a statement to the court showing what he intends to prove. Following this the defense attorney may make an opening statement, or he may choose to omit it.

The opening statement is the first opportunity for each lawyer to make an impression on the jury. An experienced trial lawyer is wary at this point, however, because he knows that the opposing lawyer will be listening for cues as to the strategy he intends to use.

Presentation of Evidence

This is another dramatic aspect of a criminal trial. The most common form of presenting evidence is to require the appearance of witnesses, who testify to certain facts of the case of which they have knowledge. Evidence may also be presented by documents, demonstrations, objects, photographs, and sometimes by recordings. Sometimes, too, a lawyer will ask the judge to take the jury on a trip to visit a place of importance, such as the scene of the crime.

Witnesses are the most common means of presenting evidence. Lawyers for either side may force the appearance of witnesses by issuing subpoenas. A person must appear as a witness in court after he has been served with a subpoena or risk punishment for contempt of court.

Witnesses are first questioned by the lawyer who ordered their appearance. This is called *direct examination.* After the lawyer has finished questioning his own witness he must allow the opposing attorney to question the witness in *cross-examination.* The cross-examination may be used to try to persuade the jury that the witness is lying, to trick the witness into a contradiction, to prove that the witness could not possibly have witnessed what he says he saw, or perhaps to persuade the jury that the witness is an unreliable person whose testimony should be considered unimportant.

SOME WAYS OF INTRODUCING EVIDENCE AT A TRIAL

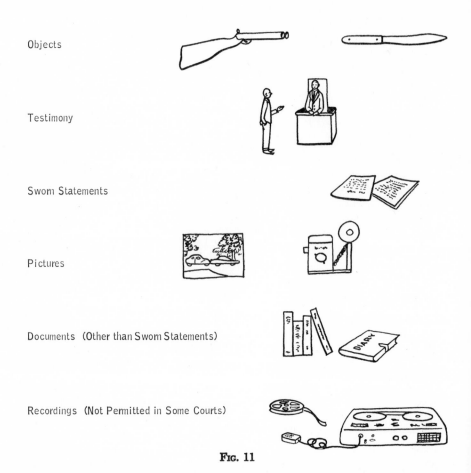

Objects

Testimony

Sworn Statements

Pictures

Documents (Other than Sworn Statements)

Recordings (Not Permitted in Some Courts)

Fig. 11

Sometimes lawyers go to great lengths to disprove the testimony of an important witness. The testimony of Whittaker Chambers was of critical importance in the trials of Alger Hiss for perjury in the 1940's. The first trial ended in a hung jury, so a second trial was necessary. This portion of a story by James Reston in the *New York Times* shows how the defense attorney in the first trial, Lloyd Paul Stryker, attempted to discredit Chambers as a witness:

Everything about Mr. Stryker and his case was most wonderfully contrived. He is noted for his trial-court maxims about getting the facts marshaled carefully before the judge calls the case, and at least yesterday he had them catalogued and indexed from Alger to Whittaker.

If there was a weakness in his technique it was that he was almost too brilliant. He put the melancholy Chambers on the stand and lashed him gently and scornfully for nearly four hours.

. . . Mr. Stryker paced gracefully up and down before the jury, measuring out his canny questions with a kind of cunning glee, and turning suddenly on the witness to demand a "yes" or "no" answer.

Sometimes he glared Mr. Chambers down and demanded the only answer that could possibly be given. But most of the time he paced elaborately, charging Chambers directly, insinuating all kinds of subtle and devious motives, but looking all the while at the jury or even turning his back on his client's accuser.

There cannot have been many more brilliant performances in this theatrical city since Barrymore played Hamlet, and yet while the opportunity for an equal trial has now improved, the case so far is one of defense by attack.

Mr. Stryker did not defend Mr. Hiss yesterday so much as he sought to destroy the credibility of Mr. Chambers as a witness. Thus the case, though it is just beginning, has not answered and may not ever answer many of the questions it has raised.

For the question that is still uppermost in many minds is not whether Mr. Hiss lied, but whether he spied, and since this is merely a trial for perjury, that point may never come to trial.

In the second trial the defense hired a psychiatrist to observe Chambers in the courtroom. Brought to the stand after several days of watching Chambers, the psychiatrist testified that Chambers was not a reliable witness, because he had admitted that he had told several small lies and because he had the habit of looking out the window when he was testifying. The prosecutor knew how important it was for the jury to believe Chambers, and he went home that night and slept little, but boned up on psychology. The next day, when he cross-examined the psychiatrist he made him admit that he had occasionally told small lies to his wife. The prosecutor then confronted the psychiatrist with a list of the number of times he had looked out the window while testifying and asked if that, in the psychiatrist's expert opinion, made the psychiatrist himself an unreliable witness. Apparently the jury got the prosecutor's idea, for the prosecution won the case.

The psychiatrist was hired as an *expert witness*. This means that, although he had no special information about the facts of the case, he was a person with special knowledge which a lawyer felt would be helpful in proving his case. Psychiatrists are often called by lawyers in an effort to prove that their client was insane at the time he committed a crime. Doctors are often called as expert witnesses to testify as to the extent of injuries suffered. Expert witnesses are used often in civil cases, too.

Documents are frequently used as evidence. Almost any kind of document may become an important piece of evidence. Letters, ledgers—any kind of writing may figure in a trial. In addition, two kinds of official documents are designed to take the place of witnesses who cannot be brought to testify in person:

1. *Affidavit.* This is a sworn statement made by a witness before an official empowered to take such statements.

2. *Deposition.* This is also a sworn statement intended for use in court. It differs from an affidavit in that a lawyer for the opposing party is present to cross-examine the person making the statement.

Demonstrations are sometimes used by an attorney to prove a point. One famous medical examiner for Scotland Yard was famous for the demonstrations he used to obtain convictions. One defendant, charged with drowning his wife in a pail of water, was arguing that it was impossible to drown anyone in that fashion. The medical inspector went to work in his laboratory and set up a demonstration to prove that it was possible. His demonstration in court was successful, so much so that he almost drowned his nurse, who posed as the victim for the demonstration.

All kinds of *objects* are entered as evidence. Often the prosecution will display the weapon with which the crime was allegedly committed.

Photographs are often used as evidence. Frequently they are introduced in evidence by requiring the presence of the photographer who took the pictures, who testifies as to the conditions under which they were made.

The use of tape or wire recordings is often barred in court because they can be faked. Under certain conditions they have been admitted, however.

After the prosecution has presented its case, the defense attorney often moves for a *directed verdict of acquittal.* In essence he is asking the judge to dismiss the case and order the defendant acquitted. Usually this is requested on the grounds that the evidence presented is not sufficient to support an action. A defense lawyer may make the motion when he is quite sure the judge will not accept it. It seems to be a psychological device designed to persuade the jury that the evidence against an accused person is not so bad after all. Of course, every once in a while a judge will agree and order the case dismissed. This is unusual, however, for most prosecutors are careful to bring to court only cases which will stand up.

If this motion is lost the defense attorney then presents his evidence. He calls witnesses and produces whatever other kinds of evidence he can to persuade the jury that his client is innocent. He, too, must allow the opposing attorney to cross-examine his witnesses after the direct examination. He tries to prove that the defendant could not have committed the crime.

The *burden of proof* is on whichever attorney will lose a point if it is not proved. The prosecution has the burden of proof, for example, in proving the guilt of the person accused; that is to say, he will lose the case if he does not succeed in proving his point. For that reason, the prosecuting attorney has the privilege of opening and closing the case. The burden of proof, however, is not always on the prosecutor. If, for example, the defense tries to establish as an alibi the point that the defendant was in another city at the time the crime was committed, he has the burden of proof on this point. That is, he will lose the point unless he proves it. Thus the burden of proof will shift back and forth during a trial. The burden of proving the major point, however, that of guilt, rests finally on the prosecution.

The Summations

After the defense has presented its evidence, both sides are given a chance to sum up their cases. The defense is first, and the prosecution closes. This, too, is often a dramatic part of the trial, with each lawyer giving all he has to persuade the jury that his side is right.

Instructions to the Jury

After the summing up the judge instructs the jury. This is the only time in most courts when spectators are not free to come and go as they please. During the judge's instructions the courtroom doors are locked, and the spectators in the courtroom at the start must stay until the judge is finished. It is the duty of the judge to help the jurors evaluate the evidence from the legal view—helping them to understand what is reliable evidence. He may tell jury members that if they believe a certain version of the evidence as presented in court, they should bring in a given verdict. If they believe another version, they should bring in another verdict. He helps the jury to decide how certain of guilt they must be to bring in a verdict of guilty. In a criminal action a juror should feel that guilt has been established *beyond a reasonable doubt*. This makes it more difficult to win a decision than in a civil action, in which juries are usually instructed to bring in a verdict which corresponds with the *preponderance of evidence.*

During the charge to the jury, the attorneys for either side may enter an objection. If the judge agrees that he has made an error in his charge he will correct himself on the spot. If he disagrees he will overrule the objection, but the lawyer has the privilege of asking that his exception be noted on the record. This simply means that the objection will become part of the record, so that the attorney can use it later as the basis of an appeal if he decides to do so. Sometimes appellate courts have refused to review a case because the objection was not in the record.

Jury's Deliberations

When the judge is through charging the jury, the members retire to a jury room and ponder their verdict. Meanwhile the court may recess to await the verdict, or it may proceed to other business in less important cases.

In criminal actions the verdict must be unanimous. A jury may bring in a verdict of guilty to a crime less than the one charged if the lesser one was included in the commission of the one charged. However, if a defendant found guilty of a lesser crime asks for and is given a new trial, he can be found guilty of the more serious crime.

Sometimes juries are out for hours, and once in a while a jury will stay out for several days, trying to agree on a verdict in an important case. The jury may return to court and ask for further instructions, or ask the judge to repeat some portion of his charge. If members of a jury finally cannot agree, the judge dismisses them and orders a new trial. This is called a hung jury. A jury which cannot agree after a trial has lasted several months costs the taxpayers a considerable amount of money, because a trial is very expensive when it runs for a long period. The defendant, too, is put to much added expense because he has to hire lawyers for two trials instead of one. For this reason judges do everything they can to make it possible for members of a jury to bring in a verdict.

During the period that a jury is considering a verdict it is kept isolated from all outsiders so that no one not on the panel can influence the verdict. Members may be kept in a hotel or, in some communities, in special quarters in the local jail. When jury members go to a restaurant for a meal, a bailiff accompanies them to make sure that no outsider talks with a juror.

Announcing the Verdict

When a jury finds a verdict, the bailiff informs the judge, who convenes court to hear it. If it is late at night, the judge may order the verdict sealed and opened when court convenes in the morning. The foreman of the jury announces the verdict. The lawyer for the losing side may ask that the jury be *polled*. If so, each member is asked in turn if he agrees with the verdict. If one says he does not the jury must retire again and try to achieve a unanimous verdict.

Sentencing

If the verdict is not guilty the judge orders the prisoner freed. If it is guilty, he may set a time for the hearing of motions for appeal if so requested by the defense attorney, or he may simply set a time for sentencing. In New York State an appeal is taken directly to the Court of

Appeals, the highest court in the state, in all cases involving the death penalty.

Appeals are based on errors in the trial, such as admission of evidence which should not have been permitted, or a judge's error in charging the jury, or a constitutional question which should be decided by a higher court.

A defendant may also ask for a new trial if new evidence was discovered or if a verdict was obtained by fraud or misrepresentation. In such cases the request for a new trial is filed with the clerk of the court in which the first trial took place.

REPORTING ASSIGNMENTS

1. Visit criminal courts in your community and write stories for local publication about the cases being tried.

2. Interview an official of one of the criminal courts in your community for a feature story about his work.

3. Write an article describing the criminal courts in your area. How many are there? What is the jurisdiction of each?

4. The Constitution provides for a "speedy" trial of persons accused of crime. With that in mind make an analysis of how long it takes, on the average, for a person accused of a felony in your city to come to trial. Write a story about your findings.

5. Interview an experienced lawyer who has defended persons charged with crime. Ask him to help you define the function of the criminal lawyer in our judicial system.

12

Punishment

Residents of Lepers' Island in the New Hebrides used to eat murderers. Modern punishments are not quite so drastic, but too often they have the same motivation—a desire for vengeance.

This vengeful attitude is one of the reasons our penal system does not work better. Other reasons are lack of public interest and understanding, inadequate resources, insufficient information, and political domination of some of our prison systems.

Modern society gives lip service to the ideal that treatment of offenders should be aimed at protecting society and reforming the criminal, but sometimes our methods of punishment do neither.

Common forms of punishment through the ages have been the infliction of physical torture, death, banishment, loss of the privileges of citizenship or forfeiture of property, and loss of liberty through imprisonment or servitude. In most societies today we use fines, imprisonment, capital punishment, and probation.

Sentencing Procedure

After a jury brings in a guilty verdict, the judge sets a date for sentencing. Usually he will have some discretion as to the severity of the punishment, although in a few states the judge may have none in the more serious offenses. Before sentencing he will often order a social worker to investigate the prisoner and his background. In California and Michigan such a presentence investigation is mandatory in all felony cases. Colorado requires the judge to order an investigation if he has any discretion in sentencing. The courts in Massachusetts and the Superior Courts in Rhode Island are required to do the same by their own rules. The practice is common in New York and New Jersey courts. In the United States district courts investigations are made before sentencing unless the judge rules otherwise.

Before he passes sentence the judge will study the report of the investigator and consider the prisoner's background as well as his offense. In some states he can specify the institution in which a prisoner will be held. In others he simply orders the prisoner sent to a reception center where a staff of criminologists and allied workers will decide what institution is best suited to handle the prisoner.

In some offenses the judge will have power to suspend the sentence or to place the prisoner on probation. We will consider these processes later in this chapter.

Mittimus is the name of the writ which the judge signs. It orders the sheriff or other local official to deliver a prisoner to a prison or reception center and orders the warden to receive him.

Places of Detention

County jails and local lockups are our most common penal institutions. They originated in sixteenth century England as a place to keep minor offenders. In 1576 Parliament ordered each county to establish such a jail. The most famous was a former palace which Edward VI gave to the city of London for use as a jail. It was in Blackfriars, London, at St. Bridgett's Well. It became known as "Bridewell," a name still used by some feature writers seeking a breezy synonym for jail.

Other types of penal institutions are reformatories, houses of correction, county penitentiaries, state and federal prison camps, and state and federal prisons or penitentiaries.

Local officials usually have custody of prisoners before and during their trial. After they are sentenced for a felony, prisoners become the responsibility of state officers. Federal officials have custody of prisoners being tried in the federal courts and may or may not use local jails on a contract basis.

A federal official who has inspected many local jails, Roy Casey, estimates the number of local lockups at about 10,000. Through them, he says, "there passes each year one American citizen out of every hundred of our population." Some stay only long enough to be booked; others spend longer periods.

Writing in the *Annals of the American Academy of Political and Social Science,* Casey gives this description of the local lockups:

> Only in a few of our biggest and best jails are provisions made for new prisoners to be examined by a physician until hours or days have elapsed after commitment and for decent standards of personal hygiene to be maintained. In the vast majority of catchall city and county jails prisoners are compelled to continue to wear their own clothes regardless of how filthy or

vermin-infested they may be; facilities for delousing drunks, vagrants, and bums are totally lacking; and too frequently hot and cold running water, soap and towels, any sort of provision for bathing or even for washing face and hands are nonexistent. Such deplorable conditions are almost universally found in our smaller city and county jails, and too often they exist in large ones which have funds to provide these necessities, but fail to do so.

TYPES OF PRISONS

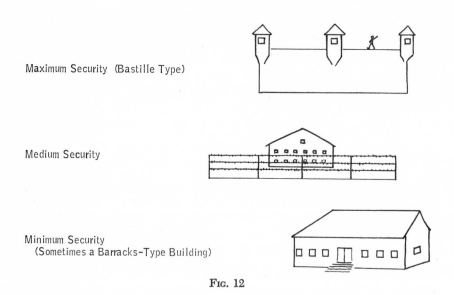

Maximum Security (Bastille Type)

Medium Security

Minimum Security
(Sometimes a Barracks–Type Building)

Fig. 12

Jailkeepers seldom make adequate provision for constructive activities by inmates, and often jailers are forced to mix all kinds of petty offenders with others who are awaiting trial and with material witnesses who are charged with no offense. Even with the best of physical facilities, it would be difficult to classify prisoners properly and keep them busy. Prisoners arrive at all hours of the day or the night without advance notice. The arresting officer bringing in a prisoner may know nothing about him, not even his name. Since many of the prisoners are awaiting hearings it is impossible to know how long they will stay, so normal work programs are impractical.

Sometimes jailkeepers change with each election, and efficient jail management becomes impossible. Poor management and unsanitary conditions are not the only criticisms. In some counties the jailkeeper, the sheriff, or his deputy, is allowed a certain sum to feed each prisoner. He can keep the difference between the actual cost and the food allowance. In many places this difference is commonly regarded as a part of the legitimate income of the jailer. It stands to reason that the jailer will feed prisoners as cheaply as possible so he can pocket a larger amount. Some jails provide adequate food, but others give their prisoners a starvation diet. The jailer should make a reasonable income from his job, but he should not have to do it by keeping prisoners hungry. The county should give him an adequate wage, then pay the actual costs of a decent minimum diet for the prisoners.

Despite the criticisms cited here some jails are efficiently run. State jail inspections have helped to raise standards. So has the work of the American Prison Association, the National Jail Association, and the Jail Inspection Service of the Federal Bureau of Prisons.

Despite their improvement our local lockups are a disgrace. Too often a few days or weeks of idleness, combined with bad companions and degrading conditions, will turn a first offender back to normal society much more of a menace than when he entered jail.

The first requirement for better jails is public interest. The real reason intolerable conditions exist is that the general public does not know about them, or at least prefers to forget about them. A newspaper which keeps reminding its readers of conditions in its local jails will eventually have some effect. An interested public will see to it that officials divert more resources to jails and employ competent people to run them. In its own interest, the public should insist on no less than the best possible jails. It takes only a little neglect to turn good jails into breeding places for disease and crime. The prisoners kept in jails sooner or later return to the community, and the bad habits and diseases they pick up in jail will be transmitted to the community. These considerations should serve to focus public interest on the jails even if humanitarian ideals fail to do so.

Even the best jails seldom exert a beneficent influence on their inmates. The second part of the problem is to keep people out of jails whenever possible, and when they must be imprisoned to keep the period as short as possible. This means speedier court action and more general use of probation and parole.

County penitentiaries have been built by a few counties to confine short-term prisoners who would otherwise be held in local jails. The county penitentiary usually has a farm and other provisions for using the labor of the inmates. Often such an institution will take prisoners from other counties on a contract basis, at a set price for each prisoner.

Reformatories are designed to house youthful offenders, and to turn them into useful citizens. The Elmira, New York, Reformatory, opened in 1876, was a model for many later institutions of its type. Individual treatment and education are used to rehabilitate prisoners. Houses of correction, "state schools," and other names are sometimes used for institutions which follow the basic plan of the reformatory.

Prison camps are maintained by the federal government and by some of the states. Prisoners about to be released are often transferred to this kind of institution to help them make the adjustment to life in normal society. There are fewer restrictions here and often there are counseling and lectures aimed at helping the men make a new start.

Penitentiaries are maintained by the states and by the federal government. They vary in the amount of security provisions from maximum to minimum. In maximum security institutions prisoners are kept under careful guard at all times, and every effort is made to prevent escape. Minimum security institutions usually have no walls, and sometimes no fences or locks. They allow a considerable amount of freedom, often making use of the honor system.

Prison Problems

The most vital problems of prisons center around the question of how well they do their two most important jobs—protect society from law breakers and help the prisoners to reform. Figures are not very conclusive. In fact, this is one of the problems of the penal system—inadequate figures.

If protecting society from the law breaker is regarded simply as keeping prisoners from breaking out, the prisons have a good record. Relatively few men escape from prison and nearly all of those who do are eventually returned. This is sometimes forgotten, because the story of a prison break is such big news that readers do not realize how unusual it is. They forget about the many prisoners who never try to escape.

Any serious consideration of protecting society must include whether the prisons return men better able to cope with normal life. It is commonly estimated that 95 per cent of the prisoners eventually are returned to society. The degree of protection given society certainly has to be measured in terms of whether these men, during their period of confinement, somehow became less likely to commit future antisocial acts.

For a certain kind of prisoner it seems unlikely that a prison term can do any good, but for many others the proper kind of treatment during a period of confinement may be helpful. The penologists talk about the number of recidivists—those who get into trouble with the law again after their release. Reports again are not adequate to supply dependable figures, but one prison authority estimates that about three quarters of those sent to jails have been in the same or similar institutions before.

The consensus is that the percentage of repeaters is high. Few reliable conclusions can be drawn from this. We can't compare the group released with a similar group who never went to prison, so we cannot condemn the prisons. Nor can we conclude that prisons are making confirmed criminals out of their inmates. About all we can do is examine the prison system and try to estimate how it might be made more effective.

One thing we do know is that overcrowding is unhealthy. More than 200,000 men and women spend some time in prison each year. The average daily prison population is over 175,000. Many of our prisons are crowded with more prisoners than they were built to accommodate. This leads to rows of cots in corridors, and jamming of three or even more prisoners into cells designed for one or two men. It leads to a breakdown in the education system and often to mass idleness with all its evils.

It may also force wardens to permit first offenders to associate with hardened criminals. Sex deviates should not be allowed to associate with other prisoners. When these logical separations cannot be made, the prison is obviously falling down on its job.

Prison Industry and Prison Costs

Most of our state prison systems are operated on the most meager budgets, although our prison costs each year run somewhere around $200 million. Despite the often desperate need for more money to run more adequate programs, the assistant director of the Federal Bureau of Prisons has estimated that less than half of the available prison manpower is constructively employed. Not only does this idleness cost the taxpayer unnecessary dollars, but it has an unhealthy influence on the prisoners, confirming them in habits of idleness.

Much of this idleness is caused by the fear of business and labor that prison products will compete unfairly with those made on the outside. Pressure from business and labor has sometimes forced the closing of prison mills and led to complete idleness for convicts in a prison, meantime increasing tremendously the burden of the taxpayers. During the period of labor shortage caused by the Second World War much of this opposition was relaxed, and $138 million worth of war goods and $75 million worth of agricultural products were produced in prisons.

Co-operation among prison officials and representatives of business and labor has sometimes succeeded in removing the opposition to prison labor, and sometimes produced positive help. It was this kind of teamwork which changed the federal penitentiary at Atlanta from a "notorious idle house" to a prison whose industry made it entirely self-supporting. Southern textile mill operators co-operated in planning a cotton mill for the penitentiary.

California officials have won much co-operation from outside interests. A textile mill at San Quentin is one result of this. Advisory committees representing some of the labor unions visit the prisons, help plan training programs, keep shop methods up to date and help released prisoners get union cards and jobs.

Most prison labor produces food and other goods used at the prison, helps to run and maintain the prison plant, or makes articles which are used by various divisions of the state government. Public works, reforestation, land reclamation, and road building are also frequently assigned to prisoners.

These are the bright spots, but the rule is still an inadequate work program which cripples the prison further by reducing the funds available for other services. A more enlightened attitude on the part of business and labor would help as much as anything in overcoming enforced prison idleness.

Education Programs in Prison

Some people get into trouble with the law because they never learned a skill which would enable them to earn a living. The work programs mentioned earlier can be very useful here. Indeed, the work programs may be an essential aspect of the educational program. Training for success in the outside world should include preparation for earning a living.

Many prisons provide some elementary education, sometimes using inmates as teachers. A few conduct high school level classes, and some encourage inmates to take college courses through correspondence when this is possible.

There is not much consistency in the programs from one system to another, and it is not possible to draw general conclusions.

Prison Discipline

Many of our jails in days gone by were run by "kangaroo courts" of inmates who did just about as they pleased, short of harming the guards or escaping. This has apparently been abated in most places, but there is still a tendency for some prison officials to allow a certain amount of prisoner control, and sometimes to abet it with special favors granted to prisoners who achieve power within the institution and thus can help in maintaining order.

The will and skill of the warden and his assistants determine the amount of inmate domination, but sometimes officials are handicapped by powerful forces outside the penitentiary which seek special treatment for influential offenders.

Austin H. MacCormick, professor of criminology at the University of California and executive director of the Osborne Association, tells of one rich man serving a term for murder in an Alabama prison. This man was given a special room where his wife and business manager visited him, and he often spent week ends at home.

Another wealthy and influential prisoner was given quarters at the prison ranch, "wore civilian clothes, ordered both prisoners and guards around, kept his car nearby, went off on frequent trips, including one to the Mardi Gras, and spent about as much time at home as he did before he was sent to prison for shooting his son, a returned veteran, during a quarrel over business matters." The quotation is from an article by Professor MacCormick in the *Annals of the American Academy of Political Science.*

Political domination of the prison system leads, too, to political appointment of the staff. This results in lowered quality, and often to such frequent staff turnover that the prison is periodically being managed by inexperienced personnel. One prison inspector told of visiting a prison whose entire staff was new on the job and without professional training. Under these conditions it is easy to understand why many prisons are poorly run.

In his article in the *Annals,* Professor MacCormick describes the ordinary prison this way:

> The great majority of our state prisons are mediocre. Their buildings are either ancient firetraps or "white sepulchers" with pretentious twentieth century buildings and nineteenth century programs. Most of them are so overcrowded that there are two men in every cell, and the makeshift dormitories are jam packed so tightly that you could ride a bicycle down the line of beds. There is nowhere near enough work for all the prisoners, and many men have less than two hours of real work a day. The educational program frequently consists of a few classes in the three R's, taught by prisoners. The "idle and unassigned" men loaf for endless hours in the prison yard or are locked up in their cells most of the twenty-four hours. Lockup time is 5:00 P.M., or sometimes 4:30 P.M., for all prisoners except those who are lucky enough to have work assignments or yard privileges that extend beyond that time. The cell doors open again at 6:30 or 7:00 A.M., the beginning for most men of another day of deadly monotony.
>
> When you walk through the cell blocks in one of these prisons in the evening, you see men lying on their beds with radio headphones on, staring vacantly at the ceiling, or trying to read by the light of a dim bulb, or swapping jailhouse chatter with their cell mates. At the end of the first month of their sentences they have had enough sleep, enough radio, enough hours in a cage four and a half to five feet wide to last them a lifetime. . . .
>
> Almost anything goes except escape. Favored prisoners are granted special privileges, and anyone with money on the books or in his pocket can buy extra food stolen from the kitchen. Prisoners with the right connections sell jobs, cell assignments, transfers to the prison farm, food, extra blankets, soap, special clothing, everything that is not nailed down. Payment is by cash in the many institutions that do not make any serious attempt to keep it out; in all prisons cigarettes by the pack or the carton are legal tender.

The author emphasizes that this is a description, not of the worst prisons, but of the average. It seems likely that readers of newspapers would profit from hearing newspaper descriptions of the prison conditions in their own areas.

What Kinds of Prison Buildings Are Needed?

As we have seen, some of the early jails in England were broken-down palaces or other buildings which happened to be available. One of the earliest attempts to plan a prison resulted in the famous building at Ghent, Flanders, erected in 1773. Eight wings radiated from a central section. Each wing contained cell blocks, and the spaces between the wings were used for exercise. The separate wings were a great improvement over previous prisons inasmuch as they allowed for classification of prisoners and separation of different types of offenders.

One principle which guided prison architecture for many years was that the entire institution had to be built to guard against escape by the most dangerous inmates. Accordingly, we have many prisons surrounded by high walls and guarded by gun towers, with inside cell blocks and elaborate locks. This "Bastille type" prison is so common that it is the stereotype most of us carry around in our heads when we think of prisons.

Into these elaborate, gloomy structures we throw our hardened criminals and also many offenders who show no desire to escape.

Modern criminologists estimate that somewhere around 25 per cent of the criminals sent to prison need this maximum security structure. For the rest the extra precautions and gloomy surroundings produce such an alien environment that they find it harder than ever to adjust to normal society when they are released. Moreover, we are spending a great deal of money unnecessarily to build and maintain more maximum security prisons than we need.

We have medium security prisons with some of the Bastille accoutrements removed, and we have a few so-called minimum security institutions in which the physical safeguards against escape are very few.

Probably the two best known minimum security institutions in the United States are the federal institution at Seagoville, Texas, and the California Institute for Men at Chino.

At some institutions of this type there are no locks on the doors, and prisoners live in barracks buildings or cottages. The only threat is that they will be hunted down if they escape, time will be added to their sentences, and they will be transferred to another institution where there are more security safeguards and fewer privileges.

Kenyon J. Scudder, superintendent at Chino, reports that there are few cells used to punish men who get into trouble. They are kept there only until they declare they can behave themselves and get along with the rest of the people. Few men stay in the cells more than 24 hours and few are locked up a second time.

At Chino the prisoners have been allowed to build a visiting pavilion with picnic tables where their families can come on Saturdays and Sundays, bring a lunch, and spend four hours with the inmates. This is in startling contrast to the usual prison visiting procedure, which limits a prisoner to a few minutes with a relative with glass and a barred window between them.

Minimum security provisions are often used in other places such as forestry or farm camps, where men live in barracks or farm buildings and have few security provisions.

PUNISHMENT AND REHABILITATION OUTSIDE OF PRISON

By Fine

By Probation

Sentence is suspended and person lives in
the community under supervision.

By Parole

Prisoner is released before his term has expired and spends the remainder of it in the
community under supervision.

Fig. 13

When the selection of prisoners for these privileges is properly made there are no more escapes from this kind of institution than from any other, and the benefits to the prisoner and so ultimately to society cannot be measured. The conservation camps in California have provided forestry workers and fire fighters who have given valiant service.

Probation and Parole

Prisons are expensive and there is some question as to whether they actually achieve any good for most of the people sentenced to them. Penologists point out that about 95 per cent of those sentenced to prisons and jails eventually return to society, and they say that many of those persons could be trained better by living under supervision in the community rather than by being banished from it. They argue that the time spent in prison often makes it harder than ever for an offender to adjust to the world of freedom. The odium of having served a term in prison makes it more difficult for a person to get a job and to be accepted in other ways in the community.

Probation and *parole* are the means we use to allow offenders to spend some or all of their time at home under the guidance of a social worker. An offender may be placed on probation by a judge at the time of sentencing. This means that he is left free but under the supervision of a probation officer, instead of being sent to prison. Certain conditions may be laid down. If he violates them he may be sent to prison to serve the rest of the term.

Parole is used after an offender has served a part of his sentence. He is set free, again on condition of good behavior, and under the supervision of a parole officer who helps him adjust to life outside prison.

One group of wardens estimated that between 25 and 40 per cent of the prisoners in their institutions could have been handled by probation. This is important because we have reached the point where an extensive program of building and renovating prisons will be necessary unless we find some way to decrease our prison population. James V. Bennett, director of the Federal Bureau of Prisons, estimated that one billion dollars will be needed for prison construction by 1975 unless more offenders are treated in the community.

Costs of keeping an offender on probation or parole seldom exceed $250 per year, while costs of keeping him in jail or prison are more than $1,000 in most places. In New York State the cost of keeping a person in a reformatory is about $4,000. Actually, with present case loads, the cost of supervising a parolee is often far below the figure cited, although by keeping it so low we make case loads too high and fail to use probation and parole to best advantage.

One of the reasons parole has not worked better in some areas is that parole and probation case workers are so overburdened that they have little time to do actual case work, but spend most of their time in the office keeping records. They are doing the most good when they are out working directly with the people they are supervising or making contacts with clergymen, teachers, employers, and others to help parolees.

How Parole Works. The federal government and about 25 states maintain boards in which the parole function is centralized. It is regarded as best practice to separate prison officials from direct parole authority, although in a few states the board which governs prisons is also the parole board.

In some states the governor and other high level officials constitute the parole board. Sometimes the state department of welfare or corrections may have parole power. Adults and youthful offenders are handled by different parole boards in California and Minnesota. In Massachusetts the two women on the parole board consider only female offenders. The President appoints the eight members of the U.S. Board of Parole with the consent of the Senate.

The federal government and about 12 states require that a prisoner serve one third of his term or at most 15 years before he is eligible for parole. Most of the states require some minimum time or portion of the sentence, but Idaho, Minnesota, Missouri, Oregon, Utah, and West Virginia require no minimum for most offenders.

Prisoners normally have no right to be paroled, although they do have a right to be considered for parole. Most systems provide for automatic consideration by the board whenever a prisoner becomes eligible. In the federal system each prison is visited once every three months by a member of the board, who talks with each man eligible for parole, and makes recommendations to the board.

Although parole officers have considerable discretion over the activities of parolees, most of the states require some restrictions. Florida, Idaho, Michigan, and New Jersey forbid parolees from drinking excessively, while 41 other states forbid the use of any alcoholic beverage. Other common requirements are monthly reports and curfew hours, usually 10:30 or 11 P.M. Two states, Kansas and Nebraska, require regular attendance at church. Often permission is required for parolees to get married, own or drive an automobile, move, travel out of the state, change jobs, or go into debt.

A special correctional employment service in New York State tries to find jobs for parolees. It also works with the prisoners before their release, teaching them skills for jobs in which workers are currently needed and telling them how to apply for a job.

In the many areas of the country where juvenile correction institutions are inadequate, we have no sensible way of dealing with young offenders except to place them on probation. Where probation facilities are lacking or inadequate the results are tragic.

The *Saturday Evening Post* described the situation in Baton Rouge, Louisiana, before probation services were enlarged. The city had only one probation officer who was swamped with hundreds of cases. When an offender was "put on probation" he was, for practical purposes, released because no effective supervision was possible under these conditions.

The *Baton Rouge Journal* aroused the citizens by describing another aspect of the story. Policemen and deputy sheriffs were bringing children into the city jail and locking them up for several days or weeks. During one year, the newspaper reported, 243 children under 17 had been jailed. More than half of them never appeared in court.

Children as young as eight or nine were lodged in steel cells; boys slept on mattresses on the floor; young girls were locked up with prostitutes.

Revelation of these conditions brought about a reform. A family court was established to handle delinquency and divorce cases. Trained officers were formed into a juvenile bureau which handled all youthful offenders. Instead of being thrown into jail, children were taken directly to court where an "intake officer" took charge of them. Now children who must be held are housed in a detention home instead of being mixed with hardened offenders.

Perhaps as important as anything was the establishment of an enlarged probation staff with adequate investigative and psychiatric personnel, so that the judge now can obtain a complete report of the background of each child before he has to reach a decision.

One result of this is that only 11 per cent of the children brought into juvenile court are repeaters. In the old days 40 per cent had been in court previously.

Since many communities are too small to afford proper facilities for handling young offenders, three states, Connecticut, Utah, and Rhode Island, have established state-wide systems. Connecticut has three judges who travel from town to town on a regular circuit to handle juvenile cases. Probation and detention services are now organized so that even the smallest hamlet has good service.

Parole and probation services are necessary in any system, but they are needed most in dealing with young offenders. Just how many criminals could have been turned into constructive citizens by proper guidance is debatable. Certainly the number is large and the chances are better with young offenders than with hardened ones.

In parole and probation work, as in prison work, there is not enough evidence to evaluate the job being done. Standards vary from one jurisdiction to another and records are not complete. Some authorities think that parole and probation have not been given a chance yet to prove their real value. Most case workers are overloaded; parole is not being used systematically in many places; and there is still a certain amount of public mistrust.

It is another area in which newspaper reporters can find true human interest stories which will help the public to understand, and perhaps generate enough public interest so that correction outside of institutions can get a real test. It is a concept which may change our ideas of punishment.

Unusual Punishments

The Constitution forbids "cruel and unusual" punishments, but occasionally judges try unusual ones that are not cruel. Sometimes traffic court judges, for example, will sentence speeders to look at the bodies of victims of traffic accidents in the morgue, or require offenders to attend a safety school.

When a judge tries this kind of sentence it is often good for a story. Reporter Lois Wille made an interesting and instructive feature of such a situation in the *Chicago Daily News:*

> Twenty pink-cheeked boys from Aurora went to prison Monday afternoon to learn a lesson. They went in chewing gum and cracking jokes.
>
> An hour later they filed out again—without the gum.
>
> But the wisecracks were fast and chilling. "What's this? You mean all these guys gotta work?" asked a freckle-faced 12-year-old, gazing around the prison textile mill.
>
> "I thought all prisoners sat in their cells and wrote books."
>
> Another said that his mother was mighty glad Justice of the Peace William H. Wake of Aurora had decreed the unusual punishment.
>
> "She knows I'll stay out of trouble all afternoon," he said.
>
> A slight boy with a thin, pale face and black leather jacket pointed to a big manhole on the prison lawn.
>
> "Hey, look," he said to his pal. "I found a way to get out—swim through the sewer."
>
> The 20 youths—most of them members of car-theft-and-burglary gangs—were "sentenced" to tour the old Joliet prison to show them where a life of crime will lead.
>
> When they assembled again after the tour, each agreed to mend his ways.
>
> "Sure, Warden, I'll be good," muttered a handsome 16-year-old, arrested for drunkenness and disorderly conduct. "I'll have just five beers tomorrow night instead of six." The warden heard neither remark.
>
> Warden Joseph E. Ragen, guide on the prison tour, was determined to show the boys the blackest side of the prison life: Isolation cells, armed guards in yellow stone towers and dreary cell blocks.
>
> Only twice in the tour were all 20 boys subdued. Those quiet, sober minutes came when two inmates—a murderer and a robber—gave them little lectures.
>
> "I'm in for 99 years—99 years," said the robber. "I was young like you when I started out. It's terrible here, boys—it's cold and I ain't got enough to eat.
>
> "Stay out of trouble, boys. Don't ever come here again."
>
> The slayer was brief:
>
> "When you lose your freedom you've lost everything," he said.
>
> Jimmy Lampson, 12, of 931 Spruce, Aurora, missed the tour because he's still in critical condition in Brokaw hospital, Normal, Ill., wounded by a trooper's shotgun.

He and a pal, James May, were stopped by gun-fire Thursday night when they tried to run down troopers with a stolen car.

Pardon, Commutation, Reprieve

These three powers are usually exercised by the executive: the President in the federal system and the governor in the states. Sometimes the power is given to a board.

The power to pardon is lodged somewhere in the government of all civilized countries. It gives flexibility to the system and sometimes is the only way in which justice can be done. If a person is serving a term for a crime and new evidence later reveals that he is innocent the pardoning power is often the only way he can be released. This is because courts in many states cannot order a new trial based on new evidence after a certain number of years has elapsed. The pardoning power is used in many criminal cases, but it becomes most dramatic and newsworthy in cases involving capital punishment. Here the governor and his advisers may weigh the political consequences and they may take into consideration circumstances that would indicate clemency. This is especially important if a judge does not have discretion, but must order the death penalty after a jury brings in a guilty verdict.

About a quarter of the states give the governor alone the pardoning power. Half give the power to the governor, but provide that he shall be advised by a board which has held hearings on the application. The governor is not bound to follow the board's recommendation, but he usually does. In another quarter of the states the responsibility for making the decision on a pardon is given to a board, with the governor as one of its members.

Pardon frees a man of all punishment, while *commutation of sentence* substitutes a lighter punishment. Usually the same authority which holds the pardoning power also has the power to commute a sentence. Most states include it in the pardoning power by statute, but where it is not spelled out it is assumed.

Commutations and pardons are sometimes given on recommendation of the judge who did the sentencing, but had no power to do otherwise. They may be given on the basis that only one of several participants in a crime was given a severe penalty, when he was not the one chiefly responsible for the crime. Sometimes the power to commute or pardon is used if evidence is conflicting, or if a district attorney has promised a lighter sentence to a defendant for turning state's evidence.

Sometimes a death sentence will be commuted to life imprisonment, and then commuted still more, so that eventually the offender can be paroled. This is not possible in all states, and is rather severely limited in those where it is possible. In Alabama and Colorado parole in commuted death sentences continues for life unless especially terminated.

Occasionally the release on parole of a killer involved in a sensational case well remembered by the public will be the source of good newspaper articles. This is always a touchy subject with much controversy and public interest. The release of Nathan Leopold from Stateville Penitentiary in Illinois, 33 years after he and Richard Loeb confessed to the killing of 12-year-old Bobby Franks in Chicago, started such a series of stories in the newspapers. Readers who were too young to remember the event were familiar with it from retellings of it. After his release Leopold dropped quietly out of the public eye, but probably the stories increased the understanding of many readers of the problems of crime and parole.

A *reprieve* is simply a delay in the execution of a sentence. Again it is the governor, or whatever pardoning agency is authorized, that has this power. It is used sometimes to insure time for an appeal to the United States Supreme Court. At other times it is used to give the governor or other pardoning authority time to examine the evidence and reach a decision on a pardon or commutation of sentence. Sometimes a reprieve is granted because the execution would otherwise fall on a Sunday, holiday, or on the prisoner's birthday.

The Newspapers and Punishment

Newspapers are sometimes criticized on the basis that they emphasize the crime and de-emphasize the punishment, thus giving a lopsided law enforcement picture. As with most blanket criticisms cases can be cited to prove or disprove this. But newspapers do need to cover punishment aspects more carefully, even though these stories lack the obvious drama of stories of the crime itself.

Stories of trials are plentiful, but we need more coverage of what happens after the sentencing. There are many stories in the case histories and figures amassed in prison files, and the records of correctional boards and social workers.

Newspapers have sometimes rendered great public service in exposing to public view unsavory conditions in the jails and prisons. The only way we will ever have the best correctional system of which we are capable is through public knowledge and public interest, and newspapers will have to play a major role in awakening such interest.

REPORTING ASSIGNMENTS

1. Visit your county jail and write a story describing it.
2. Do the same for a state or federal penitentiary in your area.

3. Interview a prison official for a story on what is done in your area to rehabilitate persons sentenced to prison.

4. Interview a probation officer to get his views on the proper use of probation in place of imprisonment.

5. Find out costs of keeping a person on probation as against keeping him in jail in your area.

6. Write a story describing procedures at your local jail. How many prisoners is it equipped to hold? How full is it most of the time? How long do prisoners stay there, on an average? How many persons put in jail are never brought to trial? What attempts are made to fill the time of prisoners with useful activity?

7. Write a story or series of stories about juvenile offenders in your community. What provision is made for their detention? What use is made of probation?

8. Write a feature story on "A day in the life of a probation officer."

13

Civil Procedure

Civil cases seldom have the drama of a murder trial, but often they are more important to readers. Perhaps because it is more difficult to dramatize them, civil cases tend to receive less coverage in the newspapers than do criminal cases.

While the criminal trial seeks to determine the innocence or guilt of a person accused of a crime, a civil action applies legal concepts and procedures to a private dispute. In a criminal action the state is always a party. Most civil actions are between two persons, or between two organizations which have the same role as private parties before the law. A corporation, for example, is sometimes a party to a suit, but its rights and privileges before the law are the same as though it were a private person.

With the distinctions between civil and criminal actions firmly in mind, a reporter must remember not to carry over into civil court stories some of the terms used in covering criminal cases. For example, no one is found guilty in a civil case, and there is seldom a prisoner. The *plaintiff* brings charges, naming another party who becomes the *defendant*.

Much of our civil law (except in Louisiana) is based on English common law. This consists of a group of principles which developed over the years as the result of many decisions. Some of them have never been written into statutes, although many states have incorporated most of them into their laws. Whether or not they are written into statutes, most courts will recognize the principles and apply them so that they have as much force as any other law.

Law and Equity

One of the important historical distinctions in civil procedure is between law and equity. In many cases it may seem to a reporter that the

205

difference is not important. However, he must understand the difference or some of the machinery of the courts will be unintelligible to him.

The distinction began in the English Common Law Courts and the Court of Chancery. The Common Law Courts (the Court of Common Pleas, the Court of Exchequer, and the Court of King's Bench) could award damages or make judgments about the ownership of property. The Chancery Court, applying the principles of equity, could make awards beyond money damages or property judgments. If a plaintiff could show that money damages would be inadequate in a breach of contract action, the Chancery Court could order the other party to carry out the terms of the contract. This is known as *specific performance.* Equity offers remedies in keeping with the wrongs inflicted, rather than assessing damages after the wrong is committed.

Injunctions illustrate the preventive action of some equitable remedies. An injunction is a court order telling someone not to commit an act. The theory is that there may be no adequate remedy at law after the act has been done, so an injunction preventing the act is justifiable if the judge is satisfied that an illegal act is likely to be committed. The use of the injunction in labor disputes will be discussed in Chapter 20. A person might get an injunction to prevent another from taking some valuable bit of property out of the jurisdiction of the court before a suit could begin.

The distinction between law and equity is recognized now more in terminology than in any other way. Some states still have separate law and equity courts, but many have merged them. In other states the same courts hold separate law and equity terms.

Actions at Law

Here are the principal types of actions at law:

1. *Torts* are private wrongs for which redress is sought. Every person has certain rights which are protected by the law. When a person's rights are violated he can appeal to a court for damages. It violates the rights of others to drive an automobile which is in a dangerous condition, and a person who is injured by the driver of such a machine can sue for damages. All of us have the right to use the streets with safety, and if another person causes us to sustain injury we may be able to collect damages. Landowners have the obligation to maintain their property so that others present on legitimate business will not be subjected to unreasonable hazards.

2. *Contracts* confer certain rights which the courts will uphold. If a householder contracts with a roofer to install a new roof, the agreement confers rights on both parties. To the householder is given the right to

a new roof of certain quality and type and completed by a given time. To the roofer is given the right to receive a certain amount of money for the job at a given time. Obviously the contract confers both rights and obligations on both parties. If one of the parties fails to carry out the duties incurred by the contract, the court will help the other party to obtain justice. This may take the form of a money settlement, or it may require the party to carry out the specific terms of the original contract. (The latter would be an equity remedy.)

3. Actions involving *property rights* are often on the civil court dockets. The law of property is complicated and important because its interpretation involves one of our basic concepts of government.

Equity Actions

Equity actions give relief to a plaintiff when there is no adequate remedy at law. They are concerned with *specific performance* or prevention of anticipated injury.

As we have seen, a court of law can award damages in a breach of contract action, but if the plaintiff wishes an order requiring the other party to fulfill the terms of the contract, he must initiate an equity action for specific performance.

An injunction may be used to force action or to prevent it. When a court issues an injunction it is said to enjoin something. It is more common for an injunction to forbid some action, but it can be used, too, to force someone to act. An equity court will issue an injunction when the judge is convinced that the act which is forbidden will do injury for which there is no adequate remedy at law. If one person constantly disturbs his neighbors' sleep at night by loud noises, for example, a judge may order him to cease, since it would be impossible to obtain adequate relief through remedies at law.

Equity courts will sometimes order the *cancellation* of a contract or will order its terms changed (*rectification*) if its original terms were in error or impossible to fulfill.

Legal processes to divide property are sometimes still conducted in equity in a process called *partition.*

Receivership is another important equity remedy. Sometimes a business which is in entirely sound condition will be placed in receivership to protect the rights of the parties concerned. A receivership puts the operation of the business into the hands of a disinterested third party who is appointed by the court. This may be done while a partnership is being dissolved, to protect the rights of a widow or other heir, and to keep the business operating until legal proceedings can settle ownership questions. None of these receiverships are as newsworthy as the one in which creditors ask a court to appoint a receiver, charging that the business is being operated inefficiently or dishonestly and that they cannot collect money due them.

Equitable remedies are used, too, to prevent unjustified law suits and to clear titles to property about which there is some uncertainty.

The tendency now is for one court to hear both equity cases and cases at law, in either separate sessions or mixed. A few states still maintain separate equity courts. Sometimes they are called *chancery* courts, harking back to their beginnings in England, and sometimes the judge of the equity or chancery court is called a *chancellor*.

A decision of a chancery or equity court is usually called a *decree* rather than a judgment.

Preliminary Procedure

The legal work done before a case comes to trial is very important in civil actions, and it can be very complicated. The preliminary work consists of the preparation, serving, and filing of papers, collection of evidence, and numerous motions.

Preliminary papers are called the *pleadings*. Copies of these papers are normally served on the opposing party or his attorney and filed in the court. As far as the court is concerned, the case begins when the first paper is served on the defendant and filed with the clerk of the court.

In a few states these preliminary pleadings, except in certain types of cases, are privileged. This is true in the federal court system and in New York, South Carolina, Kentucky, Texas, and California. In these systems a reporter can quote preliminary papers without fear of a libel action if he gives a full, fair, and accurate account. Normally preliminary papers in divorce proceedings and those involving children are not privileged even in these states. The California Supreme Court held in 1959 that even divorce court proceedings themselves can be held in secret if children are involved. In most states no privilege is attached to any of the preliminary pleadings and a reporter quoting them has to be as careful about libel as if he were using any other unprivileged source.

Preliminary papers and talks with the court clerks and lawyers furnish the material for the first story about a civil action. The reporter may summarize the contents of the first document in language which will make sense to his reader.

Preliminary Pleadings

For our purposes here we can list the preliminary papers and describe their content and purpose. This indicates an orderly progression which, in fact, seldom occurs. A lawyer has several alternatives, and it is an unusual case which follows the standard routine.

We will list the steps, however, as they are prescribed in New York State practice, then note some of the exceptions. The number of pleadings varies from state to state, but those which have codified their laws usually limit them to three or six. New York State allows three preliminary pleadings, with three more by special permission of the court.

The three pleadings ordinarily used are:

1. The *complaint*. This is the normal starting point of a civil action in New York, and, as noted above, it becomes reportable in that state without fear of libel, once it is filed in the court and served on the other party to the suit. The person filing the paper becomes the *plaintiff* and the other party is called the *defendant*.

The complaint should contain a statement of the nature of the action, the names and addresses of the parties, a statement of a right of the plaintiff and a description of how it has been violated by the defendant, and a statement of the specific damages sought. Often the complaint form will have on its back a summons form which is filled in and served at the same time. This orders the defendant to take notice of the suit and make appropriate response. Sometimes a summons may be served as a separate paper at the same time.

2. The *answer* is the defendant's reply to the plaintiff. It is the paper which is normally served in answer to the complaint, although, as noted below, it is not the only way a defendant can respond. In his answer the defendant may admit some of the charges made in the complaint, he may deny some or all, and he may make counter charges.

3. The *reply* is the plaintiff's chance to answer the counter charges which appear in the answer. He is not supposed to introduce new charges in this paper.

The purpose of the pleadings is to narrow the issues which will come to trial and, if possible, to eliminate the trial altogether. For example, a plaintiff might make eight charges in the complaint. If the defendant is willing to admit six of them, it is obvious that only two need to come to trial. Often parties see during the course of the filing that they are not so far apart as they had thought, and they reach a settlement out of court.

Although the pleadings may seem long and drawnout, they do serve their purpose—to settle as many cases as possible out of court. For every case which comes to trial, there are many others which were filed, but settled before actual trial. This saves time and lawyers' fees.

A reporter's work would be simplified considerably if all proceedings followed the routine described above—or the regular routine which parallels it in every state. Actually, nearly every case varies from it. Some of the variations are worth considering.

Dilatory Tactics

These delay the proceedings, but do not stop them. Among such tactics are:

1. A request for a *continuance*. In this a defendant, usually through his attorney, files an *appearance,* which is an acknowledgement of the suit and has the effect of putting him under the jurisdiction of the court. Then he asks for a continuance, a request for more time to answer. If the judge agrees that the grounds are valid he will grant it. Some of the valid grounds are that the material needed in the answer is not available, that the attorney is unable to prepare an answer because of the press of other work, or anything else that seems reasonable to the judge.

2. A request for a *bill of particulars,* a very common response, seeks more details on the charges.

3. *Discovery* is a request for permission to examine records in possession of the plaintiff.

Along the same line, an attorney may request the privilege of conducting a *pretrial examination.* This gives him a chance to question the plaintiff in an effort to make the charges more specific.

4. *Joinders* and *separations of parties* to the suit may be requested at this time, too. A person who knows that he is involved in an action may request a joinder so that his interests will be protected. One city, for example, asked that it be joined to a civil action between a trucking company and a neighboring town. The city's interests were involved because it had rerouted trucks leaving the city so that they had to use certain roads in the adjacent town. The town thereupon forbade trucks from using those roads, so that there was no legal way for trucks to enter and leave the city from that direction. A trucking company sued the town to force it to open the necessary roads, and the city was afraid that its interests would be neglected unless it participated in the action.

5. *Joinders* and *separations of causes* may also be requested by persons who think they may be more likely to win a case if they can get an issue separated from the others.

Grounds for Dismissal

Instead of seeking delay, a lawyer may respond to a complaint by asking to have it dismissed for one of these reasons:

1. That the facts as stated in the complaint, even if true, are not sufficient as a cause of action.

2. That the issue is already pending in another suit.

3. That the matter has already been decided in another suit. The legal term for this is *res adjudicata.*

4. That the plaintiff is not legally capable of suing. (This would be

valid if the plaintiff were under age and not suing through a guardian.)

5. That the statute of limitations has run out. After a given number of years a person may not be able to sue. The number of years will vary with the type of case and the state.

6. The court has no jurisdiction over the defendant or over the subject matter.

These pleas, if successful, will end the action, but they do not make it impossible for the plaintiff to start another suit if he can repair the weakness which caused the first one to fail.

Most of the suits which are filed in civil courts are never tried in the courtroom. They are dismissed or settled first. We would have to establish many more civil courts and elect many more judges if every case that was filed came to trial.

It is difficult to report the amount of a settlement made out of court, for the principals usually prefer to keep it secret. There is no public record of the amount unless the presiding judge, in approving it, made it part of the record.

Sometimes, to save time and money, the parties will ask the judge to render a *judgment on pleadings*. This means just what it says: The judge reaches a decision on the basis of the pleadings and without a formal trial. Sometimes the judge will issue a *summary judgment*, the effect of which is the same as a judgment on pleadings.

If a defendant fails to put in an appearance after he has been properly served, the judge may enter a judgment against him. This is called *judgment by default*.

The Trial

The clerk of each court arranges a *calendar*, which is a list of the cases expected to come up at a given term of court, in the order in which they will be heard. In many courts the list of cases expected to be tried that day is read at the opening of court. Periodically, perhaps once a week, a session will be devoted to hearing motions. These are requests that lawyers make to the judge to take certain action in relation to the cases which they are handling. There are often many preliminaries which a judge must approve before a case comes to trial and sometimes after it is over, so *motion sessions* are likely to be busy. Most of the activities do not need to be reported, although a motion concerned with a newsworthy case deserves coverage.

Lawyers watch the court calendar to tell when their cases will come up. With cases often settled just before a trial is about to begin or even after it is under way, and with lawyers sometimes pleading that they are not ready to try their case, it is difficult to know exactly when any given case will come up. When the time draws near for their cases to reach the top of the calendar attorneys may station clerks in the courtroom to give them advance notice.

When a case comes to trial the procedure is similar to that in a criminal case, with the plaintiff's attorney taking the same role as the prosecuting attorney. That is, he will open and close the case and present his evidence first. The over-all burden of proof is on his shoulders. He will lose the case if he does not prove his major points.

Evidence is presented in the same way as in a criminal trial, but there is an important difference in the way it is evaluated. In a criminal trial the jury should not convict unless it is persuaded of a man's guilt beyond a reasonable doubt, while a civil decision is based on a preponderance of evidence. It is impossible to make these terms entirely clear, but it is apparent that it should be easier to convince a jury in a civil than in a criminal case.

Equity cases are heard without a jury, but other important civil cases are heard before a jury unless both parties agree to dismiss it and let the judge decide the facts as well as rule on the law. Cases involving large sums of money are usually heard before a jury of 12, although smaller juries are often used in less important cases.

Here are the major steps in a civil trial with a jury:

1. *Selection of the jury.* As in criminal cases, each side has a certain number of peremptory challenges for which no reason need be assigned, and an unlimited number of challenges for cause, by which a lawyer can dismiss a prospective juror if he can show to the judge's satisfaction that the man is likely to be prejudiced against his client.

2. *Opening statement of plaintiff's attorney.* In this the lawyer will tell what his client is asking and, in a general way, how he intends to prove his case.

3. *Opening statement of defendant's attorney.* The defense attorney may give some idea as to his defense, but he is likely to be careful not to disclose his strategy. Often the defense does not make an opening statement.

4. *Plaintiff presents his evidence.* This is usually through witnesses, but documents, pictures, and exhibits may be used, too. Witnesses are first questioned by the side which presents them in direct examination. Then the opposition attorney may conduct a cross-examination, in which he tries to weaken the effect of the testimony by making it sound impossible or by making it appear that the witness is unreliable. There may be a redirect examination of the witness followed by another cross-examination.

After the plaintiff has presented his case, the defense attorney usually moves for a *dismissal* on the grounds that the evidence is not sufficient for a cause of action. If the judge agrees, he will dismiss the case and the effect is that the defendant has won. If the judge does not issue the dismissal the trial goes on.

5. *Defense presents its evidence.* The defense attorney presents evidence.

6. *Defense sums up.* The defense attorney reviews the case for the jury and asks for a decision favorable to his client.

7. *Plaintiff sums up.* After this the defense may again ask for a directed verdict of acquittal. If the judge grants this the case ends in a victory for the defendant; otherwise it proceeds.

8. *The judge charges the jury.* He tells jury members what verdicts they can bring in and what the law is, although he should let the jury interpret the facts for themselves. Attorneys may suggest points to be made in the charge to the jury, but the judge is not bound to accept their advice. If a lawyer objects to a part of the charge he tells the judge, who may or may not change the charge. If he does not change it the lawyer may ask that his "exception" be noted on the record in case he wants to use it later as the basis for an appeal. In more important cases the charge is usually written out in advance and read to the jury.

9. *The jury deliberates.* The jury's function will vary with the type of case and with the jurisdiction. In some cases the jury will be asked to set the amount of damages; at other times it will have the function only of finding for the defendant or plaintiff, with the judge setting the amount of damages, if any. A verdict which simply finds for the plaintiff or defendant is called a *general verdict.* When the jury reaches a decision on the facts, leaving the judge to apply the law to the facts, its report is called a *special verdict.*

Juries in civil cases usually do not have to bring in unanimous verdicts as do criminal court juries. Often only three quarters or five sixths of the jurors must vote for a verdict.

During its deliberations the jury is cut off from communications with nonjury members, so that no outsiders can influence the verdict. The bailiff takes charge of the jury, if necessary taking members to meals and seeing to it that they do not discuss the case with anyone else, and sometimes "locking them up" at night.

Sometimes when jurors reach a verdict late at night they will write it out, seal it inside an envelope, and leave it with the bailiff. Then they can go home for the night. They must reconvene and appear in court the next day when the envelope is opened and the verdict read.

10. *The verdict is read in court.* When the jury has reached a verdict it tells the bailiff, who reports to the judge. Court is reconvened and the jury foreman reads the verdict or hands it to the court clerk who reads it. The losing attorney is likely to ask to have the jury polled. If so, each member of the jury is asked whether he agrees with the verdict. The

attorney hopes that one of the jurors may change his mind so that the verdict will fall. If this happens the judge either sends the jury back for more deliberation or dismisses it and declares a *mistrial*.

A mistrial may also occur with less drama. If the jury finds that it cannot agree on a verdict it may ask for further instructions from the judge. If it is still hopelessly deadlocked, the foreman so reports to the judge and asks that it be dismissed. If the judge thinks there is no chance of the members reaching a verdict he will dismiss them and declare a mistrial. The jury is said to be a *hung jury* and the litigants must begin over.

Sometimes the judge has the power to set aside the verdict of a jury if he finds it excessive or contrary to the evidence. He may set it aside on the condition that the party concerned accept a fixed sum.

Where the judge has to apply the law to a jury's verdict the attorney for either side may present a statement showing what facts he considers established and what ruling he desires the judge to make upon them.

The losing party often is required to pay court costs and attorney's fees, or part of them, for the winner.

Enforcing Civil Decisions

If the loser (*judgment-debtor*) in a civil action refuses to pay a judgment against him, the winner (*judgment-creditor*) can apply to the court for a *writ of execution*. Such a writ ordinarily empowers the sheriff to help in the collection of the obligation. Some states still cling to a long list of special writs to cover each situation, as they developed in the common law. The major writs are either *property attachments* or *body attachments*. As their names indicate, these order the sheriff to seize a piece of property owned by the judgment-debtor or to arrest him. A judgment-creditor has a period of years in which to request such a writ. The period varies from state to state, but usually it is five or more years.

The sheriff may be ordered to seize a portion of the judgment-debtor's property and sell it to satisfy the judgment, or he may put a lien on real estate. Different states have different rules about what kind of property, real or personal, should be seized first.

Body attachments are permitted in some states, with debtors who refuse to pay a judgment being thrown into jail. This happens sometimes in alimony actions. Sometimes the complainant has to pay the expenses of keeping the prisoner in jail.

A *writ of garnishment* is an order to a third party who has property belonging to the judgment-debtor to pay it to the court to satisfy the judgment. This writ is used to compel an employer to pay part of an employee's salary to a court to satisfy a judgment.

The contempt power of the court is used to bring individuals into its jurisdiction and to punish for failure to obey its decrees.

Special Civil Proceedings

The courts described above handle a wide variety of cases. A few special kinds of cases are described in the rest of this chapter. Sometimes special courts will handle the cases. In other jurisdictions the regular courts try them.

Surrogate's Court

Most states have special courts to handle wills and the disposition of the estates of persons who have died. They are called *surrogate's court, probate court,* or *court of the ordinary.* In a few places one of the regular courts handles these matters.

In larger cities the probate or surrogate's court handles vast sums of money and the surrogate, through his power to appoint guardians and set their fees, can dispense a considerable amount of political patronage. The processes by which wills are probated seem complicated, and many people feel far removed from the activities of such courts. Actually, the affairs of many individuals are settled by the courts, which have the duty to validate wills and control the disposition of estates.

The New York Bar Association once said that the Surrogate's Court of New York County "probably affects more people more frequently than any other court of the state." The amount of money handled by the New York County Surrogate's Court in a year is in the hundreds of millions. The late New York County Surrogate James A. Foley felt that the laws under which New York surrogates' courts operated should be modernized, so he appointed members of the State Legislature and of Tammany Hall as guardians. They returned the favor by enacting laws which made fraud more difficult and increased the inheritance rights of husbands and wives, the changes asked by Foley.

Newspapers have an interest in the estates and wills because their readers are interested. In small communities nearly all wills are reported when they become available in court. In larger places only wills of unusual interest will be reported. These include those involving large estates, prominent persons, or unusual circumstances. Wills which leave money to philanthropic organizations usually receive publicity, for many readers are interested in the institutions.

Persons who died without leaving a will are said to have died *intestate,* and their property is disposed of according to the laws of the state in which they resided. The statutes will provide for the division of property among nearest surviving relatives according to a set formula, with a surviving spouse and children ordinarily receiving most of the property. If no heirs can be found the money will eventually return (*escheat*) to the government.

A will defines how a person wants his possessions to be distributed after his death. Ordinary requirements for a valid will are that it be written and signed by the *testator* while he is in sound mind and without undue pressure, and that it be witnessed by two persons who sign it. A *codicil* is an addition to a will. It must be witnessed in the same manner as the original.

A *holographic will* is one in the handwriting of the testator, but not witnessed. A *nuncupative will* is oral, made by the testator before a sufficient number of witnesses, and often afterward reduced to writing. It depends on oral testimony for proof. State law differs considerably on these two types of will. Some do not recognize them at all, some only for estates of small size, and some only if made by a person in the armed forces.

A person making a will usually names someone as *executor* (*executrix* if it is a woman). The executor can apply to the court for *letters testamentary,* which give him power to assume his role. If a person dies intestate the court may grant *letters of administration* to a relative who is then empowered to administer the estate. *Public administrators* are regular officers in some states charged with the duty of bringing up for probate the estates of persons who died without wills so that no estates remain unsettled. In other states courts appoint such administrators.

Guardians, appointed for minors who inherit property, are charged with managing the inheritance for the minor until he comes of age. Guardians usually must give bond for the faithful performance of their duties and also give periodic accountings to the court.

The will is filed with the probate court, usually at the request of an interested party. Notice is given to all who might have an interest in the estate and a hearing may be held to *prove the will,* or *admit it to probate.* The will may be proved by the testimony of the persons who witnessed it or by testimony as to the handwriting of the testator. If the will is regarded as genuine, makes no illegal bequests, and is not contested, the court will empower the executor to carry out its terms.

Some interesting stories develop from contested wills. If a relative thinks that a will has been obtained under duress or undue influence, or was written when the testator was not of sound mind, he may start proceedings to *break the will.* The surrogate, probate judge, or ordinary may sit as a judge in proceedings which resemble other trials, often with a jury. Evidence may be presented as in any other trial. Sensational trials of this kind usually are covered thoroughly in the newspapers, and often arouse more interest than other civil proceedings.

The usual story on a will becomes available when the document is filed with the court or admitted to probate. The reporter needs to note any unusual provisions, the amount of the estate if it is apparent or available from lawyers, and he needs to tie the story in with enough background so that the reader will understand it.

One of the early duties of the administrator is to itemize the estate, and in this he may be assisted by a tax official, for inheritance taxes are a favorite with state and federal governments. Federal statutes allow for credit up to a certain point for state inheritance taxes, thus encouraging the states to collect at least a minimum tax.

An executor or administrator may be empowered to carry on a business for a period, or to sell assets to pay taxes or other obligations of the estate. If a testator has drawn a will in times of prosperity and his estate does not have sufficient funds to pay bequests and legacies, the executor must decide, with the court, how much is to be paid to each beneficiary. Some testators simplify this problem by willing their property in portions, such as one half, or one quarter, or other fractions of the estate.

This portion of a story from the *Syracuse Herald-Journal* shows how the problems of a large estate may be of continuing interest to a community when large charitable gifts are involved:

> A federal court yesterday ruled that more than $2,000,000 in taxes must be returned to the Rosamond Gifford Charitable Foundation.
>
> In a decision handed down in Utica, Judge Stephen W. Brennan said $2,128,252.97 plus six per cent interest from March, 1957 must be paid back to the Foundation, which was established by the late Rosamond Gifford who died in 1953.
>
> Miss Gifford directed that the bulk of her estate of approximately $6 million be left to a corporation to be "created, managed and operated exclusively for religious, educational, scientific, charitable or benevolent uses."
>
> But the Internal Revenue Service ruled the estate was subject to federal estate taxes because it construed the use of the word "benevolent" in the will was permissive of other than charitable expenditures.

Replevin

Replevin is the seizure of property, often by a vendor who has sold it on time payments. In this kind of action the person seeking to replevy the goods must first make a demand that they be returned. Replevin is also used to restore stolen goods to their rightful owners. In such an action there is no need to demand the property first, unless the stolen goods have been sold to an innocent purchaser, who must be allowed time to determine the rightful owner before the property can be forcibly seized.

A sheriff is usually the officer who actually takes the goods. He acts when he receives from the plaintiff's attorney a written requisition to replevy certain goods, together with an affidavit stating the facts of the case, and a bond more than twice the value of the goods he is seeking to replevy.

Bankruptcy

When a businessman or a corporation is hopelessly in debt, the laws of bankruptcy may come to his rescue. In general these laws provide for the liquidation of the business and its sale, to divide the assets among creditors so that each gets a certain percentage of what is due, or an amount determined according to some formula which recognizes first the more valid claims. Sometimes the business may be reorganized under new management. The person going through bankruptcy is left clear of debts to start over again.

Section 8 of the Constitution gives Congress the power to establish "uniform Laws on the subject of Bankruptcies throughout The United States."

Congress made some attempts to implement this power by passing bankruptcy laws in 1800, 1841, and 1867, but none of them was effective and all were repealed. The first effective federal statute on the subject was passed in 1898, and since that time most bankruptcy proceedings have been held in Federal District Courts or before referees in bankruptcy appointed by federal judges and serving as their agents.

In early times bankruptcy actions came up in equity terms of the state courts, but this was an unsatisfactory procedure. Sometimes the jurisdiction of the courts was not wide enough and suits had to be initiated in several courts to get jurisdiction of all the assets of a business or to serve the needs of all the creditors. As businesses increased in size it sometimes was necessary to sue in several different states. Federal jurisdiction was the only adequate answer to this problem, as the framers of the Constitution understood.

The bankruptcy laws aim to distribute as equitably as possible the resources of an insolvent concern among its creditors, and to make it possible for the insolvent concern to be saved if possible for the greater benefit of all concerned. They also help the individual debtor to make a fresh start, rather than stagger through life with an impossible load of debts.

The remedy of a simple suit to recover money due is not very adequate in many situations, because an insolvent individual or concern is likely to owe money to many creditors. A suit for recovery would favor the first one to file such a suit rather than the one with the most valid claim.

A *petition* opens a bankruptcy proceeding. This can be *voluntary* (filed by the insolvent person or business) or *involuntary* (filed by creditors of the concern). The petition should show that the debtor owes at least $1,000, cannot pay his debts, and has "committed an act of bank-ruptcy" within the past four months. Acts of bankruptcy are: concealing or moving property to defraud creditors, moving property to give prefer-ence to certain creditors, allowing creditors to take liens on property without discharging these liens within a certain period, making a gen-eral assignment of property, permitting the appointment of a receiver while unable to pay debts, or admitting insolvency and asking to be declared a bankrupt.

The first newspaper report of a bankruptcy action is usually written from the petition. The reporter evaluates it by the same means he evalu-ates any other court document. Prominent persons or concerns, large sums of money, and unusual circumstances are the factors which are likely to make such a document worth a story. Sometimes familiar local landmarks are involved. In some cases the effect on other local concerns is important. It has happened that one important concern going bank-rupt will owe so much to other concerns that they, too, are forced into bankruptcy.

Sometimes involuntary petitions are hotly contested at a hearing. When this happens it often makes a good story. It has happened, of course, that a ruthless businessman has been able to maneuver a rival into bankruptcy and thus dispose of the competition. Probably no bank-ruptcy procedures could be devised to make this impossible. One of the jobs of the referee in bankruptcy is to see that this does not happen, and the hearing and sometimes an investigation preceding it are two of the devices he uses to make sure that the true intent of the law is car-ried out.

Usually a voluntary petition results in the declaration of the debtor as a bankrupt when the petition is filed.

The court may appoint a receiver on the motion of the creditors at the time of the filing of the petition. The receiver may take the debtor's assets to make sure they are not dissipated before a disposition can be made. He or the referee may seek to gain agreement among all the creditors to take a certain percentage of their debts, perhaps 50 per cent, and discharge the bankrupt from further obligation. Under these cir-cumstances the bankrupt can sometimes continue in business.

Once a person or firm has been adjudged a bankrupt, the receiver is replaced by a trustee who is elected by the creditors or appointed by the referee or judge. Often the receiver continues as trustee. He takes possession of the resources of the bankrupt and generally presides at the liquidation of the assets to the creditors, according to a plan approved by the referee or judge.

The referee or judge will preside at an examination of the bankrupt to determine the full extent of his resources and to make sure that none are hidden. After this the bankrupt may be discharged from further obligations.

The creditors work out with the trustee and the judge a plan for distributing the assets of the bankrupt, and the trustee administers it. The trustee makes periodic reports to the referee or judge.

Bankruptcy laws now provide that the Interstate Commerce Commission participate in bankruptcy or reorganization plans for railroads, thus tapping the expert knowledge of that body.

Small businesses which are insolvent usually have most of their outstanding debts to banks and suppliers of goods or services. Large incorporated concerns are more often indebted to holders of stocks and bonds, and it is often difficult to decide who has a right to be paid off first. An understanding of corporate structure, as explained in Chapter 17, is necessary to appreciate the problems of corporate reorganization. We should note here, however, that federal laws provide for corporate reorganization of insolvent businesses. This is somewhat short of bankruptcy, and is aimed at supplying whatever relief is possible to a corporation's owners plus, if possible, keeping the business in operation. Very often the only way that bond and stock holders can realize very much on their investment is to keep their interest in the concern and try to reorganize the business so that it will turn in a profit.

The corporate reorganization plan requires the appointment of one or more disinterested trustees who assist in obtaining a reorganization which will protect the interests of all stock and bond holders. In larger reorganizations the judge or referee must submit the plan to the Securities and Exchange Commission, which offers an advisory opinion not binding on the judge. Security holders representing two thirds of the outstanding stocks and bonds must approve the plan, and regulations attempt to protect the interests of dissenting security holders.

A reporter covering bankruptcy and reorganization proceedings finds that they often resemble other civil proceedings, with information coming from documents, officials, and the individuals involved. Once in a while a dramatic courtroom battle will occur, and this is covered much as any other case. Libel dangers are present, as they are in any court proceeding.

As in criminal coverage, it is important for a reporter not to anticipate the proceedings. To call an individual or a concern a bankrupt before the court has officially made such a finding is likely to get a newspaper into a libel action.

Appellate Procedure

Our court system provides that a person dissatisfied with the judgment of a lower court can, if he has sufficient reason, have the decision reviewed in a higher court.

Usually it is the person who loses a case who seeks the review, but sometimes both parties will be dissatisfied and will appeal.

A defendant in a criminal action has the right to one appeal, but the state cannot appeal a not guilty verdict except in a few situations. Appeals are usually granted as a matter of right, too, when the issues involve the construction of the state or the federal constitutions or statutes. The United States Supreme Court has the power to declare an act of Congress invalid because contrary to the Constitution. The high court of each state normally has the same power with regard to acts violating the state constitution.

Ordinarily a litigant must exhaust the remedies in the original court before he asks for an appeal, so he may ask the court for a *stay of execution* and a new trial. The judge may set a time for arguing the motion for a new trial. If the judge refuses to grant a new trial, the party may still ask a higher court to grant a new trial or to review certain factors of the original trial.

Appeals and new trials are ordinarily sought on the grounds that an error was made in the lower court which affected the verdict. Such errors might be the admission of evidence which should have been excluded because it was immaterial or incompetent, or the exclusion of evidence which should have been admitted, errors in the judge's charge to the jury, prejudice on the part of one of the jurors, a verdict clearly against the weight of the evidence, or a defect in the papers. Appeals are also allowed, usually to the highest court in the state system, when a lower court certifies that the case involves important questions of law.

A reporter may first learn of the intent to appeal after the verdict in the original trial. A lawyer for the losing party may then announce that he will appeal. Sometimes such announcements need not be taken too seriously, for they may be made simply for effect and without any real intention of appealing.

The first official step to be taken by a party seeking to appeal is to file with the clerk of the court of original jurisdiction and with the opposing party a written notice of the intention to appeal from the judgment or part of it. This must be done within a certain number of days (usually 30 to 90) after the original judgment.

The party seeking the appeal then becomes the *appellant* or sometimes the *plaintiff in error*. The other party may be called the *appellee*, the *defendant in error*, or the *respondent*. In a few states the plaintiff and defendant in the original action keep those designations through appellate proceedings.

The appellant has the responsibility of supplying the higher court with the record of the case or whatever part of it is necessary to consider the points he is bringing up. In many states the record must be printed when an appeal is taken to one of the high courts. This is expensive and makes it difficult for some individuals to appeal, although there is usually a provision that a "poor person" can submit typed copies of the record. A "poor person" is one who swears that he is not worth more than a certain amount of money—usually a few hundred dollars.

In some jurisdictions, a *bill of exceptions* must be filed along with the record. A bill of exceptions is a formal statement of the objections taken during the trial to rulings, decisions, or instructions of the presiding judge. Usually, too, the appellant has to post a bond as surety that he will pay costs if he loses the appeal.

Sometimes the attorney for the appellant seeks to have the case reviewed by asking the higher court to issue a *writ of error,* a *certiorari,* or a *writ of review.* Not all of these are used in all jurisdictions and they have special uses, but the effect is to order the lower court to send up the record for review.

When a federal question is involved in a proceeding in a state court, the United States Supreme Court may use a *certiorari* to order the record sent from the state court for review, to determine whether a federal right is violated. Federal questions come up quite frequently in civil rights cases because the Fourteenth Amendment provides that "All persons born or naturalized in the United States and subject to the jurisdiction thereof" shall be citizens of the United States as well as the states in which they reside. It also declares: "No State shall make or enforce any law which shall abridge the privileges or immunities of citizens of the United States; nor shall any State deprive any person of life, liberty, or property, without due process of law; nor deny to any person within its jurisdiction the equal protection of the law."

An attorney who feels that a state court has violated this provision may ask that the United States Supreme Court issue a writ ordering the state court to send up the record for review. The Supreme Court will consider the application. If it grants the motion it will review the case. If it denies the motion the lower decision is, of course, left unchanged, although it is not correct to say that the Supreme Court affirmed it—it simply left it unchanged.

The appellate court usually consists of a panel of judges who sit without a jury, since they are deciding matters of law. They may review only certain aspects of a case, such as the admission of certain evidence or the judge's charge to the jury, or they may review the case in detail. Sometimes they interpret the law and send the case back to the lower court for a finding in keeping with their interpretation.

Reporter's Problems

Perhaps the most difficult part of the reporter's job in covering civil and appellate courts is *to understand* the legal maneuvers and terminol-

ogy, but *to write* the story so that it is free from unnecessary legal terminology and unencumbered by procedural matters which the reader does
not need to know to understand the case. When a reporter develops the
expertness he needs to cover the courts properly, he is in danger of losing
his understanding of the layman's need to be told what is happening in
everyday terms.

In court actions, as in any other story, the reporter should try to report the story so that the reader will be interested and, if possible, so
that he will understand how it affects him. Not all court actions have a
direct bearing on the lives of readers, but many do. Tax cases, for example, are likely to affect the pocketbooks of many persons other than
those directly involved in the litigation. Precedent-setting cases are highly
important news and it is worth a great deal of effort to write them so
that the general public can understand them and evaluate their importance.

Standards of news values govern stories about court proceedings, as
they do any other kind of story. Famous names, large sums of money,
novel or dramatic circumstances, importance to the reader—these are the
factors which make for good news stories. One of the reporter's jobs is
to dig through the mass of detail he will find in the proceedings of any
court and tell his readers the things they need to know in terms they can
understand.

REPORTING ASSIGNMENTS

1. Visit as many civil courts as possible and write stories for local publication about the cases being tried. Use court records to supplement
your observation.

2. Interview an official of one of the civil courts in your community for
a feature story about his work.

3. Write an article describing the civil courts in your area. Name them
and tell the jurisdiction of each.

4. Write a feature story telling how wills are probated in your community.

PART THREE

Informal Areas of Public Affairs

14

Politics

Newspapers and Politics

As long as there have been newspapers they have been concerned with politics. This was true in England, where many restraints were imposed on printers because the king or members of Parliament resented criticism. They professed to believe that the public had no right to know about public business.

Benjamin Franklin got his first chance to be a publisher because of a row over a bit of political news. His brother James published in the *New England Courant* for June 11, 1722, a letter purporting to be from a correspondent in Rhode Island. One sentence read: "We are advised from Boston that the Government of Massachusetts are fitting out a ship to go after the pirates, to be commanded by Captain Peter Papillon, and 'Tis thought that he will sail sometime this month, wind and weather permitting."

The council, regarding this as a hint that the government was guilty of delay, ordered James Franklin arrested. When James admitted that he was the publisher of the offending paper, he was ordered imprisoned for four weeks. Brother Benjamin took over the publisher's duties for that period.

It was politics again that touched off the famous trial of John Peter Zenger in New York in 1735. Zenger's *New York Journal* had carried articles critical of Governor Cosby.

The American Revolution itself was partly planned in the Boston print shop of Edes and Gill, where Sam Adams met his little band of revolutionists.

After the Constitutional Convention of 1787, newspapers again played an important role in a far-reaching political decision. The Federalist papers, written by Jefferson and Madison, were clever arguments for the adoption of the Constitution. Appearing in newspapers throughout the colonies, they were given credit for turning the tide toward ratification, and thus allowing the United States to become, in fact, a united nation.

It is dramatic to tell how newspapers were concerned with politics at crisis periods of our history. However, these instances only highlight a process which is going on all the time. Newspapers, magazines, and radio and television stations are the nerve system of democracy. Without them democratic government would not work. Every election is preceded by political reporting. Stories of trends and personalities help to keep the citizens informed about political activities between elections.

We will be concerned in this chapter with many of the problems of politics. One of the most important of these is also a problem in communication. How can we interest more people in politics? This is the job of a reporter and editor just as much as it is the job of a politician.

Another problem is of basic concern to the reporter. Politics gives a reporter many chances to express his own biases. It is easy to be unbiased in reporting a scientific discovery, but hard when covering a favorite politician. The reporter's job is to tell the reader what he needs to know, without trying to make up the reader's mind. This is not easy.

Political reporting requires much practical as well as theoretical knowledge. A reporter must understand political parties and party structure. He must understand, too, how the play of personalities affects the political process. Much of a reporter's background can come from books and college courses. Much must come from first hand observation of events and personalities.

Practical economics, the "who gets what" of our society, is the motivating force for much of our political activity. Therefore, to truly understand his subject, the political reporter must understand its economic foundations.

Organization for Political Action

The purpose of political parties is to try to get their ideas adopted and their candidates elected. Of course, before they enter a campaign the members must agree among themselves on candidates and issues.

Government, particularly democratic government, is compromise, and political parties are one of the devices used to achieve this. Much argument and maneuvering precede the adoption of a platform and selection of candidates at a political convention.

Democratic government, ideally, is constantly changing to reflect new situations and new ideas, while remaining loyal to the basic concepts of free choice and individual liberty in an ordered society.

Although political parties are not perfect, they are the best system we have invented so far for achieving orderly change. In some countries change is possible only through violence. Political party activity is one of the means we use to achieve change peacefully. As such, politics deserves the interest and participation of every citizen. General participation in party politics is the only final answer to inadequacies in our party system. If the government turns out to be rotten, it is usually because the citizenry has, by ignoring it, turned it over to those who are eager to use it for private gain.

Some political scientists class all the informal decision-making machinery as part of the political process. For example, they point out that even after a party has been elected to office, policy decisions are reached by political methods—bargaining and all the rest. This is reasonable. For the political reporter, however, the concept of politics is much closer to the everyday one with which his reader is already familiar.

Parties: One, Two, or Many?

Since we live in a two-party country we are likely to regard all political activity in the light of the two-party system. Actually, one-, two-, and multiparty systems are used in different countries.

One-party countries usually are governed by a dictator. This does not always mean that only one party exists, but it does mean that the same one wins every election. Sometimes a dictator will pride himself on maintaining an opposition party to prove how democratic he is. If a true dictatorship exists the second party never wins an election. Sometimes a few members of the opposition party may be elected to a national assembly, but usually they do not receive even this much recognition.

Russia is our most important one-party country. There voters do not dare vote for anyone except candidates of the Communist party; and the man who controls the party controls Russia. Joseph Stalin sometimes held high government office; more often he had no official position. As secretary of the Communist party, he ruled with an iron fist.

In such a country the party is kept relatively small, and membership in it often entitles a person to special privileges. Elections, if they are held, merely serve a propaganda purpose.

The two-party system is found in the United States and England. In these countries two major parties dominate. Minor ones may exist, but they have little hope of gaining power. The only way a minor party can win an election is by supplanting one of the existing major parties and thus becoming a major party itself.

In England the two parties are the Conservatives and the Laborites. In the United States they are the Republicans and the Democrats.

Whichever party wins an election is charged, through its elected officials, with running the country. The losing party has the almost equally important function of serving as the opposition, questioning the government's decisions, suggesting improvements, and generally being the people's watchdog.

In England this watchdog function is more clearly seen than it is in the United States, because of the parliamentary form of government. The prime minister is a member of the House of Commons and the leader of the party in power. He can be questioned by the opposition on the floor of the House. If he loses a crucial vote he is expected to resign because that means he no longer controls the majority.

In the United States, since the president is elected independent of Congress, the "watchdog" function is not quite so easily carried out. A president cannot be called for questioning before Congress or a Congressional committee, although cabinet members sometimes appear. The president's press conference helps to fill this void, although it has no official status.

The French government illustrates the multiparty system. Several parties usually win enough votes to be influential in the French National Assembly. In the first election under the Fifth Republic, in November, 1958, 2,784 candidates representing six major and 12 minor parties or segments of parties sought the 465 seats filled by voters in continental France. Residents of Algeria and four overseas territories elected the rest of the 546 French deputies.

Many parties result in government by coalition. Since no party has a clear majority, a premier must seek agreement among several parties and appoint their leaders to his cabinet. Such a cabinet has less stability than one composed of a single party, since it can be upset if representatives of one or two parties decide to pull out. They may direct their members in the Assembly to vote against the premier, thus forcing him to resign. The new premier will have to try to form a new cabinet, often by putting together the same pieces which have just fallen apart. Thus it is the multiparty system which is at least partly responsible for the dreary record of six-month premiers and ineffectual leadership which beset France during the Fourth Republic, which ended with the adoption of the new constitution in 1958.

This constitution provided for the election of deputies from single-member constituencies, rather than a system of proportional representation which included election of deputies on a Department-wide basis. Each party would present a list of candidates equal to the number of deputies to be elected from the Department. If a party polled a quarter of the votes it was awarded a quarter of the Department's seats in the Assembly.

At times this can work to the advantage of strong, centrally-controlled parties, but it also allows minor parties to elect delegates when they might not otherwise be able to do so. Suppose in the United States, for example, it takes 20,000 votes to elect a representative to the legislature of a given state. It is quite likely that a minor party could muster 20,000 votes throughout the state and thus could elect a representative under a system of state-wide elections and proportional representation. With the state divided into election districts, however, it is unlikely that there will be enough minor party votes in any one district to elect a representative.

The multiparty system has some advantages. Most important are two:

1. It forces issues into the open where the general public can look at them. In a two-party system differences are likely to be settled in party conventions and caucuses, so that the party can present a united front in Parliament or Congress. Only the major issues, usually oversimplified, are ironed out in the arena of the Senate or the House of Commons. In France these have been fought out in the National Assembly where they have all the dignity associated with the nation's highest legislative body. This results in more thorough discussion and it gives observers a better chance to study motivations of politicians.

2. It tends to give better representation to minor opinion groups. In a multiparty system, the believers in a high tariff may be able to form a party to support that single idea. The Socialists are able to elect representatives to the legislative body. This gives their representative a better chance to get their ideas across to the electorate.

Why doesn't our two-party system gradually develop into a three- or four- or five-party system? After all, we allow third and fourth parties on the ballot and there are minor parties in many states.

The answer is that our election laws make it very difficult for a third party to gain a foothold.

We have already noticed that the major parties are constantly watching the minor ones for cues on popular issues. By adopting these themselves they are likely to win back converts from the minor parties. We have already seen, too, that our habit of geographical representation makes it difficult for a third party to achieve power.

Combine with this the fact that voting districts are drawn up by representatives of the major parties. If there is a determined group of minor party voters in a given area, it is easy in redistricting to split this segment into two or three other districts, where minor party voters will be outvoted by the major parties.

All kinds of special restrictions, too, can be brought to bear to make difficult the survival of a third party. Warren Moscow points out in "Politics in the Empire State" that the New York State election law requires 60,000 signatures on a petition before a new party can run a state-wide ticket. In New York State it might not be difficult to collect this many signatures. The joker is an added requirement that at least 50 signatures must come from each of the state's 66 counties. Two or three of the upstate counties are very small and very much under the control of the Republican organization. The control is so tight that it is very difficult for a minor party to get the required 50 signatures from these counties.

All the advantages of established position work for the benefit of the major parties, too. The strength of patronage, unavailable to minor parties, helps the dominant parties. Since the major parties already have representatives in state and national forums they can more easily keep themselves in the spotlight.

The major parties, too, can more successfully solicit campaign funds. This is extremely important in these days when campaigning is often done in paid radio and television time, and through newspaper and billboard advertisements.

All this is not to say that a minor party never becomes a major one in the United States, but this has never happened without a corresponding decline in one of the existing major parties. The last minor party to make the grade was the Republican party with the election of Abraham Lincoln in 1860. The Republicans built their party partly out of the collapse of the Whigs.

Some powerful bids have been made by third parties. Theodore Roosevelt, running as the Progressive Party candidate, split the Republican party in the election of 1912 and thus insured the election of Woodrow Wilson, the Democratic candidate.

How Are Parties Organized?

At the start we should remember that the laws which govern the organization and conduct of political parties are state laws. This means that representatives are elected to our federal government by election systems which are to some extent out of its control. This has led to some interesting questions of power politics and occasional agitation for a national election law. Some object because the qualifications of voters who elect members of Congress and our president are decided by state legislatures or in state referendums. To most people this seems one of the minor criticisms of our election system.

Because parties and election procedures are controlled by the states, it is not possible to draw a picture that applies throughout the country. The interstate similarities, however, far overshadow the differences.

Party organization usually follows governmental organization. At the bottom is the precinct committeeman or precinct captain. He may have assistants or he may work alone. In a well-organized party it is his job to know every voter and to do his best to get every voter to favor his party. In populous areas he needs helpers, and the territory may be divided into blocks, with each individual responsible for a block.

The precinct captain adapts his activities to the type of people in his precinct. In places where families are poor he does the traditional things we associate with political workers. He sees to it that no one in his block goes hungry or without heat, even if he has to pay the bill himself. He suggests that family members, in return, might vote for his party. If people get into trouble with the police he may help them over the hurdle, either by supplying legal aid or by using a "fix" arranged through party headquarters. This type of activity is more successful in bad times with many people out of work than in good times. It is more successful, too, in areas with many foreign-born citizens who have not yet learned how to get along in their new country. This kind of activity accounted for the years of domination by "political machines" in many of our major cities.

In more prosperous times and communities, the precinct captain may call on voters and try to persuade them to vote for his party's candidates. His direct service to the voter is usually limited to offers of transportation to the polls or supplying a baby sitter while the mother goes out to vote. He is a little more effective in delivering the vote for his party if he can offer summer jobs to the sons of voters in his area, but patronage has become less important.

In cities the next level of political organization is the ward. The precinct committeemen together usually form the ward committee, which is headed by a ward leader. His responsibility is to help the precinct workers and to keep the ward in his party's pocket.

In rural areas the towns are usually broken down into election districts, so that party organization follows along. The district workers report to a town leader.

The ward and town leaders usually form a county committee which elects a county chairman. In most states the county committees and the county chairmen are very influential in their state politics and so eventually in national affairs.

A state governor has the power to fill a number of good jobs by appointment. Either he or his political advisors see that the jobs are distributed throughout the state for the greatest benefit to a party. Sometimes a deserving county chairman is rewarded with a high-paying job. Sometimes he is given a chance to recommend a person from his county who is appointed to the job. This gives the county chairman increased influence with local workers.

State committees head up the state organization. These are usually composed of county chairmen, and they derive their influence from the fact that each of the members is a power in his home area.

At the top of the hierarchy are the national committees which hold the power of the party between conventions. These are headed by the national chairmen.

In addition there may be district committees based on either congressional districts, judicial districts, or other political subdivisions.

Selection of Candidates and Platforms

American party politics has provided two major means for selecting candidates and issues. These are direct primaries and conventions. A third way is the caucus.

"Caucus" is a word used to indicate various kinds of meetings of members of a political party. It is commonly applied to a meeting of all the Republican or all the Democratic members of a legislative body, perhaps a state legislature or the U.S. Senate or House of Representatives. These meetings are commonly held to decide the action to be taken by the party with regard to an issue. Less frequently a caucus is used to nominate candidates, although this was common practice in the early days of our political life.

Conventions

In the early days high state officials were usually nominated by the party members in the legislature, while the president and vice-president were nominated by the members of each party in Congress.

In 1844, as the convention system was rising in popularity, John C. Calhoun wrote this defense of the caucus:

> Objectionable as I think a congressional caucus for nominating a President, it is in my opinion far less so than a convention constituted as is proposed. The former had indeed many things to recommend it. Its members . . . the immediate organs of the State Legislatures or the people; were responsible to them, respectively, and were for the most part of high character, standing, or talents. They voted per capita; and, what is very important, they represented fairly the relative strength of their party in their respective states. In all these important particulars it was all that could be desired of a nominating body. . . . I acting with General Jackson and most of the leaders of the party at that time, contributed to put it down, because we believed it to be liable to be acted upon and influenced by the patronage of the government—an objection far more applicable to a convention.

Despite the objections of Calhoun and others, conventions were widely used in America during the nineteenth century. Usually they came under the regulation of the state governments, and sometimes that regulation was not as strict as might have been desired.

The casual quality of some of the early conventions is illustrated by the manner in which West Virginia's 14 ballots were cast in the 1836 Democratic convention in Baltimore. Edward Ricker of West Virginia happened to be in Baltimore at the time of the convention, so he attended. Being a Van Buren man, he cast the state's votes for Van Buren.

Proponents of reform in convention procedure cited horrendous details of convention irregularities. One tally of the Cook County (Illinois) convention of 1896 showed that of the 723 delegates, 17 had been tried for homicide, 46 had served terms in the penitentiary for homicide or other felonies, 84 were said by detectives to have criminal records, more than one third were saloon-keepers, 2 kept houses of ill fame, and several kept gambling resorts.

Today's conventions are much more carefully regulated by state governments and by the publicity in which they operate.

Most spectacular are the national conventions, in which the parties nominate their candidates for the presidency and vice-presidency and adopt their national platforms. In some states the convention is used to nominate high state officials, while the direct primary is used for local officials. In New York State, for example, state officers and senators are nominated in state conventions and supreme court justices are nominated by district conventions, while other officers are nominated in direct primaries.

The Direct Primary

First adopted in Crawford County, Pennsylvania, in 1869, the direct primary is now in use in some form in all states except Connecticut and Rhode Island.

The direct primary gives voters of a party a chance to vote for candidates for their party's nomination. Voters may enroll in a party when they register or at a previous election.

Direct primaries have been hailed as the answer to the problem of bringing true democracy into the nominating process. As we shall see, they function less than perfectly.

Robert La Follette, the Wisconsin liberal, became a bitter foe of conventions, claiming that voters nominated him in 1896 and 1898 in primaries, but that delegates were bought off at the conventions. He said it cost the machine $8,300 to buy the delegates at the 1898 convention.

In his autobiography, La Follette commented:

> Conventions have been and will continue to be prostituted to the services of corrupt organization. They answer no purpose further than to give respectable form to political robbery. Abolish the caucus and convention. Go back to the first principles of democracy; go back to the people. Substitute for both caucus and convention a primary election—held under the sanction of laws which prevail at general elections—where the citizen may

cast his vote directly to nominate the candidates of the party with which he affiliates and have it canvassed and returned just as he cast it. . . . Then every citizen will share equally in the nomination of the candidates of his party and attend primary elections as a privilege as well as a duty. It will no longer be necessary to create an artificial interest in the general election to induce voters to attend. Intelligent, well considered judgment will be substituted for unthinking enthusiasm, and the lamp of reason for the torchlight. . . . The nominations of the party will not be the result of compromise or evil design.

La Follette was elected governor in 1900 thanks to a rift in the party machine. In 1904 he got his direct primary law.

Often states will combine a convention and a primary system, with party voters electing the delegates to a convention. Often delegates to a convention are not legally bound to support any given candidates; thus it is questionable whether this procedure results in any real increase in influence for the voter. Some states require that a slate of delegates pledged to support a given candidate will have to vote for him until he releases them or is out of the picture. When the candidate is a "favorite son" with slight chances of being nominated, this results in the voters' power being entrusted to him, because he can control his state's votes.

The primary system has not succeeded in taking control of the nominating machinery out of the hands of the people who make a business of politics, and it is doubtful that any system will do this. Relatively few votes are necessary to control a primary election because most people think it is not very important and so do not bother to vote in it. If an election district contains 600 votes and they are equally divided between two parties, it is easy to see that only 151 votes would be necessary to control a primary election, even if all the eligible voters participated. With the general apathy about primaries, it may take considerably fewer votes than this. Often 60 votes or less will control a primary. A few workers and their families can easily account for these and thus control the party's nomination. This means that the voter's power of selection is really limited to registering a choice between the candidates presented by each of the major party organizations.

Such a process often leads to so much apathy that only one slate will appear on the primary ballot—the slate supported by the regular party organization. The fact that there is no competition means that voters have even less inclination to vote. This makes it still easier for those most interested to control the primary elections, and so the cycle goes.

The real problem is not one of machinery; it is one of interest. When local people of courage become interested in challenging a local political organization they have the machinery to do it, and sometimes primaries have been taken away from the regular party organizations. The keys are interest and energy. Usually the primaries are won by the regular party organizations. That result is only natural because the persons in the organizations are the ones who display the interest and energy necessary to win an election.

Giving More Control to the Electorate

Conscientious politicians and citizens for many years have been trying to give the electorate more power over the affairs of government. The results have been expressed in four ways: shorter ballot, initiative, referendum, and recall. These devices have sometimes seemed to serve their original purposes. Sometimes they have worked in strange and wonderful ways to circumvent their purposes.

Simplification of voting procedure has resulted in shorter ballots and use of voting machines in some states. Until around the middle of the nineteenth century printed ballots were distributed in advance by the candidates or their parties. A voter carried the ballots to the polls and deposited the one indicating his choice. Political managers could make sure voters were being regular simply by making their ballots distinctive. They used a certain color or a distinctive typographical device so they could observe who was casting ballots for their party. This was made to order for buying and selling votes.

Now in almost every state the ballots are printed by public officials at public expense. A single ballot lists candidates of all parties, and, if a voter marks his ballot in private and deposits it folded in the ballot box, it is impossible for anyone to know how he voted.

In a few states voting machines have further simplified voting. A voter enters a closed booth and flips down levers indicating his preferences. When he moves a master lever it records the votes, returns the voting levers to normal, and then opens the curtains surrounding the booth. When the polls are closed at the end of the day, election officials open the back of the machine and the votes on all candidates and issues are tabulated. This saves hours of hand-counting of paper ballots. It is more accurate than hand-counting and makes results available many hours earlier. Voting machines are not in more general use because of the heavy initial cost of installing them, and because many politicians seem to fear their adoption.

Some states have made considerable progress in shortening the ballot. This makes it easier for the voter to cast his ballot intelligently because he has a chance to study personalities and issues and vote for a dozen candidates, while this would be impossible for most people if they had to vote for 30 or 40 candidates.

During the first quarter of the present century much experimenting was done with three so-called methods of "direct democracy." Called the initiative, referendum, and recall, all were designed to put more power into the hands of the electorate.

The initiative and referendum, available in about a quarter of the states, make it possible for the voters to force through a constitutional amendment or a new statute even though the legislature may refuse to consider it.

Under this system a group of citizens proposing a new law can insist that it be submitted to the legislature or to the electorate. The procedure calls for a certain number of signatures on petitions, with various restrictions about the number that can come from each county. Sometimes the restrictions are so numerous and so complicated that the process is almost unworkable.

Arguments for the initiative and the referendum are that they enable the voters to push through a statute or a constitutional amendment which the legislature, perhaps because of the pressure of special interest groups, may refuse to pass. This has considerable merit, although it would seem more logical for the people to put the effort into electing legislators who are more friendly to the popular will.

Some argue that the initiative and the referendum make it easier to pass irresponsible laws, because the general voters can be stampeded by special interest groups more easily than the legislature. Among other arguments against them are these:

By making the ballot longer and more complicated, the referendum makes it even more difficult for the voter to take time to inform himself adequately and to vote intelligently.

The referendum may be used by the legislature as a device for passing the buck to voters on touchy issues.

There are other arguments on both sides. Whatever the reasons, the use of the initiative and the referendum has declined in states where they are available, and few states have adopted the device since the first quarter of the century.

The recall is a device used in some states by which the voters can force a new election in an effort to oust (or "recall") an official whom they consider derelict in his duties. Like the initiative, this requires a certain number of signatures on petitions. This device is more common in city than in state governments. It is different from impeachment proceedings, by which an official body may consider whether a government officer should be removed for failure to perform his duties or for misfeasance.

The real intent behind these devices is to heighten general interest in political affairs. For fairly brief periods they have been successful. For example, in referendums on hot issues the voters can become highly aroused. Over the long haul, however, little added voter interest can be laid directly to these devices. A heightened long-term interest in political affairs will have to come about through a new attitude toward politics achieved through education and the mass communication media. We will consider the newspaper's role in this educational process toward the end of this chapter.

The Campaign

The most spectacular phase of politics is the campaign and election, with the greatest public interest shown every four years in the national extravaganza by which we elect a president of the United States.

Political campaigns have fascinated writers and social scientists from the earliest days of our democracy. Voting habits was one of the early favorites for study among political scientists. Public opinion pollsters depend on the national elections every four years to demonstrate the accuracy of their predictive powers, and usually the demonstration is effective.

Electronic media of communication, radio and television, have combined with a more literate and informed electorate to change the nature of campaigning. The trend is away from personal contact, and toward reaching voters in their homes through newspapers, radio, and television.

Until the development of modern advertising and the electronic media, standard procedure was for the politician to travel as widely and as often through his constituency as his time and energy permitted. On his travels he shook as many hands as he could, and made a speech whenever he could assemble a group, perhaps only a small one on a street corner. If his electorate was small enough he would try to visit every home, take an interest in the householder's problems and those of the family, briefly tell why he should be elected, perhaps leave a cigar, and be on his way.

Presidential candidates, of course, could not campaign as intimately as this, but they followed the same pattern as far as possible. They traveled the country widely, made rear platform appearances from early morning until late at night, shook hands by the thousand, and generally used the old tried and true methods.

There were exceptions. In 1920 Republican candidate Warren G. Harding conducted a "front porch" campaign. He made a few addresses, but most of the time stayed at his home in Marion, Ohio, and received delegations from all over the country. The reporters covering the campaign got their material from statements the candidate made to the visiting delegations. Over a period this spelled out a rather complete discussion of the issues.

In the most recent campaigns the presidential candidates have done a great deal of traveling, but the heavy emphasis has come more and more to rest on the mass media, rather than on personal contact, to put across a candidate's message and personality.

Also, there is a tendency to turn a part of the campaign over to advertising agencies, and to rely fairly heavily on advertising men as advisors in all aspects of a campaign. Senator Richard Neuberger of Oregon stated the objections to this before his own election as United States Senator. The tendency, he said, is for the advertising people to look at the candidate as a commodity to sell, as they might sell toothpaste; this results in less emphasis on the issues and more on the personalities. The other major drawback is that it favors the candidate or party which has the most money. Money is used to buy the services of advertising agencies, time on radio and television stations, and advertising in newspapers and on billboards.

There is another side to this picture. When they are properly used, television and radio offer a means of achieving a more perfect democracy than we had believed possible in a country so vast as the United States.

Few presidents have held a tighter grip on popular favor than Franklin Delano Roosevelt; and no small part of his appeal was achieved by the highly skilled use he made of radio. What he might have done with television had that been available makes interesting speculation. His "Fireside Chats" made political history. He developed the technique when he was governor of New York, faced with the traditional dilemma of Democratic governors there—how to achieve a measure of control over a legislature in the hands of a persistent Republican majority.

Roosevelt got into the habit of appealing to the voters over the heads of the legislature, when the lawmakers refused to go along with him. He achieved some control over legislation by this means, and he cultivated a finished radio manner. He used it later in the White House to project his personality and ideas into millions of living rooms, with telling effect on his own political fortunes and on the trend of events in this country and the world.

All presidents since have used radio and television to report directly to the people. President Eisenhower, with the aid of his advisor, Robert Montgomery, went to the unusual length of allowing the televising of a cabinet meeting. The members heard a report from Secretary of State John Foster Dulles after he had returned from an important trip to Europe. Members were given questions to ask to add to the informality and apparent spontaneity of the occasion. The spontaneity was increased when one of the members forgot to interject his question and had to be cued by Secretary Dulles.

Another effect of the rise of television has been the deliberate attempt by both major parties to put on a good show for television viewers at the national conventions. It is doubtful whether this adds any prestige to the conventions as nominating and policy-forming bodies, but it was probably inevitable that publicity-minded political managers would seek to take advantage of the free television time offered by networks covering the conventions as news.

The changes wrought by radio and television are most dramatic on the national scene, but they are important, too, on state and local levels.

Many local politicians seem to be convinced that the most effective way of reaching voters of a city is to buy television time, either for "spot" commercial announcements lasting a minute or less, or for speeches or forums. It is worth noting that this change is not something entirely brought about or controlled by the politicians. People seem to be less willing to go out to attend political rallies. Candidates just cannot draw a crowd by having a torchlight parade or by hiring a brass band as they traditionally used to do. The voters tend to sit home and turn on the political program on television—if it has sufficient interest for them.

Covering the Campaign

The standard bill of fare for a political reporter during campaigns consists of speeches, dinners, statements, and general coverage of the activities of candidates. A feature of national elections is the candidates' special trains, which are well staffed by correspondents of the press associations and the major newspapers.

Campaigning is strenuous work for the campaigner; it is just as strenuous for the reporters who cover the campaign. In an article in "Times Talk," house magazine of the *New York Times,* Anthony Leviero tells what it's like to be on a campaign special. He is describing President Truman's campaign for Governor Stevenson in 1952:

> Mr. Truman is likely to start his whistle-stopping at 6:45 A.M. (Indianapolis, for instance). Then, if there is a crowd on hand, he'll wind up the day at 11:30 P.M. That wouldn't be a bad day. One could fit in some sleep. But along around 11 P.M. Mr. Truman's press secretary springs a prepared speech on you. It is scheduled for delivery sometime next day. Well, you had better stay up and write it then and there.
>
> In the first place, you don't dare wait until the following day because you have to spend your time hopping off and on at the whistle stops. You never can tell what may happen at the back platform. And you can't take chances on your telegraph facilities, even though Carroll S. Linkins of Western Union gets them lined up in fine shape. Forty or fifty reporters pouring out thousands of words often swamp the facilities, especially in the great Western voids.
>
> Often you get a prepared speech during the day, too. Thus you often find yourself trying to make a coherent story out of two prepared speeches and ten or twelve off-the-cuff talks that you file more or less in fragments from points in one, two or three states.
>
> Let's pause to pity the poor copy editor. He gets the fragments of copy from scattered points, and as like as not he'll receive copy filed at 1 P.M.

before the stuff that was dropped off at 10 A.M. That "dropped off" should be taken literally. Sometimes the copy is put into envelopes weighted with nuts, bolts and washers and tossed from the speeding train to an alerted Western Union man at some hamlet, and that man sometimes has to drive fifty miles to get the copy to a good telegraph point.

At Davis, Calif., Mr. Truman encountered his first lively hecklers one night, and the next filing point was San Francisco, two hours later. Mr. Linkins dropped off one of his men who telephoned all the inserts on that meeting to Western Union in Frisco. Otherwise the incident would hardly have made any morning papers.

This gives us some idea of the pace at which reporters have to work and how they go about it. A little later in the story, Mr. Leviero voices the standard complaint of reporters and campaigners on the "specials"— no chance to take a bath, get clothes laundered, or sleep.

Baths are a wonderful thing on the Truman Rocket Ship. That is, the baths are not on the train, but it is wonderful when you can get one. (Mr. Truman, but only Mr. Truman, has a shower.) Westward bound, around the third day, the people of Columbia Falls, Mont., opened their high school showers and the great unwashed were cleansed. Great place, Columbia Falls. Then there was the night the train was to lay over at Wilson Creek, Wash. But the Secret Service advised everybody to stay aboard because the train was in a rattlesnake habitat, so the bath situation wasn't investigated.

As for laundry, the collector's item is the Hotel Fairmont's (Frisco) laundry bill: $9.27. Ordinary shirts, 65¢ each; sport shirts, 90¢ each, probably because they have short sleeves and short tails.

Railroad fare for the cross-country trip alone will exceed $600, which is a lot of money to pay for the use of a berth four or five hours out of each twenty-four.

Another highly respected newspaperman is not sold on the great emphasis placed on coverage of the election special trains. In a talk before the American Society of Newspaper Editors in Washington in 1956, Roy A. Roberts of the *Kansas City Star* said, "Coverage of a campaign from the presidential candidate train is the poorest spot in the world."

He urged reporters to go out "to original sources of information, and that is the voter."

A state, city, county, or congressional district campaign can be just as strenuous for a newsman, although none of them achieves quite the glamor of a presidential campaign.

A reporter covering a local election is also likely to find that he can't do the job in a normal working day. He has the additional problem of remaining objective in the face of pressure from all kinds of local politicians, many of them important persons.

Election Day Stories

Election day ends campaigning for the candidates, but it does not end a political reporter's chores. An election, even a local election, is a big story, and the political reporter turns from the last campaign rally to write the first stories on the election as the returns begin to trickle in.

Many a newspaperman takes it for granted that he will not get to bed at all on election night. Instead he and his co-workers preside over the machinery they have set up to collect the votes and tabulate them, so that the voters can know the next day whom they have elected. Often newspapers press into service ad takers, circulation people, and part time workers. The more reporters that newspapers have scattered around at the different polling places, the quicker the returns will come in.

The general plan of election coverage is simple, but the number of details to be supervised for a one-night stand can make it extremely complicated. It is simplified somewhat when voting machines are used. The managing editor arranges, if possible, to have someone at each polling place when the polls close, to take down the totals when the machines are officially read, and then to hurry to a telephone and give the results to a clerk who records them at the office. Adding machines from the business office are often used to tally up the votes, and a running score is kept. The process is complicated where paper ballots are used, because the reporters have to wait around until the votes are counted; this may last far into the night and often the reporter has to keep checking so that he does not miss the final tally. There always seems to be one (at least) election board which becomes tired early and closes up shop, waiting until the next day to finish the count.

As the votes begin to come in the political reporter takes over again, for it is his job to tell the readers what the early returns mean. Often, too, the local radio and television stations will try to press him into service to interpret the results for their listeners and viewers.

In national elections the local scene is about the same, with added drama coming from the job of getting local results on the wire and receiving national figures back from the press associations. These agencies plan their election coverage months in advance, often basing their organization on the local newspapers. Newspapers and press services spend several hundreds of thousands of dollars to tabulate votes from 150,000 precincts in more than 3,000 counties. *Editor & Publisher* estimated that in the 1956 election 75,000 newsmen would be working, and between 10 P.M. and midnight of election night national headquarters would tabulate nearly 150,000 votes a minute.

News media in Texas have consolidated their efforts in election coverage. How this paid off in a 1957 election is described in the *UP Reporter,* a bulletin put out at that time for client papers by the United Press:

> Tabulation of the Texas senatorial election went ahead smoothly this week despite the fact that a tornado hit Dallas a few hours before the polls closed. This could happen only in Texas. In other states either the tornado coverage or the election tabulation would have suffered. The reason is that Texas has a central bureau which tabulates all election returns. This is a pooled effort by the newspapers, radio and TV. Press association wires are used to distribute the returns to all media. The wire services write their own leads based on returns which are available to all.

Unofficial returns, compiled by the news media, are invariably days ahead of the official tabulations. Without the work of the newsmen, the results of elections might not become known for days or weeks after election day.

Between-Election Coverage

After the returns are in and reported, the reporter turns back to his quest to answer *"why?"* As a nation we have a mania for trying to find out why we voted as we did. After election day every barber shop sprouts its own set of experts. The political reporter is almost forced to get into the game. He has to put his views before the public, and he is almost as vulnerable as the baseball reporter who analyzes why the local fans' favorite club failed to come through.

After the analysis of the previous election is over the political reporter relies on dope stories—somewhat similar to the between-season stories of the sports writer.

While the general interest in politics dies down between elections, the activity of the professional does not stop. As soon as one election has been won or lost, the true professional begins to plan to win the next one. There is much analysis of the previous campaign, which may lead to changes in party officials or in the platform.

This activity is only partly reportable, but a reporter with good contacts will be able to discover most of what is going on and to report at least some of it. He will also cover many of the party meetings at which new policy is activated.

Patronage and its political use does not stop between campaigns, and the reporter should tell his readers what people are given jobs, and explain the political (or other) motivation behind the appointment.

Backgrounding is one of the skills of the political reporter, and sometimes he uses information the source of which he cannot reveal. This is why he needs to be close to private sources of information. Political reporters have to be superior fact finders in often difficult and confusing situations, and they must be persons of judgment and veracity so that their stories will be believed.

The political reporter is obligated, too, to help his readers keep a running audit of how the party in power is living up to its campaign promises. Most readers do not have the time and facilities to check what candidates said and what the platform stated against what officials actually did after they were elected. A reporter can keep a constant check of action against promises, and this is one of the services he should offer readers. It is a service very much in line with our traditional concept of the newspaper as a guardian of our political liberties and a watchdog on our public officials.

Political Problems as Reporting Problems

Newspapers and magazines, and to a lesser extent radio and television stations, are sensing more and more that their responsibility in politics does not stop with reporting and interpreting events. The importance of a running account of everyday doings in politics is obvious. Equally so is the importance of background writing to make clear the significance of today's events. Editors and writers are also assuming responsibility for a more creative kind of reporting—the kind which recognizes a problem and helps to clarify it by bringing it to public attention.

As our educational level increases so will our need for more of this kind of reporting. As more sophisticated readers are turned out by our secondary schools and universities, they will demand more sophisticated reporting, as represented by coverage of problems. It seems inevitable that gradually problem reporting in politics and other areas will take the dominant role in newspapers and other public information media. This does not mean that reporting of day-to-day events will be eliminated; it does mean that it will be supplemented by a new kind of reporting.

In the following pages we will consider some of the problem areas of politics and how these problems affect political reporting.

Single-Party Domination

While we in the United States have a healthy two-party situation in many areas, we have also many places where there is only one effective party. We have only to look at the "Solid South" for confirmation. In several of our Southern states the election of a Republican official is unheard of. Areas of similar Republican domination are smaller, with even Vermont beginning to elect some Democrats.

The problem is acute on the local level; there are many cities in which one party dominates the scene entirely.

Abuses arise inevitably where one party is so strongly entrenched that it does not have to worry about the outcome of elections. Wielding the power of government is heady business—on the local scene as well as nationally. Executives and legislators make decisions which affect profoundly the lives of many persons. Many of us cannot wield such power for long without having it change our attitudes. Some officials tend after a while to confuse their own personal power with the power of the government office which has been entrusted to them. Officials who can make the separation after many years in power are the happy exceptions to the rule. Some of the heroes in *Plutarch's Lives* are celebrated because they did not give in to a lust for power.

Despite the occasional heroes who are able to withstand the character erosion which often accompanies great power, it is healthy opposition which most often keeps government in line—opposition, plus public examination, in the press, of governmental activities.

A one-party situation means that there is less opportunity for the democratic process to function. If it is well known that the candidates of only one party can be elected, there is little point in an opposition vote. This leads to further decay in the minority party, and so even less opportunity for a voter to register effective opposition to the party in power. In effect, it means that there is no way in which an individual can protest a majority party decision.

To some extent battles inside the party replace the battles between parties. In the Southern states, for example, the real contests are held at the primaries, and the regular election simply ratifies primary results. This is ineffective at best as a replacement for a living two-party system.

A one-party community may sometimes become two-party in national elections. Part of the South has sometimes bolted the Democratic party in national elections, but this revolt seldom carries over to state and local elections.

Another of the ill effects of one party rule is that legislative bodies become stagnant. The Democratic party, for example, can always count on certain states to deliver Democrats to Congress, and thus furnish a nucleus of voting strength. This may be entirely the reverse of national trends, and, combined with the seniority system in Congress, it often gets in the way of effective legislation. It leads, too, to party lines being obliterated on some issues, with Democratic conservatives (usually from the South) combining with conservative Republicans against the more radical elements of both parties.

What can a newspaper do about areas of one-party domination? From a reporting angle it can only tell what is available to it. This means describing the activities of whatever parties are making news and also describing the real effects of one-party domination. On the editorial page it can serve as an example to the electorate by selecting candidates and issues on the basis of ability and good sense, regardless of party label.

The problem is deep seated and will be solved eventually only through the substitution of reason for emotion. In the South Republicans risk becoming social outcasts. Being a Democrat is just as disastrous in a few northern communities. That this is irrational does not change the fact. This is the reason so many northern Republicans change their registration when they move south. Most of the nice people are Democrats, and they want to associate with nice people, so they become Democrats, too.

Many observers feel that too long incumbency in any office by officials of one party is a negation of the two-party system. Such an idea is implied in the following lead on the 1952 election story in the *Christian Science Monitor* by Roscoe Drummond, then chief of the paper's Washington bureau:

> Gen. Dwight D. Eisenhower becomes the 34th President of the United States in a towering, national, personal triumph which dramatically ends the 20-year Democratic rule and restores the American two-party system to vigor and vitality.

States and other districts which traditionally turn in strong majorities for either party often feel that they are taken for granted. Southern voters have complained that neither candidate in a presidential election bothers to tour the South. The Democratic candidate knows he has the votes, while the Republican knows he cannot get them. With signs of the South splitting its votes a little in national elections, however, both parties are giving it more attention.

Other wails arise from one-party areas. Here is such an expression in an editorial in the Middletown, New York, *Times-Herald:*

> By-passing of Martin Rosenblum as a nominee for the federal bench lends dramatic impact to the oft remarked fact that Orange County is so "safely" Republican that it can be ignored by party leaders.
>
> Obviously, there can be no quibble with the qualifications of any of the four proposed by President Eisenhower to serve in the Southern District of New York. Nor, let it be emphasized, are the Rosenblum qualifications open to challenge.
>
> Aside from patronage, major considerations of practical politics are geography and political climate.
>
> On such a basis, it is safe to presume that both these considerations served to shunt Mr. Rosenblum aside.
>
> Our information from respected sources is that Mr. Rosenblum was the only upstate representative among a list of eleven passed along through political channels to Attorney General Brownell for recommendation to Mr. Eisenhower.
>
> Unfortunately, as has been demonstrated in this instance, Mr. Rosenblum

is a resident of Orange County. Because the political climate of the county is so overwhelmingly Republican, leaders of that party are safe in sprinkling the largess of political preferment anywhere else.

Mr. Eisenhower's four nominees are all from the metropolitan area. In their designation, it must also be presumed that geography and political climate were decisive.

The metropolitan area is not politically "safe" for either party. The record shows that.

But it does have hundreds upon hundreds of thousands of votes which can be a determining factor in elections—and this is an election year. Patronage considerations dictate the way many of those votes will be cast, a fact which is not of major concern for "safe" Orange County.

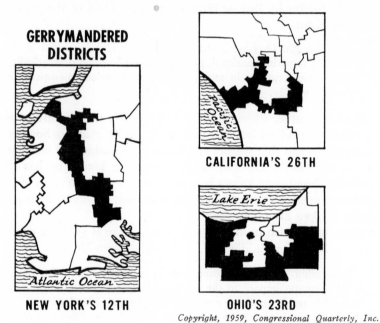

GERRYMANDERED DISTRICTS

NEW YORK'S 12TH

CALIFORNIA'S 26TH

OHIO'S 23RD

Copyright, 1959, Congressional Quarterly, Inc.

FIG. 14. Gerrymandering—drawing districts to achieve a political purpose—is an old American custom. Here are three gerrymandered Congressional districts.

Rotten Boroughs

The problem created by rotten boroughs, essentially, is that some people's votes have more power than the votes of others. Senator Richard L. Neuberger cites an example in *Adventures in Politics:*

The 4,125,000 urban residents of Los Angeles County have one Senator in the California legislature. Equal Senate representation with them is enjoyed by the 13,560 rural inhabitants of Mono and Inyo counties. What rare quality, perhaps peculiar to the remote Sierra Nevada Range, renders an Inyo County sheep rancher worthy of at least 300 times the strength in the California Senate of a Los Angeles surgeon or trolley conductor?

California is fairly typical. In most of our states the rural population dominates the legislatures. In New York the upstate voters constitute roughly 47 per cent of the population and elect 57 per cent of the members of the State Assembly. In New York State the Senate is even more tightly controlled by upstate voters, although there is more justification for that on the theory of area representation in the upper chamber.

Every ten years, after new census figures are available, seats in the House of Representatives are reapportioned, with states gaining or losing seats according to shifts in population. The state legislatures have power to arrange the boundaries of the new congressional districts. This is usually done to further the political ambitions of the members of the state legislatures. Since the rural influence predominates in the legislatures, it is very likely that it will predominate again in the districting for Congress, and so the rural influence is transplanted.

Senator Neuberger cites some dramatic figures to show inequities in representation in the House of Representatives.

For example:

The California 26th district has 480,827 residents; the 16th, only 223,703.

The Texas 8th has 806,000 residents; the same state's 17th has 226,000, giving citizens in the 17th between three and four times as much power per vote.

This underrepresentation in the cities leads to lack of interest in the House in problems of metropolitan areas, and to advantages for rural sections. Just as important, it makes it easier for the city voter to think that he might just as well forget about voting, since his vote counts for so little anyway.

Newspapers carry stories about redistricting haggling when it is taking place. This seems hardly enough attention to the problem, since it has much importance for everyone. It is likely to become more aggravated, too, if the trend continues for the population to migrate to metropolitan areas.

Voter Apathy

Why don't more people vote? This is a question politicians, newspaper editors, and citizens have been asking each other for a long time. The answers are not very clear yet, but it is clear that large numbers of our people just don't bother to go to the polls.

Our presidential campaigns are great shows which stir up more interest than any other political event, with the exception of an occasional hot local contest. Even in a presidential election, we are doing well when 60 per cent of the eligible voters cast a ballot. Only 51.5 per cent of the eligible voters went to the polls in November, 1948, the lowest per cent in several elections.

It is easy to think that it is the ignorant and uninformed citizens who fail to vote. That is not always true. A check in Syracuse, New York, of 4,000 members of 16 luncheon clubs and trade associations showed that 35 per cent failed to vote in an election for mayor and United States senator. The 4,000 whose names were checked on official election records were among the leaders of the community. In the following election the clubs put on a concentrated drive, and reduced the stay-at-homes from one out of three to one out of eight.

Whatever the cause, the apathy of voters raises some important questions. For instance: How successful are we if we just get more voters to the polls, without seeing to it that they are informed? In other words, is a large turnout at the polls a real measure of participation in the election process? However, there is logic to the argument that a person who votes is more likely to inform himself.

Intelligent voting by a high percentage of voters is the goal. This is of special interest to reporters of political affairs, for they are the ones who must funnel the information to prospective voters. If they do not adequately inform the readers, then the voting will be lighter and less intelligent.

Among the political reforms suggested to get more people to vote is permanent personal registration. Urged by the League of Women Voters and other groups, PPR, as it is called, is making real headway. It means that voters will not have to make two trips to the polls to vote. In most of our cities voters have to register a few weeks before election day. This means another trip to the polls, and those who don't bother to register cannot vote.

Permanent personal registration requires election officials to canvass periodically the lists of qualified voters. In this process they would eliminate the names of persons who have moved away or died. Thus it would not be necessary to open the polls before every election to make sure the voting list was honest.

Corruption in Politics

Politics and government are power centers of our society, so politicians are sometimes subjected to great pressures to profit from their positions. Some writers have built careers on exposing corruption in politics and other places. Lincoln Steffens and Ida Tarbell came to fame this way in the early days of "muckraking."

The exposé makes such dramatic reading that it often overshadows the good things being achieved by politicians. It often leads to larger head-lines and wider readership than does the more stodgy news of civic im-provement. This is not a fact of newspaper life so much as it is a fact of human life—newspapers emphasize what interests readers.

From this emphasis in the reader's mind on corruption has developed over the years a notion that all politics is dirty business and all politicians crooked. This is not only erroneous, it is harmful. It keeps many sensitive people from participating in politics and so saps the vigor of our de-mocracy.

Machines control some areas, and sometimes we find evidence that one man controls the political life of a city or even of a state—as Huey Long once ruled in Louisiana. Once such a combination has entrenched itself it is difficult to remove it. Even reporting its activities may be more than difficult—it may be plain dangerous. Some political leaders will go to great lengths to avoid adverse publicity. Bribery may be tried; threats are not uncommon; and some reporters have been subjected to violence.

Huey Long induced the legislature to impose special taxes on all the newspapers in Louisiana over a certain size. This put the larger papers at a serious disadvantage, and it was no coincidence that larger papers were fighting the Long machine. The United States Supreme Court de-clared the tax discriminatory and therefore unconstitutional.

Heady though the fight against corruption may be, the reporter faces almost as hard a job in making people appreciate the virtues of honest politicians. And yet this story is just as important as the tales of vice and corruption.

Why Do People Vote as They Do?

Dr. George Gallup and the other prophets of the "new science of public opinion polling" pose some problems for the editor and the politi-cal reporter.

Dr. Gallup and others have made a science of public opinion measure-ment, and in so doing have severed its relationship with "straw polls" of earlier days. Straw polls were as unreliable as their name seems to indicate. Their chief method was lack of any method in the scientific sense. Anyone who asked a few persons for their opinion and reported the results qualified as a straw poller.

Unreliable as straw polls were, they satisfied human curiosity and so they flourished. The most famous of the straw polls was that of the *Literary Digest*. After the poll's debacle in picking President Herbert Hoover to win again in 1932, it became one of the causes of the demise of the *Digest*.

Dr. Gallup was well prepared, with statistical understanding and systematic method, to step into the breach created by the fall of the *Digest* poll.

A political reporter who does not understand at least the rudiments of current public opinion polling techniques is not equipped to write many of the best stories on his beat.

A poll is conducted in three steps:

1. Selecting the cross section.
2. Interviewing.
3. Analyzing and interpreting the results.

THE CROSS SECTION. Perhaps the most important concept behind modern polling procedures is this one. If enough samples are drawn from a universe by pure chance methods the resulting sample will reflect the characteristics of the whole. The term "universe" means all the elements under study. For example, if a pollster is trying to predict a presidential election in the United States his universe is all qualified voters in the United States. If he is trying to predict an election of the governor of Illinois his universe is all the persons qualified to vote for the governor of Illinois.

Statisticians illustrate the principle of chance sampling this way: If you put an equal number of black balls and white balls into a jar, mix them thoroughly, and then pull out a sufficient number of balls purely by chance, you will have an equal number of black and white balls.

Just as you would get an equal number of black and white balls, you would, by pure chance methods, obtain a sample (cross section) of voters whose behavior would reflect the behavior of the entire group. Thus you can predict the reactions of many by talking with a few, provided, of course, the few you interview represent a true cross section of the universe.

Pollsters have devised various methods to obtain cross sections. Obtaining a sample by pure chance is much more complicated than it sounds. If a reporter walked out into a city and talked with 500 voters as he happened to meet them, the one sure thing about his sample would be that it was not a chance sampling. The reporter's predilections would prevent that. Chance requires that every voter in the city have as much chance as any other to be interviewed. If the reporter simply walked out and started interviewing people as he met them, obviously the people who were in town that day would have a better chance to be interviewed than those out of town. People who happened to be on the streets the reporter traversed would have a better chance. Perhaps people with whom the reporter was acquainted would have a better chance of being interviewed.

If a pollster has a list of the people in his universe, it is not hard for him to draw a sample of the names by a chance process, although finding the people may be difficult and expensive.

Because it is so difficult to achieve a cross section through pure chance, many pollsters use a quota system to select their cross section.

In a national poll, Dr. Gallup uses certain quota controls to decide whom to interview. These are age, sex, section of the country, socio-economic status, and population density of a person's home area. In selecting a sample he will make sure that if his universe contains 51 per cent women and 49 per cent men, his interviewers talk with 51 per cent women and 49 per cent men. When this process has been carried through all the quota controls, Dr. Gallup feels that he has obtained a sample which truly reflects the characteristics of the universe. That he is correct is testified to by the success of his election predictions.

CONDUCTING THE INTERVIEWS. Once he has selected his sample, the pollster has to see that his interviewers talk with the right persons, and that the interviews are conducted so that a true opinion is recorded, not a reflection of the interviewer's prejudices. The questionnaire must be carefully drawn to avoid biased questions, and the interviewers trained in its use.

INTERPRETING THE FINDINGS. In this process the pollster has to tabulate the answers and find out what they mean. He must be careful not to draw generalizations unsupported by facts, and he must give his reader enough information about how the poll was conducted so that the reader can evaluate it for himself. The pollster should realize that sometimes he may not have enough interviews to draw conclusions about small portions of his group. For example, his cross section will have to be larger if he is trying to predict voting behavior of persons in their early twenties, in addition to calling the shots in a national election.

This brief outline of the steps in a poll does not begin to present the problems. Perhaps the most adaptable to local newspaper use are the methods of Samuel Lubell, who has combined skilled reporting with sampling methods to produce new insights on the opinion-forming process in politics.

A reporter covering politics should be a thorough student of polling methods and current polls, so that he can help his reader evaluate them, and can use the results as background for his own writing.

What Should a Newspaper Do About Polls?

Political reporters should report all polls which their studies convince them are reliable. The results should be presented to readers in such a way that the reader is helped to understand them and to evaluate the poll.

The polling errors which resulted in the prediction of a victory for

Governor Thomas E. Dewey in 1948 over President Harry Truman did some good. The pollsters were not only forced to evaluate and improve their methods, but they were forced to try to explain them better to the public. The polls pointed so strongly to a Dewey victory that the entire country was misled. This would not have been nearly so likely to happen if the pollsters had taken care to explain their methods better, and if the general public had thoroughly understood them. It was an error of only a few percentage points which led to the wrong prediction. It was enough to make the pollsters and the rest of the country wrong.

Since then pollsters have not been regarded so much as secret practitioners of a magic art. They have been more careful to tell how they achieve their predictions, and the reading public somewhat more critical.

Dr. Gallup and Elmo Roper, who sometimes sell national poll stories to newspapers, have suggested that newspapers might well conduct local polls. The *New York Daily News* for many years conducted a New York State poll which was highly regarded for its accurate election predictions. Other newspapers have done the same thing.

But political reporters should not feel that their responsibility for reporting pre-election trends has been usurped by the polls. The polls make standard coverage more important than ever. Most reporters followed the polls in 1948 and predicted an overwhelming victory for Governor Dewey. President Truman's triumph brought some soul-searching from reporters and editors.

Joseph and Stewart Alsop wrote, "There is only one question on which professional politicians, polltakers, political reporters and other wiseacres and prognosticators can any longer speak with much authority. That is how they want their crow cooked."

Roy A. Roberts, president of the *Kansas City Star,* gave this advice to reporters: "In the future, don't get politis. Pay more attention to basic facts and get down to grass roots and the lower east side with hardboiled reporters searching for changes in mass thinking."

The consensus was that reporters should do their own looking, talk with more people, and be hard-headed enough to state their own conclusions even if they differ from those of the pollsters. It goes back to honest reporting—good advice in any field.

Politics and Objectivity

Reporters in any area need to strive for objectivity. Political reporters are more likely than others to be criticized for lack of objectivity because they work in one of the most controversial fields.

J. R. Wiggins, executive editor of the *Post and Times Herald* of Washington, gave his staff some advice in covering the 1956 election:

A lack of objectivity, of which a given writer or reporter is not aware because of his own slant on affairs, can be forgiven and corrected. The deliberate effort to insinuate bias into the news is another matter. Those guilty of this offense usually leave a great many finger marks about. It does not take a very astute analyst to find out that a partisan is at work when views that are the reporter's own are slyly attributed to "sentiment in the state," "prevailing opinion," "reliable sources," "competent observers," "diplomatic quarters," or other handy retreats into anonymity. Whenever you think "prevailing opinion" indicates a "Democratic" or "Republican" landslide, or like political phenomena, make sure that it prevails somewhere other than in your own mind.

Even in writing interpretively it is a good thing to avoid total judgments on men or events, or parties. Much is expected of individual reporters and editors. They are not expected, on the basis of each day's news, to give the reader the current total estimate of the relative merits of contending candidates or parties. It is better not to attempt it.

During political campaigns a conspicuous weakness of American reporting becomes especially noticeable. I am referring to our weaknesses in reporting public speeches. A published account of a speech—political or otherwise—ought to try to disclose to the reader the total view of the speaker, insofar as he exhibits it, and not just a fragment. This doctrine sometimes seems to be at war with our news techniques. We look for a lead—usually the most provocative, inflammatory, controversial thing the man says. From that lead we tail off into as much additional comment as we have room for. Let us exercise caution in trying to keep the controversial phrase in context. If the speaker hedges, let us say he hedged, at the expense of the sharp lead or good headline.

It is our duty, of course, to report the utterances of candidates for office, whatever the merit of what they say, but the fact that a campaign is in progress does not suspend the laws of libel. The degree to which privilege extends to such matters varies with the incident, but it is not wise to assume that any privilege exists. When someone is charged with criminal acts great care must be taken in reporting. If we are satisfied that the matter is not libelous or is privileged (by reason of being uttered in the Senate or House or under other privilege) we should take care to see that accusation and answer are printed in the same editions of the newspaper, if possible.

In closing days of a campaign, we must be especially careful that we do not help float groundless accusations and libelous rumors to which the persons accused cannot answer before the election. The news columns are the proper forum for debate, but the debate there, as elsewhere, must be conducted with regard for the rules of fairness.

Election day editions ought to be confined to the real news of the election and should shun speeches and statements making last-minute charges, the truth or falsity of which cannot be simultaneously presented. If sensational developments occur, decision on whether to publish or withhold should be put up to the Managing Editor.

Objectivity in political reporting, as in any other work, is a frame of mind. It comes from being able to separate fact from opinion, and from being aware of one's own biases. Given these two qualities and the desire to be objective in presenting news, the reporter can give a fair picture of two sides of a controversy without resorting to the deadpan accounts which some newspapers have excused as "objective."

Objective writing is not synonymous with colorless writing. It can have strength and vigor. It results when the reporter does his level best to present a fair picture of an event, regardless of his opinions.

REPORTING ASSIGNMENTS

1. Visit your election commissioner, or whatever official is in charge of election arrangements, for a story on election procedure.

2. Interview a party official for a story on how one goes about becoming a candidate for public office.

3. Interview an official or an active member of a minor party for a story on the purposes of the party, how it implements them, and what difficulties it faces because it is a minor party.

4. Write a story on voting trends in your county over the past few years. Note changes, seek an explanation from politicians, political scientists, or others competent to understand, and write your story.

5. Interview an old-time politician on how campaigning methods have changed in his memory.

6. Cover a political rally.

7. Visit several polling places on election day and write a story about what goes on. Visit, too, the local headquarters of both major parties for an election night color story.

8. Interview a member of your state legislature for his views on whether your state has any problems with "rotten boroughs."

9. Interview an official of a political party to get his views on the value of polls to the practical politician.

10. How many qualified voters reside in your county? What percentage of them voted in the last four elections? How does this compare with state and national averages?

15

Pressure Groups

Why Pressure Groups?

One of the reasons pressure groups exist in the United States is that our election laws encourage the domination of two parties, and thus make it necessary for each of them to appeal to voters with widely varying interests. In countries which have multiparty systems a party may be able to thrive just by blasting away at one issue, but in the United States it can afford no such luxury—it has to put together the most attractive bundle of issues possible to snare the votes of citizens with widely differing opinions.

It is small wonder, then, that parties tend to put the election of candidates ahead of the promotion of issues. Issues are discussed by candidates and they are pondered in the writing of the party platform, but they still tend to be used as a means of electing candidates, rather than as a primary objective.

Since our major parties are almost forced to put issues in second place, the way is left open for the formation of groups dedicated to promotion of single issues. But there are other reasons for the formation of pressure groups.

Our representative system is based on the idea that officeholders represent the people, not groups nor interests. This means that a legislator seldom openly espouses the cause of one interest group or another, unless he can identify it with "the common good." In other words, he is the representative of the people, but not of any of its subgroups.

Some of our theorists think it would be better to represent interest groups—workingmen, small businessmen, industrialists, retired people, and others—rather than individuals. Actually, these groups are represented in our government indirectly through representatives elected by the people, although the representation is thrown somewhat out of line by underrepresentation of some individuals and overrepresentation of others, as we have seen in Chapter 14.

Our theory is that legislators represent the whole people, and that the objective is the general welfare. Ideally, at least, this is what makes for the most equitable government, but it leaves interests unrepresented directly in our government.

It is small wonder, then, that people with special interests often band together to promote them, and that often these people try to influence government decisions which affect them.

Sometimes this activity is called lobbying, a term that is often used disparagingly. Just the same, lobbying is essential activity, from the point of view of the government as well as that of the special interests concerned. Some lobbyists have engaged in undesirable activities, and these have tended to give the whole process a bad name.

In the rambunctious nineteenth century, lobbyists for the business interests sometimes controlled state legislatures and exerted much influence in Congress. Thurlow Weed, one of the founders of the Whig and Republican parties and a powerful political leader, was an open lobbyist for some business interests. His success was built originally on his control over the Republican party in New York State, but where business interests were involved he cut across party lines. He extended his influence to Washington through a wide acquaintance among office holders.

Glyndon G. Van Deusen, in his book, *Thurlow Weed: Wizard of the Lobby,* gives a picture of Weed as go-between of business and politics:

> The story of Weed's activities as a business agent gives only a fragmentary picture of the extent to which, as a powerful political leader, he was tied up with the business interests of state and nation in the eighteen-fifties. He was on friendly terms with Cornelius Vanderbilt. When Seward went abroad in 1859, it was through Weed that the Commodore offered passage on his steamers, out and back, to the traveling statesman. A few months later, Weed was acting as mediator in the cutthroat rate war over sea transport to California between Vanderbilt and Pacific Mail. Russell Sage, running for Congress in 1852, asked Weed to exert pressure on Collins and Law to keep them from contributing to the campaign chest of Sage's Democratic opponent. The request was eminently reasonable, for Weed was on good terms with Edward Knight Collins, head of the Collins line of steamships; and George (Liveoak) Law, shipowner, ferry operator, and speculator extraordinary, a man whom Weed himself described as doing everything "for a consideration," had such friendly relations with the Albany leader that he could ask repeatedly for the passage or blocking of bills that affected his business ventures. More important still was Weed's close con-

nection with other New York shipowners and businessmen, such individuals as Moses H. Grinnel, Robert B. Minturn, James Bowen and Simeon Draper.

The connection with these pillars of New York City's economic life had begun in the eighteen-thirties, and had grown firmer with the passing of the years. The merchants provided a steady source of money for campaign purposes, and Weed returned their golden favors by keeping a watchful eye over legislation that touched their interests, and by listening sympathetically to their views in the matter of political appointments. Wharfage bills, steamboat bills and other similar measures were a source of frequent correspondence and consultation. So was the choice of men for offices that bore on the interests of the merchants, and Weed always did his best to meet the demands that arose from the countinghouses and the directors' offices that multiplied at the mouth of the Hudson.

Later in the book the author shows that the technique of the lobbyists sometimes is transferred to another setting and becomes the technique of the statesman. In describing Weed's efforts on a mission to sway opinion to favor the North, Van Deusen says:

> The influence which Weed exerted upon the London press, save for the redoubtable *Times* was due in considerable part to the contacts that he made among influential people. He cultivated the friendship of Edward Ellice (founder of the Reform Club and a power in Whig politics), and was on friendly terms with Palmerston's son-in-law, the Earl of Shaftesbury, and with Seymour Fitzgerald, Under-Secretary for Foreign Affairs. He also became well acquainted with Emerson Tennant of the Board of Trade, Bright, Cobden, Nassau Senior and other notables. The result was an entree to the clubs and a strenuous round of breakfasts and dinners whereat the Northern point of view was duly and skillfully presented. "I work all day and dine nearly all night," Weed wrote to Frederick Seward. Such efforts, undertaken with the full concurrence of Adams, were bound to produce results.

Lobbying and other activities designed to influence government decisions are protected by one of our fundamental rights—the right of petition. This holds that any citizen or group has an inalienable right to address his government to seek redress of wrongs or the granting of rights which are due.

Most of us make use of this right, either directly or indirectly, rather frequently. Almost everybody helps support at least one or two lobbyists. Auto clubs, hunters' groups, church groups, social betterment organizations, business and professional groups—all these and many others support lobbyists. We petition our governments directly and we support lobbyists, so few of us can condemn the practice. All we can do is ask that it be conducted fairly and sufficiently out in the open so that the public can judge whether it is being done honestly.

What Are Pressure Groups?

In a broad sense any group which tries to change the world is a pressure group, but we shall limit our discussion to the groups which try to change government policy. We need to make another fundamental distinction, too, between groups which are organized primarily to influence government decisions, and those which have some other purpose and try to intervene only occasionally in governmental decisions.

In the category of groups which mainly try to influence government are many of the retail trade groups and professional and labor organizations. The variety of purposes is so great that it is not possible to generalize, but some of these groups do little except organize their members to support or oppose legislation which affects the group's welfare. Many other organizations, not primarily pressure groups, sometimes exert pressure on government to gain ends which they regard as desirable. Social groups may be interested only vaguely in government, but once in a great while they may be aroused to pass a petition among members and send it to some arm of government.

In the middle ground are most of the organizations we will consider. They are formed to promote the interests of their members or of some specific cause, and promote these interests in any legitimate way they can. Grocers' associations, for example, may give members of their group suggestions on how to run their stores more efficiently, and how to hire help; they may hold conventions once or twice a year which are social as well as business events. They are very likely to become interested in legislation, and they may become so interested that they send a member or an executive secretary to the state capital or to Washington to try to influence the decision on legislation. They may instead hire a professional lobbyist, already on the scene, who takes on the additional job just as an advertising agency or public relations man might take on a new account.

Pressure groups are so varied that few generalizations can be made about them, although four are valid for most.

1. They tend to work in the background. Even pressure groups with the highest principles are seldom eager to have publicity turned on all their methods. The methods may be entirely honest, but the group's purposes are often better served by background operation. One reason for this is that government officials know they are expected to serve the general public, and voters, if they think officials serve one of the "interests," may turn the officials out. Therefore, a quiet contact with a legislator often is most effective.

2. Usually pressure groups represent a single interest. Most people belong to more than one pressure group, but each group normally is

interested in promoting just one general program. Parent-teacher groups usually limit themselves to advocating better schools, and seldom try to better the lot of the workingman or lighten the burden of the industrialists. Similarly labor groups seldom concern themselves with the problems of the schools, and try to help the industrialists only when they think it will preserve their jobs or fatten their pay checks. Industrialists' groups, too, are usually preoccupied with their own problems.

There are some genuine exceptions to this rule. The general public, for example, may become so concerned with some problem, such as bettering the schools, that every group becomes interested.

3. Usually the pressure group represents a minority. With a large population and many interests, a pressure group can seldom honestly claim that it represents a majority of voters even in a small area. If the group truly represented a majority whose interests could be aroused, the group could achieve its ends and thus would put itself out of business.

4. More often than not pressure group activity is concerned with the pocketbooks of members. Local pressure groups watch zoning regulations which affect the value of property, the tax rate, and other money matters. On state and federal levels the interest tends to be about taxation and its impact on special groups, and about subsidies, protective tariffs, and other pocketbook measures. There are many exceptions. Some of the best known examples are the China lobby, the Anti-Saloon League, and the Women's Rights Movement, although even the last did have a property angle.

Since pressure groups cannot be defined very accurately, it is impossible to say how many there are or how big they are. Congress requires that all lobbyists register and report their expenses each year, and many of the states have similar rules, but this information is incomplete. Many groups which intervene in government only occasionally are not required to register, and it is impossible to decide what is a lobbying expense. For example, if an attorney who goes to Washington to represent the interests of a city in a certain bill gives a party for congressmen from his state, should this be charged up as a lobbying expense? The attorney might insist that these men were his personal friends and he might be prepared to prove that the expense of the party came out of his own pocket.

Some insight into the variety of pressures which can be exerted is given us by Professor Donald C. Blaisdell in his book, *American Democracy Under Pressure*. In a table he lists more than 80 separate groups which attempted to influence the nature of one single revenue act. With such a number, it is not to be wondered at that some of our tax bills seem to resemble more a compromise of many separate interests rather than the general interest.

One of the interesting aspects of pressure groups is that sometimes one part of the government itself acts as a pressure group, trying to get a favorable decision out of another part of the government. It is common practice for administrators in departments of the federal government to appear before Congressional committees to persuade them that appropriations requests are valid. It has been shown that some government departments have sought to build up pressure throughout the country to persuade Congress that certain government programs should be continued or expanded.

Any legislative body is full of internal pressures, with members trying to persuade each other to vote for or against a given bill. Every once in a while this activity begins to resemble lobbying, when a certain member is always identified with a given interest.

Where Do They Operate?

We are used to thinking about pressure groups as operating in legislative bodies, but they are at work in the other branches of the government as well.

Pressure groups must take action in executive and judicial, as well as legislative, branches of the government because public policy is made in all three branches. This is the regular business of the other branches as well.

Administrative officials are often given wide discretion to make policy decisions. The Federal Reserve Commission has the power to control the amount of money in circulation—a decision of vast significance to business and thus to everyone. The State Department makes many decisions involving important public policy, and the President is charged, as is the mayor of a city, with much policy-making in his position of party leadership as well as in the administrative phases of his work.

The courts interpret the law, but the highest courts often determine public policy as well. The interpretation of fundamental law depends to some extent on the frame of reference which the interpreter brings to the task. If it were otherwise we would have few Supreme Court decisions except unanimous ones, so public policy is determined here, too.

Where public policy is determined, naturally the pressure groups must work.

How Do They Work?

The effectiveness of a pressure group is determined by several factors. Among them are these:

SIZE OF GROUP. With other factors equal, the larger the group, the more influential it will be. The more votes a group can control, the more weight it will have.

INTENSITY OF INTEREST. Mere size may be outweighed by interest. A group may be huge, but if interest is small it is unlikely to be successful. There is much speculation about the ability of labor leaders to deliver the vote of rank and file members. Political leaders are always considering the labor vote, and union chiefs may threaten to withhold the support of their members if a legislator does not vote "right." The late Senator Robert A. Taft of Ohio was re-elected in an industrial state after being denounced by labor leaders for his sponsorship of the Taft-Hartley Act, but there are other indications that labor leaders do, sometimes, deliver the vote of their members. If labor leaders really can do this, they are a formidable political force, for theirs is the largest organized group in the country. One important factor is that union members also belong to other groups, whose influence on the members may be as strong. Like most other people, they belong to churches, lodges, parent-teacher groups, hunting clubs, and many other groups which may also have an interest in politics.

QUALITY OF LEADERSHIP. A capable, aggressive leader is likely to make the difference between success and failure.

FINANCIAL SUPPORT. Money-raising for a cause is a skilled occupation, but better than a skilled fund raiser is a membership so vitally interested that it pays dues promptly, or a large treasury to devote to a cause. Tightly knit professional groups such as the American Medical Association usually can raise the money needed to finance a campaign. So can a labor union by requiring dues from members. A large business is usually well situated in this matter because it has access to company funds. Small organizations and those whose members are only mildly interested in a cause suffer most from lack of financing.

The nature of the organization determines the method it uses. An organization with few members and a considerable amount of money may not be in a position to threaten a state legislature with defeat at the polls, so it may have to offer other reasons for voting its way.

In essence the job of the pressure groups is getting the ear of the policy-maker, and then persuading him that he should support or reject a certain proposition.

Sometimes a group of property owners will get together to protest a zoning change or something else that affects their interests. Few would call the resulting action lobbying, but it is pressure politics and a fairly pure expression of the right of petition. This Associated Press story from the *New York Times* illustrates the point:

LEVITTOWN, L. I. Oct. 4—The down zoning of two dwellings here has touched off a controversy between civic leaders and officials of Hempstead Township.

Julian Kane, president of the Levittown Property Owners Association, charged that the Town Zoning Board had approved the down zoning despite the unanimous objection of home owners in the area. Both buildings are on Hempstead Turnpike at the corner of Hamlet Lane. They are to be used for professional offices.

Three civic associations representing a total of 4,500 home owners opposed the down zoning. A petition signed by 1,000 residents was submitted to the Town Board.

Mr. Kane termed the board's decision a "flagrant example of spot zoning" that might set a precedent that would damage business interests and lead to slum conditions in Levittown.

His statement was made in a letter to Allan C. Miller, chairman of the Nassau County Planning Commission.

Edward P. Larkin, Presiding Supervisor of Hempstead Town, acknowledged that there had been strong opposition to the zoning change. He explained, however, that the Town Board had made it a practice to zone business along Hempstead Turnpike on a "consistent and dynamic zoning plan." He said this plan had made Levittown "one of the best-zoned areas of the nation."

Sometimes a pressure group tries to assure itself of a "friendly" town council or state legislature even before election time. It may contribute to the campaign funds of one or both of the major parties, and help select, nominate, and elect candidates. This process usually results in a candidate who is friendly to that interest. If a pressure group can do this in enough districts in a state it assures itself of a considerable amount of voting strength in the legislature.

Getting into office men whose only commitment is to the general welfare is one of the problems of politics. Election campaigns cost money. Usually this has to come from contributions, and it is difficult for a candidate to feel that he has no obligations to those who contributed to the fund which helped elect him.

Sometimes pressure groups have enough voting strength to achieve somewhat the same result without contributing to the candidate's campaign fund. A standard technique is to circularize candidates before or after the primary, or both, to ask them how they stand on a given set of issues of interest to the pressure group. Sometimes a promise is demanded before a group will recommend that its members vote for a candidate. The promise may encumber a candidate after he is elected just as much or more than a campaign contribution would have.

One governor of New Jersey, trying to find new sources of revenue, found that some legislators had promised not to vote for one kind of tax, others, not to vote for another, and so on until it was impossible to work out a plan to keep the state solvent without asking some of the legislators to break their pre-election promises.

Anyone with a legitimate errand can find a way to reach the ear of a legislator, and a good lobbyist who knows his subject can expect a hearing. With many lobbyists this is the standard approach, and there can be little objection to it. After all, it is the job of the legislator to balance interests. Some lobbyists use threats and sometimes they work, although the blustering lobbyist of earlier days has just about disappeared.

Various ways have been devised by pressure groups to present a show of strength. One is to bring a delegation to see members of the legislature, and perhaps to sit in the balcony and watch proceedings as their favorite bill comes up for consideration. The delegates often work themselves into an emotional state, and do themselves and their cause as much harm as good by irrational and emotional appeals, or by gallery demonstrations that detract from the dignity of the legislative body.

Picketing is also used to attract attention. Legislative chambers have been picketed; so have the White House and the homes and places of business of state legislators. This usually wins space in newspapers because it is difficult to ignore, but it is questionable whether it achieves results.

Appearing before a committee or an administrative hearing is a common practice of lobbyists.

Often lobbyists can help a legislator by supplying information which it might be hard for him to assemble, especially if he is in one of the states which allow legislators very limited funds for research help.

The late Robert M. La Follette, Jr., in a *New York Times Magazine* article emphasizing the information function of lobbying, said:

> . . . lobbying is directly related to the complexity of the legislation under consideration. The more complex or technical a bill may be, the more need there is for expert advice and assistance on details. Often the person directly affected can give the best information on practical application, as contrasted with the academic approach of the public administrator less familiar with details, even though such "practical" opinion often needs to be discounted to eliminate personal bias or generalized to meet a broader application. Tax legislation most certainly falls in this category.

Information may be presented in testimony, in private conversations with legislators, or through written or printed material. Most legislators seem to welcome it when it is presented intelligently.

A few states pay their legislators so little, and give them so little in the way of information services and fact-finding help, that they are at the mercy of the lobbyists for information and sometimes for help in bill drafting. It is no secret that many of the bills passed by some of our state legislatures were drafted by the interests which were most affected by them.

Not so long ago one of the favorite devices of the lobbyists was to pass the word to the "people back home" to write their congressmen. Those lobbyists supported by groups interested enough could produce a flood of letters or telegrams on order. This is still done, but much of its effectiveness has evaporated. Too often the letters bear the same wording; sometimes they are sent on the same kind of paper and in similar envelopes.

The more modern counterpart of this technique is the "grass roots approach" in which the lobbyist uses his connections in a legislator's home district to work on him when he is home. This is regarded by some as the best way to influence a legislator's decision.

A ground swell of public opinion favoring the position of the pressure group is a powerful weapon, so many lobbyists use public relations techniques. One important phase of this is the attempt to use the mass media of communications to put over the pressure group's views. Personal contacts are made with editors, news events may be staged, and all the familiar devices employed. Much of the resulting information must be published because it is newsworthy, but the editor has to protect his paper from becoming just a sounding board for pressure groups. Good reporting covering all aspects of an issue is the only answer to this. News stories and editorials favoring the lobbyists' side are carefully clipped by pressure groups as evidence of the importance of their viewpoint. The professional lobbyist likes clippings, too, for they are a tangible result which he can show the people who sign his paycheck.

Often a group will seek to impress the public with the group's views by making a statement. The prominence which it receives in the news media is commensurate with the editors' judgment as to the importance of the situation and of the person or group making the statement. Here is an example from the *San Francisco Chronicle:*

> The Board of Regents of the University of California called yesterday for limiting enrollments at UC "to the number of students that can be given high quality instruction with the faculty and facilities available."
>
> But at the same time the regents said there should be no raising of admission standards "to prevent unwieldy enrollments."
>
> The regents found a way out of this seeming impasse by urging "every effort" to provide new campuses for the University "so that enrollment pressures at Berkeley and Los Angeles do not threaten the high quality of instruction and research to which the University is committed."
>
> The general statement issued by the regents yesterday also called for maintaining a program of study at Berkeley and Los Angeles grounded in "research and in the intellectual disciplines."
>
> "Clear distinctions," the regents said, should be made between the program at the two main campuses and the "other worthy educational objectives" at the six other campuses of the University.

The statement said the policy at Berkeley and Los Angeles should emphasize graduate and upper-division instruction, with the lower-division program being continued "on a substantial basis."

Sometimes lobbyists resort to unethical or illegal methods. Bribery was not uncommon in state legislatures of former years. Apparently it is much less common now.

Many subtle forms of persuasion are questionable, although not illegal. Many states pay their legislators so poorly that they have to work at other jobs even during the legislative session. Lawyers are often elected to the legislature because the position enhances their professional reputation, and because they can adjust their time to do the legislative work more easily than can people in many other vocations.

"Conflict of interest" problems are subtle. If a legislator-lawyer's firm handles a public utility account, is his vote on utility regulation suspect? Is it unethical for a member of the legislature to work as a paid consultant for a group which is interested in a piece of legislation?

Social lobbying is as subtle as any. Washington is a great social as well as political center, and state capitals have a certain amount of social life. It is not uncommon for representatives of interest groups to be lavish entertainers, and often members of various branches of the government are entertained along with others. If the government official enjoys himself at a party, this is likely to make him feel friendly toward the individual who gives it. This is not a matter of buying votes. Few government officials, in or out of the legislatures, would sell a decision for an invitation to a party. Obviously no one can or should try to control the social life of government officials. Just the same, the fact that lobbyists are often splendid entertainers has some significance.

How Important Are Pressure Groups?

The effect of pressure groups on governmental decisions can be assessed only very generally. There is no question that they have a vast influence. This is inevitable, for they represent important interests.

Pressure group activity can result in abuses, but so can other ways of arriving at political decisions. In most cases part of the abuses can be removed by public awareness of what is going on. This was the purpose of the Legislative Reorganization Act of 1946, which required registration of lobbyists and periodic statements of their expenses. These reports are printed quarterly in the Congressional Record, but they are pretty much ignored by the general public.

The point of publicity is that many of the undesirable practices would disappear if they were generally known. The requirement that lobbyists register and reveal their expenditures has not accomplished this, and it is probably impossible to frame new legislation which will focus publicity steadily on lobbyists. The right of petition is fundamental, and any attempt to abridge it would take away some of the basic rights of every citizen. Pressure group activities are of such significance in formulating public policy that it is not clear whether they can remain outside more formal public regulation. Political parties were not envisaged by the framers of our Constitution and so were not mentioned in it. They became necessary for a successful government, and for a while operated with few legal restraints. They have become increasingly subject to regulation as their importance has been recognized. It is entirely possible that the same thing will happen to pressure groups.

Identifying Pressure Groups in the News

Part of the problem of controlling pressure groups would be solved by more reporting in depth. It is not too difficult to report the surface movements involved in legislation. Committee hearings and debates on the floor can be covered by an accurate observer with an understanding of procedure. Readers need to know, too, what forces are at play beneath the surface events. This is another place where the "why" becomes the answer to better government as well as to better reporting.

Identifying pressure groups, and describing their activities in connection with a given piece of legislation or an administrative decision, would help. Sometimes this is easy to do; more often it is difficult because the pressure groups may dislike having their methods revealed for fear such revelation will impair their success.

A story or series analyzing the impact of pressures on a given government decision will increase public understanding more than many spot stories. This requires a considerable amount of time, and a resourceful and understanding reporter. Newspapers have both and often use them for projects of this caliber. Too often the job of analyzing social pressures has been left to social scientists. This has helped in a general understanding of the situation, but sometimes the information does not reach the public.

A newspaper reporter can add to his skills the techniques of the social scientist, and come up with articles of value to the specialist as well as to the general reader. Timely reports of these pressures will increase their interest to the general reader, and help secure the public understanding which must be achieved if we are ever to resolve the pressure conflicts into a true pattern of public interest. The pressures are likely to become stronger as the means of mass persuasion and group action become more widely available. Understanding is the first step in channeling the pressures for their most productive use.

Woodrow Wilson phrased the ideal concept of power control on a large scale in an address to the Senate on January 22, 1917:

"There must be, not a balance of power, but a community of power; not organized rivalries, but an organized common peace."

REPORTING ASSIGNMENTS

1. Interview an official of a labor group in your community to find out how his organization tries to influence legislation at the local, the state, or the national level.

2. Do the same for a professional organization.

3. Interview a member of your city council to find out what pressures are brought to bear to influence his vote on questions before the council.

4. Interview the mayor or one of his top assistants. Ask how citizens try to influence the mayor's decisions.

5. Interview a member of your state legislature. Find out how much members are paid and how much time they have to put in on their job in the legislature. Ask him to estimate how many of the legislators have other jobs. Ask him his opinion of the place of the pressure groups.

16

Volunteer Agencies

Types of Groups

People accomplish changes through government, business organizations, and labor or trade groups. People also join in private organizations of all kinds. Some of these are dedicated to socially desirable objectives, and they operate in the public interest fully as much as do any of the other more official agencies.

These groups are a public concern because they often have a profound effect on social action. The public often underrates the importance of such groups because they usually work much more quietly than government agencies, and in a much more varied form than do business concerns or labor groups.

Groups of this sort differ from pressure groups, discussed in Chapter 15, in that these groups are nonprofit organizations dedicated to social progress, while the pressure groups have a financial or business motive of their own, or else represent organizations which have such an aim.

It is difficult to classify volunteer agencies, because they may range from a loosely organized group of local business and civic leaders who meet occasionally to discuss local problems, to a giant foundation which spends millions a year on research. The classification problem is further confused by pressure or public relations organizations which adopt the terminology of charity or independent research groups to hide their real propaganda or commercial purposes.

Lack of public understanding exists partly because it is difficult for newspapers to report adequately the activities of such agencies. This in turn breeds lack of public interest, which results in further neglect in the news columns. There are other good reasons for insufficient coverage. It may be difficult to obtain stories on some agencies because there is little material of public record, and we are not in the habit of thinking about these groups as a regular source of news, comparable to the agencies of local government. Nevertheless, the nonpublic agencies often shape public decisions fully as much as do the public agencies which are forced to operate in the light of publicity.

It is hard to draw the line, too, between purely social organizations and those which have more serious purposes. Many of the luncheon clubs, for example, do very useful things for their communities, although most of them appeal to members primarily as a social organization.

Since we cannot discuss all the kinds of organizations of this nature, we will consider four types in this chapter: fraternal or social, charitable, foundations, and churches. It is worth remembering that stories of local importance often come from similar private organizations which do not fall into any of these categories.

Fraternal or Social Organizations

Organizations of this nature have some solid achievements, and may be social or fraternal mostly in their trappings. Others are organized mostly for social purposes. At any rate, these organizations usually have two objectives—promoting community interests, and serving as a social club for their members.

Such organizations often become good copy when they hold conventions, as this story from the *Chicago Sun-Times* shows:

> One hundred thousand Shriners settled down to the serious business of running the largest, most detailed and most expensive convention in the history of the fraternal order Wednesday.
>
> Having put the show on the road Tuesday with a day of glamor and gaiety, the Nobles put their fezzes together to make important plans. . . .
>
> The first order of business was the election of officers at an Imperial Council session, and the unanimous selection of a new boss for Masonry's 800,000 Shriners throughout the United States, Canada and Mexico.

Later one of the Shriners' important projects is mentioned when the new imperial potentate is quoted as saying that the Shriners' hospital for crippled children will get most of his attention.

Charitable Organizations

We all know about charity drives. Twenty-five million of us participated in a recent year as volunteer solicitors in fund raising campaigns. The amount collected runs into billions.

We are familiar with United Fund, Community Chest, and Red Cross drives, and with the Mothers' March on Polio, but these are only among the better known ones. At least 600 national organizations make annual appeals to the public for financial support. In addition there are thousands of local ones. New York City has 1,100 local fund raising charities.

With the scope of the fund drives and the amount of money collected, it was inevitable that abuses should crop up once in a while.

A Detroit organization, the National Cancer Hospital of America, was permanently enjoined by a New York Supreme Court from soliciting funds in that state, because the court found funds were handled carelessly and that there were "unexplained shortages."

The large number of honest charities is very much interested in exposing undesirable ones, and the principal weapon is public knowledge of the working and financing of the good ones. The National Information Bureau in New York City was established in 1918 to provide information to prospective contributors to charitable organizations. It publishes a Giver's Guide. The organization has suggested 11 standards for charitable organizations:

1. The organization should have a responsible governing body meeting regularly and serving without pay.

2. Its purposes should be legitimate, and it should not duplicate the work of another organization which is doing a reasonably good job.

3. It should be efficient.

4. It should not maintain solicitors paid on a commission basis.

5. It should not try to raise money by sending merchandise or tickets to prospective donors through the mail, asking them to pay for the merchandise or return it.

6. It should stage no benefits in which the costs exceed 40 per cent of the gross proceeds.

7. Statements made in publicity material and in personal calls should be honest, presenting an accurate picture of the organization.

8. It should co-operate with other welfare agencies in its locality.

9. It should make available each year an audited, detailed statement of income and expenditures, made by an independent certified public accountant or trust company.

10. It should issue detailed annual budgets.

11. It should not solicit for funds from the general public by telephone.

Since many charitable organizations depend on public donations, they are likely to actively seek publicity. Most newspapers give large amounts of space to charity drives which the editors deem honest and useful. Community fund drives in many places have replaced most of the other drives. This means that there is one annual campaign for funds, which are then distributed among the various charitable and social service agencies in the area.

Some national organizations vigorously oppose joining such a community fund drive on the basis that they tend to lose their identity when they do not make separate appeals. Nevertheless, the united fund drives have answered most of the problems formerly caused by many different drives throughout the year. A large number of drives tends to confuse the public, and since the drives compete with each other they eventually discourage contributions.

Often newspapers will give space daily to the progress of united fund drives, and quite frequently newspapers will run individual articles about each of the charities which benefit. In this way the public is kept informed on the various social service organizations in the community, and interest in fund raising is kept alive. The newspaper needs to tell its readers, too, what services are available. Most people know about the Salvation Army, but many services, such as free clinics and aid to unwed mothers, may be unknown to people who need them desperately.

Some newspaper editors refuse to print articles about fund drives of organizations unless they are well known in the community, or the organizations submit independently audited statements of their financial condition.

Modern charitable organizations in some respects resemble a business organization, with its board of directors, executives, and professional and public relations staff.

There is room for good feature writing in describing the activities of various agencies, and the human interest material is built in. Reporting and writing problems center around the fact that it is sometimes hard to find different angles, so that the stories do not sound the same year after year.

Among the stories on local fund drives are those which give the names of the prominent citizens who are heading the drives. Here is an example from the *Pittsburgh Post-Gazette*:

> A 20-man group of labor, education, business and industry representatives has been appointed as the United Fund's Fair Share Plan Committee.
>
> The committee, headed by Philip A. Fleger, chairman of the board of Duquesne Light Company, will try to raise the number of "Fair Share givers," in the coming fall campaign for 9,715,907.

Foundations

Foundations are often confused with the charitable and social service agencies described in the preceding section, but there are important differences.

In the first place, true foundations do not make a public appeal for funds, because one of their characteristics is that they have a fund (corpus) already. The person or organization which creates the foundation normally gives it money or stocks which provide income. The foundation is nonprofit and maintained for either specific or general socially desirable purposes.

Foundations are less likely than the social service organizations to attempt direct aid to individuals in need. Instead they may sponsor research activities designed to discover the causes of poverty, and so help to alleviate it. Much of our progress in medicine and science has been made possible by the research grants from foundations. Social science research, too, has benefited from foundation grants. Educational, charitable, and religious institutions frequently are aided by foundation funds.

Very often a foundation will start out as a means for a wealthy person to channel his giving. Ordinarily this means that the foundation will receive a gift each year from the donor, and frequently a large sum on the donor's death.

Sometimes a fund may be given nonvoting stock in a business enterprise. This gives it the income from the stock, but keeps the control of the enterprise within a family or small group of common stockholders. This is sometimes a convenient way for a donor to reduce his estate to manageable size after his death. When family enterprises have grown to monstrous proportions, the estate taxes sometimes are so large that it is difficult or impossible to find the liquid assets to pay them. Giving part of the stock to a nonprofit organization may ease the problem.

Taxes are often credited for the creation of foundations, but this cynical view is not always justified. Some of our large foundations were organized before the tax benefits were so great.

Frank Emerson Andrews, in *Philanthropic Foundations,* a study published by the Russell Sage Foundation, lists six types of foundations:

1. General research foundations. These include the Rockefeller and Ford Foundations, the Carnegie Corporation of New York, and the Commonwealth Fund. These get most of the public attention, and so tend to form the average citizen's idea of the foundation. Mr. Andrews estimates that there are no more than 150 of these, but that they control more than one-half the assets of all the foundations.

2. Special purpose foundations. These tend to be small, and there is the danger that the founder will define the purpose so narrowly that the foundation will become outmoded. The "Emma A. Robinson Horses' Christmas Dinner Fund" of Olathe, Kansas, is an example.

Another fund with a narrow purpose was the Samuel G. David Fund, established in Mashpee, Massachusetts, in 1930, to reward Mashpee students for "good, kind manners." In 1938 the trustees asked the courts for permission to use the money to build schools, because the town officials "can't find enough mannerly boys to reward."

3. Family or personal foundations. These are usually small and de-

signed as a buffer between the donor and seekers after donations. Sometimes they grow into large foundations. They may not have a large amount of capital, but are replenished annually out of the donor's current giving.

4. Corporation foundations. Since 1936 business corporations have been allowed to deduct up to 5 per cent of net income for charitable gifts. This tax deduction and the growing social consciousness of business have combined to increase the amount of corporate giving, and often this has been channeled through a foundation set up by the corporation.

5. Community trusts. This type of foundation or trust fund usually is established within a given city or county, to make funds available for local social welfare purposes under community control. Normally the trust department of a local bank or trust company administers the money, paying it out on the order of a committee of local citizens. Many such organizations exist more on paper than anywhere else, but some have attracted local contributions and have made significant contributions to their communities.

The first such organization was the Cleveland Foundation established in January, 1914, by Frederick H. Goff. It financed important surveys in Cleveland on education, recreation, and crime.

A brief quotation from the document forming the Community Trust in Mount Vernon, Ohio, will give an idea as to the purposes and organization of such a fund:

> Whereas there is a need in this community for the creation of a general fund permitting of flexibility in the power of distribution, to assist public educational, charitable, or benevolent enterprises;
>
> Now, therefore, to accomplish this purpose, the Board of Directors of the First-Knox National Bank and the Board of Directors of The Knox County Savings Bank, both of Mount Vernon resolve. . . .

The resolution is to accept gifts for the purposes listed. The distribution committee was to consist of five members, to be appointed by the boards of directors of each of the two banks, the chamber of commerce, the city council, and by joint action of the judge of the court of common pleas of Knox County and the judge of the probate court.

6. Government foundations. It has often been suggested that Congress should establish independent foundations, but it has done so only once. That was when it ordered the creation of the National Science Foundation in 1950, to promote the progress of science and advance national health and welfare. It has concentrated on the physical sciences, granting sums for basic research, for improvement of science teaching, and for the exchange of scientific information.

A foundation, as a nonprofit organization operating in the public interest, is tax exempt, and this fact brings with it responsibility to the public. The extent and nature of the responsibilities have never been well defined.

Mr. Andrews, in the study cited above, has this to say about accountability of foundations:

> . . . it seems wholly proper that the foundation or trust should be held accountable for its stewardship. The availability of the new social asset should be made known promptly, at least to public authorities and possibly widely. Society should have the means of protecting itself against the theft, squandering, or unreasonable withholding of the promised benefit. Finally, the operations of the exempt organization should be fully and regularly reported, with adequate provision for review by a public authority possessing power to correct abuses. This constitutes accountability.

Mr. Andrews makes it clear that by accountability he does not mean public control.

In testimony before a congressional committee, a representative of the Russell Sage Foundation suggested a three-part program to promote greater public accountability of the foundations:

1. Provide uniform state legislation requiring all foundations and charitable trusts to register.

2. Require annual reports, including a full financial statement and a description of activities. These statements would be open to the public.

3. Institute review of such reports by a public authority with power to correct abuses. The logical place for such review would be the offices of the state attorney generals.

Actually, only a few states have laws which set forth very strict requirements about registration and disclosure of information. New Hampshire and Rhode Island are among the exceptions to this.

Foundations which are granted tax exemption must file a form with the district directors of internal revenue. This form includes such information as gross income, expenses, disbursements, accumulation of income at the beginning of the year, contributions received, and a balance sheet at the beginning and end of the year. Part of the form is kept on file at the district offices, and part is forwarded to Washington. Much of the information on the two parts is the same, although the list of contributions is not included in the part which is filed at the district offices. The copies in the district offices are open to public inspection, but those in Washington are not generally available without a special order of the President. This makes country-wide reporting difficult, but it does make it possible for a newspaper to report a local situation by studying forms on file at the office of the nearest district director of internal revenue.

Some foundations seek publicity on the theory that it will increase public understanding and acceptance of their work. Others shun it because it always brings more requests for grants, and they already have many more than they can fill.

The larger foundations tend to spend a great deal of money telling the public what they are doing. The Rockefeller Foundation issues quarterly reports in addition to detailed annual reports. The preparation of these involves much time by highly skilled personnel, and the expense of publishing them is considerable. The foundation officers believe that this is part of their public responsibility.

The role of the foundation in our society is more important than many of us realize. The very fact that they have money to spend with no strings attached other than the public interest, puts foundations in a position to be uniquely useful to society.

The success of their operations is sometimes dramatic. It was foundation money, for example, which enabled Dr. Jonas Salk to discover and perfect his vaccine against poliomyelitis. At other times, and especially in dealing with the social sciences or human resources, the success of a foundation is impossible to measure. Sometimes foundation officers authorize the foundation to pay for the publication of findings with which they disagree, and which they know will bring severe criticism on the foundation. If the work is honestly done and is a viewpoint which needs to be presented to the public, most foundation officers will go ahead and publish it.

Courageous foundations are one of our most useful agencies in helping people to think in broad new ways. New ways of thinking are seldom popular, and so government often cannot finance such undertakings. Men of vision in foundations sometimes manage to find and support projects which otherwise could not be undertaken. It is small wonder that the foundation funds are so often called the "venture capital of society."

Churches

Churches are another great force in reaching social decisions. Too often newspaper coverage of the religious life of its community is routine and dull—unnecessarily dull.

Activities centering in the church itself are often worth covering, as are those beyond the church walls. Some churches are becoming social service centers by sponsoring homes for the aged, youth programs, and psychiatric services.

A newspaper adds to its own prestige and helps its readers of different religions to live together in harmony by an understanding coverage of religious affairs in its community.

Walter Froehlich, who covers two diverse beats, traffic safety and religion, for the *Buffalo Courier-Express,* describes his reaction to religion writing in these words in answering the question, "Is it a satisfying job compared with other reporting assignments?"

> I would say yes, BUT there is not a single reporter in our newsroom who would seriously ask to get my job, in fact, most reporters will try to dodge when I need a substitute. . . . The reason, I believe, is that church writing calls for tremendous detail work and holds none of the thrills of covering a banner-line front-page story.
>
> But I believe that religious misunderstanding is great and causes many unnecessary tensions. I believe there is a need greater than in practically any other field, to explain the community to the community on religious lines. While I skirt theological arguments, I don't hesitate to explain the convictions of the people I interview—and explain them from *their* point of view—controversial as these may be.
>
> I have long had a deep interest in community relations work . . . and I believe that religion writing can do much toward easing tensions between groups and knitting the community into a more coherent entity. And I believe this is a real challenge and, indeed, satisfying work compared with practically anything you can name.

One of the problems Mr. Froehlich faces in covering the more than 1,000 churches in the Buffalo area is to help the church people get in routine stories speedily and with all essential details. The *Courier-Express* has printed a pamphlet with suggestions to clergymen and church publicity chairmen about handling regular stories and being alert to feature possibilities.

The *Courier-Express* covers the regular church news, but concentrates, too, on features with a high human interest value, features which will appeal to readers of many faiths and even to those who do not attend any church. Religion stories often appear in the Sunday Pictorial section as well as in the daily editions, but the backbone of the church coverage is the Saturday Religious Page.

This features a weekly story about local churches or church people told in a way that is likely to interest many readers. Here are headlines on a few of these articles from the *Courier-Express:* "Space Scientist Teaches Bible Class," "Three Describe Renewal of Faith," "This Bishop Works a 6½ Day Week," "Cleric's 'Tuesday Club' Here is Unusual Group," "There's an Art in Being an Usher," "WNY Churches Short of Clergymen," "Church Bulletin Has Vital Function," "Cleric 'Fee' Policy Varies Widely," " 'Sickroom's My Parish,' Hospital Chaplain Says," "Preparation of Sermons Nothing But Hard Work," "Acting Talents Help Tell Passion Story," "Buffalo Rabbi Attains Stature as Spokesman."

The opening paragraphs of Mr. Froehlich's story about the preparation of sermons illustrates an informal but dignified style which is likely to attract many readers:

Those sermons you hear in church each Sunday morning are a lot harder to prepare than to listen to.

Take it from some of Erie County's best-known clergymen: For each minute of preaching, there usually precedes at least one hour of preparation.

Even clergymen with many years of pulpit experience say it is not unusual for them to spend more than 20 hours preparing a 20-minute Sunday morning sermon. And most of these hours are filled with as much perspiration as inspiration.

In fact, some local clergymen recite their sermons in front of a mirror to eliminate unnecessary gestures. Some talk into a tape recorder to find flaws in their delivery.

Covering Volunteer Agencies

The reporter who covers the news discussed in this chapter is likely to find that he is surfeited with information from one group of agencies which grasp for every last shred of "publicity." From another group he is likely to hear nothing, and to be greeted as if he had leprosy if he goes to it seeking a story. There are some in-between agencies which are glad to co-operate with reporters and are not too demanding, but the pressures caused by the first two may make the reporter forget the ones which do not give him any special problems.

Social service agencies are gradually being converted to the public relations point of view. This, briefly, holds that an agency should tell its story to the community, or to the various subgroups in a community, and that newspapers furnish one channel for this information.

Public relations workers imbued with this idea can be very helpful to a newspaper reporter, but do not excuse him from his reporting chores. Reporters need to remember that their viewpoint is basically different from that of any public relations representative. The public relations man is trying to create a favorable image in the community of the organization he represents. The reporter is trying to find out what is most important for his reader to know, and to give him this information. In other words, the reporter represents his readers' interests.

This is true even though many of the stories presented by a press agent are valuable. He can often help a reporter to obtain stories which he might not otherwise find. At the same time, there may be stories which the public relations man would like to keep out of the paper, but the reporter feels his readers need to know.

REPORTING ASSIGNMENTS

1. Write a feature story about an organization which conducts an annual fund drive in your community. Tell how the campaign is organized and directed, how much money is collected, and how it is spent. What

percentage of the amount collected is used to defray costs of running the campaign?

2. Write a story about an agency which derives its support, or part of it, from your community's United Fund or Community Chest drive. Tell what the organization does and how it is run. Try to make your reader feel as though he had visited the agency.

3. Does your community have any foundations? If so write a feature story about one of them.

4. Interview the head of a charity agency to find out what he thinks about the treatment his agency is accorded in local newspapers and on local radio and television stations.

5. Write a story or a series about the number of fund drives each year in your community. Is there any overlapping?

6. Interview a few householders to find out whether they think they are overburdened with fund drives.

7. Find a feature story of general interest in one of the churches of your neighborhood.

8. Write an article or a series about "religion in our community." Consider such things as the number of churches and variety of denominations, the number of church members compared with the population, and the upward or downward trends in church membership.

9. Seek out and analyze local indicators which show the extent to which local church groups co-operate with each other. Write a story on your findings.

PART FOUR

Industry Is Public Affairs

17

Business Organization

Need for Public Confidence

The fortunes of American business determine the fortunes of everyone in America. When business is good nearly everyone's pocketbook is full. When business is bad everyone feels it. This is why business news is often front page news. This is why reporters translate ponderous documents such as SEC reports into stories which make sense to a factory worker who reads the paper during his coffee break.

All of us earn our living, one way or another, as a result of business enterprise. Business and industry produce our wealth—the material things we enjoy.

Many of us are paid directly by business and industry as workers, managers, owners, or investors. Doctors receive their fees from people who earn their money in industry. Public employees are paid with money raised from taxes on industry and employees of industry. Parallels could be drawn for nearly everyone with an income; it comes directly or indirectly from business. In our free enterprise system the private entrepreneur is the source of wealth, because he owns and controls the organizations which transform raw materials into the goods we need and want.

When government produces wealth, perhaps in the form of electrical energy, it performs the same function as business and thus moves into a new relationship beyond its role of referee.

The public's stake in business is big, but the business world's life is dependent on the confidence of the public. When the public begins to doubt, the business world shakes. E. S. Banks, financial editor of the *Philadelphia Inquirer*, puts it this way:

It is this lack of understanding of economics on the part of the average individual which is responsible, to a large extent, for the large swings upward or downward of the economy.

If we can make the public understand just what makes the economy click—what things to watch for—we feel that we can eliminate the major portion of the main cause of recessions and the depressions—the fear psychology.

Confidence, or lack of it, is reflected perhaps most rapidly in stock market fluctuations. In 1933 the public had a good demonstration of what confidence means to our banks. It is common knowledge that much of our business is transacted by credit arrangements, and that vast wealth may be transferred without any money actually changing hands. In 1933 only about $6.5 billion of actual currency existed, although our economy was operating on the basis of $46 billion. This worked fine as long as the public had confidence in the banks. Then, as today, a bank which had, say $5 million in deposits, would keep on hand only a small portion of that amount in currency. If all the depositors should demand their money at once, the bank obviously could not supply it. Early in 1933, as people began losing confidence in their banks, they began to withdraw their deposits. Soon the banks ran out of cash and had to close down their paying windows.

This caused confidence to drop even lower. State after state declared "bank holidays"—periods in which banks were closed to prevent more runs on them. By March 3, 1933, 24 states and the District of Columbia had either declared bank holidays or stringently limited the amount that any depositor could withdraw from his account. This was followed by federal action.

The *New York Daily News* explained the situation in a page 3 story this way:

Twenty-four States yesterday decided to declare new bank moratoria, or to grant bankers permission to restrict withdrawal of cash from their institutions to a total of around 5 per cent or took steps to make bank moratoria legal. . . . Bankers declared that heavy withdrawals in recent weeks by nervous depositors who had no reasons for worry about the safety of their money forced these States to act in order to protect the structure of their credit system. In plain language, that means the people of the States and the District pulled their money out of the banks and stuck it in the sock at home, forcing an unnecessary banking crisis. . . .

Confidence in and understanding of our banking, business, and industrial system are just as necessary in good times as they are in bad. Business news is a necessity, and it must be written so that it will be understood by the general public. The days are gone when a newspaper can afford to slant business news just for the businessman and the investor.

What does this mean in terms of reporting and writing? It means simply that business reporters must work just the way the good police or court reporter works—to find out what business stories are most important to the public, to get the stories, and to write them so that they will interest general readers. It means more emphasis on personalities in the business world, and better physical presentation through dynamic pictures and charts that speed a reader's understanding.

Ken Hand, a former police reporter who took over as business editor of the *Dallas Morning News,* told his staff: "Remember, lads, business men are people—regardless of what you may have heard to the contrary. So treat them like people. Remember that they will go for an interesting, well written story the same as the next guy."

Here, as an example of Mr. Hand's style, is part of a column he wrote when Lee Bristol, president of Bristol-Myers, visited Dallas:

> Toothpaste advertising has gone through some interesting phases since people began to rely on a dentifrice to do other things besides clean the teeth.
>
> So let's pass over all this gobbledegook about sales impact and impulse buying and get down to a clean little cottage where Joe Blow, like all creatures, returns at eventide.
>
> Blow, I'm sorry to say, is loaded to the scuppers. But he gives seven playful raps on the door with the confidence of a man who knows that chlorophyll toothpaste removes all unpleasant odors including those arising from over indulgence.
>
> Mrs. Blow, a realist, is not deceived . . . and there begins to form in Blow's clouded thinking the conviction that chlorophyll holds too great a promise, not completely fulfilled.
>
> And, adds Lee Bristol, president of Bristol-Myers Company (Ipana for the Smile of Beauty) there is no record of its having prevented a man from staggering.

This introduces a discussion of the serious problems of the toothpaste companies.

Not all newspapers carry the feature angle as far as Mr. Hand does, but most will admit that the feature approach is vital in telling the story of the business world.

Bernard Kilgore of the *Wall Street Journal* reaffirms the point. "Business news," he says, "can be as dull as dishwater. . . . In the hands of incompetent reporters, hacking away in the jargon they have picked up to conceal their ignorance, all these subjects can be made almost literally repulsive. . . . On the other hand, business news . . . is essentially interesting."

Bring out the human interest, Kilgore urges. Time and talent are essential to produce good stories, he adds. Newspapers must invest more money in recruiting reporters, and then give them time to do a quality job—that is, to report in scope and depth, with perception and illumination.

Agreement is general that our newspapers need more thorough reporting of business and better writing of business news, because business is increasingly important to each of us.

THREE WAYS TO ORGANIZE A BUSINESS

1. As a proprietor:

Owner does business in his own name.

2. As a partnership:

Two or more individuals pool their resources in a common undertaking.

3. As a corporation:

Many people become owners by buying stock. (In some closed corporations only a few persons own stock.)

Fig. 15

Patterns of Organization

Businesses are organized in three basic patterns: (1) Proprietorships, (2) partnerships, and (3) corporations.

PROPRIETORSHIPS consist of individuals doing business as individuals. Most small stores are owned and operated by single proprietors. If the owner wants to borrow money to expand, he goes to a bank and borrows money as an individual, perhaps using the assets of his business as collateral. If the business becomes involved in a law suit, or if it fails and the proprietor is unable to pay his debts, he may lose all his personal possessions—house, car, jewels, nearly everything of value—to satisfy the judgments against his business.

Many small concerns are organized this way because it is the least expensive way; no charter is required and there may be no need to hire an attorney. On the other hand, few businesses operated as single proprietorships become very large without changing to another form of organization. It is hard for a proprietorship to borrow money in large amounts.

PARTNERSHIPS have the same liabilities as individual proprietorships, with each partner's private possessions being held liable for any judgments against the business. This leaves each member at the mercy of the others. If one defaults, all the others may have to sacrifice their personal property to make good.

Partnerships usually have more working capital because there are two or more partners to put up cash, and with property to be used as security for bank loans.

CORPORATIONS are associations of persons who buy *stock* in an enterprise and, in fact, become the owners. Most big businesses are corporations. A corporation can increase the amount of working capital by selling more stock; it is also easier to borrow money in other ways which we will consider shortly. Each investor (an owner if his investment consists of common stock) is liable for company debts only to the extent of his investment in the concern. Thus a person who owns a part of a corporation need not lose his personal possessions if the concern goes bankrupt. There may be tax advantages, too, to the corporate setup.

A disadvantage of the corporation is that it is more expensive to establish—a charter must be granted by the state. This involves the payment of fees to the state and usually high attorney's fees. Another disadvantage in some cases is that corporations are usually subjected to more strict regulation. One aspect of the regulations requires public disclosure of specified information.

Corporations are an important part of our life in the United States today, but they are not an American, or even a modern, invention. Some historians say there is reason to think that corporations existed in Babylonia in 2200 B.C. Lawyers refer to corporations as "legal persons." By this they mean that corporations can sue and be sued in the courts just as though they were private individuals. Corporations have lives of their own, independent of the lives of their owners, and they may be chartered without any time limitation. Bracton, an early English jurist, commented on this characteristic in 1260 when he compared a corporation to a flock of sheep, "always the same flock, though the sheep successively depart." Blackstone, another great English jurist, put it this way in 1765: "All the individual members that have existed, or that shall ever exist, are but one person in the law, a person that never dies, as the river Thames is the same river though parts are changing every instant."

Corporations are created by franchise granted by the federal government or a state. This document describes the powers granted and the conditions upon which they are given. Not only private businesses, but many government functions are carried on by corporations. City governments, for example, are corporations.

Among the grants usually made to a corporation is the power to raise money by selling stocks, and to borrow money, either by selling bonds or borrowing directly from banks.

Two kinds of stock are ordinarily offered for sale—common and preferred.

Common stock is the most speculative, which means its owner has a chance to make a larger gain, but he will be in the last group to be paid off if the organization fails. The common stockholders control the corporation by voting for members of the board of directors. When affairs are going smoothly this is mostly a formality, with only one slate of candidates up for election and therefore the same group assured of control.

Battles for control develop once in a while, and they make good stories. A person or group seeking to gain control of a corporation gets control of all the common stock possible by buying it, persuading friends to buy it, and by trying to persuade everyone who owns common stock to vote for his slate of candidates for the board of directors. This group sets policy, so control of the board means control of the organization.

Newspapers gave much space to the efforts by which the late Robert R. Young gained control of the New York Central Railroad. Mr. Young and his friends owned much of the stock, but the outcome of the voting was in doubt for days after a hectic meeting of the stockholders in the Armory at Albany. The balance of power rested with the owners of small amounts of common stock. Mr. Young, as well as the previous controlling group of the Central, used all the techniques of public relations to persuade these small owners to vote "right." Organizations specializing in this work were hired to telephone stockholders in advance of the meeting to get them to vote for Mr. Young's group.

This story, from the *New York Times,* concerns a battle in the making for control of a concern:

> Robert H. Morse, president of Fairbanks, issued the following statement yesterday:
>
> "The more stock Mr. Silberstein announces as owning, the more his financial gyrations are revealed. I repeat, it is not the stock of which he claims ownership today which will count, but the number of shares which he will be able to vote legally at the annual meeting of Fairbanks, Morse stockholders on March 27."

In another development, Charles H. Morse, Jr., grandson of the founder of Fairbanks and a former director, announced he would form a committee to "disseminate information concerning the need for change of management of Fairbanks, Morse."

Mr. Morse said he had no intention of soliciting proxies personally, but would support Penn-Texas, if it should decide to do so. Mr. Morse resigned in December, criticizing the lack of a consistent management program for employes. He supported Penn-Texas in its unsuccessful bid last year to obtain control of Fairbanks.

The speculative aspects of common stock are more important to some financiers. The value of any stock at any time is determined by the amount a prospective buyer is willing to pay as against the amount that a seller is willing to take. Since the income from common stock is less certain than that from other forms of investment in corporations, it stands to reason that it will be subject to more price fluctuation.

The other kind of stock often traded in the market is *preferred*. This is a more stable investment than common because it normally pays its holders a given return on the investment, and this must be paid before any of the owners of common stock are given a dividend.

Bonds are a third way of investing in corporations. Bonds differ from both common and preferred stock in that persons buying bonds are not considered to be owners of the company, but simply individuals who have loaned money to it. The bonds will be carried on the company books as a debt. Bonds normally form the steadiest income of the three types of investment. They pay a stated rate of interest and run for a stated number of years. Bondholders have no voting privileges.

If a corporation goes bankrupt the bondholders are paid off first, because they hold a debt against the company. Next come the holders of preferred stock. If anything is left after these groups are paid, the common stockholders divide it.

One of the most significant facts about the corporate ownership pattern is that, while it was invented thousands of years ago, it is the factor which makes big business and economic democracy compatible. Organizations have to be fairly large these days to survive and make progress, if only because a large amount of expensive equipment is needed to produce efficiently. A shoemaker of long ago, for example, could do all the work in making a pair of shoes himself, with some simple equipment. This method of making shoes is still possible, but to bring down the price so that we all can afford several pairs, the modern manufacturer must make them in large numbers by using expensive machinery. This means a heavy investment in machines and a large payroll.

Few persons can afford to own a large business, but many small investors can buy stocks and together they can own a large enterprise.

Through their voting of common stock they can control its policies. This is the only practical way that we have found so far to spread among many the ownership and control of the large concerns which today's production methods demand. By buying stock in the company which employs them, the workers can become part owners. Many businesses encourage their employees to buy company stock to keep them more interested in their jobs and help them produce better.

Corporations are not the perfect solution to the problems of big business and democracy. Abuses may develop when a small portion of the stockholders controls the concern. Many stockholders may be too busy or too poor to attend stockholder meetings, so the control, as in government, is held by the interested minority.

Minority control can have far-reaching effects when holding corporations pyramid power so that a few persons control many corporations. As an example, if Company A owns a controlling interest in Companies B, C, D, E, and F, the few persons who control Company A control a vast amount of wealth which they do not own. Companies which deal in the stock of others are known as holding companies, and their affairs are regulated more strictly than those of other corporations. The Federal Trade Commision and the Anti-Trust Division of the Department of Justice have done much to distribute control more evenly.

Business Problems and the Reporter

Business today is as sensitive to the attitude of the public as is the politician. Many businessmen feel that, while a politician has to be elected once a year or once in two or four years, a business concern has to ask every day for a new vote of confidence. Certainly public confidence is an essential need of any business. No concern stays in business long if the public does not have enough confidence in its product to buy it, but product advertising is just one phase of a campaign for a friendly public attitude.

Community relations is a new field, but it is growing rapidly. In general, it is concerned with the attitude of people living in the community in which a concern is located. Most business managers want people in their communities to feel friendly toward the concern. An unfriendly community makes it harder for a company to hire workers, may result in unfavorable local tax policies and lower sale of company products, and may injure the company in other ways. The positive advantages of friendly neighbors are just as obvious.

The community relations manager and his assistants are concerned with building up a favorable impression of the business in its home community. Their activities range from trying to gain favorable articles in the newspapers and on radio and television stations, to planning plant open houses and community-wide events.

Other plant officials are concerned with gaining goodwill from others who are important to the business. Stockholders and potential stockholders are important to any corporation, and many individuals are making a career of this one phase of business public relations. The people who are actual or potential investors in a concern can facilitate expansion, and provide adequate operating capital and good reserves. An unfriendly feeling from investors will limit management in many ways. Executives concerned with stockholder relations plan the annual stockholders' meetings, prepare reports, answer stockholders' questions, and take any other avenues they can to build up a friendly feeling among the people who have money to invest.

Also important to any business is the goodwill of the people who work for it. Workers who like their employer tend to become unofficial boosters. Disgruntled workers can do much harm. Labor relations specialists try to make workers happy in their jobs and proud of their company. This involves friendly and speedy handling of complaints, fringe benefits, arranging pleasant working conditions, and often an array of social programs, descendants of the old-fashioned "company picnic."

The interest of business in creating a "favorable image" of itself in the community often makes his job easier for a reporter, but it can also complicate his job.

A good public relations man will be a tremendous help in supplying the routine stories of a business which make good local copy. The news of promotions, personnel changes, building programs, and many other things comes in to the newspaper office in professional form from the company's public relations office. Since much of this is worthwhile news for a local paper, it helps everyone concerned. One cannot expect company public relations men to be eager to disclose news which is detrimental to their concern. However, many will help a reporter obtain this kind of information if it is newsworthy on the theory that, in the long run, an honest news policy is helpful to a company. Others may try to block the news unfavorable to their employers, and thus complicate the job of the reporter who is trying to get the story and cannot afford to play favorites.

Business is so all-pervasive in the United States that its problems often affect the public interest. Many of our historic struggles have centered around the use of our natural resources. We are inclined to think that the public as a whole has an inherent claim on the basic raw materials—water power, minerals, timber, and the rest. Lumber companies in the past have been accused of wanton use, for their own benefit, of vast amounts of timber. Many companies are now careful to publicize their practice of managing their forest lands so that the timber supplies are constantly replenished. Disputes over the years as to ownership of off shore oil resources in the Gulf of Mexico illustrate another aspect of the same general problem.

The dispute is more likely to be expressed today in conflicts over whether government or private industry shall be allowed to develop electrical energy from water power. Pretty much the same problem is involved in a consideration of whether public or private agencies shall take advantage of nuclear energy, after government paid for the basic research and development which made it possible.

Some of the other problems of business are discussed in other chapters in this section. The general reporter is likely to find himself covering varied business news more often in the future, and he needs to write the stories so that the general public will understand. More and more workers in the middle income group are setting aside some of their savings to become investors. This, plus the general tendency to regard business as a public trust, is frequently moving business stories from the business page to the general news sections.

The news magazines often do a good job in reporting business news in simple terms. This item from *Newsweek* is an example:

> As big pension funds grew bigger, an argument has raged about how much economic power they could wield over the nation's corporations through their investments in common stocks. As a practical matter, not much, pension-fund expert Robert Tilove concluded this week.
>
> In his "Pension Funds and Economic Freedom," a study prepared for the Fund for the Republic, Tilove predicts "self-insured" pension funds (those not administered by insurance companies) will have $17 billion to $20 billion invested in common stocks by 1965, and, if current practices prevail, most of the money will be in 200 to 250 favorite issues. Nevertheless, he sees "no 'clear and present danger,' nor even an implied threat for the near future," that pension funds—or the trust companies which control their investment programs—will try to use their holdings to gain control of other enterprises.
>
> Among his reasons: (1) It would hurt a trust company's reputation if it became known that it had used trust assets for "self-interested purposes," (2) legal complications, (3) it is just not smart investment policy to build up too large a portfolio in any one security.

REPORTING ASSIGNMENTS

1. Find a local business which is run as a proprietorship. Interview the owner to find out why he keeps it a proprietorship.

2. Do the same for a partnership.

3. Interview an official of a corporation. Find out why his organization benefits from being incorporated.

4. Talk with a bank official to obtain material for a story on "the bank's need for public confidence." Find out what percentage of deposits the bank keeps on hand to meet demands for cash; how it invests the rest; how it cultivates the confidence of the public.

5. Obtain the annual report of a corporation and write a news story from it.

6. Interview a stock broker for his ideas on the value of the mutual investment funds.

7. Interview the public relations manager of a business for a story on the nature of his job. Find out how he handles stories which are unfavorable to his firm.

18

Security and Commodity Markets

Anyone who can scrape together a few hundred dollars can buy a piece of American business. Stocks and an active stock market make this possible. When a person buys a stock he does not loan money to a company— he becomes one of its owners. If he owns one-hundredth of the company's stock, he owns one-hundredth of its real estate, manufacturing facilities, goodwill and all its other assets.

Need for the Markets

Active stock markets make it practical for people with a small amount of money to invest some of their savings in stocks. Beset by a sudden financial need, a small investor can quickly convert his stocks into cash by using the facilities of the New York Stock Exchange or one of the other exchanges. The market is usually fluid enough, that is, there is enough buying and selling, so that stocks can be turned into cash with little delay.

Most famous of the American stock markets is the New York Stock Exchange. It began when a group of men gathered under a buttonwood tree to buy and sell bonds of the new United States government and some of the banks. After a while the Exchange moved into a coffee house and eventually went into its own building on Wall Street.

It has grown into a complex organization which affects and reflects the business life of the whole nation. Persons authorized to do business on the Exchange are said to have seats on it. Transfer of seats is by sale, and in recent years the price has run into many thousands of dollars. Most of the firms which maintain seats are brokers; that is, they buy and sell stocks and bonds for other people, known as principals, although some investors use seats on the Exchange only for their own operations.

The commodity markets, which deal in agricultural products, likewise perform a public service; they provide a place where prices can be determined through the laws of supply and demand. The commodities most likely to be traded are those which have a wide market, are produced in large quantities, and can be accurately graded and kept for a reasonable period. These include potatoes, wheat, barley, corn, oats, rice, rye, cotton, wool, flaxseed, butter, and eggs.

Important commodity markets are situated in Chicago, Duluth, Kansas City, Los Angeles, Minneapolis, New Orleans, New York, Portland, St. Louis, San Francisco, and Seattle. In addition there are many regional markets which are important in their areas.

One of the most famous commodity exchanges, the Chicago Board of Trade, was the subject of an article in the *New York Times* on the Board's 110th anniversary in 1958:

CHICAGO, April 3—For the first time since World War II trading stopped briefly today on the Chicago Board of Trade.

During the war, trading stopped each day for one minute at 11 A.M. for a silent prayer for victory. Today the halt was a recognition of the exchange's 110th anniversary.

The City Council adopted a congratulatory resolution and Mayor Richard H. Daley read it from the public gallery overlooking the floor of the exchange.

The Board of Trade is one of Chicago's oldest institutions, tracing its start to a period only eleven years after Chicago became a village. It is the cradle of futures trading in grain. At the time, instead of passing resolutions praising the new exchange, the City Council was busy passing ordinances prohibiting horse racing on the wooden sidewalks and against the keeping of pigs in the dirt streets.

Contrasting its small beginning with the role of the exchange today, Robert C. Liebenow, president, said that within the walls of the exchange nearly 90 per cent of the world's grain futures business is transacted.

Moreover, he added, it has the only lard futures market and does practically 100 per cent of the world's soybean futures business, 90 per cent of the crude soybean oil futures trade and more than half of the trade in soybean meal futures. It is also the world's largest market for cash corn and soybeans. In 1957 the total dollar volume topped $25,000,000,000.

The board's first meeting, Mr. Liebenow said, was held in a room over Gage & Haines flour and feed store facing what was then South Water Street, now the corner of Clark Street and the lower level of Wacker Drive.

The eighty-two Chicago merchants who founded the board wrote into their constitution the sentiment that they wanted "to promote uniformity of customs and usages of merchants and to inculcate principles of justice and equity in trade."

Until uniform grading standards were established, the board's standards were used by many other grain marketing centers. Trading in contracts calling for the delivery of grain at some future date had its beginning here.

From time to time, the Board of Trade is attacked as a group of speculators whose activities harm farmers and consumers. Mr. Liebenow said that the board provided the country with an economical marketing system and of every dollar spent for food made from grain, less than 2 cents goes for marketing costs.

He said that his exchange provides a means of recording price, and helped minimize risk of financial loss from adverse price changes.

Market Operations

Most investors do business on the New York Stock Exchange through brokers in their own cities who maintain contacts with member New York firms. New York brokers maintain branch offices, too, in many cities.

When an investor tells his broker to buy so many shares of stock, the order is sent on leased wires to the firm's trader on the floor of the Exchange. The trader goes to the trading post where the stock is being traded, and buys the stock at the lowest possible price. A sell order is handled in the same way, with representatives of buyers and sellers meeting at the trading post on the floor of the Exchange. When a sale is consummated, it is reported at once to the brokers for the principals and to the stock record clerk of the company whose stock changed hands.

The buyer will receive a bill in the mail for the price of his stock plus the commission due the broker. Or he may receive a monthly statement.

Every stock issued has an assigned value. This is the price paid by the original purchaser of the stock. After that the laws of supply and demand determine its value. The Exchange supplies a trading place, but it does not determine the value of stocks. The price is determined by what someone is willing to pay and what someone owning the stock is willing to accept. Of course, value of stock is determined over a period by many factors, including the earning history of the stock, the success of a company's management, the outlook for this particular type of industry, and the general business outlook. Stock prices are regarded as a reliable long-term indicator of the business picture, although they are too sensitive to events such as strikes, unsettled international conditions, and even national elections.

Some of the common terms used by traders are:

Bull market is a rising market created because many investors are optimistic. The buying increases and therefore prices rise.

A *bear market* is just the opposite. If many investors think prices are too high, they will sell. This depresses the market. To be *bullish* is to believe that stocks will go up; to be *bearish* is to believe they will go down.

An *investor* is a person who buys stocks planning to keep them for a while, and hoping to profit from dividends.

A *speculator* buys stocks intending to make a quick profit by taking advantage of price fluctuations. Many persons have criticized speculators on the grounds that they do not perform any service. Actually, a speculator performs a valuable service by keeping up the volume of trading, thus furnishing a ready market for stocks that an investor may want to liquidate.

The grounds for criticism arise when a speculator tries to manipulate the market to suit his own convenience. For example, a speculator or a group of speculators may create a false activity by heavy buying, hoping to induce others to buy the same stock. This will force the market higher and give the speculator a chance to sell when the market is high. This practice is fairly well regulated on most exchanges.

Round lots are shares bought and sold in 100-share units. Smaller orders are handled by odd-lot brokers, who charge a small extra commission for their services.

Short selling, is, in effect, selling securities you don't own and borrowing them to deliver to the buyer. This practice has been used in an effort to control the market, but essentially it is a normal and necessary operation. Similar arrangements are common in other types of selling. A farmer, for example, may agree to sell his corn crop to a canner even before the seed is in the ground. An automobile dealer may agree to sell an automobile in a month even though he does not have it in stock and it is not even in production at the factory. Book clubs agree to supply a given number of books each year, many of which are not yet in print.

Short selling and dealing in futures generally are even more common to the commodity markets than they are to the stock markets. Agricultural goods which are produced in large quantities and which keep reasonably well are often traded this way.

Buying on the margin is borrowing part of the money the customer needs to buy stocks. After a customer's credit is established with a broker, he may extend credit in this way. Usually the agreement includes a provision which empowers the broker to sell the stock when it drops below a given point, so that his investment is protected. In periods when many people are buying stocks on the margin there is real danger that a sudden drop in the market will wipe out many speculators, especially amateurs. Many professionals as well as amateurs were ruined by the 1929 market crash.

Wide-scale margin buying can cause the market to rise higher than it would normally, because many persons are enabled to borrow to double or treble their holdings, thus increasing demand and forcing prices higher.

One of the regulatory devices that resulted from the 1929 crash was the power granted to the Federal Reserve Board to regulate margin requirements. A purchaser is required to put up a certain minimum percentage of the amount he is spending for securities. In October, 1934, this was set at 45 per cent. It has ranged from 40 to 100 per cent in the years since. When members of the Federal Reserve Board think that the volume of credit is excessive, they will raise the margin requirements so that each buyer must put up more of his own money to purchase stocks. This makes less money available for speculation and so helps to cut down the volume of business on the exchanges. The Federal Reserve Board can liven up a slow market by allowing buyers to borrow more money for speculative purposes.

Watered stock is overvalued in terms of the assets which support it. Thus a concern's total outstanding stock can be valued at a higher price than its total worth. Such stock obviously is not a very sound investment.

Methods of Buying Stocks

Investors buy stocks by establishing credit with their brokers as they might establish credit at a department store, and then telling the brokers when they want to buy or sell. This can be done by a telephone call, a letter, or a personal visit to the broker's office. The most common method is for the investor to call his broker and give him the order, perhaps after getting a quotation on the price.

The buyer may use some special kinds of orders if they fit his purpose:

A *limit order* tells the broker to buy or sell at a specific price. For example, the investor might tell his broker to buy 10 shares of a given stock if and when it comes down to $45 per share. The broker could not pay more for the stock, but would buy it at $45 or cheaper if he could. Sellers use the order the same way. An order to sell at $45 means that the broker should sell if he can get $45 or better.

Stop orders tell the broker to sell if a stock drops below a given price. Investors use this device to protect themselves from heavy losses or to protect profits. If a stock were selling at $45, the investor might order his broker to sell at $42. If the price of the stock declined to $42 the broker would sell at that price or the best price he could get.

Such orders can be limited to any period—a day, a week, or a month— or they may be good until cancelled.

Monthly investment plans are becoming popular with people who want to buy stocks out of current income. This means that a person agrees to invest a certain amount each month. The broker invests this as directed. When shares are purchased under this plan, they are sent to the buyer, or kept for him at the broker's office.

Research services are furnished by many brokerage houses, which spend large sums of money each year to maintain staffs to study market trends and help their customers invest wisely. This information is supplied without extra charge.

Regulation—Internal and External

The New York Stock Exchange exercises strict control over its own operations and over its members, and it maintains certain requirements for companies whose stock is listed on the exchange. These restrictions, together with the government-imposed controls, have done much to keep order in the security market and consequently to stabilize the entire business structure.

Before a company may list its stocks on the New York Stock Exchange, its officers must satisfy the governors of the Exchange that it is a succesful concern, with substantial assets and earning power. Its stock should be distributed widely throughout the country among at least 1,500 stockholders, with 300,000 shares. The company should show at least $1 million in earnings in the preceding year.

It must agree to issue regular financial statements. Most of the companies publish financial statements every three months; a few publish only once a year. Those which report annually are seasonal businesses, and quarterly statements would have no significance.

In addition a company must agree to keep a transfer agent and registrar in New York City. The transfer agent keeps a record of the name and address of each stockholder, and the registrar keeps a constant check to see that a company's stock is not overissued. The Exchange supervises the quality of the engravings on the stock certificates, the tangible evidence of ownership, so that investors will be protected against false certificates.

Officials of the exchange report that normally about 100 companies inquire each year about listing their stock on the Exchange, and that, of these, about 20 qualify. Despite the rigid controls, the number of stocks listed has grown steadily. Until 1869 the controls were highly informal. If a member presented a stock for trading and the majority of members agreed, the stock was placed on the list. In 1869 the Exchange required that it be notified of all stocks issued and valid for trading.

Officials of the Exchange have expressed their philosophy regarding controls in these words:

"The investor or trader who owns, buys or plans to purchase listed securities is entitled to information about the corporation which will help him to make his investment decisions intelligently. Failure of a company to disclose all information specified by the Exchange may result in its suspension from the list."

Corporations are willing to live up to the standards prescribed by the Exchange because of the prestige gained from a listing there, and because of the added facilities for raising money which such a listing provides.

Controls over Members

Membership on the New York Stock Exchange is a tremendous business asset and is highly prized, with seats selling in recent years for as much as $113,000. The initiation fee is $4,000 and dues are $750 a year. Until 1952 the Exchange had 1,375 members, but membership is being reduced gradually to 1,325.

Member firms are required to inform their customers regularly of the condition of their accounts, and to supply customers with the firm's financial statement on request. Firms must have adequate capital, must supply information to the Exchange at given times, and must submit at least once a year to a surprise audit of their books. Employees of member firms who do business with the public are registered with the Exchange, and are required to pass a written examination after a period of training. Penalties used to enforce these requirements are suspension or expulsion.

Securities and Exchange Commission

The Securities and Exchange Commission spends between $5 million and $7 million a year to administer a series of federal regulations established by the Securities Acts of 1933 and 1934. In the process it investigates each year from 1,000 to 2,000 security transactions of which it is suspicious. The general privisions of the Securities Act require full disclosure of information about new securities offered to the public, for the prevention of frauds in connection with such listings. This information is required for securities listed on any of the national exchanges, or offered through the mails or in interstate or foreign commerce. Included, too, are most *over-the-counter* dealings—stock and bond transfers not involving one of the exchanges.

In addition to registration with the SEC and adequate disclosure of information, the Securities Acts forbid manipulative operations. These include the formation of pools to force prices of securities up or down, faked sales, and use of misleading information.

The Securities and Exchange Commission is also given power to insist on revision in the rules of exchanges in the public interest.

Other Markets

This country's largest stock market is the New York Stock Exchange, but it is only one of the important markets. The American Stock Exchange (formerly called the Curb Exchange) also operates in New York

City. Other stock exchanges are in Toronto, Montreal, Chicago, Baltimore, Detroit, Los Angeles, San Francisco, New Orleans, St. Louis, Spokane, Salt Lake City, Washington, D. C., and several other cities.

The New York exchanges deal in nationally traded stock, but for a financial reporter in another city, the coverage opportunities are great in his own local exchange. The local exchanges deal in regional stocks, and many important concerns in an area may list their stock only locally. This means that much of the business news of a given area develops from the regional exchanges. Since this is the most important financial news of all to many readers, it is important news for every paper in the area.

Federal law requires that all exchanges attempting to do business through the mails or in interstate commerce be registered with the Securities and Exchange Commission, unless the body specifically exempts them. Such exemption may be granted when the Commission finds that the volume of business is so low as to make registration impractical, unnecessary, or inappropriate.

Over-the-Counter Security Markets

Many stocks and bonds are not traded on the organized exchanges, but are handled by brokers who buy and sell for themselves and for their customers. Brokers may maintain an over-the-counter business, in addition to facilities for trading on one or more of the exchanges.

Maintaining an active market is obviously more difficult in over-the-counter securities, since there is no central place where trading occurs. Brokers who deal extensively in over-the-counter securities keep elaborate records of owners of various stocks, of potential buyers, and of bid and asking prices.

Most of the stocks and bonds handled in over-the-counter transactions are as reliable as those traded on the exchanges. It may be convenience or custom which dictates this method of marketing securities. Regional stocks often are traded in this fashion. Stock offerings of smaller companies may not be large enough to justify the expense of listing on one of the exchanges. New concerns must rely on over-the-counter operations to market their stock, because they are not well enough established for one of the exchanges to be interested in handling their stocks.

Wide dispersal of the dealers and lack of a central clearing house has made regulation of over-the-counter dealings extremely difficult. Such outlets used to be good hunting grounds for swindlers, because there was not the formal control which could be maintained by an exchange.

Control problems were so difficult that the Securities Acts of 1933 and 1934 did not try to enforce specific regulations. Instead they provided general powers of regulation, and required the SEC to investigate operations and recommend future legislation.

Specific regulation was provided in 1936 and 1938 in amendments to the Act. Now all dealers must register with the SEC unless their business is entirely intrastate, or unless they deal entirely in securities which are exempt from SEC regulation. They must, in filing, furnish information about themselves and their business, including the types of securities in which they deal. This information must be kept up-to-date. The Commission is empowered to stop certain manipulative practices.

Traders have been required to join organizations which provide self-regulation under the general supervision of SEC officials. The most prominent of these organizations is the National Association of Securities Dealers, Inc. This provides detailed regulations for its members, which regulations have been approved by the commission. Expense of self-regulation is paid out of dues charged to members. The organization also serves as a clearing-house for information and provides a list of bid and asked prices on the more important over-the-counter securities.

Regulation of Commodity Markets

The regulation of the commodity exchanges has been of the same type as that of the securities markets, although Congress began earlier to regulate trading in commodities. Abuses centered mostly about futures trading, and the regulations have concerned that primarily.

Important commodity markets are in Chicago, New York, Kansas City, Minneapolis, Duluth, Portland, New Orleans, St. Louis, San Francisco, and Seattle. All markets doing business in interstate commerce or through the mails are required to register with the Commodities Exchange Commission. Disclosure of information is required and specific regulations imposed.

Forbidden activities include:

1. Getting a *corner* on a market. This is done by a trader or group of traders who buy up enough of a commodity so that any one buying it has to deal with them, thus allowing them to control the price.

2. *Wash sales.* Traders sometimes try to make the market look more active than it really is by buying and selling the same commodity at the same time.

Purchases larger than a certain size are forbidden to traders for speculative purposes.

The amount of price increase or decrease in a given time may be controlled. Thus, for example, the price on a bushel of a certain commodity may not be allowed to increase or decrease more than five cents in a day.

Fluidity of Capital

This brief review of the markets will serve as a starting point for a reporter interested in covering the financial news of his own community.

Most reporters do not cover the New York Stock Exchange or the Chicago Board of Trade. They still need to understand these markets, because they help to control general business conditions and thus affect every business in the land. Moreover, more and more readers are interested in the great central markets because they are investing their money through them.

Out of this general picture of the financial institutions, three things become apparent:

1. The importance of these institutions to the entire economy has made a certain amount of control necessary. Overcontrol is as much a mistake as undercontrol, because too much control can take away the great contribution of any market: the chance for prices to seek their own level based on what people are willing to pay and the price at which owners are willing to sell.

2. A significant contribution of the markets is that they make possible a free flow of capital. As we have seen, they make it practical for the small saver to invest in securities, because he knows he can readily convert them back into cash if that becomes necessary. These markets also make it possible for the speculative investor to take his chances with new concerns and new industries where the risk and rewards are greater.

3. The public, as it becomes more investment-conscious, will seek to know more about these institutions. This gives newspaper writers and editors a duty and an opportunity. Successful newspapers will find and print the stories most in demand.

The free flow of capital is a real part of the free enterprise system. Without it there would be little chance to start new businesses, for few people could finance ventures large enough to compete with established big businesses.

Free flow of capital and freedom to do the work of one's choice are the basic ingredients of free enterprise. One is as important as the other.

REPORTING ASSIGNMENTS

1. Interview an official of your local produce exchange for a story on how the exchange works.

2. Visit a local stock broker to find out how he handles stock purchases and sales for his customers.

3. Find out from a local broker what local stocks are for sale and how the sales are handled.

4. Interview a grocery wholesaler to find out how prices are set on the commodities he handles.

5. Interview a bank official to get his views on how fluctuations on the New York Stock Exchange affect business in your community.

19

Business Barometers

Importance of Barometers

How do you know when times are good? When times are bad?

How can you predict the future state of the economy?

Mr. Average Man does it by the feel of his pay envelope on Friday, by the thickness of his pocketbook, by the size of his rent or tax bill, by the price of steak or hamburger.

The financial reporter uses all these criteria, but he also follows others which are not so obviously related to his own welfare.

Among the most sensitive indicators of our economic health are the stock and commodity markets.

Bernard Baruch, who demonstrated his understanding of the stock market by making millions in it, put it this way in an article in the *Saturday Evening Post:*

> Actually, the stock market could be termed the total thermometer for our civilization. The prices of stocks—and commodities and bonds as well—are affected by literally anything and everything that happens in our world, from new inventions and the changing value of the dollar to vagaries of the weather and the threat of war or the prospect of peace. But what actually registers in the stock market's fluctuations are not the events themselves, but the human reactions to these events. In short, how millions of individual men and women feel these happenings may affect the future.
>
> Above all else, in other words, the stock market is people. It is people trying to read the future.

When people are confident they buy stocks and bonds, and, in answer to the law of supply and demand, the market goes up. When people lack confidence they sell, and the market goes down.

The stock market is perhaps the most sensitive indicator we have of business activity. But it is not the only one, and many other indicators help in predicting trends. Indeed, the individuals who buy and sell on the stock market and thus determine its activity base their decisions on many other indicators.

Production indexes are among the most significant. Obviously, if we produce more goods this year than last, our business has been more active. Production of various goods is reported regularly. Automobile, steel, and agricultural production are among the important indexes of business activity. Steel production is important because so much of our industry uses steel. When orders for steel are high, then most of our other businesses are producing in high gear, too. Automobile production is such a large segment of our economy that it, too, offers a good index.

To persons interested in any particular branch of the economy, production figures in that field are valuable.

Money being spent for industrial expansion is also highly regarded as an indication of business health. This reflects the confidence level of the industrial leaders.

Donald I. Rogers, business and financial editor of the *New York Herald Tribune,* discusses this indicator in a column for his newspaper:

It's easy to be fooled by the figures. When the Commerce Department and Securities and Exchange Commission reported that American business is going to boost its spending for new plant and equipment 6½ per cent this year to $37,361,000,000 it sounded as though we were off on another boom-tide of prosperity. Indeed we may be. Probably the most significant factor in a boom is the amount of money spent for expansion.

There's a factor which should not be overlooked, however—and that's the high cost of building anything these days.

Any one who has bought a house in recent years knows that real estate values have soared beyond the inflationary rise reflected in other markets. It's equally tough, perhaps tougher, in the heavy construction industry, when they build commercial buildings or manufacturing plants.

This reporter asked the people at Turner Construction Co. if they could document the boost in building prices. Turner should know, after all, for the outfit constructs some of the biggest and most important buildings in the nation.

Did you know that a house which could have been built in 1939 for $10,000 would cost $31,000 today?

Or that a house which could have been built in 1948 for $10,000 would cost $15,000 to duplicate today?

Of course, the $10,000 1948 house would not be nearly so commodious and well-built as the $10,000 1939 house.

The reason for this disparity (certainly most other values have not inflated so much) is that in the building industry today's dollar is worth 33 cents when compared to a 1939 dollar considered to be worth 100 cents. This is a greater erosion than in most other industries.

After further elaboration Mr. Rogers concludes by reminding his readers that "At these prices, and with this water, the expansion isn't as great as it seems."

This column is an illustration of what any qualified business reporter should do. He not only needs to report the indexes, but he should make a conscientious effort to explain and evaluate them.

Price Indexes

Price indexes are widely followed as barometers which reflect the state of our economy. Indexes are means for comparing a price (or almost anything else which can be expressed in figures) with a base period. Usually the base period is arbitrarily set at 100; prices below those in the base period will be less than 100; prices above it will be more than 100.

The Bureau of Labor Statistics of the United States Department of Labor constructs one of the most widely-used indexes. It is based on consumer prices in the 1947–1949 period. This means that prices in that period are pegged at 100. Higher prices in other periods are higher than 100, lower ones below 100.

The consumer price index, or cost of living index, as it is popularly called, is widely publicized, and it is used as the basis for wage adjustment in some labor contracts which tie wage rates to the price level.

The following Associated Press story, which appeared in the *Syracuse Post-Standard,* is fairly typical of those stories which regularly report the cost of living index, and to some extent interpret it.

WASHINGTON, Aug. 22 (Æ)—The cost of living rose in July and for the 11th straight month set a new record, the government reported today.

The July increase was one-half of one per cent, raising the Labor Department's consumer price index to 120.8 per cent of the 1947–49 level. A department spokesman indicated that no great decline was expected for August.

The latest jump means a wage increase for some 1,300,000 workers whose salaries are tied to the index. The increases will range from one to six cents an hour, with the bulk of the workers getting an additional three cents.

Most of the workers whose pay will go up are in the auto, farm equipment and electric industries. The big three auto-makers announced an increase of three cents for 700,000 hourly workers and increases for 188,000 salaried workers.

Smaller groups in local transit, metal industries and trucking are due to get raises. About 120,000 are in Westinghouse Electric plants.

Average spendable earnings of factory production workers went up 15 cents a week in July, the Labor Department said, but the increase was canceled out by price rises.

The July average spendable pay for a worker with three dependents was

$75.46 and for a worker without dependents $68.05. Considering the price increases, purchasing power of these workers declined by three-tenths of one per cent as compared to June but was still 1½ per cent above a year ago.

The Labor Department pointed to food as the villain in the latest price rise—particularly the breakfast staples, bacon, eggs and fresh fruit.

Food makes up about 30 per cent of the government's price index, and its price rose by a full one per cent on the average. That boosted the food index to 117.4 per cent of the 1947–49 average, and topped the previous record high of August 1952.

The 70 per cent of the items that make up the rest of the price index showed an over-all increase of only one-fifth of one per cent.

Housing prices remained stable from June to July.

One of the misleading things about a price index is that it is easy to accept it because it is presented with the finality of figures, when in reality the index is only a human estimate. The precise figures make it sound like an exact indicator, although no one makes any such claim for it. There are so many points in building an index where human judgment enters, that no two people working independently would be likely to achieve indexes which correspond exactly.

Some of the important decisions which have to be made in constructing an index are these:

1. What period shall be selected as the base? This is important, for the implication seems to be that the base period is somehow "normal." The consumer price index is based, as we have said, on the 1947–1949 period, although this base period is sometimes shifted. Prices higher than this base period are over 100 and tend to look "high"; prices under it are lower and tend to look "low." Obviously, current prices would look much higher if 1910 prices were used, and higher still if 1870 prices formed the base. Conversely, prices would seem to be not so high, as expressed in the index, if the base were 1953–1954. Prices would *be* the same; only the base would be different. Economists understand that, and so do all well-informed readers. Just the same, a high price index is sure to seem worse than a low one. This is an important factor when one remembers that an administration may rise or fall on the basis of low or high prices.

The people who construct the consumer price index are well aware of this problem. They simply have to use some period as the base. The fact that it can be a little misleading for readers who scan a story in a hurry is an inherent fault of the index system, not of those who produce the index.

2. How much weight shall be assigned to various elements? If one were developing an index showing the fluctuation in the price of a given

grade of butter at a given store packaged in a certain way, this element in the index might not be so troublesome.

In an index which tries to indicate the general cost of living, it is sure to be difficult. The story quoted above says "Food makes up about 30 per cent of the government's price index." Why did the men and women who make the index decide to allow 30 per cent for food? They probably decided on the assumption that the average family spends 30 per cent of its income for food.

This may very well be the most logical decision, but a little consideration will show that this, too, is an inherent weakness in a price index. Obviously, some families will spend more than this for food, others less. If a family spends only 20 per cent of its income for food, the index will not be accurate for that family. How about workers who eat in restaurants? The index will be somewhat out of line for them. This is another point at which human judgment will affect the final figure.

3. How are prices to be determined? The Bureau of Labor Statistics sends out shoppers. This is the logical procedure, but it raises many questions. Shall the shoppers price goods in expensive delicatessens or in supermarkets? Should they shop the big department stores or the little drygoods shops? How shall they adjust the prices for various grades of goods, and how shall they allow for the value of different kinds of packaging? For example, should they price butter dished up out of tubs, or butter sold in neat waxed boxes and divided into quarters for easy serving? Prices vary from one part of the country to another, so how will the economists adjust for this?

These are not insurmountable problems, but again they require skillful judgments on the part of the specialists who put the indexes together. Our information is not sufficiently well developed so that different experts are very likely to make exactly similar judgments.

These questions are not presented with the intention of disparaging the consumer price index or any other index. There is no question that they are valuable tools. Just the same, the reporter needs to understand the human judgments which enter into the compilation of figures which appear so mechanically exact because they are reported in tenths of percentage points.

Indexes are often used to indicate changes in prices, wages, rents, property values, taxes, and almost everything else which can be expressed in numbers. It is a summary device, by which a statistician can present the significance of a vast amount of information so that its importance is apparent at once.

The story quoted earlier illustrates this, too. The lead presents a fact which all of us can understand—it costs more to live now than it did last month. It became apparent only after a tremendous amount of time and labor spent in collecting information, and countless hours spent by highly skilled experts in arranging the data and making the decisions necessary to interpret them. Thus the price index summarizes a vast amount of data and makes it understandable. As such, the index is an extremely valuable device for a reporter covering business.

It is widely used in interpreting stock, bond, and commodity market trends, and it might well be used more often in local stories. Probably the reason that it is not used more widely on the local level is that it requires much work by highly skilled persons.

Another government index is reported in this story from the *New York Times:*

> WASHINGTON, Aug. 27—Wholesale prices appear to have resumed their upward creep after six months of stability.
>
> The Department of Commerce, making its monthly report today on business conditions, noted that increases for all major categories of wholesale prices contributed to an over-all rise of six-tenths of 1 per cent in July.
>
> The stability in wholesale prices for the first half of this year was a major reason for the hope of many government economists that the current inflation was nearing its end. They are known to be disappointed by the July and early August figures.
>
> No matter how the wholesale price index is broken down, the figures for July, and, to a lesser extent, for June, indicate a change in trend toward the upside.

Other indicators on the national level are such items as the number of freight cars loaded, wholesale and retail sales volume in various fields, gross revenues of national concerns, net profits, dividends declared, and many others. The newspaper which reports and evaluates the most indicators is doing the best job. However, no newspaper pretends to make valid predictions. It reports all the indications it can and gives what additional background it can, including expert opinion. Then the reader has to draw his own conclusions.

Local Sources of Business News

Newspapers which subscribe to one of the large press associations usually have available more material on national and international business news than they feel they can print. The quality of coverage of the local business, labor, and financial picture varies widely from one newspaper to another, and both quality and quantity sometimes leave much to be desired.

In a speech before the New York State Society of Newspaper Editors, Vincent S. Jones, a high executive of the Gannett Newspapers, said that newspapers should do a better job in telling the story of business and industry—especially in playing up local angles. "How many of you editors," he asked, "localized the profound effects of the recent increase in interest rates on loans and on home building? A 20 cent raise for bricklayers probably means much more to your readers than a $2 rise in the price of General Motors common. Prevailing wages for domestic help (if you can find any), the number of plasterers and plumbers out of work, how to get a raise, changing to a better job, borrowing money,

Economic Signposts

REPORTED WEEKLY	Date Reported	Latest Figures	Previous Figures	Year Ago
Bank clearings (26 cities)	6/19	*$27,391,136	*$23,100,295	*$28,591,599
Business failures	6/16	295	314	254
Coml & indust loans	6/18	*$31,238,000	*$31,005,000	*$29,305,000
Construction awards	6/19	$546,131,000	$522,793,000	$429,875,000
Crude oil production (bbls.)	6/18	7,009,975	7,032,325	6,334,885
Electric power production (kw. hrs.)	6/18	*13,503,000	*13,023,000	*12,109,000
Freight carloadings	6/19	709,139	682,624	622,686
Herald Tribune Business Index	6/18	206.1	205.1	172.4
Steel operations	6/16	92.0%	93.7%	64.0%
Wholesale Commodity Price Index	6/20	119.4	119.4	119.0
Wholesale Food Price Index	6/18	$6.09	$6.09	$6.63
REPORTED MONTHLY				
Building permits (217 cities)	5/22	$708,940,061	$710,994,544	$590,547,983
Consumers' Price Index	6/20	124.0	123.9	123.6
Cotton consumption (bales)	6/20	702,362	716,820	600,256
Employment	6/11	66,016,000	65,012,000	64,061,000
Unemployment	6/11	3,389,000	3,627,000	4,904,000
F. R. B. Industrial Production Index	6/16	152	150	128
Manufacturers' sales	6/ 2	*$30,836,000	*$30,564,000	*$25,248,000
Manufacturers' inventories	6/ 2	*$51,003,000	*$50,626,000	*$51,595,000
Manufacturers' new orders	6/ 2	*$30,706,000	*$31,843,000	*$24,254,000
Avge. wkly. hrs. per worker, all mfg.	6/11	40.5	40.3	●38.7
New business incorp's (48 states)	6/19	16,660	17,554	11,943
New York Stock Exchange:				
Brokers' loans	6/ 9	*$2,872,000	*$2,888,000	*$2,515,000
Short interest (shares)	6/19	3,244,393	3,322,332	5,803,605
Personal income	6/18	*$376,200,000	*$373,200,000	*$347,300,000
Pig iron production (tons)	6/19	7,747,996	1,392,606	4,073,796
Steel ingot production (tons)	6/12	11,600,581	11,281,920	6,301,159
Rail net operating income	6/ 6	$82,337,327	$79,139,549	$37,013,809

*000 omitted.

Fig. 16. Business barometers as reported weekly by the *New York Herald Tribune*.

and countless other problems of Mr. Average Reader should provide a rich field for local coverage."

Here Mr. Jones gives us the key to effective local business reporting— answer the reader's inevitable question, "What does this mean to me?" This is one of the keys to any kind of good reporting. In business news it is usually easier to answer the question than it is in other kinds of news, but not enough newspapers take the trouble to do it.

What do people want to know about the local business, labor, and financial scene? Countless things, and the only agency adequately equipped to find the answers and tell them is the local newspaper.

Young men and women getting out of school want to know how to get a job and where to look. What kind of workers are needed? In what fields is there an oversupply? How much training and what kind of training do you need to get a certain kind of job? What does it pay locally? What jobs are covered by union contracts? What does the union do for its members? What businesses have records of offering stable employment? What fringe benefits are offered by local concerns? What employment agencies will help a person find a job? How much do they charge? Who offers vocational counseling? What do people in various jobs think about their own work? Where are courses available to prepare one for a given job?

The list could go on and on. Any competent reporter could answer such questions to the benefit of his readers and his paper. Answers to these questions would come from public and private employment agencies, from personnel directors of local concerns, from high school principals and guidance people, from union leaders, from rank and file workers. Stories answering these questions are highly important information; they are also high in human interest because they answer the question, "What does this mean to me?"

Local businessmen have their questions, too. These questions cover such things as the available labor supply, the prevailing wage rate in various skills, the availability of transportation and how much it costs, the availability of housing for new workers, the general tone of a community and whether it will help business attract the kind of workers and executives it needs, the community's record in labor strife, and many others. Again, the answers are available—all that is needed to get them is competent reporting.

Everyone who lives and works in a community is interested in local business news because it affects his pocketbook. Much help can be given through localizing stories of national scope. When the press wires tell that interest rates are going up, the local reader wants to know, "How is this going to affect me?" The local newspaper is in a good position to answer this question, because it requires local reporting. The effect will be different on readers in Chicago, Dallas, and San Jose. The press wires can give the clue, but the local newspaper has to fill in the local angle. It is not difficult to find local answers to the questions about how the higher rate will affect local people who want to buy cars or houses, and how it will affect sales of furniture and all of the other items which customers buy "on time."

Everyone is interested in how prices in his town compare with those somewhere else. In other words, how does the cost of living index apply here at home?

Everyone wants to know the condition of local business and industry. If things are good the merchants can order larger stocks, the worker can know his job is secure, the restaurant owner will expect a good season.

Reporters can find from personnel directors, from state and private employment services, and from labor leaders whether the local concerns are laying off or hiring workers. Many concerns will tell about new orders and the size of their backlog of orders. Annual reports of local concerns provide much material which can be made significant for local readers.

Another worthwhile indicator is the degree to which local industry is diversified. Economists say that the greater the diversity of industry, the greater the community's resistance to depression. If the community has concerns in all the basic branches of industry, it is in a better position to weather depressions than a "one-industry town" or a "two-industry town."

Tied in with this question is a related one: "Are local interests trying to get more industry here and to increase the diversity of our industry?"

Answers to these questions come from local chambers of commerce, industrial groups, manufacturers associations, from public officials, official and unofficial research agencies, and from local universities which often conduct studies on these matters.

Some of the sources of local business news have been discussed in connection with the questions, and a reporter covering the business beat will soon have many good sources.

In addition to the primary sources there are others which are useful in providing tips about what is going on, as well as furnishing primary information of their own. These sources include lawyers who sometimes can suggest the availability of certain information without violating confidences. Real estate dealers often know of new developments because they handled the transactions, or know the people who did. Bankers are good sources of news and tips. Insurance people often know what is going on in the business community.

Whenever national indexes can be localized, a good story results. If national figures are available on department store sales, it is interesting and valuable to local persons to know how the local stores compare. Production indexes can be localized. So can the impact of new processes and inventions on local pocketbooks and industry.

The housewife reads busines news when it concerns her interests. Food prices—indeed, prices of all consumer goods—are vital to her. She buys at the local level, so she needs to know price trends at that level. The coffee crop in Brazil, and anything which affects wholesale prices, is sure to be of interest to her if the reporter goes to the trouble of finding out and reporting how it concerns her family exchequer.

Yes, business reporting on the local level should produce copy that everyone in the community will read because it concerns them. More and more, good local business reporting is likely to become one of the great backbones of American news coverage.

Mr. Jones quotes *Time* as saying that the *New York Times* economic reporting "widens out from the fat business section and nourishes the whole newspaper." This should be true of more newspapers.

The business reporter who understands his subject and can write in everyday language about how it affects his readers' pocketbooks is sure to be much in demand.

REPORTING ASSIGNMENTS

1. Visit offices of public and private employment agencies for an article on job openings in your town.

2. Interview an officer who supervises hiring in one of your town's larger industries for a story on whether the area has an adequate labor supply.

3. Watch the newspapers for a story reporting a price index or some other national economic trend. Find out how it applies to your own area and write an article about your findings.

4. Investigate local costs of building new homes compared with the national average.

5. Compare local department stores sales with national figures.

6. Report on what is being done to attract new industry to your area.

7. Write a story on the degree to which local industry is diversified.

8. What is your community's record in labor strife?

9. Write a feature story on how one local family spends its income. Do not disclose the identity of the family.

10. Is the tax structure in your city favorable or unfavorable to industry, compared with neighboring cities?

20

Labor Unions

Growth of Unions

As mass production has necessitated big business enterprises, it has made inevitable the rise of big labor unions. When businesses were tiny each worker could deal directly with his employer, and often was a personal friend. Gradually this changed, and now top management people can know only a few of the thousands who work for a large concern.

Today an individual worker in a large enterprise cannot bargain effectively with his bosses. The importance of each worker, as a single unit, is so small that individually he has no way to bring pressure. To equalize the situation workers have formed labor unions.

Unions have been so successful that they have grown along with business, and today many big businesses face big labor. In some industries the power differential has not only been equalized—the tide has turned to favor labor.

Before the American Revolution there were a few local unions in the United States, although no labor organization of any size developed until after the Civil War. During the intervening years workers in some trades formed national unions which still exist. Membership in the labor movement rose with good times and fell with bad, achieving no lasting stability.

The Noble Order of the Knights of Labor was organized in 1869 as a secret organization aiming at eventual replacement of the wage system with a cooperative society. Its immediate objectives were shorter hours, higher pay, and abolition of child labor. By 1886 it had 700,000 members, but it lost ground rapidly after that, coming down to 100,000 members by 1890.

The American Federation of Labor was formed in 1886 from a re-organization of the Organized Trade and Labor Unions, which had started in 1881 as a league of autonomous affiliates designed to influence legislation. The AFL made it more of a union by adding wage demands to its objectives. Thus the AFL started out with 138,000 members.

By 1904 the labor movement in the United States had completed the most spectacular period of growth it was to achieve for another 30 years. It had in that year 120 nationally affiliated unions with two million members. These two million represented most of the nation's skilled workers. Growth in membership was stymied until it became feasible to organize less skilled workers in mass production industries.

In 1915 labor unions had only slightly more than two and a half million members. Labor shortages and friendly government policy enabled unions to double in size, reaching five million in 1920. This gain was mostly in the established unions, with relatively few new ones added. The early twenties, however, cut membership back to about three and a half million by 1923.

Two laws enacted in the early days of Franklin Roosevelt's administration speeded the cause of unionism.

One of the hot political controversies of 1933 was over the famous Section 7a of the National Industrial Recovery Act. This required employers to allow workers to bargain collectively through representatives of their own choosing without interference. The Supreme Court declared the act unconstitutional in the Schechter decision in 1935, but Section 7a's provisions were re-enacted that same year in the Wagner Act.

Officially called the National Labor Relations Act of 1935, the Wagner Act put teeth into its collective bargaining requirements by establishing the National Labor Relations Board. The Board was assigned as a watchdog to protect labor's rights.

With the national government playing big brother, the unions prospered.

Craft vs. Industrial Unions

Labor's fortunes improved, too, with the settling of a dispute in the AFL over the virtues of the craft (horizontal) vs. industrial (vertical) unions. Most of the AFL unions were composed of skilled workers grouped by their skills. For example, in a newspaper plant the printers would have their own union, the stereotypers theirs, the pressmen theirs, and so on. Vertical unions organize all workers in a given industry into a single union, regardless of their particular skills. Thus the United Auto Workers organized all the workers in the automotive industry without regard to their particular skills or whether they had any skill at all.

The issue came to a head in 1934, after Section 7a made it feasible to organize mass production workers. In November, 1935, eight AFL unions, led by John L. Lewis of the United Mine Workers, established a Committee for Industrial Organization to organize mass production workers. Two other unions soon joined it, and it became the Congress of Industrial Organizations in 1938. At this time its membership of four million was about 400,000 higher than that of AFL.

By 1940 union membership stood at nearly nine million. The industrial expansion of the Second World War aided the union movement, bringing membership in 1960 to around 16 million. During the next decade membership increased slowly.

The AFL and CIO agreed to merge again in 1955, although leaders of each side seemed to retain their own opinions as to the relative advantages of craft and industrial unions. Horizontal unionists claim that their type of organization breeds more pride in craftmanship, because a person is required to have a skill before he can join such a union. For example, a man who belongs to the International Typographical Union can go into a shop, put on an apron, and go to work. He served years of apprenticeship before he was admitted to the union.

The arguments for industrial unions are compelling, especially to a national leader. Unskilled workers would be excluded from skilled horizontal unions. Vertical unions are the only way to organize this vast number of workers.

In labor disputes, too, industrial unions have advantages. Only with them can the national leader hope to outmaneuver his management opponents. For example, if the national leader of the United Auto Workers wants to push for higher wages in all of the major plants, he may be able to play off the manufacturers against each other. He may call out Chrysler workers if Chrysler does not meet his demands. He leaves workers in production at Ford and General Motors, but collects a strike fund from their pay. This assessment, plus the union's reserve fund, makes it possible to pay the Chrysler workers high enough weekly strike benefits so that they can stay out on strike for a long time. Chrysler management realizes that Ford and General Motors are gradually picking up the share of new car sales that formerly went to Chrysler. Under such circumstances even a determined management is likely to give in to the union demands. Once Chrysler has capitulated, the national union leader can put it back into production, call out the workers at Ford, and apply the same strategy all over again.

This is the type of national power bargaining which is much more effective with industrial than with craft unions. It works because industrial unions can shut down an entire plant, and because they are somewhat more susceptible than skilled unions to national direction.

Craft unions can cripple an industry, but sometimes they cannot shut it down. There have been several printers' strikes, for example, which failed to shut down newspapers. Cold type processes made it possible to publish presentable papers without a single printer. A strong union weapon, the sympathy strike, often makes it possible to close a plant. In such a strike the other unions not directly involved in a dispute will strike against an employer to help another union enforce its demands. Sometimes when mailers are striking against a newspaper publisher, printers, stereotypers, engravers, and even editorial workers may walk out, too.

Union Structure

The international is the basic unit of labor union organization in this country. The international aspects of the organization usually mean that it has affiliates in the United States and Canada, although some of the "internationals" are confined to the United States. The more than 200 internationals in this country are composed of locals. This is where the rank and file members come into contact with their union, in meetings and conversations with officials. Internationals are usually close-knit structures with much control over locals.

Most of the internationals are affiliated with the AFL-CIO, which has a few elected officials at the top who direct the affairs of the organization with the help of an executive committee. This group makes policy decisions which cannot wait for the annual convention. Otherwise major policy is determined by vote at the convention.

Two unions claim memberships of more than one million. They are the International Brotherhood of Teamsters, Chauffeurs, Warehousemen and Helpers of America whose president, James R. Hoffa, reported a million and a half members, and the United Automobile, Aircraft and Agricultural Implement Workers of America with 1,124,000.

Some of the other unions which frequently get into the news are:

United Brotherhood of Carpenters and Joiners of America with 750,000 members in nearly 2,800 locals.

United Steelworkers of America, 931,000 members.

International Brotherhood of Electrical Workers, 492,500 members.

Hotel and Restaurant Employees and Bartenders International union, 300,000 members.

International Ladies Garment Workers' Unions, 373,500 members.

Amalgamated Clothing Workers of America, 288,000 members.

The Big Four Railroad Brotherhoods consist of Railroad Trainmen, Locomotive Firemen and Enginemen, Locomotive Engineers, and the Order of Railway Conductors and Brakemen, with a total of nearly 300,000 members. All were independent until 1957 when the Firemen and Enginemen and the Trainmen joined AFL-CIO.

The United Mine Workers of America, headed by John L. Lewis, has somewhere around half a million members. Its catchall District 50 was active for a time attempting to organize wherever an opportunity opened—dairy farmers, railroad workers, construction workers.

Labor Legislation

The federal and state governments have been interested in regulating the relations between labor and its employers for many years. Congress and state legislatures have set maximum hours and minimum wages. The maximum hour protection was first extended to women and children, but gradually the limitation has been set on nearly all employment. The limitations are still especially strict, however, on the number of hours worked by women and children. Child labor is banned except under certain conditions in most states.

Another important area of labor legislation centers around the protection of the worker from the hazards of unemployment, destitute old age, industrial accidents, and sickness. This is commonly called social security. The United States government and the states were slower to adopt these devices than most of the countries of Europe, but since passage of the Social Security Act for 1935, progress in this direction has been rapid, with more and more workers becoming eligible for benefits which have been increased in size and variety over the years.

The basic plan of the 1935 federal social security legislation was to make it attractive for states to inaugurate unemployment insurance plans. The pressure was so strong that all the states adopted such measures.

The Social Security Act also started the first general old age insurance program in the United States, with provisions designed to protect the entire family against impecunious old age, and to provide subsistence benefits to families whose wage earner dies.

The security legislation is highly important as an expression of enlightened public policy intended to protect workers from the hazards which historically have hung over the heads of all except those with a considerable amount of property. Banishment to life in the poor house no longer is a fear to haunt workers as they begin to pass middle age.

Also important, and currently even more newsworthy, is government policy in relation to collective bargaining. This policy decides, in large measure, how much of the profits of industry goes to workers and how much to the investors.

Legislation is only part of the picture. Judicial interpretation of the statutes has sometimes made them wholly or partially ineffective. On the other hand, friendly interpretation by the courts has sometimes strengthened a law.

Much of the pioneering work has been done by state legislatures; sometimes state laws which have proved workable have served as models for federal legislation. A reporter covering labor affairs needs, of course, to be familiar with labor legislation in his own state. Also important is the federal legislation. A few of the landmark laws passed by Congress are these:

The *Sherman Anti-Trust Act* of 1890, although it was not designed primarily to regulate unions, had far-reaching significance for many facets of our economy. One of its major provisions was the outlawing of conspiracies or combinations in restraint of trade. This affected labor unions, because the courts frequently held that they were acting in restraint of trade. It is logical to hold that a strike is in restraint of trade, for its effect is obviously to curtail the activities of the plant or industry struck. Courts have sometimes held the secondary boycott illegal under these provisions. This is a refusal to handle the products of another plant whose workers are on strike. The use of the injunction under the Sherman Act was limited by the Clayton Act.

The *Clayton Act* of 1914 decreed that the antitrust laws should not be construed to forbid the existence of labor unions or the implementation of their legitimate objectives. The Clayton Act resulted in judicial decisions on the whole more favorable to labor, but did not free the unions entirely from regulation under the antitrust laws.

The *Railway Labor Act* of 1926 reflected popular confidence in the Brotherhoods of Railway Workers, giving them freedom to select their own representatives and to bargain collectively. This was the first time such a specific provision had been incorporated into federal legislation.

The *Norris-LaGuardia Act* of 1932, resulting from further public opinion shifts in favor of labor, limited the use of injunctions in labor disputes. It declared collective bargaining to be good public policy, and made unenforceable in federal courts "yellow dog" contracts. These were devices, particularly hated by labor, by which an employer required workers to agree not to join any noncompany union.

The *National Industrial Recovery Act* of 1933, a broad law affecting much of industry at a time of economic crisis, reflected the philosophy of the F. D. Roosevelt administration. Famous Section 7a required that all codes of fair competition include the provision that workers should be allowed to bargain collectively.

The *Wagner Act* of 1935 (the National Labor Relations Act) was widely hailed as labor's Magna Charta. It gave all employees in interstate commerce the right to organize, to bargain collectively through representatives of their own choosing, and to engage in supporting activities. It created the National Labor Relations Board to enforce its provisions. Although the act covered only workers in interstate commerce, the courts have interpreted this so broadly that the vast majority of workers are included.

The *Taft-Hartley Act* of 1947 represented another current in ever-shifting public opinion. The increased protection and power given to the unions by the Wagner Act had led to some union excesses and a resulting less favorable public attitude toward labor. The Taft-Hartley Act was the natural result. It imposed restrictions which made it somewhat more difficult for organized labor to achieve its objectives. It included bargaining procedures which will be discussed later in this section. Three specific limitations were imposed on labor:

1. The Act outlawed the closed shop and made the union shop more difficult to attain. The closed shop and the union shop, particularly the closed shop, have been two of organized labor's main objectives. Understandably so, because they put a tremendous amount of power into the hands of union leaders. The closed shop requires an employer to hire only union members. The power this puts into the hands of the union is quite obvious; in the long run it gives the union control over the hiring policies of an employer, since he can hire only persons who have been admitted to the union. In some industries this has logically resulted in a situation such that an employer needing workers simply notifies union headquarters, which dispatches the workers. Some employers say they favor this system because it simplifies their hiring problems. Recruiting and negotiating are done through union officials. Many employers have objected to the closed shop, however, on the ground that it gives too much power to the union. It was public acceptance of their philosophy which was reflected in the Taft-Hartley Act.

The union shop is related to the closed shop, but it places less power in the hands of the union. It allows the employer to hire whomever he selects, but requires the new employee to join the union within a certain number of days. The Taft-Hartley Act made it more difficult for labor to attain a union shop, because the Act set up a complicated procedure which had to precede bargaining for the union shop. Thirty per cent of the workers had to sign a petition asking for such a shop; then a majority of all the workers (regardless of the number voting) had to vote in favor before negotiations could begin.

2. The second important limitation of the Taft-Hartley Act on labor unions was its provision that the injunction could be used under certain circumstances to prevent picketing. This was a reversal of the trend of the preceding legislation, which had limited the use of the injunction to prevent picketing.

3. In its avowed effort to equalize the position of business and labor, the Act provided that employers could initiate a collective bargaining election in an effort to replace the existing union. The law allows such an election to be held during a strike, requires that pickets shall have no vote, and that new workers hired to replace strikers shall be allowed

to vote. This makes labor's position much less secure than it was under the Wagner Act.

Other provisions also tended to limit labor's powers. Health and welfare plans were limited; secondary boycotts were prohibited, as were strikes and boycotts in jurisdictional disputes. This last provision was an attempt to cut down time lost in strikes because two or more unions cannot agree as to who shall be permitted to do a certain kind of job. In construction work, for example, it may be difficult to determine whether a mason or a carpenter should do a certain job, or whether a plumber or an electrician should install appliances which use electrical power to perform functions normally thought of as being in the plumber's realm. Such strikes may appear ridiculous to the general public. To a union they involve important principles. Normally these issues are ironed out in negotiations between heads of unions, but on occasion the disputes have erupted into long-term strikes. This leaves a contractor powerless because he has no interest in the point at issue, and so can make no concessions even if he wants to.

There seems to be no question that the Taft-Hartley Act has slowed to some extent the growth of the union movement in this country, and that it has made it more difficult for unions to win concessions from employers. On the other hand, it has not rendered the unions powerless. Under its provisions unions have made very important progress toward one of their long-term goals—the guaranteed annual wage. This will be discussed later in this section.

This brief review of some of the important labor legislation shows that in this area, as in most others, our laws tend to swing back and forth as public opinion swings, somewhat like a pendulum, from a position tending to favor labor to another tending to favor management. The quest is for equal opportunity for labor and for management. Just what our notions of equal opportunity turn out to be is governed by our social concepts. In a socialistic state private industry would have no privileges because it would be nonexistent. In a complete *laissez-faire* economy, organized labor would get no particular protection. We can expect our own national policy to fluctuate between these extremes.

Labor Goals

The goals of the American labor movement have been primarily economic—to win more of the industrial return for its members. This has not been its only concern. Working conditions, health insurance, and pension plans have been important demands made by labor leaders at bargaining tables. Unions have helped to agitate for laws requiring minimum safety precautions in mines and factories.

In recent years labor leaders have been making solid progress toward one of their dreams—the guaranteed annual wage. This has not been achieved, but in 1955 the United Automobile Workers won substantial concessions along this line from motordom's big three, Ford, General Motors, and Chrysler. The concessions were not a guaranteed annual wage, but amounted to an increase in and liberalization of unemployment insurance benefits supported by company funds. The Supplementary Unemployment Benefit Plan, as it was called, is subject to court review and cannot be used in a few states because it runs counter to their laws. There have been few extensions of it since then, but it still marks a significant step.

In *Editor & Publisher* for June 18, 1955, Robert Perrin, labor editor of the *Detroit Free Press*, told the story of the problems faced by reporters who covered the negotiations. Here are some excerpts from his report:

> The new contracts include a little item called the modified guaranteed wage which can evoke reams of happiness or apoplexy, depending upon the source.
>
> However, to the reporters who sweated out this business to the end, the most important thing about the pacts is that they run for three years.
>
> The editorial writers call this "three years of industrial peace." We labor reporters think of it as three years to catch up on our sleep, restore proper feeding habits, reacquaint ourselves with our families and get our arches jacked up.
>
> . . . I recall asking UAW President Walter P. Reuther in 1950 at the signing of the first GM-UAW five-year contract what the union's next major goal would be.
>
> "Why," said Walter, "we will seek the guaranteed annual wage."
>
> Those few words have occupied well over half our time for the past five years.
>
> First there was the tremendous outpouring of propaganda as the union built its case and sought to convince its own members as well as the general public.
>
> From the start reporters were handicapped by a lack of specific approval or disapproval from the auto industry itself.
>
> Everyone else got into the act, but the people with whom we wanted to talk—at GM and Ford—weren't talking.
>
> As the contract expiration dates moved closer, we scrutinized every speech or comment by Ford and GM officials to detect some clue to their thinking. This usually got us into the position of writing something along the line of "while he didn't actually mention the guaranteed annual wage, he sure as hell was thinking of it when he said . . ." etc.
>
> Meanwhile "outside" newsmen were drifting through town, each dropping off a series of articles on GAW at the home desk.
>
> . . . The GM contract expired May 29 and the Ford pact on June 1, meaning more or less simultaneous negotiations to cover.

. . . Which talks should the labor editors cover on any given day? We finally adopted the practice of following Reuther to whichever session he was attending. Some days he hit both.

When official negotiations began early in April, the labor reporters would sit outside the door in solitary splendor, a far cry from the mobs of newsmen who showed up for the climax.

Jack Crellin, of the *Detroit Times*, Asher Lauren, of the *Detroit News*, myself, and sometimes a wire service reporter in the early stages, would drift from the GM building to the Detroit Leland Hotel and back.

Our major accomplishment during those days was to set up the "oldest established permanent floating poker game in Detroit" which went into temporary limbo during the early morning hours of June 13. But it will be revived.

GM provided us first with a table and chairs in the fifth floor lobby of its building, just outside the conference room. At the Ford talks, however, we were treated with a hotel suite.

GM later opened up a press room after non-GM tenants of the floor complained that their clients were faced with a "bunch of bums playing poker" when they got off the elevators. We admit to the poker.

The major difference between the GM and Ford press rooms was that the former had a refrigerator full of cheese and Cokes and the latter had a bathtub full of beer.

All was not play, of course, if any of the waiting hours can be considered that. But actual coverage of the talks was not helped at all by the participants.

At GM, for example, the company and union established from the start a policy of not talking about bargaining table developments without first giving each other 48 hours notice.

The only official breach in the curtain was the settlement announcement at 3:15 A.M. June 13.

The no-talking edict was in force at the Ford talks, also, but it didn't last quite so long.

In addition to the news blackout, other precautions were taken by negotiators.

After a *Life* photographer boosted up his camera and took a picture through the glass transom of the GM conference room, the transoms were replaced with wood. For some reason, wood panels also were substituted for the translucent glass in the doors.

Naturally, this quickly became known as the "wooden curtain"!

A Ford security officer was posted at all times outside the door of their conference room in the hotel, to keep reporters out of earshot.

Even the UAW was taking precautions after it found a reporter blithely sitting in the union's hotel caucus room during a recess in the Ford talks. The union then placed a couple of guards to block off an entire corridor of the hotel leading to office and sleeping rooms.

The union even gathered up all used carbons, stencils and other waste and burned it.

Top negotiators at both locations were swarmed upon whenever they left the conference rooms and were followed right down to the rest rooms. But all we got was "no comment."

. . . Despite the blackout, however, the Detroit papers scored many laudable news beats on what was going on.

Everyone, including the negotiators, was in a near state of collapse when the break finally came.

Such are the problems of reporters who cover labor-management negotiations, although sometimes the conferees are more communicative.

Once the agreements have been reached, reporters have other stories to write. After the agreement described above, calculations began at once on the effects of the agreement on the auto companies, other industries, the unions, and the American economy. This is only natural for such a new concept in American business. In a matter of such importance the most informed opinion was of prime news importance.

The questions which reporters sought to answer included these:

Is this agreement likely to set a pattern for other industries?

Is it likely to push prices higher?

Is it likely to stabilize the economy by providing purchasing power during slack periods and thus evening-out "humps" in the business cycle? How many workers will it affect?

Can we ever achieve a stable enough industry so that skilled, semi-skilled and even unskilled workers can depend upon a steady year-around income?

Business reporters, of course, busied themselves with the problems of management in trying to stabilize employment the year around.

All of these questions were important and still are. Some reporters come up with enlightening answers.

Sumner Schlicter concluded in the *Atlantic Monthly* that larger public unemployment benefits are needed before such a program will have an appreciable stabilizing influence on the economy. He came to this conclusion by estimating that the new benefits would reach only a quarter of the workers covered by government unemployment compensation plans.

Furthermore in the very spots where unemployment is most serious, in declining industries and among weak firms, unions will have the greatest difficulty in negotiating agreements of the Ford-General Motors type.

Mr. Schlicter, in the same article, summarizes his concept of the value of such plans.

An adequate system of unemployment compensation would not only add to the security of workers—it would also add to the security of business enterprises and would enhance the value of the investment in American industry and the value of every farm. It is amazing that the businessmen and farmers have not sought to stabilize their markets by insisting that the government provide an adequate system of unemployment compensation.

Collective Bargaining

Terms of employment in unionized industries are governed by a contract, which is the agreement reached after differences have been reconciled by collective bargaining. This hard-earned right of labor is a simple procedure, although the job of reporting it may be difficult, as we have seen.

Bargaining may be conducted at several levels, and the actual bargainers will often vary with the levels.

In local bargaining, an employer talks with all or a portion of his employees, or there may be city-wide agreements. At the regional level, larger areas are covered and negotiations may result in uniform employment conditions for several manufacturers and all the workers in a given trade in the area. National bargaining determines employment conditions for workers in a given industry for the whole country.

Employers and union representatives have not made up their minds entirely as to which type of bargaining they prefer, although there is a tendency for employers to prefer local bargaining, while unions would rather bargain on the regional or national level. Rank and file union members have more control over the outcome of talks when they are conducted locally. They can watch proceedings more carefully, can require frequent reports from their representatives and can more readily make their opinions felt. At the local level, the entire membership usually has to ratify an agreement before it can take effect. In some unions, however, even agreements covering large segments of the industry require ratification by the membership. This is true of the National Maritime Union.

Who Does the Actual Bargaining?

The people who sit around the bargaining table are important sources of information to a reporter. Quite often they try to keep the progress of negotiations secret, apparently thinking that this is likely to promote harmony more quickly. Almost always reporters are barred from the talks. Sometimes briefing sessions will be held at the end of each day's sessions. At these meetings representatives of both sides appear to summarize the progress of the day and to answer questions. Sometimes the only source of information is a press release, supplied by labor and management together or by either side. Without any of these advantages, the best a reporter can do is sit outside the bargaining rooms and try to buttonhole participants when they enter and leave the sessions.

Sometimes the coverage conditions are difficult, but both management and labor are becoming more responsive to public opinion. They have at least learned to expect the presence of reporters when important negotiations are being conducted. The public's stake in the outcome of some labor talks is so large that it is difficult to see how information can be bottled up.

Participants in the talks vary with the customs of the unions and owners and with the level at which the talks are conducted.

A plant owner may bargain with a part of his workers, the ones who are members of a given union. This is done in plants where the workers are organized by skills into several unions. In newspaper plants, for example, the publisher bargains separately with printers, stereotypers, pressmen, and editorial workers because they are organized in different unions.

In industries organized by industrial or vertical unions the plant owner bargains with representatives of all his unionized workers. The plant owner may do the bargaining himself, perhaps with the advice of his lawyer, or he may be aided or represented by other people. His industrial relations manager may conduct the talks or assist the manager. If the owner is a member of an association of related industries, the association may help with the bargaining or may actually conduct the sessions. For example, owners of newspapers in New York and many other states are members of publishers' associations. The executives of the association frequently sit in on bargaining sessions with union employees.

Union representatives at local bargaining sessions usually include local officers. If the union has a business agent he is almost invariably an important member of the union's bargaining committee. Sometimes the president of the local will appoint the bargaining committee.

In regional or national talks the union is often represented by its national officers, who may also advise the union in local talks. Some internationals require that the national officers must approve any local contract before it is signed by the local representatives.

Some negotiations have special importance because they tend to set the terms of other agreements in the same and related industries. The negotiations between the United Steel Workers and "Big Steel" have this "generating" or "bellwether" tendency. An exception to this general rule resulted in one of the bitterest labor disputes in our history, in 1937.

In March, Big Steel, represented by our largest steel concern, United States Steel Corporation, had agreed to deal with the United Steel Workers on specified matters. This was a surprising victory for the steel workers, and they set out to gain the same concession from "Little Steel"—Youngstown Sheet and Tube, Inland, and Republic. Little Steel refused to follow the bellwether this time, and the result was violence and bitterness seldom repeated in our history of labor-management relations.

Agreements reached by Big Steel, the Big Three in the automotive world, and other basic industries, influence the terms of the contracts in many other industries. For example, when the United Auto Workers won a modified guaranteed annual wage, there was widespread prediction that similar agreements would follow in other industries, although that has not happened to any large extent. Agreements which follow patterns set in other negotiations are called "satellite" agreements.

Trend of Labor-Management Agreements

As one would expect from the previous discussion, there has been a discernible trend in labor contracts over the years. It has been toward shorter hours, higher pay, better working conditions, and more "fringe benefits," such as longer vacations, hospitalization, pension plans, and the like.

One fairly recent development has been the tendency to tie wages in with the cost of living. As the living cost index rises, workers are given an automatic wage boost. Similarly, they take a cut when the index drops. This plan has been criticized by some representatives of both unions and management. Management spokesmen argue that an automatic increase tends only to increase the inflationary spiral, and that workers will not accept a wage cut on the basis of a drop in the cost of living index. Union spokesmen have sometimes argued that such a program tends to freeze wages at a given level. Despite this criticism, the plan has influential adherents. One of the problems is determining an equitable measure of the cost of living.

How Disputes Are Settled

Labor contracts run for a given period—usually from one to three years. State and federal law, as well as the contracts themselves, spell out the means of settling disputes which arise under terms of a contract. Despite these provisions, strikes sometimes result from disputes which normally should be settled under the contract without interrupting production.

Three methods are used to settle disputes: conciliation (including mediation), arbitration, and fact-finding boards.

Conciliation, strictly defined, means bringing the parties together, while *mediation* is the added step of trying to guide bargaining sessions into productive paths. Actually the terms are used interchangeably. Conciliation and mediation are voluntary processes. A third party aids the bargainers in meeting and in reaching agreements. The mediator has no authority to impose solutions, but he may suggest them. Often a skilled and understanding mediator can avoid strikes or speed their settlement.

Anyone accepted by both parties to a dispute may serve as a mediator. Often prominent citizens are asked; their prestige may make it possible for them to be effective, since both sides trust their integrity and judgment.

The federal government and many state governments have conciliation services, and sometimes government agencies can participate of their own volition.

Most important of these agencies in the national government are the Federal Mediation and Reconciliation Service and the National Mediation Board. The first of these deals with any type of industry. The second is concerned with work stoppages in the transportation industry.

State conciliation services in New York and Massachusetts antedate federal agencies, having been established in 1886. New York's State Mediation Board has seven members with headquarters in New York City, and district offices in Albany, Buffalo, and Syracuse. The Board functions at the request of either party to a dispute, or it may enter a dispute of its own volition or at the direction of the governor.

THREE METHODS OF SETTLING LABOR DISPUTES

Conciliation (with Mediation)

Brings parties together (conciliation) and tries to help them reach an agreement (mediation).

Arbitration

Arbiter hears both sides and hands down a decision.

Fact-Finding Boards

Impartial board conducts its own investigation and issues a report.

Fig. 17

Arbitration is provided automatically in some contracts. Each party to a dispute agrees to an arbiter, and each party agrees to accept the arbiter's solution after they have submitted the facts to him.

The use of a *fact-finding board* is an attempt, usually by the government, to force a solution through the pressure of public opinion. Often these boards go beyond a pure "fact-finding" role and suggest solutions. The Railway Labor Act provides "emergency" boards, in an effort to settle disputes which may deprive some section of the country of essential transporation. The Taft-Hartley Act of 1947 gives the President power to appoint fact-finding boards in disputes that "imperil the national health and safety." Such boards have power to investigate and issue a public report, but they are prohibited from making a recommendation.

Similarly, New York State law provides that the State Mediation Board may inform the industrial commissioner of a dispute which vitally affects the public interest. The commissioner then may approve a board of inquiry, which has power to investigate and issue a factual report. In its investigation it may hold public or private hearings, subpoena witnesses, and take testimony and receive evidence.

Grievance Procedure

Once an agreement has been reached and a contract signed, it becomes important to see that both parties adhere to its provisions. The system by which disagreements are ironed out is called grievance procedure. This varies, of course, from plant to plant, but the general pattern goes like this:

1. The worker, usually with his union representative, presents his complaint to the foreman. At this point most grievances are adjusted.

2. Two or three appeal steps are provided for cases not settled by the foreman. As the appeals go higher, more important plant officials participate, and the employee is represented by a grievance committee. Business agents enter the picture during some of these steps, and eventually the international representatives of the union may participate.

3. In the final appeal representatives of the international usually represent the workers, and a member of top management represents the company.

4. If the appeal steps do not result in a settlement, arbitration is used. Contracts usually provide for the submission of the disputes to arbitration, and usually the federal or state mediation and conciliation services are asked to supply an arbiter. Machinery may be permanent or established as needed.

Grievance committees, business agents, and shop stewards have an important function in maintaining terms of the contract. Frequently stewards are paid by the company or the union for time spent in this work.

Most union leaders regard their activities as part of the free enterprise system, and a smoothly functioning union shop may very well take much of the strain of labor relations off management's shoulders. On the other hand, unreasonable and willful union agents can have the opposite effect.

Right To Work Laws

Labor reporters will have to spend more of their time in the days to come covering the controversy over "right to work laws." These, in effect in more than a third of the states, provide that membership in a union shall not be a condition of employment. This outlaws all three of the union security provisions: closed shop, union shop, and maintenance of membership. The first two are discussed earlier. Maintenance of membership means that an employer is required to dismiss an employee who, having joined a union, fails to continue his membership.

Proponents of right to work laws say that they are needed to protect a worker's freedom to join or refuse to join a union. This is guaranteed in the Constitution, they say, but is abrogated when a person is forced to join a union to get or keep a job. A union shop, they say, is a yellow-dog contract in reverse.

Corrupt union bosses, the argument runs, can never be overthrown unless a worker has freedom to join or stay outside a union. Some unions, they say, hold their members in slavery, for they have to abide by the dictates of the union bosses or lose their jobs.

The union leaders say that right to work laws are not designed to improve unions, but to eliminate them so that industrialists can exploit the workers. "Freedom" granted by these laws, they say, is freedom to starve.

Right to work laws open the door for the free-loader who takes advantage of union benefits without contributing dues, union men argue. The unions are compelled by law to bargain, not only for their members, but for all workers in the unit. It is unfair to let some benefit by union activity without contributing to it, they say. Those who favor the laws say that the unions want to be bargaining agents for all the workers in order to protect their own position, and this is no reason to force all workers to join unions.

Unions also argue that workers have to choose between being dominated by employers and, by participating in unions, controlling their own actions. The unions are the more democratic method, they argue.

Supporters of the laws report that the fastest gain in industry and wage rates is in the states which have adopted right to work laws. They can show that industry is more interested in moving to states which have such laws. Ralph J. Cordiner, president of General Electric, told a group of Virginians that one of the reasons GE is interested in establishing plants in their state is because it has a right to work law.

Union leaders say that the increase in such states is not significantly larger than in states which do not have the laws. Such gains are to be expected anyway, they say, because most of the states having the laws are underdeveloped now and so are sure to grow more rapidly than the rest.

Whatever the merits of the arguments, they will be much heard and much reported in the next few years.

The Reporter and Labor Stories

Reporters have special difficulties in all highly controversial areas, and labor coverage is no exception. Feelings run high in labor disputes, violence sometimes occurs, and facts are hard to get.

Labor stories are an important part of the news, and they are worth the extra time and the hard work it often takes to get them. In years past, reporters have often found that it was hard to get labor's side of the story because the labor leaders mistrusted them and often refused to talk. This, coupled with friendly treatment and access to information from management, sometimes resulted in stories favorable to management. Recently labor leaders, too, have realized the value of an accurate report of their side of the story, and often they are as cooperative with reporters as is management. This has helped to even up the coverage.

In labor stories, as in all others, reporters must work to report both sides of the controversy. If one side or the other is hard to deal with, this does not excuse the reporter from doing his best to get that side of the story. His job is to tell the public what is going on, and one side of the story is not enough. If he does his level best to report both sides and still gets only one, his story should let his reader know that an effort was made to get both.

A local demonstration of labor's increasing interest in direct political action was reported in this story in the *Buffalo Evening News:*

> LOCKPORT, Oct. 31—Leaders of organized labor in Niagara County are making a maximum effort to keep a Democrat in control of the Sheriff's Department.
>
> In the closing hours of one of the most feverish local contests in Niagara's history, the work of the AFL-CIO Committee on Political Education (COPE) on behalf of Sheriff James K. Murphy, 48, of Lewiston, is a most unusual development.
>
> Mr. Murphy . . . is opposed by William J. Redmond, 36, of Lockport, a former deputy.
>
> Political activity by COPE is nothing new but, as one top Republican

pointed out: "This is perhaps the first time in the state that a labor unit has replaced a Democratic County Committee as the main support for a candidate."

"Certainly we're working hard for Mr. Murphy," says William S. Hilger of Lockport, a CIO international representative and COPE chairman in Niagara County.

"And let's be practical about it," Mr. Hilger went on. "It takes money and lots of it to elect someone in this day and age. Certainly we're underwriting some of the bills. We have to. The Democratic organization in this county is broke."

The labor leader said that about 25,000 AFL-CIO members in 40 union locals in Niagara County are members of COPE.

They become members by voluntary contributions of $1. That would mean a war chest of $25,000 in Niagara County alone.

In addition, COPE raised about $3,200 earlier in the campaign at a $10-a-plate dinner sponsored in Lockport for Gov. Harriman.

One member of the COPE staff said: "We've got the money to spend and we're spending it like water."

In their search for the dramatic, newspapers have too often ignored labor controversies until they flared into violence. Thus, a community would wake up some morning to see a picket line and possibly violence, without being warned in advance, when good labor reporting would have indicated that a strike was brewing. Sometimes, if the public is made aware of a dispute before it erupts into violence, community leaders can help to settle it without an interruption in production.

Most of our larger papers give continuing coverage to labor affairs. Too many of the smaller ones persist in spotty coverage. This is like covering fires every time the siren wails, but ignoring every fire hazard until it bursts into flame.

Industrial harmony will be achieved through community-wide awareness of the problems, because this will force management and labor to be more reasonable. Without such community awareness harmony may never come.

Readers have a right to expect something more than a tally of the heads bumped in a picket line. A necessity today is day-in, day-out coverage of the maneuvers, the conditions, the negotiations, the principles involved. These are just as important as the violence of the picket line. One of the reporter's skills is to present them so clearly and in such perspective that people will read and understand.

REPORTING ASSIGNMENTS

1. In a story or series report the local labor organizations in your area. Tell the size, characteristics, leadership quality, and general record of the organizations.

2. Select one of the organizations for an intensive study showing how one labor unit works.

3. Interview a labor leader for his views on whether the legislation in your state is friendly or unfriendly to labor and why.

4. Interview a business leader for the same kind of story.

5. Analyze political activity of local labor groups in a feature story.

6. Interview someone who has arbitrated labor disputes and write a story illustrating how arbitration works.

21

The Power Triangle

Power Points in Society

Government, labor, business—these are the three power points in our society. On the interaction among them depends the kind of country we live in.

These agencies are only the channels through which human beings seek to focus power for change. Each agency is composed of many subgroups, often with conflicting ideas, so it is important for a reporter to look below the surface. To understand and interpret this interplay of forces a reporter needs all the usual tools, plus a special acumen for finding significant undercurrents and a deep understanding of the practical methods by which we arrive at social decisions.

In a socialist state the distinction among forces is less clear, for the government is in charge of production, and all workers become government employees. This does not necessarily mean the end of labor disputes, but it does mean that the employer has added methods of enforcing his will.

Our own economic freedom is limited, as is our political and social freedom, by government control. The extent and type of government control varies in democratic countries and with the times, although it is not hard to see a trend toward increased government control over both labor and business. In our own country part of F. D. Roosevelt's New Deal was the establishment of "yardstick" operations in certain areas, in which government entered fields formerly held by private enterprise, such as utilities. In England the Labor party advocates steadily increasing government ownership of industry, and during its periods in power it moves the government in that direction.

Government intervention in the economic area often takes the form of aid rather than restriction. The purpose of a tax on goods entering our ports from foreign shores is often to protect our own industries. The Department of Commerce of the federal government and similar units in state governments are designed to aid business.

Why Government Regulation?

In the ideal situation, no government regulation of business or labor would be necessary. Nevertheless, we have a considerable amount of

THE POWER TRIANGLE

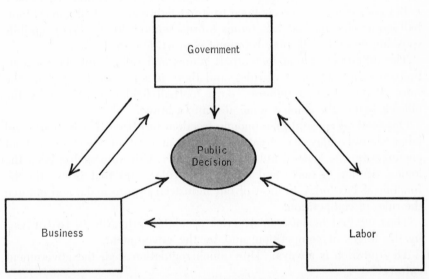

FIG. 18. Three of the great decision-influencing factors in our society are government, business, and labor. Each tries to shape public decisions. The picture is complicated by the shifting of people and ideas from one group to another, and by the fact that one person may belong to government, business and labor groups all at once.

regulation in this country and it is increasing. Is this good or bad? Is it necessary? Is government regulation of labor unions necessary? Is it desirable for government to aid struggling businesses and to protect labor unions from forces which might otherwise destroy them?

Pure *laissez-faire* economic theory argued for unrestricted business and industrial activity. This has never worked out, for it has led to practices which the larger part of the population would not tolerate. Sometimes labor disputes and disputes between rival industries led to the use of physical force, not much different from any other hoodlum antics.

Adherents of the *laissez-faire* theory placed their faith in the regulatory power of competition. Competition, they argued, would permit only the efficient producers to stay in business. Competition would regulate prices, because a concern which overpriced its products would find customers going to lower-priced competitors. Competition would give workers the best possible price for their work, because efficient workers would naturally gravitate to the place where they could get the best wages.

The trouble with unrestrained *laissez faire* is that the tendency is for competition to take on all the unattractive characteristics of a street brawl. Many, in their unholy haste to look after themselves, resort to dirty fighting. If they know no dirty fighting techniques in the beginning, they learn rapidly or are destroyed. Unrestricted economic competition, like unrestricted gang wars, leads, not to utopia, but to domination by bullies.

But competition is not confined to street fighting. Baseball games, football games, boxing matches, tennis tournaments, bridge tourneys, public speaking contests—all these represent competition, too.

The difference is that in football games and other contests, the participants abide by a set of rules, and there is a means of enforcing the rules. "Unnecessary roughness" on a football field is penalized by the officials before the game degenerates into a brawl.

Our general concept of economic freedom has been that business and labor should enjoy the greatest possible amount of freedom without endangering the general public or each other. Government has been the logical agency to make and enforce the rules, and that is exactly the function it has today in most of our industrial life—to make and enforce the rules of competition.

Thus we find business in America regulated primarily in two ways— by the forces of competition, and by the government.

The question is always: "How much regulation shall the government enforce?"

In theory the question is answered by studying how effectively competition is working in a given situation. Some industries, for example, develop into monopolies. The question the government has to answer is whether the monopoly is one which is advantageous to the public. If it is, the government will foster it, but regulate it. If it is not, the government will break it into smaller units so that competition can again become effective.

Public utilities are the classic examples of monopolies which are not only tolerated, but often fostered. It would often be impractical to have two competing bus companies in one city, so the government grants franchises to only one concern, and then proceeds to regulate it. It is likely to control the charge for a ride, the number of buses on a given route, the routes themselves, the safety precautions, and many more items which would be considered "socialistic" if applied to other businesses.

This article from the *San Francisco Chronicle* shows the result of rate regulation by a public utilities commission:

> Western Greyhound Lines asked the State Public Utilities Commission yesterday to let it put into effect a zone fare plan for the Peninsula that it estimated would increase its revenues about 3 per cent.
>
> The plan was submitted to the commission last February, after it had ordered Greyhound to study the feasibility of reducing the number of its present 48 fare points from San Francisco to San Jose. The commission took no action on it.
>
> The proposal would set up 13 zones. Generally fare from one zone into the next would be 20 cents, and for each succeeding zone 10 cents more.
>
> The 20-ride commuter fare would be $4 for travel from one zone to the next, and in most cases 50 cents more for each additional zone.
>
> Sample 20-ride fares from San Francisco would be $4 to Daly City, unchanged; $5 to San Bruno, up 50 cents; $5.50 to Burlingame, unchanged; $6 to San Mateo, up 25 cents; $6.50 to San Carlos, up 25 cents; $7 to Menlo Park, unchanged; $7.50 to Palo Alto, up 50 cents; $8 to Mountain View, unchanged; $9 to Sunnyvale, unchanged; and $10 to San Jose, unchanged.
>
> No date has been set for hearing Greyhound's proposal to put the plan into effect.

We usually think of public utility commissions as regulating concerns to protect the consumer, but sometimes the businesses concerned will seek price regulations to protect themselves from competition, as this story from the *San Francisco News* shows:

> San Francisco's 500 independent service stations will press for state control of gasoline prices, The News learned today.
>
> They will ask an assured profit of 8¢ per gallon of gasoline by the State Public Utilities Commission "as protection against big company price control."
>
> Wallace Pettigrew, treasurer of the San Francisco Petroleum Retailers Assn. and vice president of the California Federation of Service Stations, said he has polled independents here as part of a statewide move.
>
> "All of the dealers we've discussed it with think it's a good idea," Pettigrew said. "Everybody in the milk business is making money. We feel that if it's good for them, it's good for us."
>
> Pettigrew said California's milk control act would be used as a model for one governing gasoline prices.

The antitrust laws are used to regulate concerns which become too big in the opinion of government specialists.

What is "too big" or what is a "natural monopoly" are questions for debate. Should a concern be broken down into smaller units if it controls 20 per cent of the business in a given field? Should a city permit one, two, three, or an unlimited number of taxi companies to haul passengers in its streets? These are questions which are asked in all kinds of situations, and how they are answered has much to do with the kind of society we have.

We will examine government control in a few areas, although we can cover only a minute sampling, for government, industry, and labor are in constant collision.

The Antitrust Laws

The Sherman Anti-Trust Act was passed in 1890, and, although it was not enforced very strenuously until the presidency of Theodore Roosevelt, it has been of tremendous importance in shaping our policy toward business.

The two general provisions of the Act forbid combinations in restraint of trade and make monopolies illegal.

The language of the law is general, and much interpretation is required from the courts. The Supreme Court first interpreted the act in the Sugar Trust Case (United States vs. E. C. Knight Co.) in 1895. The government sought the dissolution of the American Sugar Refining Company. The Supreme Court held that the trust was not illegal because it was engaged in manufacturing. The assumption was that it would have been illegal had it been engaged in interstate commerce. This distinction is not followed in more recent decisions.

The Standard Oil case was perhaps the most dramatic one ever fought under the Sherman Anti-Trust Act. Standard Oil of New Jersey, controlled largely by John D. Rockefeller, by 1904 had so thoroughly beaten down its competition that it produced 90 per cent of the country's refined oil. It was a true industrial empire, with pipelines and refineries scattered throughout the country. It was able to dictate prices it paid for crude oil, to exact rebates from great railroads for its business, and to control prices of the finished products.

After a five-year battle through the courts, the United States Supreme Court handed down a unanimous decision in 1911 which ordered the dissolution of the empire. This was a victory for the government, but it left the same individuals in control of the component parts.

The Sherman Act has been amended several times (notably in the Clayton Act in 1914 and the Robinson-Patman Act in 1936). The amendments sharpen it and exempt certain activities of labor or agriculture.

Most states, too, have laws designed to control monopolies and conspiracies in restraint of trade. The federal and state laws are enforced with varying amounts of vigor according to the temper of the times and the view of the policy-maker. Antitrust legislation, however, continues to be an important part of our society. The nature of these laws and how they are enforced determines how big we allow our businesses to become, and thus how much power and wealth we allow individuals to accumulate.

Public Service Commissions

State public service commissions affect the readers of every newspaper, and more intimately than most readers realize. These commissions control agencies which perform vital services. Transportation companies, telephone and telegraph companies, and similar utilities are subject to regulations concerned with the quality and amount of service they offer and the rates they charge. All business is subject to regulation with regard to health and safety practices. Public utilities, however, often have monopoly position and special privileges such as use of city streets and other rights of way, and therefore they are subjected to special regulation.

This story from the *Albany Times-Union* illustrates one kind of regulation:

> The Public Service Commission has extended the deadline for the New York Central Railroad to install automatic flashing light signals at the Lincoln Ave. crossing in Colonie to Sept. 1. The railroad must continue 24-hour watchman service until the lights are in operation.
>
> Harold Kemm of Westmere and his daughter, Cynthia, were injured June 12 at the crossing when a train struck their car. The accident led to a new ruling by the PSC yesterday that railroads must provide round-the-clock watchmen at grade crossings if installation of protective devices is not completed on time in cases where the railroads are ordered to install the devices. This covers installation of warning lights or gates.
>
> The New York Central was ordered last October to have the light signals at the Lincoln Ave. crossing by June 1. After the train-car smash, the railroad blamed an "inadvertent slipup" in inter-departmental communications for failure to meet the June 1 deadline; and the PSC then blamed a "time lag" in its inspection program for its failure to discover the railroad had defaulted in installation of the warning lights.

This story from the *Chicago Daily News* illustrates the same general kind of regulation:

> The 13-track "death crossing" of the Indiana Harbor Belt railroad in Melrose Park was closed Tuesday.
>
> Railroad officials ordered the closing—with a temporary barricade constructed of railroad ties—after receiving an Illinois Commerce Commission order.
>
> A permanent barricade will be erected by Thursday, a railroad spokesman said.
>
> The ICC ordered the crossing at 25th Ave. barricaded last Friday after the recent deaths of four youngsters there in auto accidents.

Interstate carriers are subject to regulations by the Interstate Commerce Commission as well as by state agencies.

Public Health and Safety

Health and safety regulations affect almost every industry. Manufacturers are required to maintain minimum safety and health conditions in their plants. Usually inspectors from a state labor department see that these provisions are observed. These are requirements such as safety devices on machinery, adequate light, ventilation, and toilets.

Another area in which health laws affect business is in enforcing minimum standards for living units offered for rent. The force with which these laws are occasionally applied is clear in the following story from the *Chicago Daily News:*

> "I wish I'd never seen that property."
>
> Thus Ira J. Clements, 47, summed up his feelings about a slum building he owns at 4949 Indiana.
>
> He was arrested for failing to pay a . . . fine imposed by Municipal Judge James J. Geroulis for various building, electrical and sanitary violations.
>
> Clements was seized in his home at 1139 North, Deerfield. Neighbors there knew him under the name of Khayyami, but Clements refused to say which was his real name.
>
> "I've been expecting you people," Clements told Floyd Vourret, deputy building inspector, and Charles Larson, Lake County deputy sheriff, when they arrived to arrest him.
>
> Clements was held at the Chicago detective bureau overnight then taken to the House of Correction.
>
> Louis Wexler, assistant corporation counsel, said Clements will serve 18 months on three fines. . . .

The story of how government affects business is one of the most important that newspapers have to tell their readers. The brief description in this section is meant only to be suggestive. Obviously, volumes could be filled on the subject. Every reporter will find that all the knowledge he can get of business and government will be needed to help him find and write stories in this increasingly significant area.

REPORTING ASSIGNMENTS

1. Interview an official of your local bus company to find material for an article on how it is regulated by government agencies.

2. Do the same for officials of other local public utilities such as the power company, the telephone company, and a railroad or airline which serves your community.

3. Interview the labor relations manager of a local concern and a local union official for a story on government regulation of the relations between worker and management.

GLOSSARY

Glossary

I. Government and Metropolitan Area Terms

Annexation. The process by which a municipality takes in an area adjacent to it.

Assessment. The value placed on a piece of property, usually for tax purposes. (Also the process of estimating the value.)

Australian ballot. A ballot, printed by the government, which lists the names of all candidates and provides for secret voting. Originated in Australia, it was first adopted in this country in 1890 by the state of Massachusetts.

Authority. A semi-independent government corporation usually having power over just one activity (for example, flood control or housing), and sometimes crossing boundary lines of regular governments (such as cities, counties, or states).

Borough. In Pennsylvania, Connecticut, and New Jersey, an incorporated part of a township, similar to a village.

Capital reserve fund. Money held in reserve to pay for major public works.

Charter. The document, issued by a state government, which creates a municipal government and defines its powers.

Committee of the whole. A meeting of a public body from which the public is excluded. Similar to an executive session.

Consolidation. The merging of governments (such as city or county) or the joining of service divisions of two governments into one agency (such as a city-county health department).

Debt limit. A ceiling on the total amount that a government can owe at one time.

Environmental sanitation. The removal or control of health hazards.

Equalization. The process of adjusting tax burdens among towns or counties to even up the results of differing assessment practices.

Executive session. A meeting of a legislative body from which the public is excluded. Similar to a committee of the whole.

Exurbia. The area immediately beyond the suburbs, usually part of the metropolitan area formed by a city and its suburbs.

Federation. A joining of several units of government under a central unit which administers area-wide functions. Each local unit retains control of purely local matters.

General unit of government. An agency which has power to engage in all activities appropriate to it, as opposed to a special unit which usually has power to conduct just one governmental function.

Grand list. A compilation of the taxable assets of a town. Used chiefly in New England.

Grant-in-aid. A payment by one level of government to another for a specific purpose. Usually it is withheld unless certain conditions are met.

Home rule. A movement designed to give local governments more power in solving their own problems.

Impeachment. A criminal proceeding against a public officer. It is initiated by a document called "articles of impeachment."

Incorporated area. A district (usually called a municipality) with a government which has certain powers granted to it in a charter from the state.

Industrial hygiene. Control of health hazards in business and industrial establishments and the encouragement of good health habits among workers.

Initiative. A system by which voters can directly propose a new law or a constitutional amendment. After the required number of signatures is obtained on a petition, the issue is put to a public vote in a referendum.

Metropolitan area. A county or group of contiguous counties which has at least one city of 50,000 or more population and meets other requirements of the Census Bureau. In New England, the Census Bureau uses towns instead of counties as the basis for determining metropolitan areas.

Mill. One tenth of a cent. Sometimes tax rates are expressed in mills per hundred dollars of valuation.

Municipality. An area with a local government which exercises powers granted by the state in a charter.

Ordinance. A city law.

Planning. Development of a program for the orderly growth of a community, considering all such pertinent factors as population trends, transportation needs, health hazards, etc.

Precinct. A political subdivision of a city ward. Also a police district of a city.

Public utility. A private concern given certain powers (such as eminent domain) or certain privileges (such as a franchise) to function adequately. It is charged with the duty of serving the public without discrimination.

Quarantine. Isolation of persons who have a contagious disease or who have been exposed to it.

Resolution. A formal statement of the opinion of a legislative body or other group. Certain kinds of business can be transacted by resolution.

Revenue bonds. Public obligations issued as acknowledgment of money borrowed to finance an improvement, such as a water system or sidewalks. Revenues from fees or special assessments are pledged to repay the loan.

Rider. A provision attached to a bill which may not have a logical connection with the bill. The rider is sometimes used by a legislative body to pass a provision and avoid a veto by the executive.

School board. The official body (usually elected) which controls the schools of its district. Other names for it are: board of education, school district directors, and board of trustees.

Selectmen. The chief officers of a town. Used in New England.

Speaker. The presiding officer of a legislative body (usually the lower house or assembly).

Special assessment. Taxes levied against property owners who benefit directly from public improvements, such as sidewalks, water systems, and sewers.

Special district. A government unit formed to provide one specific service (such as water supply) as opposed to a general unit of government. It is similar to, but usually smaller than, an authority.

Special session. An extraordinary meeting of a legislative body, usually called by the executive head of the government (mayor, governor, or president).

Strong mayor. A type of city government in which the mayor has much power.

Suburbs. The urban-like area surrounding a city and tied to it by economic and cultural bonds. Sometimes called "suburbia."

Tax anticipation warrants. Short-term notes by which a government pledges uncollected taxes for loans to meet operating expenses.

Town; township. Sometimes a division of a county with limited powers of self-government. Most important in New England where it is sometimes incorporated and functions like a small municipality. The term "town" is sometimes used loosely as a synonym for village. In some areas "town" and "township" are used interchangeably. In others, they have different meanings, with "township" referring to a geographical subdivision of a county.

Urban renewal. The clearing and renovating of blighted city areas.

Urban sprawl. The city-like areas stretching out from cities and sometimes meeting similar projections from other cities.

Veto. The power vested in the executive head of government (mayor, governor, or president) to void an act of the legislative body by refusing to sign it. Usually the legislative body can still make the act effective (pass it over a veto) by a large preponderance of votes (two thirds or three quarters).

Village. In some states a small, incorporated area. In others, simply a place containing a few houses and perhaps a store or two.

Ward. A political subdivision of a city.

Weak mayor. A type of city government in which the mayor has comparatively little power.

Zoning. The limiting of certain areas to specific uses. For example, one part of a city may be limited to one-family houses, another to light industry, another to multidwelling structures, etc.

II. Legal Terms

Adjective law. Rules governing procedure.

Affidavit. A sworn statement made before an official empowered to take such statements. Affidavits are sometimes introduced as evidence in court proceedings.

Amicus curiae (friend of the court). A person who advises a judge in a case, but is not a participant in it. Also a person who has no right to participate, but is given permission to file a brief to protect his own interests.

Amnesty. An act absolving persons from guilt. Usually it applies to political crimes, and may be conditioned on a return to submission to authority. (For example, participants in an unsuccessful revolt may be absolved from guilt if they agree to submit to authority.)

Answer. The defendant's paper filed in response to a complaint in a civil proceeding.

Appearance. Putting one's self under the jurisdiction of a court.

Appellant. The party seeking an appeal of a court decision. Sometimes called plaintiff in error.

Appellee. The party (usually the winner of a case in a lower court) against whom the opposing party takes action in seeking an appeal. The appellee is, in some states, called the defendant in error or the respondent.

Arraignment. The calling of a prisoner before the court to hear the charge against him and to answer it.

Arrest. Taking custody of another person to hold him for legal action.

Bail. The sureties which are pledged in court to gain the freedom of a prisoner. If the prisoner fails to return at the specified time, bail is forfeited.

Ballistics. The scientific study of firearms.

Bankruptcy. The liquidation of a business and its sale to divide the assets among creditors, according to some formula recognizing their valid claims.

Bill of exceptions. A document which often must be filed with a request for an appeal, stating the objections or exceptions taken to the rulings of the judge in the lower court. Exceptions may also be taken to the judge's instructions to the jury.

Bill of particulars. A request for more details of a charge.

Bind over. To order a prisoner held for action by the grand jury or a higher court.

Body attachment. A judicial order to a sheriff directing him to arrest a judgment debtor for nonpayment of a judgment.

Booking. Recording essential information about a prisoner in police headquarters. This step follows arrest and precedes arraignment.

Breaking a will. Abrogating the terms of a will through legal action.

Certiorari. A writ from a higher to a lower court ordering the record of a trial sent up for review. Similar documents used in some jurisdictions are called writs of error or writs of review.

Chancellor. The judge of a court of equity or chancery.

Citizen arrest. The taking of a person into custody by a private citizen rather than by a police officer.

Civil law. Legal rules governing relationships between individuals.

Codicil. An addition to a will.

Common law. As recognized in the United States, this means that part of English law which was in force here at the time of the Revolution. It is also used to refer to the body of law which gains its authority from long-established traditions, rather than from statutes.

Commutation. The executive's power to substitute a lighter punishment for the original one.

Compact. A general agreement sometimes used as basic law. The Mayflower Compact is an example.

Complaint. A statement of rights and how they were violated. In many states it is the first paper filed in a civil action.

Constable. A police official with powers similar to those of the sheriff, but with less authority.

Constitution. A statement of the structure and powers of government. The basic law of a country.

Contempt of court. An act which impedes the course of justice, embarrasses a court, or holds it up to ridicule.

Continuance. A postponement of an action pending in court.

Court of the ordinary. The term used in some states for the court which has jurisdiction over wills and the estates of persons who have died.

Criminal law. Legal rules defining crime, and prescribing punishment and procedures to be used in meting it out.

Cross-examination. The questioning of a witness by the opposing attorney.

Decree. The judgment of a court in equity or admiralty. Also sometimes an executive order.

Defendant. The party against whom charges are brought in a civil or criminal action.

Deposition. A sworn statement intended for use in court. Lawyers for both sides are present to question the person making the statement.

Dilatory tactics. Procedures which delay an action, but are not pleas to the merits.

Direct examination. Questioning of a witness by the attorney who ordered his appearance.

Discovery, bill of. An order permitting one party to a suit to see certain records in the possession of the other party.

Double jeopardy. Being tried twice for the same offense.

Equity. A branch of jurisprudence which was originally exercised by certain English courts other than common law courts. Usually equity is preventive in nature.

Escheat. The process by which the property of persons who have died will eventually be turned over to the government if no heirs can be found.

Executor (fem., **executrix**). A person named by a testator in a will to carry out its provisions.

Felony. A more serious crime. The criteria which separate felonies from misdemeanors vary among the states. Often a felony is a crime serious enough to require a convicted person to serve a term in a state penitentiary or undergo a more severe punishment.

Garnishment. A writ ordering a person who has property belonging to a judgment-debtor to turn it over to the court to satisfy the judgment. Sometimes an employer is ordered to pay part of an employee's wages to a court.

General verdict. A jury is said to have brought in a general verdict when it simply finds for the plaintiff or for the defendant, leaving the judge to specify the amount of damages.

Holographic will. One in the handwriting of the testator.

Hung jury. A jury which cannot agree on a verdict.

Ignoramus (Lat., "We are ignorant," or "We ignore it."). Grand juries sometimes write this on bills of indictment if the evidence, in their opinion, does not justify a trial. A grand jury may be said to ignore the bill.

Indictment. A written accusation returned by a grand jury to a court charging that the person or persons named committed a crime.

Information. Similar to an indictment, but filed by a district attorney or similar official without any action by the grand jury.

Injunction. An order requiring a person to refrain from some act.

Interlocutory judgment. A judgment which is not final. It may become final when certain conditions are met. For example, after a certain length of time has elapsed.

Intestate. A person who dies without leaving a will is said to have died intestate.

Joinder. A uniting of issues or parties so that all may be settled in one suit.

Judge's charge. After the attorneys have made their closing statements, the judge charges the jury by explaining the law to jury members and telling them what alternatives they have.

Judgment by default. A decree entered against a party to a suit because he failed to appear at a trial.

Judgment-creditor. A party to whom money is owed as a result of a law suit.

Judgment-debtor. A party who owes money to another party as a result of a law suit.

Judgment on pleadings. A judge reaches a decision on the basis of the papers filed in a suit (pleadings) and without a formal trial.

Jurisdiction. The area of control of a court. A court's jurisdiction is usually defined by describing the kind of cases over which it has control.

Kangaroo court (col.). A group of prisoners who, through lax prison administration, are allowed to control some aspects of inmate discipline and mete out punishments for infractions of their rules.

Letters of administration. A document given to a person empowering him to administer the estate of a person who died intestate.

Letters testamentary. Documents issued by a court giving the executor power to assume his role in carrying out the terms of a will.

Misdemeanor. A crime less serious than a felony. Often punishable by a fine or a term in a county jail.

Mittimus. A writ signed by a judge ordering a sheriff to deliver a prisoner to a prison and the warden to receive him.

Motion session. A session of a court devoted, not to formal trials, but to hearing motions.

No bill. A phrase sometimes written on a bill of indictment when members of a grand jury think there is insufficient evidence to support the charge. Newspapers sometimes report that a grand jury reported a no bill in a certain case.

Nuncupative will. An oral will made by a testator before a sufficient number of witnesses and usually reduced to writing later.

Pardon. The executive's power to exempt a person from punishment for a crime.

Parole. Release from prison before a prisoner has served his full sentence on condition of good behavior and under supervision of a parole officer.

Partition. An equity process sometimes used to divide property.

Plaintiff. The person who brings charges in a civil action.

Plaintiff in error. A term used in some states to designate a party seeking to reverse the decision of a lower court by appeal.

Pleadings. The preliminary papers in a civil action.

Polygraph. One of several devices used as lie detectors.

Precedent. Decisions in earlier cases which guide a judge in a given case.

Presentment. An accusation by a grand jury. It differs from an indictment in that it is made by the grand jury of its own motion, while an indictment is drawn up by the district attorney.

Pretrial examination. An opportunity sometimes granted a defendant to examine the plaintiff to make the charge more specific.

Private law. Law governing the relationship between individuals. The term is used to distinguish between private and public law.

Privilege. In the law of libel, privilege is an exemption from liability for libel because of a public duty which was involved in the publication. There are two kinds of privilege, absolute and conditional (also called qualified).

Probate court. The term used in some states for the court which has jurisdiction over wills and the estates of persons who have died.

Probation. A process by which a person convicted of a crime is allowed to stay out of prison, under the supervision of an official and with certain specific conditions.

Proclamation. An order by an executive. Often it has the force of law.

Property attachment. A judicial order to a sheriff directing him to seize a piece of property owned by the judgment-debtor to satisfy a a judgment.

Public law. Law which is concerned with the state in its governmental capacity. It includes constitutional law, administrative law, criminal law, and international law.

Receivership. Placing a business in the hands of a court appointee to protect the rights of all owners and persons to whom the business owes money.

Replevin. An action brought to repossess goods which were illegally taken or are illegally held.

Reply. A preliminary paper filed by the plaintiff in a civil action.

Reprieve. A delay in carrying out a sentence.

Res adjudicata. The term is used to refer to a question which has already been settled in a previous suit.

Separation. The division of issues or parties into different actions.

Special verdict. A jury reaches a decision in answer to specific questions of fact, leaving the judge to apply the law to the facts.

Specific performance. An equitable remedy by which a person is ordered to carry out the terms of a contract.

Substantive law. The body of rules which the court administers. The term is used to differentiate the body of rules from the adjective law.

Summary judgment. A court decision issued without a formal trial. Permissible under certain conditions.

Surrogate. An official who has charge of wills and the disposition of estates of persons who have died. He presides over the surrogate's court.

Suspended sentence. A person convicted of a crime is allowed to remain free on good behavior. He may be required to report periodically to a probation officer, and there may be other specific conditions.

Talesmen. Persons added to a jury panel.

Testator. A person making a will.

Tort. A private wrong which involves the violation of the right of another person, but not a right granted by a contract.

True bill. If a grand jury brings in an indictment, it is sometimes said to have found a true bill. The expression comes from the practice in some places of writing the words "a true bill" on the bill of indictment.

Veniremen. Members of a jury panel.

Writ of execution. A judicial order to a sheriff directing him to help in the collection of an obligation.

III. Terms of Politics and Informal Areas

Canvass. The process, by an official agency, of counting and examining the votes at a public election to verify the count, and sometimes to eliminate fraud.

Caucus. Any of various kinds of meetings of members of a political party. Its purpose may be to select candidates or determine the party position on an issue.

Closed primary. One open only to registered voters of the party.

Coalition. An alliance among several political parties.

Committeeman. A political party leader in charge of a district, such as a county, ward, or precinct.

Convention. Meeting of a political party designed to nominate candidates and draw up a party platform.

Corpus. The fund administered by a foundation.

Cross-filing. Permits candidates to enter the primaries of more than one party.

Cross section. A pollster's sample drawn from the universe (all the elements of a group he is studying).

Direct primary. A system of nominating candidates for public office by an election open to all enrolled members of the party.

Electoral college. A group of persons, selected by the voters of each state, who formally elect the President and Vice-President, in accordance with the vote in each state.

Gerrymandering. Splitting an area into voting districts designed to give an advantage to one political party.

Initiative. A system allowing a group of citizens to initiate a law or constitutional amendment.

Lobbyist. One who tries to influence governmental decision by intervening directly with legislators or other officials, or by influencing others to intervene.

Logrolling. An informal system by which legislators swap support for pet issues. One legislator or bloc agrees to support the issues of another in return for similar help.

Majority leader. The person who heads the majority party's delegation in a legislative body.

Minority leader. The person who heads the minority party's delegation in a legislative body.

Parliamentary form of government. The system of government under which the executive is a member of the legislative body and the leader of its majority party.

Patronage. Favors granted by officials in return for political support.

Plank. One of the issues stated in a party platform.

Platform. A statement of the principles of a political party.

Political machine. The political organization in a given area is sometimes called "the machine." The term is often used in a disparaging sense.

Poll tax. An assessment collected from individuals before they are allowed to vote.

Precinct captain. A person responsible for representing a political party in a precinct. Sometimes called a committeeman.

Presidential form of government. The system of government under which the executive is elected independent of the legislative body.

Pressure groups. Organizations outside the government which try to influence governmental decision.

Pro tempore. Temporary, for the time being. Usually refers to the temporary presiding officer of a public body, as president pro tempore.

Quota system. One of the methods used by pollsters to draw a cross section.

Random sampling. One of the methods used by pollsters to draw a cross section. It relies on chance.

Reapportionment. The process of redistributing the number of representatives from the states, or election districts within a state, in accordance with population shifts.

Recall. A system by which the voters can cast ballots on whether to dismiss (recall) a public official.

Referendum. The submission of a bill or constitutional amendment to an election of all qualified voters.

Registration. The signing by a voter of the election roll. In a periodic registration system voters are required to appear at the polls and sign before every election. Under permanent personal registration voters sign once and then can vote in all elections until they change their residence. Under this system election officials have the duty of keeping lists of voters up-to-date.

Rotten boroughs. Areas which are not represented or are underrepresented in a country's election system.

Whip. A member of a legislative body selected by his party to keep members in line and get them on the floor for important votes.

IV. Business and Labor Terms

Accrued dividends. Payments to stockholders earned, but not yet paid.

Amortization. The process of paying off a long-term debt.

Arbitrage. The practice of buying a security on one exchange and selling it on another.

Arbitration. The submission of a dispute to a third party (an arbiter), with agreement by both sides to accept his recommendations.

Articles of incorporation. The papers by which a state or the federal government establishes a corporation. Also known as a charter.

Assets. The face value of a company's property.

Assigned value. The price paid by the original purchaser of a stock.

Balance sheet. A company's financial statement summarizing the year's operations and showing its assets and liabilities.

Balance of trade. The relationship between a country's imports and its exports.

Banker control. Presence of investment bankers on the boards of industrial, public utility, or railroad corporations.

Bear market. A falling market. To be bearish is to believe the market is about to fall.

Bond. A certificate of indebtedness of a corporation. It is a negotiable security, but gives its owner no control of management. In case of a corporation's failure, bondholders will be paid off before stockholders.

Book value. An estimate of the price a security would bring if it had to be liquidated.

Broker. A person who is in the business of buying and selling securities or commodities for others.

Bull market. A rising market. To be bullish is to believe the market is about to rise.

Buying on the margin. Borrowing part of the money needed to buy stocks.

Chain banking. Control by one person, or a group, of the stock of more than one bank. Chain banking is declining with the development of branch banking.

Closed shop. A contract provision by which the employer can hire only union members. This is outlawed by the Taft-Hartley law.

Commodity exchange. A place for organized trading in grains, cotton, hides, sugar, coffee, copper, rubber, or other raw materials.

Common stock. Certificate of ownership in a corporation. It carries voting rights.

Company union. An association of workers sponsored by the employer.

Conciliation. Bringing together the parties to a dispute.

Cornering a market or **getting a corner on a market.** The process by which a trader or group buys up enough of a security or commodity so that anyone buying it must deal with him. This allows him to control the price. This practice is forbidden by federal regulations.

Corporation. An association of persons who buy stock in an enterprise and thereby become its owners.

Cost of living index. The popular name for the consumer price index which is prepared by the federal government.

Craft union. A labor organization which is composed of workers with a given skill.

Delisting of securities. The Securities and Exchange Commission may order securities to be withdrawn from listing or registration, for the protection of investors.

Fringe benefits. Advantages (for example, health insurance and paid vacations) given to workers in addition to pay.

Futures contract. An agreement to purchase a commodity at some specified time in the future at today's price. This provides a hedge, so the processor does not have to assume the risk of price changes in the basic raw material.

Grievance procedure. The processes by which disputes between a worker and his employer are settled.

Group banking. Several banks controlled by a holding company. This practice is declining with the development of branch banks.

Holding company. A corporation which deals in the stocks of other companies, usually operating companies.

Horizontal union. Another name for craft union.

Industrial union. A labor unit which attempts to organize all the workers in a given plant.

International. The unit at the top of the structure of most unions in this country.

Investment trust. A company or trust which sells shares of ownership or bonds to investors and uses the proceeds to invest in the securities of other companies. It differs from a savings bank in that it generally holds common or preferred stock, in preference to high-grade bonds. Unlike the holding company, stock ownership is for investment, rather than for control. Types of investment trust are: (1) *management trust*, in which the management can invest funds as it pleases, buying and selling at will; (2) *fixed trust*, which is established with a certain number of shares in specified stocks or bonds; (3) *semifixed trust*, in which the trustee has some discretion to trade when the stocks do not pay dividends, or when stocks fall in value.

Investor. An individual who buys securities planning to keep them for a while, hoping to make a profit from dividends and growth in value.

Limit order. A direction to a broker to buy or sell when a security or commodity reaches a certain price.

Local. The "chapter" of a labor organization in which members meet.

Market value. The amount a security would bring if sold on the market. This value is likely to vary from day to day as the market changes.

Mediator. A third party who sits down with the parties to a dispute and tries to help in reaching a settlement.

Odd lots. Shares of stocks in less than 100-share units.

Option. An agreement, for a consideration, to deliver or buy securities in the future at a price fixed in the agreement.

Over-the-counter dealings. Transfer in ownership of securities without the use of an exchange.

Par value. The price paid by the original purchaser of a security. Also called the assigned value.

Partnership. Two or more individuals doing business under an agreement which describes the extent of their participation and responsibility.

Pit. The place where trading takes place in a commodity exchange.

Pools. An association of speculators for the purpose of trading large blocks of securities. Sometimes speculators mass their buying in certain stocks to create an active market and encourage others to buy. When the price is high enough, pool members liquidate their holdings.

Preferred stock. Certificate of ownership in a corporation. It usually carries no voting privileges, but its owners will be paid dividends before owners of common stock.

Price index. A device by which prices at any given period can be compared with a base period.

Production index. A device by which production in various periods can be compared.

Prospectus. As required by the SEC, this document should summarize the important information about a security for investors. Although a prospectus is supposed to be brief, some run 200 pages long.

Proxy. A document by which a stockholder authorizes another to vote his stock at a stockholders' meeting.

Rating bureaus. Co-operative organizations financed by insurance companies to establish equitable rates.

Registrar. A corporation employee kept in New York City by every corporation whose stock is bought and sold on the New York Stock Exchange. He keeps a constant check to make sure that his concern's stock is not overissued.

Reserve ratios. The amount of cash which a bank must keep on hand or on deposit in other banks to promptly meet demands for withdrawal of deposits.

Round lots. One hundred-share units of stocks.

Scab. An uncomplimentary term sometimes used to mean a strikebreaker. It has been held to be libelous in some states.

Section 7a. A famous provision of the National Industrial Recovery Act of 1933. It required employers to allow workers to bargain collectively through representatives of their own choosing.

Securities and Exchange Commission (SEC). A federal agency in charge of administering the series of regulations established by the Securities Acts of 1933 and 1934. The Act applies to the "public offering" of securities.

Short selling. A speculator is said to sell short when he agrees to sell stocks or goods which he does not own, borrowing them to complete the sale. He has to replace the stock later.

Speculator. An individual who buys stocks intending to make a quick profit by taking advantage of price fluctuations.

Stock exchange. A place where common and preferred stocks of business corporations, and sometimes other types of securities, are traded.

Stock split. Increasing the amount of stock issued by a company by dividing those outstanding in some ratio.

Stop order. A special kind of limit order by which a speculator tells his broker to sell if a stock drops down to a certain price.

Street (Wall Street). The New York financial district.

Transfer agent. A corporation employee who keeps a record of the name and address of each stockholder.

Union shop. An establishment in which a new employee is required to join the union within a certain time after going to work.

Wash sales. Trying to make the market look more active than it really is by buying and selling the same commodity at the same time. This practice is now forbidden.

Watered stock. A security which is overvalued in terms of the assets which support it.

Yellow dog contract. An agreement by a worker not to join any union (other than a company union) while he is working for the employer.

Suggestions for Further Reading

PART ONE: METROPOLITAN PROBLEMS

Alderfer, Harold F.: "American Local Government and Administration," New York, Macmillan, 1956.

Baker, Benjamin: "Urban Government," Princeton, Van Nostrand, 1957.

Bollens, John C.: "The States and the Metropolitan Problem," Chicago, Council of State Governments, 1956.

Bromage, Arthur W.: "Introduction to Municipal Government and Administration," New York, Appleton-Century-Crofts, 1957.

Chapin, F. Stuart, Jr.: "Urban Land Use Planning," New York, Harper, 1957.

Hinderaker, Ivan (Ed.): "American Government Annual, 1958–1959," New York, Holt, 1958.

Kneier, Charles M.: "City Government in the United States," ed. 3, New York, Harper, 1957.

MacDonald, A. F.: "American City Government and Administration," ed. 5, New York, Crowell, 1954.

"Municipal Finance Administration," ed. 5, Chicago, International City Managers' Association, 1955.

National Committee on Urban Transportation: "Better Transportation for Your City," Chicago, Public Administration Service, 1958.

Ringgenberg, Clayton L.: "Your Job as Councilman," Iowa City, Institute of Public Affairs of the State University of Iowa, 1954.

Schut, F. Baker: "Problems of Expanding Towns," The Hague, International Union of Local Authorities, 1957.

Snider, Clyde F.: "Local Government in Rural America," New York, Appleton-Century-Crofts, 1957.

Sweeney, Stephen B. (Ed.): "Metropolitan Analysis," Philadelaphia, University of Pennsylvania Press, 1958.

"Traffic Congestion in the City Centre," The Hague, International Union of Local Authorities, 1957.

"Urban Development and Urban Transportation," Princeton, Princeton University Press, 1957.

Webster, Donald H.: "Urban Planning and Municipal Public Policy," New York, Harper, 1958.

Young, Roland: "The American Congress," New York, Harper, 1958.

PART TWO: LAW AND LAW ENFORCEMENT

Barnes, H. E., and Teeters, N. K.: "New Horizons in Criminology," ed. 2, New York, Prentice-Hall, 1951.

Blume, William W.: "American Civil Procedure," Boston, Little, Brown (for Prentice-Hall), 1955.

Borchard, Edwin M., and Lutz, E. Russell: "Convicting the Innocent," Garden City, Garden City Pub. Co., 1932.

Kaplan, Benjamin, and Hall, Livingston (Ed.): Judicial Administration and the Common Man, *Annals of the American Academy of Political and Social Science,* vol. 287, 1953.

Mars, David, and Kort, Fred: "Administration of Justice in Connecticut," Storrs, Conn., Institute of Public Service, University of Connecticut, 1957.

Reynolds, Quentin: "Courtroom," Garden City, Garden City Pub. Co. (by arrangement with Farrar, Straus & Young), 1951.

Sellin, Thorsten (Ed.): Prisons in Transformation, *Annals of the American Academy of Political and Social Science,* vol. 293, 1954.

Wood, Arthur Evans, and Waite, John Barker: "Crime and Its Treatment," New York, American Book Co., 1941.

PART THREE: INFORMAL AREAS OF PUBLIC AFFAIRS

Andrews, Frank Emerson: "Philanthropic Foundations," New York, Russell Sage Foundation, 1956.

Blaisdell, Donald C.: "American Democracy Under Pressure," New York, Ronald Press, 1957.

Bone, Hugh A.: "Party Committees and National Politics," Seattle, University of Washington Press, 1958.

McKean, Dayton David: "Pressures on the Legislature of New Jersey," New York, Columbia University Press, 1938.

Moscow, Warren: "Politics in the Empire State," New York, Knopf, 1948.

Neuberger, Richard L.: "Adventures in Politics," New York, Oxford, 1954.

Redding, Jack: "Inside the Democratic Party," New York, Bobbs-Merrill, 1958.

Schlesinger, Joseph A.: "How They Became Governor," East Lansing, Governmental Research Bureau, Michigan State University, 1957.

Van Deusen, Glyndon G.: "Thurlow Weed: Wizard of the Lobby," Boston, Little, Brown, 1947.

PART FOUR: INDUSTRY IS PUBLIC AFFAIRS

Barbash, Jack: "Taft-Hartley Act in Action, 1947 . . . 1956, and Essentials of a New Labor Policy," New York, League for Industrial Democracy, 1956.

Dimock, Marshal E.: "Business and Government," New York, Holt, 1949.

Hayes, Douglas Anderson: "Business Confidence and Business Activity: A Case Study of the Recession of 1937," Ann Arbor, University of Michigan Press, 1951.

Hurley, Morris E.: "Elements of Business Administration," New York, Prentice-Hall, 1953.

McNaughton, Wayne, and Lazar, Joseph: "Industrial Relations and the Government," New York, McGraw-Hill, 1954.

Mueller, Stephen J.: "Labor Law and Legislation," ed. 2, Cincinnati, South-Western Pub. Co., 1956.

Petro, Sylvester: "The Labor Policy of the Free Society," New York, Ronald Press, 1957.

Straus, George: "Unions in the Building Trades, a Case Study," Buffalo, University of Buffalo, 1958.

Taylor, Albion Guilford: "Labor and the Supreme Court," Ann Arbor, Braun-Brumfield, 1957.

Thole, Henry C. (Ed.): "Business Action in a Changing World," Chicago, Public Administration Service, 1956.

Weyrauch, Martin H.: "Fundamentals of Labor Law," ed. 2, Brooklyn, Brooklyn Law Bookstore, 1957.

Index